Crystal Reports Encyclopedia Volume 2:

.NET 2005/2008

by Brian Bischof

Crystal Reports Encyclopedia Volume 2: .NET 2005/2008

Copyright © 2008 Brian Bischof

ISBN-10: 097495361X

ISBN-13: 978-0974953618

Sample reports for this book are available at www.CrystalReportsBook.com.

Individual sales and bulk discounts are handled through Independent Publishers Group. 814 North Franklin Street, Chicago, IL 60610. (312) 337-0747

Proofreaders:	Anita Bischof
Headshot Photo:	Maria Pablo, www.MaluPhotography.com

To Lynn Luker and Karen Loeser. You are wonderful sisters as well as friends and fill my life with many great memories. I love you both.

Table of Contents

Acknowledgements

Like my previous books, my mom proof-read every chapter to ensure that they were free of any grammatical errors. As usual, I gave her the chapters much later than I should have and she had to work non-stop near the end to get finished by the deadline. As hard as it is to believe, she actually read the book twice, from cover to cover, while editing it. Thanks for everything, Mom!

Maria Pablo took a great photo for my headshot on the back cover. You can find out more about her photography at www.MaluPhotography.com.

About the Author

Brian Bischof, CPA, MCSD, is the author of the best selling book, "Crystal Reports .NET Programming", "Crystal Reports Encyclopedia, Volume 1", and "The .NET Languages: A Quick Translation Guide". He is the President of DotNet Tech, Inc.

Brian discovered a marketing niche early in his career; many software consultants were adequate working with software applications but did not understand or know the corporate language to discover a company's true needs. Contrarily, business managers knew that they wanted to improve their business processes but did not know how to communicate this information to a computer "tech". After spending years developing software and working in the accounting field as a financial auditor, Brian created a software development and training firm that provides a unique merger of business expertise and technical knowledge using Microsoft's .NET technologies.

In 2008, after SAP acquired Business Objects, SAP contacted Brian and chose him as an SAP Mentor in the SAP Developer Network. Only 1/100th of 1% of all members are selected each year. Brian also received a Top Contributor award in 2008.

You can learn more about the author and DotNet Tech, Inc. by visiting the company's website at www.DotNetTech.com.

PREFACE

This book is for programmers who are new to Crystal Reports as well as programmers who are experienced with Crystal Reports. If you are new to Crystal Reports, you are shown how easy it is to quickly create your first report and add it to your project. As you want to learn more reporting features, you can turn to the appropriate chapter and see how easy it is to make your reports more professional.

If you are experienced with Crystal Reports, you will be interested in learning what the .NET version of Crystal Reports lets you do as well as what its limitations are. Learning how to perform runtime report customization will let you take your reporting solution to the next level.

.NET Version Differences

When Business Objects updated Crystal reports for Visual Studio .NET 2005, they made many significant improvements over the 2003 release. The user interface was cleaned up, database connectivity was significantly improved, and many new features were added. However, when .NET 2008 was released, very little was changed. The biggest difference is that Crystal Reports now supports LINQ objects, ClickOnce deployment, and 64 bit development. It is also compatible with Windows Vista and Windows Server 2003.

Business Objects also renamed the version of Crystal Reports that comes with Visual Studio as, "Crystal Reports Basic 2008". I still frequently refer to it as "CR.NET" because it's easier and I'm sure they will change the name again in the next version anyway.

This book was written with Visual Studio .NET 2008. There are a few minor differences in menu options and screen shots, but the two products are practically the same. You will be alerted when something only works in .NET 2008 and not .NET 2005.

How the Book is Organized

This book is divided into two parts: Part I - Designing Reports and Part II - Programming Reports. Each part is designed for two different types of report development.

Part I - Designing Reports is for the user who has never used Crystal Reports before or has used a previous version and wants to get up to speed on the .NET version. It walks you through the steps of creating reports using the report designer. You are also shown how to add sophistication to your reports by learning how to program with Crystal Syntax and Basic Syntax.

Part II - Programming Reports is for the advanced programmer who has mastered the art of designing reports and wants to take their reports to the next level by customizing them during runtime. You will learn the intricacies of how the Crystal Reports object model is designed. This lets you take control of the report during runtime. Unlike Part I which is focused on using the Report Designer, Part II focuses on writing code with either VB.NET or C#.

Which Language: VB.NET or C#?

One thing that makes .NET so interesting is the fact that VB.NET and C# are almost equal. Choosing the programming language used on a project becomes more of a personal decision rather than a technological decision. However, this really complicates things for the authors of .NET books. When planning a new book, it seems that one of the biggest decisions a publishing company makes is deciding which language to focus on.[1]

In this book, I've decided to use both languages. The first listing is always VB.NET and the second listing is C#. There are a few instances where I show just the VB.NET code, but this is only when the code is one or two lines long and the C# listing is identical (except needing a semi-colon at the end).

While learning Crystal Reports object model, it's easy to get confused as to which namespace a class belongs to. All the examples in this book declare object variables using the fully qualified class name. This lets you see the complete namespace that is used to reference a class. The downside of doing this in a book is that it can make the variable declarations very long and harder to understand. It is often impossible to fit the entire namespace on a single line in the book. This requires putting the remainder of the namespace on the next line. In VB.NET this isn't syntactically correct and you will have to modify your code so that the code fits on a single line. I suggest that you either use the VB.NET Imports statement or the C# using statement to reference the namespaces directly. This will condense your code and make it easier to read.

Installing Crystal Reports

Crystal Reports for .NET is included with Visual Studio .NET. When you install Visual Studio .NET it is one of the tools installed by default. After installation, Crystal Reports is listed as one of the components that can be added to a project.

Crystal Reports for .NET is not included in the VB.NET or C# Standard versions. You need to purchase one of the Visual Studio .NET packages to get Crystal Reports.

Installing Service Packs

It is critical that you periodically go to the support site to check for new downloads. In fact, you should put the book down right now and install the lastest service packs.

---

[1] I worked on a book for Wrox where halfway through the project they decided that everyone should switch the examples from C# to VB.NET. Arghh!

There are two types of downloads available: Service Packs and Hot Fixes. Service packs are released every six months. They include comprehensive bug fixes and additional features. Service packs have also been regression tested. Hot fixes are released at the beginning of each month. They include minor bug fixes and have not been as thoroughly tested as service packs. The download URL is:

https://websmp130.sap-ag.de/sap(bD1IbiZjPTAwMQ==)/bc/bsp/spn/
bobj_download/main.htm

Download the Sample Code

The sample code for this book can be found at www.CrystalReportsBook.com.

Online Forum Community

The book's online forum is available to everyone. You can read the threads, or register to post questions and answers. Registration is free. The more you participate, the better the forum becomes! The forum is at the following URL:

www.CrystalReportsBook.com/Forum

Amazon Book Reviews

As a self-publisher, I don't have a team of marketing people or inside connections to the computer magazines to get book reviews. It's just me and my laptop. I rely upon my readers to help spread the word about my books. If you like this book, please take a moment to go to the Amazon website and make a short comment about it. This will help tremendously and I will really appreciate it. If you don't like the book, please send me an email and tell me your thoughts. I take this very seriously and will make corrections in the next edition. In fact, this edition had some major changes made to it because of comments I received from the last book. I worked very hard to make this book the best that it could be, and I want everyone to be a satisfied reader.

How to Contact Me

I can be reached via the book's online forum. There is a section called Speak with the Author where you can post messages to me that are not related to Crystal Reports problems.

PART I
Designing Reports

Learn how easy it is to design your first report and integrate it into a .NET application. After designing a couple sample reports for both Windows and ASP.NET, you begin to understand report layouts and adding new report objects. You'll quickly move beyond the report wizards and create reports using grouping and sorting, running totals, and subreports. If you want to perform dynamic formatting of report objects, learn how to program in Basic syntax or Crystal syntax. This chapter takes you from being a novice to intermediate report designer.

The code samples in Part I are deliberately kept simple so you can focus on learning how to design professional looking reports. When you're ready to tackle .NET runtime customization with VB.NET or C#, move to Part II of the book.

Introducing Crystal Reports

Visual Studio .NET is the first Windows development environment that gives developers a fully integrated and robust reporting solution. Crystal Reports is now installed with Visual Studio so developers can write applications that have reports seamlessly integrated into them. Starting with Visual Basic 3.0, Crystal Reports was included with the language, but not part of the default installation. It was also a stand-alone product that was independent of the programming language.

Over the years Microsoft has been including Crystal Reports with each version of Visual Basic. With version 6, they even wrote a Data Report component that was supposed to be a replacement for Crystal Reports, but it failed miserably.

With the release of Visual Studio.NET, Microsoft finally woke up to the needs of developers. They licensed Crystal Decisions to write a version of Crystal Reports to be the default reporting solution installed with .NET.[2] Built into the IDE, Windows developers now have the tools to write presentation-quality interactive reports.

Creating Your First Report

Before you learn about all the features of Crystal Reports, it is best to start by creating a quick report. This gives you a good overview of how easy it is to create a report as well as to see some of its functionality in action. Open Visual Studio and create a new project. This can be either VB.NET or C#, and it can be either a Windows Application or ASP.NET. Designing reports with Crystal Reports is independent of the project type. The following steps are the same for both types of applications.

Once the project is open, select Project[3] > Add New Item. This displays the list of available templates. For a Windows project, the left side has a Categories list where you can click on Reporting and then select Crystal Reports on the right. For an ASP.NET project, Crystal Reports is already near the top of the list of templates. After selecting the template, enter the name "Employee List". Figure 1-1 shows this dialog box for a Windows Application. Click Add to create the report.

---

[2] Crystal Reports for .NET is a set of Runtime Callable Wrappers (RCW) around modified Crystal Reports 10 DLLs.

[3] Select the menu option Website for an ASP.NET project.

Figure 1-1. The Add New Item dialog box.

When the Crystal Report Gallery dialog box appears, accept the defaults of "Using the Report Wizard" and "Standard". This is shown in Figure 1-2.

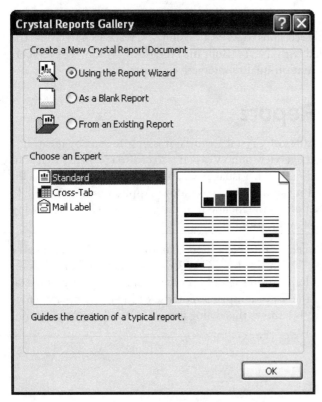

Figure 1-2. The Standard Report Expert dialog box.

The first page on the Crystal Reports Gallery dialog box is the Data page. Select the Xtreme Sample Database (it comes with Crystal Reports) by clicking on Create New Connection and then the OLE DB(ADO) option in the Available Data Sources list. This brings up a new dialog box. Select Microsoft Jet 4.0 OLE DB Provider. On the next dialog box enter the database name (database name is the fully qualified file path). By default, it is located at C:\Program Files\Microsoft Visual Studio 9.0\Crystal Reports\Samples\En\Databases. Select Finish.

You are back at the Data page of the expert. Click on the Tables node to expand and double-click on the Employee table name to move it to the window titled Selected Tables (or drag and drop it). Click Next.

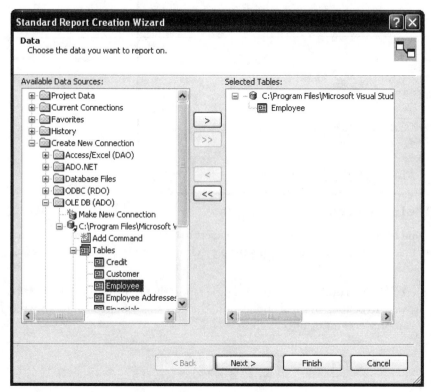

Figure 1-3. The Data page of the report expert.

To display fields on the report, you have to select them on the Fields page. Double click on the following fields to add them to the right window: Employee ID, Last Name, and First Name. This is shown in Figure 1-4.

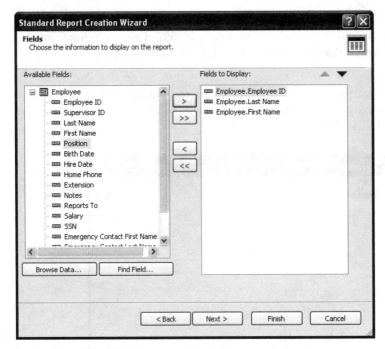

Figure 1-4. The Fields page of the report expert.

At this point, you could continue with the report expert to do things such as grouping and selecting which records to print. But, for this simple example, ignore those tabs and click Finish.

The report expert closes and builds a fully functioning report that is ready to run (Figure 1-5). If this report were to be used in a real application, the next step would be to modify the form so that it can preview and print the report.

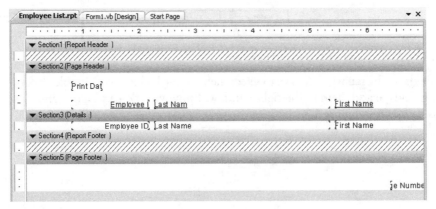

Figure 1-5. Employee List report in design mode.

Previewing with a Windows Form

After creating the Employee List report in the previous section, you can preview it using either a Windows Form or an ASP.NET application. This section shows you how to preview it from a Windows Form. Previewing it with ASP.NET is covered in the following section.

Previewing the report requires modifying an existing form. When you created the new project, Form1 should have been automatically added to the project for you. Open Form1 in design mode and add a CrystalReportViewer control to it. This is normally listed in the Reporting section near the bottom of the Toolbox. Resize the viewer so that it fills up the entire form. Do this by finding its Dock property and clicking on the drop-down box. Click on the middle square so that the property is set to Fill.

The viewer control has many ways to preview reports.[4] This example uses the Smart Tasks button to add a new report to the viewer control. If you click on the viewer control, you'll see a small arrow in the top right corner. This is shown in Figure 1-6.

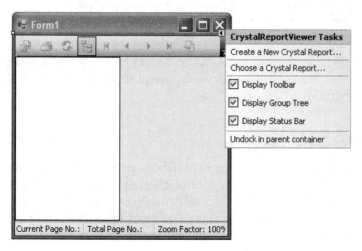

Figure 1-6. The ReportDocument dialog box.

Click on it to get a list of the Tasks available. Select the task Choose a Crystal Report. In the next dialog box, select the Employee List report and click the OK button. This adds the ReportDocument component to your form.

The viewer immediately shows you a preview of the report. You don't have to run the application to see how it will look. However, the viewer buttons have no functionality until you run the application. Go ahead and run the report. Form1 will open and show you the report. You can click on the buttons on the toolbar and test some of its functionality. The preview of the Employee List report is shown in Figure 1-6.

---

[4] Chapter 3 gives a complete explanation of using the viewer control.

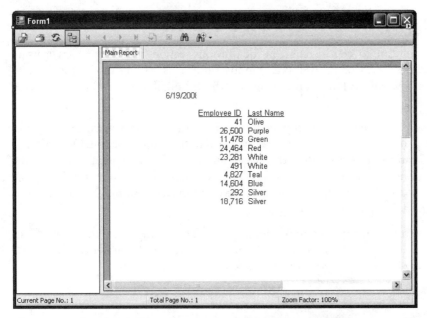

Figure 1-7. Employee List report output in preview mode.

You can see that this quick report isn't perfect and could use better formatting. As is usually the case, the report expert gives you a good basis for writing a report, but you still need to make some changes to clean it up.

Previewing with ASP.NET

Previewing a report with ASP.NET requires adding a CrystalReportViewer control to the web page and attaching it to a CrystalReportSource control. Create a new web project and open the default web page in design mode. Add a CrystalReportViewer control to it. The viewer is located in the Reporting tab near the end of the Toolbox. Once you add it to the form you will see a medium sized rectangle on the web page.

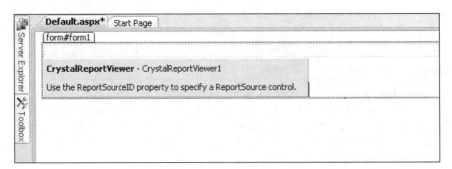

Figure 1-8. The ASP.NET report viewer control.

Notice that the web viewer control looks totally different than the Windows viewer control. The web viewer is simply a placeholder where the report will be displayed.

Click on the viewer control and notice that it has a small arrow in the top right corner. Click on this to open a list of smart tasks. This is shown in Figure 1-8.

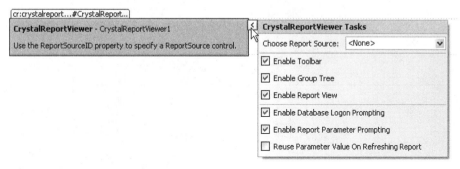

Figure 1-9. The ReportDocument dialog box.

Click the drop-down box for Choose Report Source and select <New report source>. This opens the Create Report Source dialog box. It lets you specify a name for the report source and pick the report to use. Click the bottom drop-down box and choose the CrystalReport.rpt report.

Click the OK button to create the report source control and link it to the viewer control. This automatically previews the report in design mode of your ASP.NET application.

Run the web application and you'll see the Employee List report automatically previewed when the page opens.

Figure 1-10. The Employee List report shown in an ASP.NET application.

Examining the Report Designer

Each report within your application is just like any other component that your application uses. It is listed in the Solution Explorer window as a class in your project. When you double-click it, it opens the report in design mode and you can make changes to it.

Each report starts with five sections: Report Header, Page Header, Detail, Page Footer, and Report Footer. These sections are described in Table 1-1.

Table 1-1. Report sections.

Section	Description
Report Header	Appears at the top of the first page of the report.
Page Header	Appears after the Report Header on the first page. On all the remaining pages it appears at the top of the page.
Group Header	Appears at the beginning of each new group.
Details	The row that displays the record information. There is

	usually one detail row for every record in the table.
Group Footer	Appears after all records of a group have been printed.
Page Footer	Appears at the bottom of each page.
Report Footer	Appears at the bottom of the page for the last page in the report.

To the left of the report layout is the Toolbox as shown in Figure 1-10. When you have the report designer open, there are only a few controls available in the Toolbox. They are the Text Object, Line Object, and Box Object. These are the most basic of the controls available.

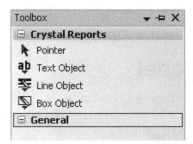

Figure 1-11. Crystal Report's toolbox.

Oddly enough, there are more controls that can be used on a report, but they aren't listed in the toolbox. You have to select the menu options Crystal Reports > Insert (or right-click on the report and select the Insert menu option). This menu is shown in Figure 1-11. There are ten controls on it that can be added to a report as well as a lot of special fields that display report specific information (e.g. page number, print date, etc.). These controls are described in Chapter 2.

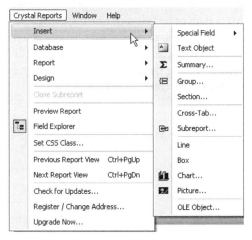

Figure 1-12. Crystal Report's Insert menu.

In the bottom right hand corner of the IDE is the Properties window. As expected, these properties are only applicable for the control that has the focus.

The CrystalReportViewer Control

The CrystalReportViewer control is used on a form to display a report. You have to use this control when you want to preview and print a report.[5] It is found in the form's Toolbox as the last control listed. To access it, you have to use the down arrow to scroll down to it.

The CrystalReportViewer control is fully customizable. Since it is the only way to display a report in your application, you may need to customize it for some applications. You don't want a user to feel like they are looking at a third-party control when using your application. Each of the buttons can be turned on or off in design mode or during runtime. You can also add your own buttons to a form and have them manipulate the report layout and respond to user events. This is described in Chapter 2.

Two-Pass Report Processing Model

It's quite possible that one of the most important parts of learning how to use Crystal Reports is understanding how Crystal Reports reads data and processes formulas while building a report. This is called the two-part report processing model and it is the reason why you can and can't do certain things in a report. While it is certainly possible to create basic reports without understanding the internal workings of Crystal Reports, it won't be long before you find that some subtotals don't seem to be calculating correctly and that certain formulas aren't available when you want them. This is due to the order in which report objects are processed. Throughout this book, I will warn you when these situations can cause you problems and I refer back to this section for more information. Understanding the two-pass report processing model will help you make proper design decisions and avoid problems later.

Crystal Reports processes reports in two stages. This is called the Two-Pass Report Processing Model. The first pass creates the primary data to be printed. During the second pass, Crystal Reports processes grouping data and formulas that can only be calculated while the report is printing. Figure 1-12 shows the two-pass report processing model diagram found in the Crystal Reports documentation. Along the left side of the diagram is the pass number. To the right are the actual processes performed during each pass.

---

[5] If you want to send a report directly to the printer without previewing first, this is discussed in Chapter 2.

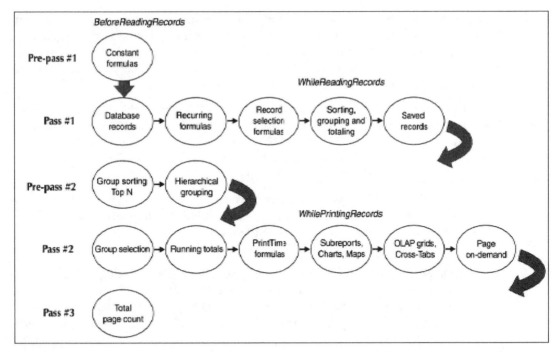

Figure 1-13. Two-pass report processing model

The first thing you might notice is that it looks like a lot more is going on here than just two passes. This is because the diagram also shows "pre-passes" that get the data ready for the pass. There is also a third pass shown, but this is only used when the report prints a total page count at the bottom of each page. Semantics aside, there are two primary passes that are performed for the majority of reports.

The first pass reads individual records one at a time from the database and calculates any formulas that use them. This pass will only calculate the formulas that are based on raw data within a record or that perform simple calculations. As each record is read and the formulas are calculated, the results are stored in a temporary file to be used during the second pass.

After the first pass is finished, Crystal Reports performs a second pass where it evaluates all summary functions on the data and selects the data to be displayed for groups. This wasn't possible during the first pass because all the data had not been read yet. During the second pass, all the raw data has been read into the temporary file and it can be evaluated and summarized as a whole.

The key to getting the most out of this diagram is to look at the relationships between each step and see where a process appears within the hierarchy. The steps are processed from top to bottom and from left to right. For example, in pass #1 the first step is to read the database records. After that, it will calculate formulas and the record selection formula. You certainly can't calculate the formulas prior to reading the data.

A rule of thumb is that formulas should only reference formulas from a previous pass. For example, a formula that is calculated in pass #1 can't reference a formula calculated in pass #2. The formulas calculated in pass #2 generally involve using more than one record and the formula's value hasn't been calculated yet in pass #1. Formulas that reference a formula in the same pass can cause unpredictable results as well.

For example, if you have Formula A and Formula B and they are both calculated in pass #1 you can't be certain which one gets calculated first. If Formula B makes reference to Formula A, the calculation might be wrong because it's possible that Formula A doesn't have a value yet. Luckily, there are ways to fix this so that your formulas are accurate. We talk about this more in the chapters on formulas.

Many times, Figure 1-12 is used to explain why you can't do something rather than explain why you can do it. For example, you can't chart the value of a summary formula. This is because summary formulas and charts are both processed in pass #2. Since they are on the same level, the summary formula hasn't been calculated yet.

Let's define exactly what types of formulas and data are processed during each pass. This makes it easier to categorize your own formulas and determine how they can be used in a report. In many parts of this book, you'll find that certain types of formulas aren't allowed with certain report objects. You can refer back to this section to quickly identify which formulas are being referred to.

Pre-Pass #1

Pre-pass #1 calculates formulas that don't reference any database fields. This usually involves simple math or assigning constants to a variable. For example, the next two formulas are both calculated in pre-pass #1.

```
X := X + 1;
Pi := 3.14;
```

Pass #1

Pass #1 reads in data from the database one record at a time. After each record is read, the record selection formula evaluates whether the data should be printed or if it should be filtered out. Formulas that only reference database fields from the current record are calculated next. The last step is to perform sorting, grouping and building cross-tabs. When finished, all the data is saved to a temporary table for use in pass #2.

In summary, the primary steps that happen during pass #1 are:

- Reading the data from the database.

- Filtering records using the record selection formula.

- Calculating formulas that use database fields.

- Sorting and grouping data.

Pass #2

Pass #2 has steps that involve more complex data processing. The data is grouped, running totals are calculated, charts and maps are built, and complex formulas are calculated. As a general rule, the steps in pass #2 are performed while the report is printing data. All the data used during this pass is read from the temporary table created in pass #1 and the database isn't read anymore.

The key aspect of pass #2 is understanding which formulas get processed during this stage. The list of formula types that get calculated in pass #2 is extensive. Formulas that have the following characteristics are processed in pass #2:

- Using the WhilePrintingRecords function. This forces a formula to be calculated while the report is printing the individual records.

- Using summary functions such as Sum, Count, Average, etc.

- Using Print State functions such as Previous, Next, TotalPageCount, etc.

- Using shared variables with subreports.

Tip

An easy way to determine whether a formula is calculated in pass #1 or pass #2 is to let Crystal Reports tell you. First, make sure the formula is being used somewhere on the report (if not, temporarily add it to the Details section until you are finished with this tip). Right-click on the formula and examine the pop-up menu. If you see the Insert menu option (for summary formulas), the formula is a first pass formula. If Crystal Reports doesn't list the Insert option on the pop-up menu, it is a second pass formula. Summary calculations can't be performed on second pass formulas, and therefore, Crystal Reports won't give you that option on the pop-up menu.

Pass #3

In pass #3, Crystal Reports only calculates the total number of pages in the report. If your report doesn't print the total number of pages on each page (e.g. "Page 1 of 20"), this pass isn't run. For optimal report performance, you don't want to print the total number of pages in the report because Crystal Reports has to internally generate the entire report prior to printing the first page. If you do need to print this on your report, it's best to leave it off while you are designing the report so that testing of the report goes faster. Put it on the report once you feel that the report is finished.

Since Crystal Reports is fully integrated with Visual Studio .NET, you may be tempted to think that creating a new report is a simple matter that only takes a minute or two. While this is true after you had a little experience, creating a report the first time can be confusing if you don't follow the proper steps. This chapter shows you what steps are required and how to do them, providing you with a foundation for all chapters to follow. After writing a couple of reports, these steps become second nature. There are two parts to learn: creating a report and printing a report.

Creating a Report

Reports are files that must be created with the Visual Studio IDE. This requires opening a project and building the files within it. Adding a report to a project involves 5 steps. Each step has different options that you need to consider before implementing it.

Table 2-1. Steps for writing a report.

Step	Description
1. Creating a new report file	From the menu, select Project/Add New Item. Follow the prompts to select the report type.
2. Running the report experts	Use the different report experts to identify the tables and fields to print and get a good start in the right direction. This is optional.
3. Setting the designer's defaults	Make sure your development environment is the way you want it before working on your report.
4. Adding report objects to the report	Add the different objects that your report needs. These objects consist of textboxes, fields, etc.
5. Formatting the objects	Set the properties of the objects so that they are formatted properly. These properties consists of fonts, sizes, etc.

Before you add a report to your project, you need to know what your reporting goals are, and how the report will help fulfill these goals for your application. None of the options presented here are complex, you just need to be aware of what they are in advance. The following sections explain each step in detail and tell you what you need to consider when doing each one.

Creating a New Report

To create and print a report, you need to create a new report for your project. Once it is created, you can modify it using the report designer and then call it from your application.

Creating a new report is done in two different ways. The first is to select the menu options Project > Add New Item. The other way is to right-click on your project name in the Solutions Explorer window and select Add > New Item. Both of these methods open the Add New Item dialog. Scroll down near the bottom to select Crystal Report, type in a report name, and click Add.

The Crystal Report Gallery dialog box opens (see Figure 2-1). You are given the option of using the report expert, creating a blank report, or creating a report using an existing report. If you choose the Report expert option, you can tell it the type of report expert to use in the list box below the options. If you choose to start with a blank report, the gallery goes away and a new report is created. This report gives you the five basic report sections and each is empty. Add report objects to the proper sections and format them to build your report.

You can also create a new report based on an existing report by selecting Project > Add Existing Item. This skips the Gallery dialog box and immediately shows you the Open File dialog box. A copy of the report is saved in the same folder as your application. All changes are made to the local copy and do not effect the original report.

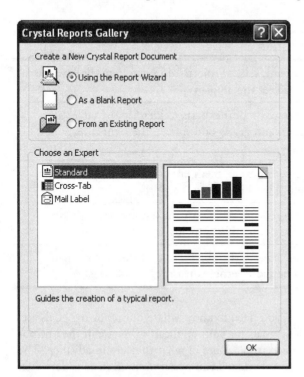

Figure 2-1. The Report Gallery dialog box.

Using the Report Experts

Depending upon your needs, creating reports can be a simple or complicated process. For example, it is very easy to print mailing labels from an address database or a form letter to a list of subscribers. On the other hand, it can be very complicated to write a report that uses multiple sub-reports which are based on user entered parameters. Fortunately, the report experts that come with Crystal Reports make it easy to quickly produce a variety of reports. The experts are useful for writing complex reports because they give you a way to quickly make a professional looking report template that you can customize for your specific needs.

Crystal Reports uses different experts to create three types of reports: Standard, Cross-tab, and Mail Label.

Since experts are designed to be easy to use, you might be wondering why this chapter needs to explain them. The problem with experts is that they are supposed to be simple to use, but often a tool that is simple is generally not very useful. As a result, today's applications are designed so that not only can you quickly answer the questions presented and create the final product, but you can also click on various buttons and checkboxes to add advanced functionality. This gives you the best of both worlds: a simple to use interface with extra features for advanced users.

Each expert consists of a multi-tabbed dialog box. Many of the tabs on each expert are used elsewhere within the main functionality of Crystal Reports. This chapter summarizes each tab and the details are covered in later chapters.

Using the Wizard's Design Pages

Each report expert uses a combination of different pages to question you about how to build your report. Each expert presents a slightly different combination of these tabs. This section describes how to use each page and explains any aspects of it that may not be obvious. The report expert pages are called Data, Link, Fields, Groups, Total, Summaries and Group Sorting, Chart, Record Selection and Report Style.

The Data Page

The Data tab is the first dialog box presented after you select which type of report you want. It lets you select the database and tables that store your data. The database can be a standard data source such as SQL Server or a non-standard data source such as an Excel spreadsheet.

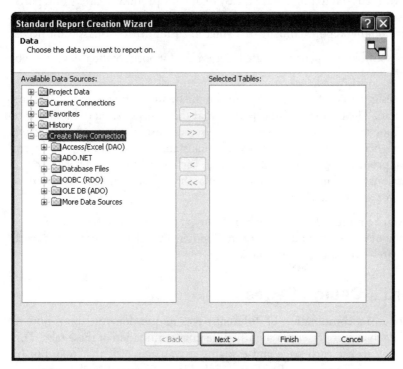

Figure 2-2. The Data page of the report wizard.

The Link Page

Reports that use two or more tables need to have the tables linked so that data can be pulled from both of them. The Links tab lets you set the fields for creating relationships between the tables. Crystal Reports automatically attempts to link the tables together by using common field names. If two tables have a field with the same name and the data types are compatible, then Crystal will link them using this field.

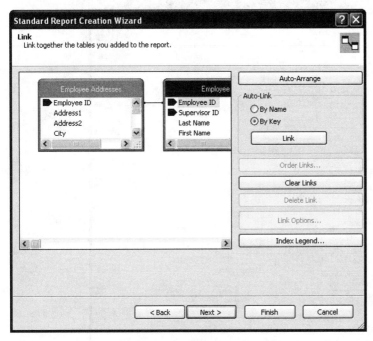

Figure 2-3. The Link page of the report wizard.

The Fields Page

After selecting which tables you want to use for your report, the Fields tab allows you to select which fields will be shown. Adding and deleting fields is done in the standard manner of dragging and dropping them between windows or selecting a field and clicking on the appropriate arrow button.

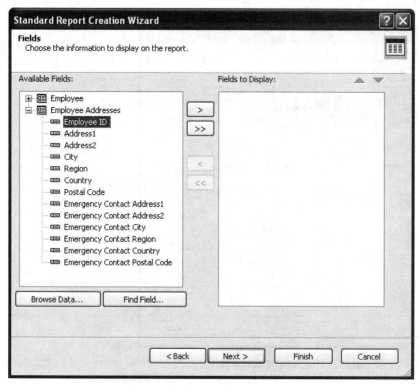

Figure 2-4. The Fields page of the report wizard.

After you add all the necessary fields to your report, you are free to reorder them by using the arrow buttons above the window. Select the field to move and click the up or down arrow to reposition it.

The Grouping Page

Some reports have so much data on them that they can be a little hard to understand. When reports are dozens or even hundreds of pages long, you need to organize the information in a way that makes it easier to absorb the data in smaller pieces. You do this by creating groups within the report. Groups can be based on many things. Some examples are grouping on months of the year or the names of the different branch offices for a company.

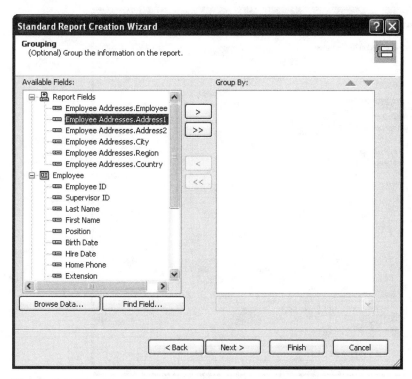

Figure 2-5. The Grouping page of the report wizard.

The Summaries Page

It is very common for reports to calculate sub-totals and other summary calculations on the numeric fields. The Total tab, shown in Figure 2-6, is where you define the summary calculations for the different fields. The left listbox shows all the available fields. The right listbox shows the fields that will have summary functions calculated for them.

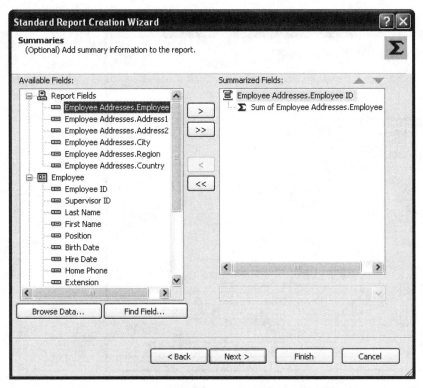

Figure 2-6. The Summaries page of the report wizard.

The Group Sorting Page

When adding a group to a report, you probably assume that every record within the group will be displayed. In most circumstances, this is the case. However, you can tell Crystal Reports to only display a certain number of records based upon their rank. For example, you could have a top salesperson report where you show the top 10 salespeople in your office. You could also have another report that shows the bottom 10 salespeople. The Top N tab lets you do this by sorting the groups based on a summary field.

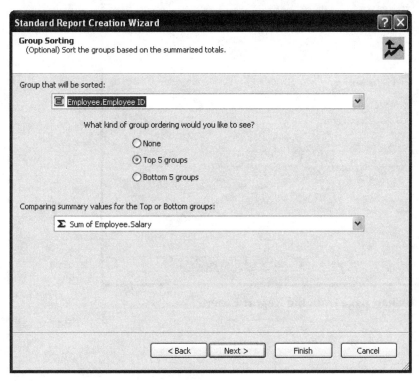

Figure 2-7. The Group Sorting page of the report wizard.

The Chart Page

This tab lets you add a chart to your report.

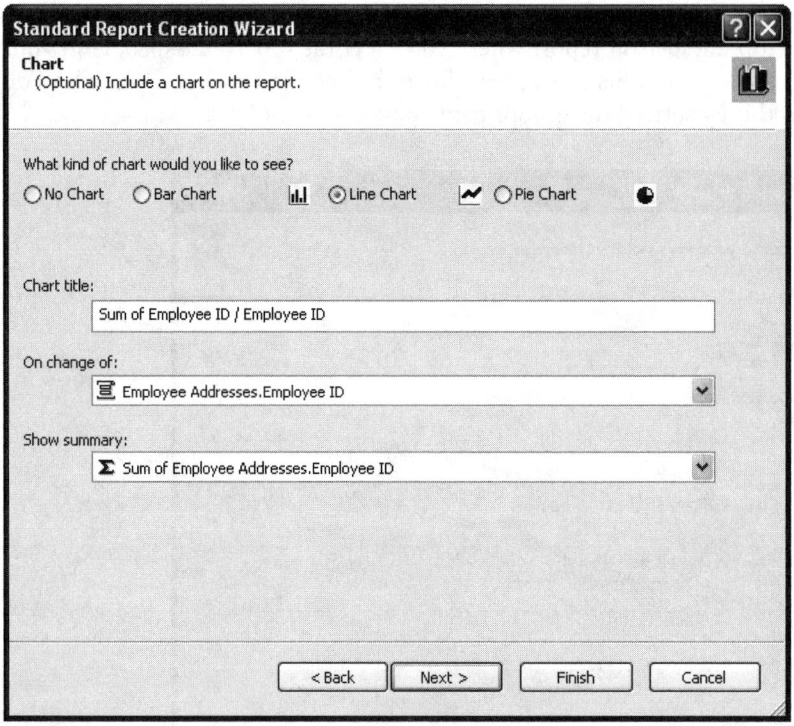

Figure 2-8. The Chart page from the Report Expert.

The Record Selection Page

Some reports need to only show a sub-set of all the data that is in a recordset. For example, a financial report may only show the corporate data for a single quarter or a range of quarters. To filter out certain data so that you limit how much information is shown on a report, use the Select tab shown in Figure 2-9.

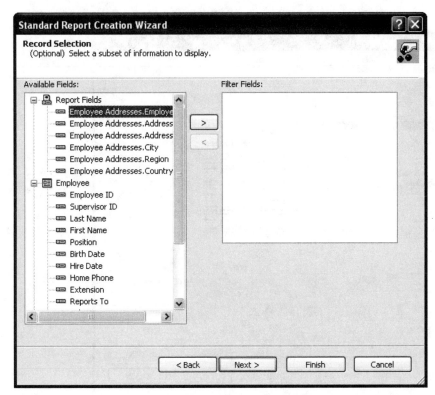

Figure 2-9. The Record Selection page from the report wizard.

The Report Style Page

After specifying the report details, use the Style tab to format everything so that the report has a professional look to it. This tab, shown in Figure 2-10, lists 10 different pre-determined formats that can be applied to your report. These styles make it easy for you to take some raw data and spice it up enough to make everyone think you worked really hard on this report!

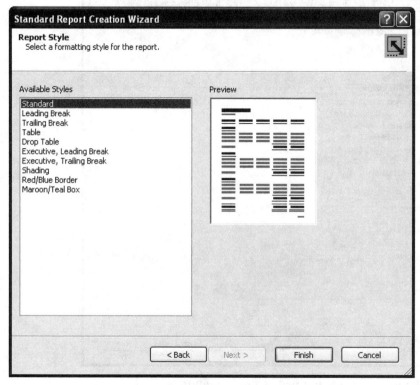

Figure 2-10. The Report Style page from the report wizard.

The Cross-Tab and Customize Style Pages

These tabs are only available when using the Cross-Tab Expert. They let you modify the cross-tab data for what appears in the rows and columns. Modifying these tabs is very involved and is explained in detail in Chapter 11.

Setting the Designer's Defaults

The report designer is where you will spend all your time creating reports and modifying them. There are many different default settings that you can set that control how you interact with the report designer as well as controlling how you access and display data on a report. Knowing what the different options are will not only make you more efficient, but it can also save you a lot of headaches. It is very likely that once you set these default values you will not come back to this step. However, when starting a new application, it would be beneficial to set the default values for how different report objects are displayed. For example, if you decide to always make group headers a certain font, you can set that to be the default and you won't have to modify it every time.

To modify the default settings, select the menu options Crystal Reports > Design > Default Settings. The Options dialog box appears. There are seven different tabs that control the default settings. Each tab affects different parts of the designer and report output.

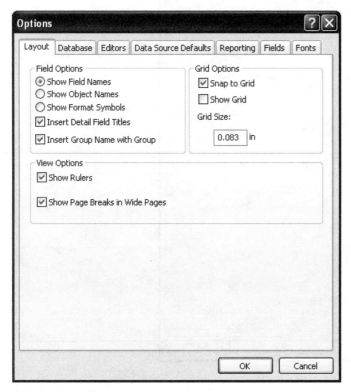

Figure 2-11. The Options dialog box.

The Layout Tab

The Layout tab effects your interaction with the report designer. The Field Options frame sets how fields are shown on the designer. You have the option of showing the names of the fields that are being displayed, the names that were assigned to each object, or format symbols. Showing the format symbols is useful for seeing how the different numbers will be formatted and seeing the maximum width that a string can use.

The Grid Options frame will be discussed in the Adding, Resizing, and Moving Controls section. It lets you turn the grid markers on and off and set whether objects must align with them. The View Options frame sets what is shown in design mode.

The Database Tab

The Database tab effects how items are displayed in the Field Explorer and it has settings for tweaking performance. See Figure 2-12. The settings for changing the Field Explorer are many. They consist of deciding what types of objects are to be displayed and how the items will be sorted.

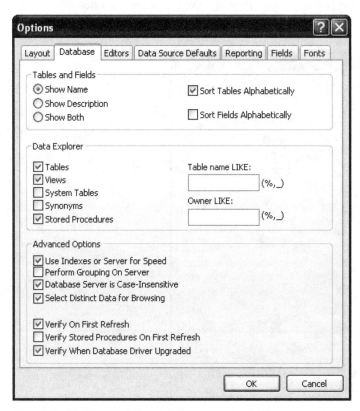

Figure 2-12. The Database tab.

Performance related settings are listed in the Advanced Options frame. The setting to use indexes on the server is set by default. Using indexes on the server gives you better performance because the server is optimized for doing this. The other performance related setting is to perform grouping on the server. Just as performing indexes on the server is faster, so is having the server do the grouping. Unfortunately, you can only use this option for accessing SQL tables directly. It isn't available when reporting off queries.

The Editors Tab

The Editors tab modifies those fonts that the Formula Editor and SQL Expression Editor use to display the programming code. You are free to customize the different programming elements to your heart's content.

The Data Source Defaults Tab

The Data Source tab lets you specify a default folder where the database files are located. This is used with the Data tab of the Report Expert. When selecting Database Files, it will display the Open dialog box and default to the folder you specified.

The Reporting Tab

The Reporting tab affects the output of your reports. See Figure 2-13. The top frame lets you set how data is read from the data source. You can automatically convert DateTime data to a String, a Date, or keep it as a DateTime data type. See Chapter 8 for a discussion of the date data types. Within this frame, you can also convert NULL fields to their default value. This is very useful for ensuring that numeric fields are printed as a zero and not an empty field.

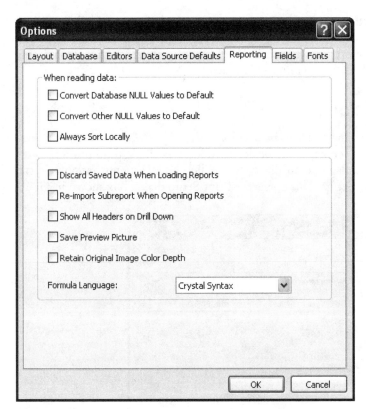

Figure 2-13. The Reporting tab.

The bottom frame contains miscellaneous options. Reports can save their data so that they don't have to reload and process the records every time (this really improves printing speed). If you want your reports to discard the old data and always re-query the data source for the latest data, turn the option on. You can also tell it to re-import subreports so that they are always refreshed when printing a report.

You can set whether drill-down reports will show the column names for the drill-down data. A preview picture (thumbnail) can be saved every time you run a report. The last option lets you set the default formula language as will be discussed in Chapter 8.

The Fields Tab

Every data type that can be displayed on a report has a default display format. For example, the default for displaying a number is to use two decimal places. The Fields tab lets you set the default formats for all the available data types (see Chapter 8 for a list of data types). By changing the default here, every new object that is added to your report after changing the default will use this setting. Any objects that were added before you made the change will not reflect the new format.

The Font Tab

Just as the Fields tab sets the default format for the different data types, the Font tab sets the default font for the different fields on a report. For example, you can make field titles appear in italics while group names appear in bold. Once again, these changes will only affect objects that are added after you make your changes.

Page and Printer Options

The first aspect of a report that needs to be decided is the page size and orientation. You can also specify whether the report should be designed for a specific type of printer. These properties are set with the Page Setup dialog box. Click on the menu options Crystal Reports> Design > Printer Setup. This opens the Print Setup dialog box shown in Figure

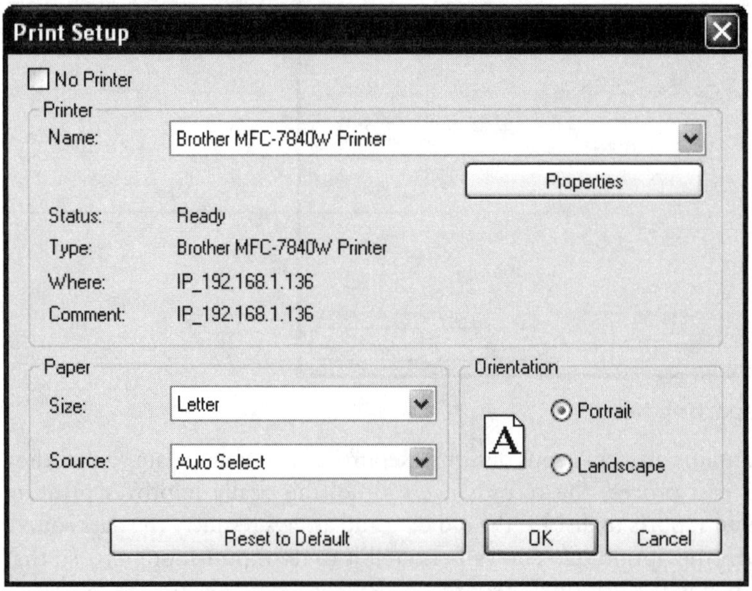

Figure 2-14. Page Setup properties.

The Print Setup dialog box is pretty self-explanatory. In fact, it's similar to the Printer Page dialog box you see in most Windows applications. It lets you select which printer to send the report to, the paper size, and the orientation.

Best Of The Forum

Question: I want to print my report on A6 paper, but the Size dropdown box doesn't have this option listed. How can I design my report for A6 paper?

Answer: The Print Setup dialog box only lists paper sizes for the selected printer. If you want to print on a specific paper, you need to install and select a printer that supports that size.

The first option, in the top left corner, is the most interesting of them all: No Printer. Even though you may assume that most reports will be sent to a printer, there are times when it's beneficial to not specify a default printer. Let's look at how this works.

We first need to talk about printer drivers. Although you might assume that each report will look the same no matter which printer it is printed on, this isn't the case. Each printer has a software driver associated with it that determines how something gets printed. There are very small differences between each type of printer and that can change the output just slightly. Although this probably seems insignificant right now, when you are creating reports that require each object to be in a precise location on the paper (e.g. forms based reports), even a small variation can have a big impact. Another time this is important is when a report tries to print so much data on a single page that you try to squeeze everything down to fit. You shrink the report so that when it prints on your printer everything is sized perfectly. But then you distribute the report to the rest of the company and people start complaining that the digits of some numbers are getting chopped off. When you investigate the problem you find that they have a different type of printer than you do and the fonts are slightly different than your printer. This wastes all the time you spent sizing everything perfectly. In some circumstances you will find that the person has the same printer as you do, but they haven't downloaded the latest printer drivers like you did and this messes things up as well. So you can see how print drivers can have a big impact on a report's output.

There are two options for using the No Printer setting. When it is checked, the report is optimized to be displayed on the screen. When the No Printer option is not checked, the report uses your computer's default printer driver to display the report preview.[6] This gives a more accurate representation of how it will look when printed on your specific printer. If there is a specific network printer that everyone in the office uses, click the Printer button and select that printer from that list. This optimizes the report to be printed on the office printer. If you want to use a type of printer that your users have but you don't have access to, you need to at least install the printer driver so that Crystal Reports can use it for the

---

[6] Your computer's default printer is set through the Windows Control Panel.

report preview. Although you won't personally print on that type of printer, Crystal Reports will format the report just for that printer driver.

Please note that all this worrying about printer drivers is overkill if your reports are printing fine. This is only a concern when precise placement of report objects is required and people are complaining that their reports don't look quite right. Then you can go back to these printer settings and test whether changing them improves the output or not.

Tip

If your users all have different types of printers then it is sometimes best to choose the No Printer option. By telling Crystal to not format the report according to one particular type of printer then you aren't locking the report into a specific printer driver. Setting the No Printer option keeps the formatting generic enough so that the report prints fine on all types of printers. This can be your best bet for solving those tough printer problems.

Summary Info

Each report has summary information associated with it. This makes it easy to determine who designed the report and what its purpose is. The Document Properties dialog box is where you enter this information. Open it by selecting the menu options Crystal Reports > Reports > Summary.

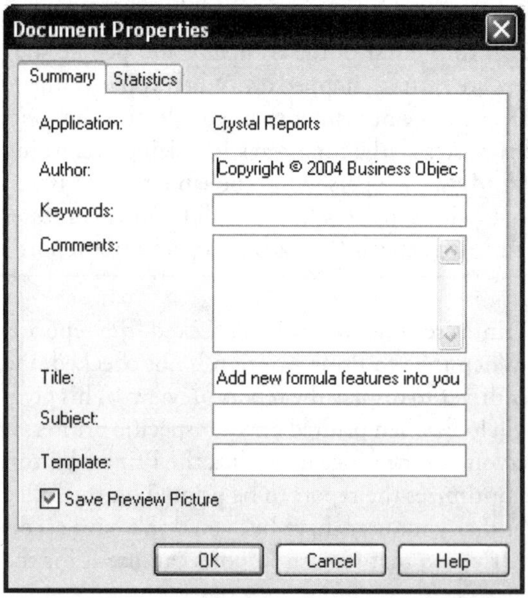

Figure 2-15. The Document Properties dialog box sets the summary info.

The fields you can enter information for are: Author, Keywords, Comments, Title and Subject. Entering good descriptions into the Comments and Subject fields makes it easier for someone else to look at the report and quickly see what the report does. Entering your contact information into the Author field makes it easy for them to locate you for more information.

The Save Preview Picture checkbox sets whether or not to save a snapshot of the first page of the report with the report file. This is saved in the reports's metadata.

There is one interesting benefit to entering this summary information. If you are using the stand alone version of Crystal Reports, e.g. Crystal Reports XI or 2008, this information is displayed in the Open File dialog box. This makes it easy to find out about a report and see a preview of it before opening it. Considering that report file names sometimes use cryptic abbreviations, this makes it easier to determine which report to open.

Miscellaneous Report Options

The last location for setting report options is the Report Options dialog box. It lets you set a variety of different options such as database optimization settings, using report alerts, the handling of grouping data, etc. I hesitate to mention this dialog box at this point in the book because all these options are advanced settings and aren't appropriate for an introductory chapter. They are all discussed within the appropriate chapters later in the book. However, just so that you see what I'm talking about, you can get to the Report Options dialog box by selecting the menu options File >Report Options. It is shown in Figure 2-16.

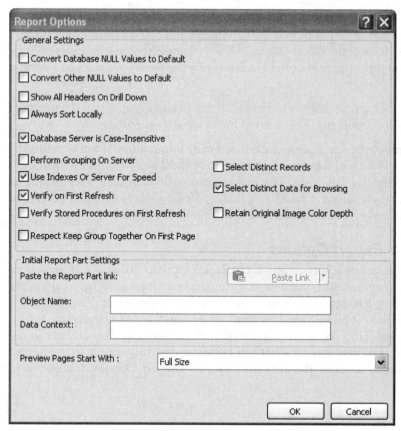

Figure 2-16. The Report Options dialog box.

Using the Report Objects

A report is very similar to a Windows form. Just like a form, the report is listed as a separate object under your project in the Solution Explorer window. There are various controls that can be added, and it is a class that has to be instantiated before using it. The objects that are added to a report are also similar to the ones you use when building forms. This section describes the different objects and how they are used. It also gives you a reference for the properties of each object. Every property isn't listed because that would require reprinting the MSDN documentation.[7] the properties you'll need to use on a regular basis are highlighted here.

There are three controls in the report toolbox (see Figure 2-17). You can access these and many others by selecting the menu options Crystal Reports > Insert (see Figure 2-18).

---

[7] There are already too many .NET books that consider printing out the MSDN tables to be quality writing. I don't want this book to be put in that category.

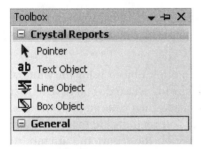

Figure 2-17. The control Toolbox.

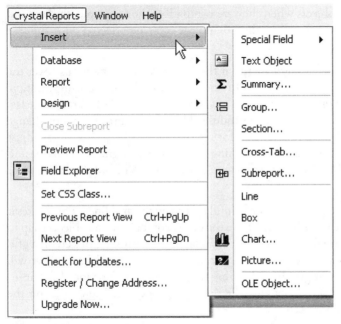

Figure 2-18. The Insert menu option.

Adding, Resizing and Moving Report Objects

The objects on a report work the same as the controls on a form. The objects that are listed in the toolbox can be added to the report by dragging and dropping them onto the proper section of the report. You can also double-click on them and they will be automatically added to the section that has the focus (its header bar will be blue while the other header bars will be gray). If you have an existing control that you want to reuse and it has already been formatted, you can highlight it and copy and paste it. This creates a copy that is attached to your pointer and will move around as you move your mouse. When you have it positioned properly, click the mouse button to drop it there. You can also select multiple objects for copy and paste.

Selecting multiple objects is done by holding down the control or shift key and clicking on the individual controls. You can also draw a temporary window on the report and any controls that are included in the window get selected. Do this by holding down the mouse button and moving the mouse to enlarge the box. Let go of the mouse when the box is complete and the objects will be selected.

There is a strange behavior to be aware of when selecting multiple objects using the window technique. You can't draw a window if another object is already selected. You have to first click anywhere on the report to unselect the current object and then you can draw the box. For example, assume that you selected a textbox object. You then decide that you really wanted to select multiple textboxes so you click elsewhere on the report and attempt to draw a window. Unfortunately, nothing will happen. It only results in the textbox getting unselected. You need to click the mouse again to start drawing the window.

You can only select multiple objects when they are compatible. For example, the box and line objects can be selected together, but the box object can't be selected with the text object.

Resizing a control is done by selecting it to give it the focus. Position the mouse over the sizing handles on any side and drag them to the new location. When resizing multiple objects, the sizing handle will only appear on the last control selected. As you resize the last control, its new size changes as you move your mouse. The other controls will not change until you release the mouse button. An option for resizing objects is to let Crystal adjust their size to be the same for each one. After selecting all the objects, right-click on one and select the Size menu option. From there, you can choose Same Width, Same Height, or Same Size.

When moving objects on the report, it can be helpful to display the grid lines. This makes it easier to line up objects with each other. You have the option of making the objects snap to the grid lines. This means that when you move a control, its edge must be placed on a grid line. It can't be placed between grid lines. When you release the mouse, the object will automatically snap to the nearest grid line. Turning the grid lines feature and the snap-to feature on and off is controlled by changing the designer properties. Right click on the report and select Design/Default Settings.

An easy way to align multiple objects is to use the Align menu option. After selecting the objects, right-click on one of them and select Align. The options to choose from are Tops, Middles, Bottoms, Baseline, Lefts, Centers, Rights, and ToGrid. Each of these options aligns multiple objects to a single object. The object that is used as the basis for alignment is the last object selected. You can identify the last object selected by seeing which one has the sizing handles on it.

Formatting Strings

String output can be formatted in a way similar to formatting a cell in a spreadsheet. You can modify its font and border. There are also formatting options that are specific to Crystal Reports. These options consist of suppressing the field, letting the width grow, rotating the text, paragraph specific formatting and hyperlinks. Almost every option on this dialog box can be set using formulas. This is discussed in more detail in Chapter 7. The formatting options are available for textbox objects, formulas, report fields, and special fields. Access the formatting dialog box by right-clicking on the field and selecting Format.

The first tab of the Format Editor dialog box is the Common tab (see Figure 2-19). The properties shown on this tab are common to most of the report objects available. These properties are described in Table 2-2.

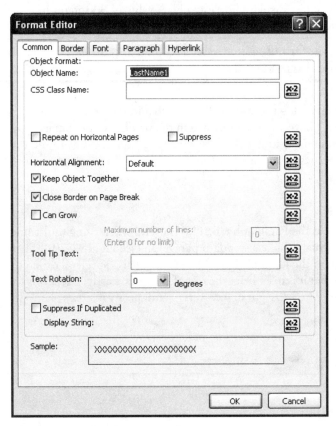

Figure 2-19. The Common tab.

Table 2-2. Properties of the Common Tab

Property	Description
Can Grow	Allows the field to expand if the object isn't big enough to hold the data. The field will only expand vertically and result in the height increasing. The width does not expand.
Close Border on Page Break	If a field has a border, and the field extends to another page, this closes the border on the first page.
Horizontal Alignment	Sets the alignment to Left, Right, Center or Justified.
Keep Object Together	Do not let the object cross over into another page.

RepeatOnHorizontalPages	Repeat the object on horizontal pages for cross-tab reports.
Suppress	Hides the object.
Suppress If Duplicated	Hides the object if it had the same value in the prior record.
Text Rotation	Rotates the text to a specified angle. A value of 0 is the default and the text displays horizontally. A value of 90 rotates it vertically upward. A value of 270 rotates it vertically downward.
Tool Tip Text	Uses the formula editor to set a string that is displayed when the mouse hovers above the field.

The next two tabs on the Format dialog box are the Border tab and the Font tab. Both of these tabs are simplistic and don't have anything unusual in them. The Border tab lets you specify which sides should have a border and it also lets you change the shading around the object. The Font tab has properties to change the font and use different effects such as strikethrough and underline.

Formatting Paragraphs

The fourth tab of the dialog box is the Paragraph tab. This is useful when using multi-line objects and you want it to be formatted like a standard paragraph (see Figure 2-20). It lets you customize the indentation on the left and right sides. You can also specify a different indentation for the first line so that it is inset from the rest of the lines. Lastly, it lets you set the line spacing, the reading order (left to right or vice-versa), and specify if it uses plain text or text formatted as RTF.

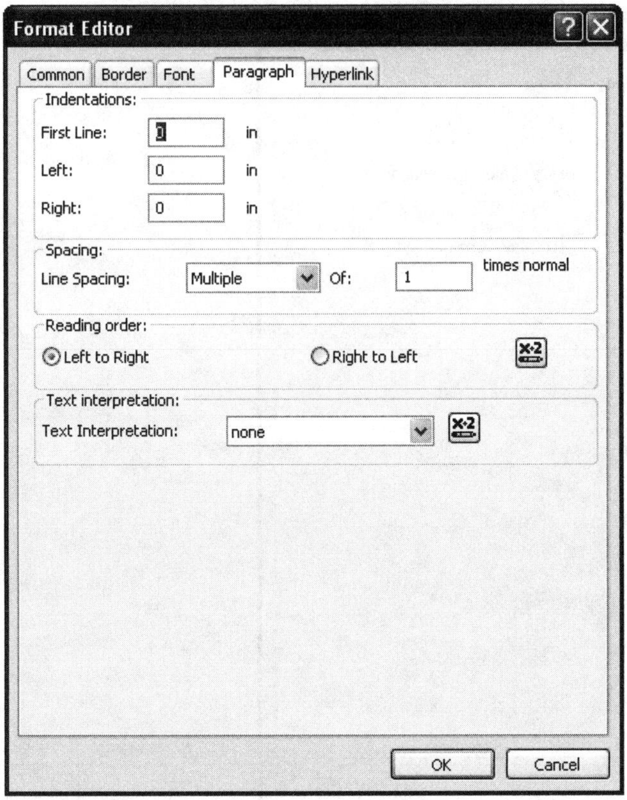

Figure 2-20. The Paragraph tab.

Formatting Numbers

Numbers are very similar to regular text objects in that they display characters on the report. The difference being that they can only display numeric characters. Thus, while they have similar formatting features (fonts, borders, etc.), they also have their own unique formatting settings (currency, number of significant digits, etc.).

The Number tab of the Format Editor, shown in Figure 2-21, displays the most common ways of formatting numbers in the Style list.

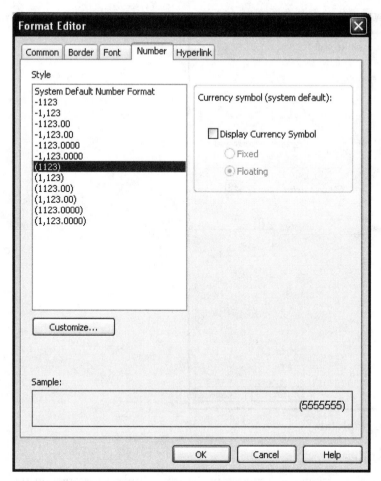

Figure 2-21. Formatting number with the Number tab.

To format a number, look in the Style list and find the format you want and click on it. To the right of the Style list is the Display Currency Symbol option. Check it to format the number as currency. You can make the currency symbol fixed (it always stays along the outermost edge of the field) or floating (it stays directly next to the numbers).

At the bottom of the Numbers tab is the Customize button. Click this button when you need more precise formatting than what is available in the Styles list. Clicking on the Customize button opens the Custom Style dialog box shown in Figure 2-22.

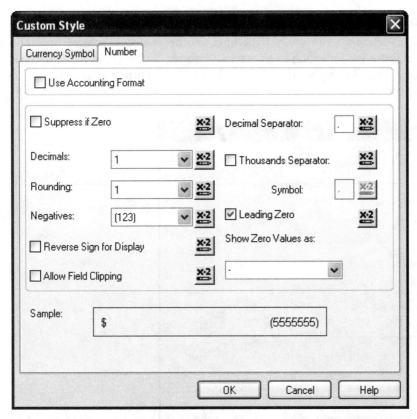

Figure 2-22. Custom Style dialog box for formatting numbers.

The Custom Style dialog box initially opens at the Number tab. It has a lot of information on it, but it is pretty simple nonetheless. You can set how many decimals to display, what the decimal separate should be, whether it should be suppressed when zero, etc. As you make changes to the number format, a preview of what the number looks like is shown at the bottom.

An important setting is the Allow Field Clipping checkbox. This tells Crystal Reports to chop off the leftmost digits if the number is too big to be displayed within the size of the report object. Unfortunately, this is a very dangerous setting because you can lose significant digits and not realize it. For example, the number "599,000" could be displayed as "9,000". When Allow Field Clipping setting is unchecked and the number is too big to fit on the report, Crystal Reports displays "######" instead. This alerts you to the fact that you need to resize the report object so that it is large enough to display the full number.

The Custom Style dialog box also has a Currency Symbol tab. It is simple to use as well. It lets you set the character to use for the currency symbol, specify where it is located and set whether it is fixed or floating.

Adding Hyperlinks

Crystal Reports lets you assign fields to be hyperlinks to other sources of information. The most common example is a hyperlink to an external website. But, you can also link to an email address or a file. Clicking on the Hyperlink tab of the Format Editor, shown in Figure 2-23, lets you makes these settings.

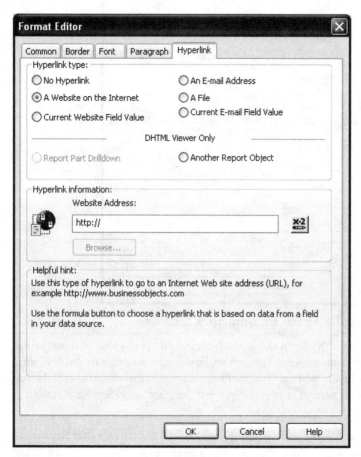

Figure 2-23. Hyperlink tab of the Format Editor dialog box.

The top section of the Hyperlink tab is where you set the hyperlink type. After specifying the link type, the Hyperlink Information section in the middle changes according to the link type. It lets you enter a website's URL, a file name[8] or an email address. If the link information is based upon the underlying data, click the Formula button to create a formula which returns the appropriate link information. For example, an international sales report could have a link to a website that shows the current monetary exchange rate for each currency. The formula can create a dynamic link based upon the country being printed. As

_____

[8] This can be the name of a data file or an executable program.

another example, you can have a hyperlink on the company name that links to the corporate headquarter's location on the MapQuest.com site.

Many databases store company website URLs and employee email addresses within the table. When this is the case, you can select one of the two options, Current Website Field Value or Current E-mail Field Value. This tells Crystal Reports that the field's current value is also the link information.

If the hyperlink opens a file, you have the option to give the user a confirmation prompt before opening it. This lets them change their mind if they decide that the file might take too long to open. The setting that lets the user confirm whether they want to open the file or not is found by selecting the menu items File > Report Options. The setting is called Prompt For Hyperlinks. It is selected by default. Uncheck it if you want the file to open with no user confirmation.

When you are previewing the report and you want to click on the field to open the hyperlink, the report might act a little funny. As you move the mouse around and it passes over a field with a hyperlink, the icon turns into a hand with an extended finger. This lets you know that you can click on the field to jump to the hyperlink.

```
Link
http://www.google.com
http://www.yahoo.com
```

After you view the hyperlink and go back to the report, you can't click on that same field to open a different hyperlink. After the first click, Crystal Reports thinks you are trying to edit the object instead of open the hyperlink. What you have to do is right-click on the field and choose Go To Hyperlink on the pop-up menu.

The problem is that Crystal Reports doesn't let you jump to a hyperlink for objects that are already selected. After you click on it the first time, you can't do it again unless you click somewhere else on the report. This can also be observed by going to the Design tab and selecting a field that has a hyperlink. Then, click on the Preview tab and try to click on that field to go to the hyperlink. It won't let you do it because it was already selected the first time from the Design tab. Fortunately, this isn't a major cause for concern. It's just an interesting behavior that might cause you confusion if you aren't aware of it.

The Text Object

The text object is used to display text, database fields, and special report fields. Each text object can display one of these or a combination of all three. After adding a text object to the report, click on it to edit it.

When writing form letters, using the textbox object with a combination of text and database fields is very helpful. Text in form letters is different than standard reports because it doesn't follow the standard format of showing individual rows and columns. It is displayed in paragraph format with a single space between each word/number. The textbox makes this possible by automatically trimming the spaces around each word and number. Thus, you can insert database fields in with standard text. Any extra spaces around the database fields are not shown. If you have ever programmed in HTML, then you are familiar with this concept. Within HTML, no matter how many spaces you put between words, they will be separated by only one space.

The properties that apply to the Textbox object are covered in the section Formatting Strings.

The Field Object

The standard field object displays data from a table or a formula. The field object is added to your report by dragging and dropping it from the Field Explorer window onto your report. The Field Explorer window is normally docked on the toolbar to the left side of the screen. If you don't have it there, you can pull it up by clicking on the menu items and selecting View > Document Outline. The properties that apply to the field object are covered in the Formatting Text Objects section.

The Line Object

The line object does exactly what you expect; it draws a line. There isn't a whole lot you can do with this except change its color, the width and its style (single line, dashed line, etc.) It does have one interesting feature that solves a common problem with line objects. The problem occurs when you draw a vertical line on a detail section. There are times when the detail section has a field that can grow down the report and make the section longer than expected. You expected the line to be unbroken down the report and now that isn't the case because the line is too short. To fix this, set the property ExtendToBottomOfSection to True. This insures that no matter how short your line is, the end point will be the bottom of the section. If it is a horizontal line, this always moves it to the bottom of the section.

The Box Object

Like the Line object, the Box object is pretty simple. You can change its color, width and style. One nice feature about it is that you can change its properties to round the edges. Depending on how you set the properties, you can make it elliptical or even turn it into a circle. The properties that affect this are CornerEllipseHeight and CornerEllipseWidth. Rather than modify these directly using the Properties window at the bottom right hand corner of the screen, it is much easier to use the Format dialog box. The second tab is the Rounding tab. It has a picture of what the box looks like and below it is a slider. As you move the slider from the left to the right, it increases the curvature of the edges. When the slider is at the far right, the box has turned into a circle. Once you click OK, the dialog box modifies the corner ellipse properties for you.

The Picture Object

The picture object is used for displaying the following image file formats: BMP, JPG, TIFF, and PNG. It doesn't display GIF files. The formatting options are similar to the other controls in that it has the tabs Common, Border, and Hyperlink with similar functionality.

There is a Picture tab, shown in Figure 2-24, that lets you resize, scale and crop the image. If at any point you feel that you resized or scaled it improperly and you want to restore it to its original size, click the Reset button.

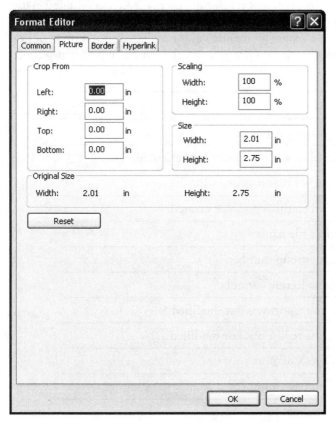

Figure 2-24. The Picture tab of the Picture object's dialog box.

The Chart Object

The Chart object lets you add a chart to your report. There are a variety of options to choose from so that you can customize the chart however you need to. There is so much to cover with this object that it was given a separate chapter. See Chapter 10 for more information.

The OLE Object

The OLE object lets you embed objects inside of your report. Some examples are embedding Word documents or Excel spreadsheets. This is a feature that was brought forward from previous versions of Crystal Reports. It isn't used much anymore.

The Special Field Object

The Special Field object is used for printing all report-related information. For example, it can print the current page number or the total number of pages. This field was created as a catch-all for all the miscellaneous types of report information that you need. Table 2-3 lists the available fields and what they mean. These fields are treated the same as a database field object. They can be added to the report by themselves, or included in a textbox object. They also have the same formatting options described in the Formatting Strings section.

Table 2-3. Special Fields.

Special Field	Description
DataDate	The date when the report was last refreshed.
DataTime	The time when the report was last refreshed.
FileAuthor	The file author that is stored with the report.
FileCreationDate	The date when the report was created.
Filename	The report's file name.
GroupNumber	The current group number.
GroupSelection	The group selection formula.
ModificationDate	The date the report was last modified.
ModificationTime	The time the report was last modified.
PageNofM	Prints "Page X of Y".
PageNumber	The current page number.
PrintDate	The date the report was printed.
PrintTime	The time the report was printed.
RecordNumber	The current record number.
RecordSelection	The record selection formula.
ReportComments	The report comments that are stored with the report.
ReportTitle	The report title.
TotalPageCount	The total number of pages.

Multilingual Support

Crystal Reports prints localized date, time and number formats according to the system's regional settings. These settings are found within the Windows Control Panel. For web requests, the viewer will take the locale from the "Accept-Languages" HTTP header and translate it into a Win32 LCID.

Integrating Reports

After creating a report and formatting it to your satisfaction, the report needs to be integrated into your application. Understanding the best way to integrate reports into your application is essential for designing the best reporting solution. This makes chapter 3 one of the most important in the book.

There are a lot of different ways to integrate a report into an application, and some of the ways can be combined. The different combinations create an interesting matrix of possibilities for you to choose from. If this is your first experience at writing reports with .NET, it may seem a little overwhelming. To try to make this as easy as possible to understand, I first give you an overview of each option. This lets you see the big picture. Afterwards, I break down each option and show the steps to integrate it into your application. This is done for Windows applications as well as ASP.NET applications. Although the differences between Windows and ASP.NET can sometimes be minor, they are important and need to be addressed separately.

Sound good? Now let's get started!

The first reporting related decision is whether the report is previewed before it gets printed. Many users like to see the report prior to printing it so they can verify that it will print the information they are looking for. This is especially true for reports that let the user choose how to filter and display the data. For other reports, you may not want to give the user the option to preview the report. An example is a reporting application that runs a batch print job at a scheduled time during the night. Requiring user intervention would cause the program to hang indefinitely until someone arrives to push the right button. Another example is a group of standardized reports that get printed every month. It is quicker for the user to select the reports to be printed by clicking on checkboxes and printing them all at once. Since the format and filters never change, making the user preview each report is unnecessary.

Previewing reports can be done in a Windows application as well as an ASP.NET application by adding a CrystalReportViewer control to the form/web page. Using the viewer control gives you many benefits. The first is obviously that the user can see what is going to be printed prior to printing it. If it isn't exactly what they want, they can close the preview window and modify the report parameters until the report delivers the necessary information. No waste and another tree gets to live. Another benefit is that the viewer control has numerous built-in reporting functions that save you a lot of work. Rather than writing the code to export reports in different formats, the viewer has a button on the toolbar that does it for you. In fact, the viewer is so useful that I would guess that most of the applications you write are going to use it.

Of course, the viewer isn't ideal for every situation. It requires user intervention for it to be useful. Another downfall of the viewer is that it can only view one report at a time. You can't pass multiple reports to it. Displaying multiple reports simultaneously requires using multiple viewers.

If you decide to send reports directly to the printer, you are going to have to write the programming code to implement the functionality that you need. This could include writing code for printing the report, selecting the page range, and exporting the report to other formats. That's a lot of work! Of course, this book makes it easy by showing you all the programming code to do this, but it's still your responsibility to implement it in the application and test it. See the end of Chapter 14 for more information.

Summary of report integration options

Whether you use the viewer control to preview reports or write the code to send them directory to the printer, there are many options for integrating reports into your application. They range from the simple drag-and-drop to the more complex coding techniques of working with the ReportDocument object model. The one you choose depends upon your needs as well as how comfortable you are working with the ReportDocument object model. Of course, the more code that you're willing to write, the more functionality that you can give the user.

The following list is a quick summary of each reporting option available to you. This gives you an easy overview of what you can do and helps you decide which is best for you. Afterwards, each option is explained in more detail so that you can implement it in your own project. To start being productive right away, you should read through the following summaries and go directly to the section you need.

Smart Tasks Panel

A Smart Tasks panel is a set of shortcuts on the viewer control which automatically sets the properties you need. Use the Smart Tasks button in the top right corner of the viewer control to open the panel and quickly attach a report to your form. This requires zero coding and is the fastest way to integrate reports into your applications.

CrystalReportDocument Component

This component lets you add a report to a form without writing any code. You can have it point to any report and associate it with the viewer control. If you are using the Smart Tasks panel, this automatically gets added to your form and points to the report you selected.

Note

In Visual Studio .NET 2005, The CrystalReportDocument component is called ReportDocment.

Non-Embedded Reports

Non-embedded reports let you load physical report files from your computer using a fully qualified filename. Since the reports are stored separately from your project, they can be shared among users via a common networked drive. Non-embedded reports can be used with the Smart Tasks option or by writing code For ASP.NET applications; this is your only option for using reports.

Embedded Reports

When adding a report to a Windows application, Visual Studio automatically creates a class to represent the report and includes it in your project files. This class inherits from the ReportDocument class. It is called an embedded report because it is part of your application. Updating a report requires recompiling and redistributing the application.

ReportDocument Class

If you don't use the Smart Tasks panel to quickly attach reports to the viewer, you're going to have to use the ReportDocument class to declare and instantiate a report object variable. Whether you use embedded or non-embedded reports, you are still working with the methods and properties of the ReportDocument class. Luckily, in its most simplistic form, it only takes a couple lines of code to instantiate a report and preview it. We'll cover how to use the ReportDocument class in Part II of this book when we look at the details of advanced report customization during runtime.

Printing to the Printer

Crystal Reports doesn't need the viewer control to print reports. You can send reports directly to the printer without requiring the user to preview it first. Although not as common, this is useful when the user has standard reports that get printed every month or when printing batch reports that are processed during off-hours. This involves more coding than using the viewer control. Just like the ReportDocument class, this is covered in Part II of this book since it involves writing code.

The following sections take each option and show you the exact steps for implementing each one in your application. Remember that you don't have to read and understand each method. Each one is simply a different way of producing a report within your application. Focus on the one that meets your requirements and learn it first. Of course, it's always good to understand all the options available to you, but you can come back to this chapter later if you feel that all this information is a bit overwhelming right now.

Smart Tasks

Visual Studio gives you a tool that makes programming applications easier. This tool is called a Smart Tasks panel. When you add a control to a form, a little arrow appears in the top-right corner of the control. Clicking on it triggers a panel to appear with a short menu list of common tasks and properties. The items on this panel are typically things that you will most frequently need. There can also be shortcuts that make it easy to perform certain operations. Using the Smart Task panel in a Windows application produces auto-generated code in a hidden class file called a partial class. When doing it in a web application, it produces auto-generated XML in the ASPX page. Using the Smart Tasks panel is the quickest way to integrate a report into your application because it doesn't require writing any code. This rapidly speeds up development time.

Although the Windows version is very similar to the web version, there are some differences. In fact, you might recall from Chapter 1 that we used the Smart Tasks panel to create both a Windows app and Web form. To make it easier on you, I copied the figures from Chapter 1 here. Figure 3-1 is the Smart Tasks panel on a Windows form and Figure 3-2 shows it on a web form.

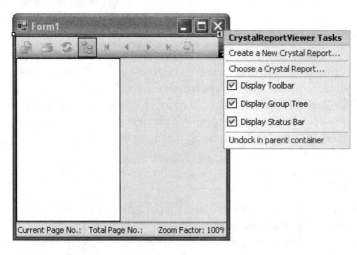

Figure 3-1. Smart Tasks panel on a Windows form.

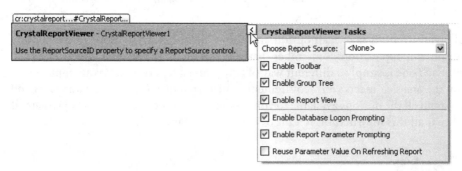

Figure 3-2. Smart Tasks panel on a web form.

You can see that the two panels are very similar, but the web version has a few more options. The first option(s) on each panel lets you either attach an existing report to the viewer control or create a new report from scratch. For some reason, the Windows version uses two links to do this and the web version uses a drop-down list where you choose the option you want from the list.

Upon completion, the web designer automatically creates a CrystalReportSource control and places it on the web form. The CrystalReportSource control enables the tag based application development model, which makes it possible to open the report using XML embedded into the ASPX page. If you are working with a Windows application, you can have the viewer's ReportSource property reference the embedded report class directly or point to the physical report file located on your computer.

Upon completion of selecting/creating the report, both viewer controls will update themselves to show you a preview of the report. Being able to preview a report in design mode is a feature that wasn't available in previous versions of ASP.NET and was a very popular feature request.

The next set of options lets you turn certain viewer features on and off. For example, you can show/hide the toolbar, group tree, status bar and report view. The option to display the status bar is only available on the Windows version because the web report viewer doesn't have a status bar. The option to enable the report view lets you show/hide the report preview in design mode. Although you can preview a report in design mode in both Windows and web forms, the option to disable that feature is only available on the web version of the panel.

The web Smart Tasks panel gives you the option to prompt the user for the login credentials and setting parameter values. In previous versions of ASP.NET, Crystal Reports would crash the web page if you didn't properly supply the user credentials and report parameters via the ReportDocument class prior to showing the report. New for Visual Studio .NET 2005 is that there is a pre-defined web page that is shown to the user if either of those items weren't set correctly. The Smart Tasks panel gives you the option to disable this new feature if you wish.

The last checkbox on the web Smart Task panel lets you persist parameter values between page refreshes. When this is enabled, the user is not prompted to enter the parameter values a second time because they are cached and reused. If this option is disabled, the parameter choices are discarded upon report refresh and you will have to write code to manually populate them via the ReportDocument object model.

Connecting to Secure Databases

If your report's data source is a secure database, you need to take an additional step to pass the user credentials to the report. Otherwise, the user will always be prompted to enter their login information every time they preview the report.

To connect to a secure data source, first make sure to open the form with your report viewer on it. Drag and drop an SQLDataConnection control onto the form. This control is found in the Toolbox window under the Data tab.

After adding the SQLDataConnection, click on its Smart Tasks panel (it has one too) and walk through the steps of setting the security credentials necessary to open the report.

The last step requires that you create the SQL SELECT statement that extracts data from the report. You have to specify the tables, linking properties, and fields that will be printed. Figure 3-3 shows the Configure Data Source dialog box where you enter this information.

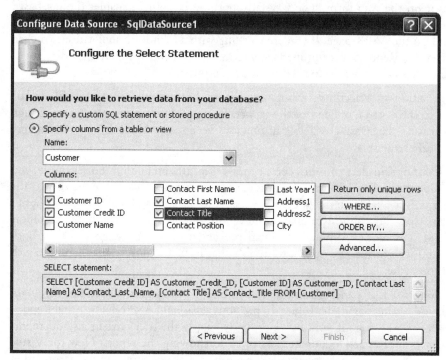

Figure 3-3. Selecting data with the Configure Data Source dialog box.

This dialog box lets you build the entire SQL statement and it displays the actual Transact SQL statement at the bottom as it is created. It doesn't take much thought to realize that this is going to create a huge maintenance nightmare for you. Every time you add tables or fields to your report, you will have to modify the SQLDataConnection object to match the report's data source. Not very practical, if you ask me.

Non-Embedded Reports

When you save a .NET project, each report in the project is saved as a separate ".rpt" file. Although these files are saved in the same folder as your .NET application, they are independent of the project. In other words, you can copy them to another folder and use them in another project. These reports are called non-embedded reports because they are separate from your application. They give you flexibility because you can copy them to a reporting library to be shared among many applications.

Embedded Reports

When you create a report within a Windows application, .NET automatically creates both the report (an .rpt file) and a report class within the current project. The report class has the same name as the report file (without the .rpt extension). Reports that are referenced by their class name are called embedded reports. To use an embedded report, declare and instantiate an object variable of the report class. This lets you open the report, set its properties, and print it.

Unfortunately, embedded reports are not available for ASP.NET applications. When you create a report in ASP.NET, it creates a separate .rpt file and nothing else. In previous versions of Visual Studio 2002 and 2003, embedded reports were available for both Windows and ASP.NET applications, but not any longer. However, if you upgrade an older project, you can still use the embedded report classes and not change your code. But, any new reports that you create will not have the associated report classes created for you.

Non-Embedded -VS- Embedded Reports

Each report type has its own benefits and drawbacks. Non-embedded reports are useful for applications that let the user choose from a dynamic list of reports. An example of this is when the user browses to a directory location and selects which report to print. You can also use non-embedded reports to share reports between different applications. This lets you create a reporting library that is shared on the network. Another benefit is that if you distribute an application and later find that you have to modify a report, you can change the report without rebuilding the application.

A drawback of using non-embedded reports is that when deploying your application you have to remember to include each report file in the deployment project (unless it's stored on the network). If you are writing an ASP.NET application, you also have to make sure that the security settings let you access the report. If you forget either of these steps, you'll wonder why your application runs but printing reports gives you errors.

Embedded reports are the easiest to work with in your application. Since the class is already part of your project, it is pretty simple to reference it by name. You also get the benefit of having the report compiled within the application's executable and you don't have to distribute the report file. However, there are two limitations to using embedded reports. First is that you can't reference reports designed by other applications or by the Crystal Reports stand-alone designer (e.g. Crystal Reports 2008). The second drawback is that modifying a report requires you to recompile and redistribute the application's executable to your users.

Note

Report types are not mutually exclusive within an application. Choosing to open a report as an embedded report doesn't mean you can't open other reports as non-embedded reports. For example, your application can have a set of embedded reports built specifically for that application, but it can also reference non-embedded reports stored in a shared reporting library. Each report can be opened in the way that is best suited for it.

In this chapter, the nuances of non-embedded reports versus embedded reports isn't as important because you are still at the beginning stages of learning how to integrate Crystal Reports into your application. The CrystalReportDocument control doesn't differentiate between the two because it lets you select either one as the report source. It hides the complexities from you. This topic is much more important in Part II of the book where we look at how to do runtime report customization using the ReportDocument object model. Starting in Chapter 14, we'll look at how to write the code which opens a report manually and modifies its properties. This is where the choice between non-embedded and embedded reports becomes more significant.

Previewing Reports in Windows

Most applications give the user the ability to preview a report before printing it. With Crystal Reports, this is controlled by the CrystalReportViewer control. In fact, using the viewer is the only way to preview a report in your application. The viewer is found in the Toolbox at the bottom of the other components. Double-click on it to add it to your form.

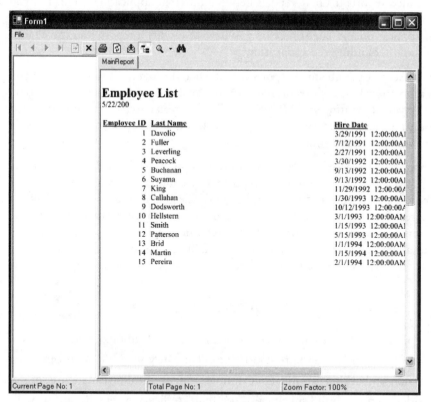

Figure 3-4. The CrystalReportViewer previewing a report.

Figure 3-4 shows the viewer previewing a report. Along the top of the viewer is a toolbar with a variety of navigational buttons. In the center is the report preview window with a

Group Tree window to the left of it. Along the bottom is a status bar that shows the page number information and the current zoom factor.

By default, the toolbar buttons and Group Tree window are all enabled. Each of these features has a corresponding property that can be set in design mode, as well as during runtime, so that you can turn them on or off. For example, a report that doesn't have any groups certainly doesn't need to show the Group Tree window. You may also want to turn off all these features so that you can create a customized preview form using your own buttons. Having a customized preview form lets you control the user interface by using your own style of buttons. This ensures that your application has a consistent look and feel across all forms.

Table 3-1 lists the properties of the CrystalReportViewer. The properties let you enable or disable the features of the viewer. Table 3-2 lists its methods. The methods let you implement the viewer's functionality by calling them from your own buttons. Most of these are self-explanatory, but the tables make good reference material.

Table 3-1. CrystalReportViewer Properties

Property	Description
BackgroundImage	Displays a System.Drawing.Image object in the background of the viewer.
BackgroundImageLayout	Uses the System.Windows.Forms.ImageLayout enumeration to set how the background image is displayed (Tile, Center, etc.).
DisplayBackgroundEdge	A background edge creates a border around the edge of the report page in preview mode. Setting this to **False** makes the edge of the page flush against the viewer's window.
DisplayGroupTree	Toggles the Group Tree window on and off.
DisplayStatusBar	Toggles the status bar at the bottom of the viewer.
DisplayToolbar	Toggles the toolbar on and off.
EnableDrillDown	Sets whether the user can drill down on reports.
EnableToolTips	Toggles the ability to show tooltips when the mouse hovers over a report object.
ShowCloseButton	Sets whether the Close button is available.
ShowExportButton	Sets whether the Export button is available.
ShowGotoPageButton	Sets whether the GotoPage button is available.
ShowGroupTreeButton	Sets whether the GroupTree button is available.
ShowPageNavigateButtons	Turns page navigation on/off.

ShowPrintButton	Sets whether the Print button is available.
ShowRefreshButton	Sets whether the Refresh button is available.
ShowTextSearchButton	Sets whether the Search button is available.
ShowZoomButton	Sets whether the Zoom button is available.

Table 3-2. CrystalReportViewer Methods

Method	Description
CloseView()	Pass a null value to close the current view. Pass a view name to close a specific view.
DrillDownOnGroup()	Drill down on a specific group. See Chapter 12 for details on implementing this method.
ExportReport()	Show the Export dialog box.
GetCurrentPageNumber	Return the page number being viewed.
PrintReport()	Show the Print dialog box.
RefreshReport()	Refresh the report view. The user will be prompted for the parameters and logon information again.
SearchForText()	Pass a string to search for. If found, it returns True and moves to the page that has the string.
ShowFirstPage()	Move to the first page of the report.
ShowGroupTree()	Shows the Group Tree window. It doesn't take any parameters. There is no corresponding method to hide it.
ShowLastPage()	Move to the last page of the report.
ShowNextPage()	Move to the next page of the report.
ShowNthPage()	Pass an integer to move to that page number.
ShowPreviousPage()	Move to the previous page of the report.
Zoom()	Pass an integer to set the zoom level.

Binding Reports to the Windows Viewer

The viewer needs to be told which report to display. This is called binding the report to the viewer. The property used for binding is the **ReportSource** property. There are three ways to set the **ReportSource** property: using the **CrystalReportDocument** component, passing it a non-embedded report filename, and passing it an embedded report class name. Using the CrystalReportDocument is covered in the next section, and the other two methods are covered in Chapter 14 where we discuss runtime report customization.

Using the CrystalReportDocument Component on the Viewer

Adding a CrystalReportDocument component to the form is the easiest way to specify which report to print. Everything about it is visual and there is no code to write. Add it to your form by going to the Reporting section of the Toolbox and double-clicking on it. It will automatically display the Choose a ReportDocument dialog box. This lets you select which report to display. The dropdown control lists all the reports that are part of your project. You can also select the Untyped[9] Report option and set the Filename property. Once you select which report to use, the dialog box closes and the component gets added to your form.

Note

The CrystalReportDocument component has to be on the same form as the viewer control. The viewer can't reference a CrystalReportDocument component on another form.

After the component is added to the form, tell the viewer to use it by clicking on the viewer's **ReportSource** property and selecting the CrystalReportDocument's name from the dropdown list. When you run the application and open the form, the viewer automatically displays the report to the user.

Previewing Reports in ASP.NET

The CrystalReportViewer control is the interface for previewing reports in an ASP.NET application. Adding a viewer control to a web page is as simple as dragging the control from the Toolbox onto the web page. After it is added to an ASP.NET page, it is represented by a simple rectangle.

---

[9] An untyped report is the same as a non-embedded report. This was its name in Visual Studio 2003 and it appears that this menu option was missed when updating the name for Visual Studio 2008.

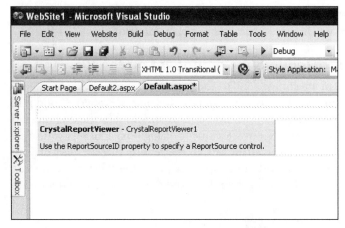

Figure 3-5. The viewer control as positioned on an ASP.NET page.

If you previously worked through the Windows example where you added the viewer control to a form, you will now notice that the ASP.NET viewer looks different than the Windows viewer. When you add the viewer to an ASP.NET page, it only displays a simple rectangle. It doesn't show you a template of what the viewer looks like. However, once you attach a report to the viewer, it will show you a mock-up of what the final report looks like on the web page.

Although the viewer control is very small when you add it to the web page, when you run the application it automatically grows to fill the remainder of the web page. It expands horizontally across the page as well as vertically down the page. This ensures that the report is readable when the page is displayed. This is controlled by the **BestFitPage** property (default value of **True**). If you set this property to **False**, the viewer control will not resize itself and the report will be displayed within the bounds of the viewer. Setting it to **False** is useful when you want to limit the amount of space on the web page that is allocated to viewing reports. Obviously, if you decide to set **BestFitPage** to **False**, you should resize the viewer to make it large enough to comfortably display your report.

When **BestFitPage** property is **True**, the control does not expand upward. It only expands downward and across. Any information above the viewer control remains intact and properly formatted. This makes it an ideal location to put your own controls because you know that they won't be overwritten by the report.

Note
If the Page Layout is set to **FlowLayout**, all information below the viewer will be pushed down the page so that it appears after the viewer control. If the Page Layout is set to **GridLayout**, the information after the viewer control will not be pushed down. The ASP.NET controls will overlap the viewer control. This could either make for a very messy report or you could get creative and implement some interesting formatting effects.

As you can see in Figure 3-6, when the viewer is displayed in an ASP.NET page, it looks very similar to the report preview that you've seen with Windows applications.

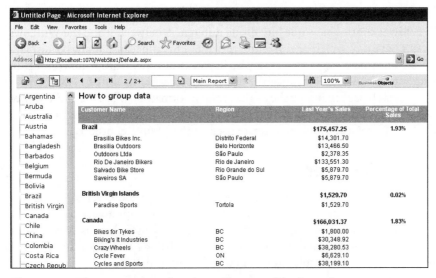

Figure 3-6. The report preview in an Internet Explorer browser.

Best Of The Forum

Question: I want the viewer to have the same look and feel of my website. How to customize the formatting of the viewer

Answer: The viewer control is formatted using a cascading style sheet. If you look at the HTML source for the web page, you'll see the reference to the file default.css. If you want to modify it, the HTML source show you the full file path to the default.css file. You can either modify it directly, or make a copy of it, rename it, and modify the copy. The viewer has a property called CSSFilename that you should change so that it points to the new .css file. The report viewer also supports ASP.NET Themes for a web page. Any changes made to a Theme are extended to the viewer control.

Question: I want to show multiple reports within one viewer control and have a separate tab for each one. How do I do that?

Answer: The viewer control can only preview one report at a time. It doesn't support multiple tabs with a different report on each tab. As a trick, you can use the ASP.NET MultiView control on your form and place multiple View controls within it. Each View control can have one report viewer on it. For example, if you wanted to show three reports on a single web page, you would have three View controls on it and each view control would preview a different report. You can add buttons to the web page to navigate between the different reports.

The ASP.NET viewer control has some interesting differences between it and the Windows viewer. It doesn't have any tabs that run along the top. This is because it always displays new information on a new page. For example, if you drill-down into a new group in Windows, it creates a new tab to display the group information in. But in ASP.NET it simply opens a new web page that only shows the group information. The ASP.NET viewer replaces Windows tabs with a drop-down box in the center of the toolbar. This drop-down box is called a ViewList. Click on it to navigate back to the Main Report area.

Printing from the Browser

Printing has been improved with Visual Studio .NET 2005. In previous versions, you had to use the browser's print button to print the report. This gave you a very poor quality report and everyone complained about it. With the latest release, there is now a print button on the viewer's toolbar and it opens a custom print dialog box (shown in Figure 3-7) and creates a PDF file that is diplayed in a new browser window.[10]

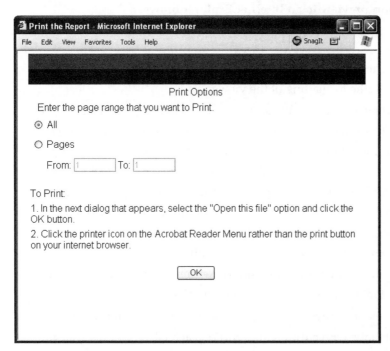

Figure 3-7. ASP.NET custom print dialog box..

---

[10] The user needs to have Adobe Acrobat installed on their computer to view the report.

The last thing you might notice is the "Business Objects" icon at the top right corner of the toolbar. Although this is totally harmless, many people don't like it appearing on their reports. You can get rid of this logo by setting the property HasCrystalLogo to false.

Crystal Reports has the option to print using an ActiveX control. When printing using the ActiveX control, a pop-up window appears (the ActiveX control) and it processes the report. When finished, it opens the Print Dialog box so that the user can choose which printer to print to, as well as set other print options (e.g. the pages, paper orientation, etc.) Be aware that, like all ActiveX controls, the user has to have permission to install and run the ActiveX control on their computer.

To switch how the viewer prints a report, click on the viewer and find the PrintMode property in the Properties window. By default, it is set to "PDF" You can change it to "ActiveX" if you want the report sent to the user's printer.

Note

There is no way for an ASP.NET page to send a report directly to the printer without first letting the user preview it. If you call the PrintToPrinter() method, discussed in Chapter 14, it is printed on the server side printer. If you export the report to another format, discussed in Chapter 19, the file is saved to disk prior to the user being able to print it.

Web versus Windows

The properties of the Web viewer control are similar to that of the Windows viewer control. It has properties for changing the look of the viewer by hiding the toolbar, hiding the toolbar buttons, and hiding the Group Tree window.

Although the Windows and Web viewer controls have properties that perform the same functionality, they often have different names. There are also certain properties that are unique to each control. Table 3-3 compares the common properties of each control so you can see the similarities and differences.

Table 3-3. Comparing the property names of the two viewer controls.

Windows Viewer	Web Viewer
DisplayGroupTree	DisplayGroupTree
N/A	DisplayPage
DisplayToolbar	DisplayToolbar
Dock	BestFitPage
EnableDrillDown	EnableDrillDown

N/A	DrilldownTarget
N/A	HasCrystalLogo
N/A	HasDrillUpButton
N/A	HasViewList
ReportSource	(DataBindings) | ReportSource
SelectionFormula	SelectionFormula
ShowCloseButton	N/A
ShowExportButton	HasExportButton
ShowGotoPageButton	HasGotoPageButton
ShowGroupTreeButton	HasToggleGroupTreeButton
ShowPageNavigationButtons	HasPageNavigationButtons
ShowPrintButton	HasPrintButton
ShowRefreshButton	HasRefreshButton
ShowTextSearchButton	HasSearchButton
ShowZoomButton	HasZoomFactorList
N/A	HyperlinkTarget
N/A	PageToTreeRatio
N/A	ReuseParameterValuesOnRefresh
N/A	SeparatePages

Both controls have properties for hiding the different buttons, but they use different names for them. For example, the properties of the Windows viewer that hides the toolbar buttons are prefixed with "Show", but the web viewer properties are prefixed with "Has". The **Dock** property of the Windows viewer is similar to the **BestFitPage** property in the Web viewer.

The web viewer also has properties that are HTML target values. When initially opening the report's web page or opening a sub-report, you can set whether the new page opens in the same browser window or in a new window. Table 3-4 shows the possible values. These values can be assigned to the **HyperlinkTarget** property.

Table 3-4. HyperlinkTarget values.[11]

Target String Value	Description
_blank	Opens the page in a new, unframed window.
_parent	Opens the page in the immediate frameset parent.
_self	Opens the page in the current frame.
_top	Opens the page in a full, unframed window.

The Windows viewer uses tabs along the top of the form to display different pages of data as the user drills down into the report for more information. As mentioned earlier, there are no tabs in the web viewer control. When a user drills down into group details and sub-reports, a new web page is generated to display the information. Rather than using tabs to look at the different pages, the user can click on the drop-down box or use the Back and Forward buttons. If you have multiple groups on a report, the user can click on the DrillUp button to immediately navigate to the main report. Both navigation options can be turned on or off. The property HasViewList toggles the drop-down box which displays the different groups the user has visited. The property HasDrillUpButton toggles the visibility of the DrillUp button. When the report is at the top-most level, this button is automatically disabled.

The PageToTreeRatio property sets how wide the Group Tree control is. It represents the relationship between how wide the viewer is compared to how wide the Group Tree is. The number entered for this property tells how many units the report page is compared to one unit of the Group Tree control. For example, if the number is 1, then the two areas have a 1:1 ratio and they are equal sizes. Thus, the page is split in half. If the number is 4, the two areas will have a 4:1 ratio, which makes the width of the Group Tree control use 20% of the total browser width.

The SeparatePages property determines whether the report uses different pages or not. If the property is set to True, each web page displays a single report page. If the property is False, the entire report is displayed on a single web page and the user has to scroll up and down.

Caution

Setting the SeparatePages property to True is the most efficient because Crystal Reports only has to process enough information to display one page at a time. Setting the SeparatePages property to False can cause a long delay to rendering the page. Crystal Reports has to process the entire report before it can display it.

---

[11] These are the standard target values used with HTML hyperlinks.

Both Windows and the Web handle refreshing reports somewhat differently. The Windows viewer has a refresh button on the toolbar that the user can click to update the report data. The Web toolbar also has a refresh button, but it is turned off by default. You have to set the property HasRefreshButton to True. The Web viewer has a property called ReuseParameterValuesOnRefresh which tells the viewer that the user shouldn't be prompted when the report is refreshed. The parameter values will be reused. Oddly enough, the Windows viewer doesn't have this property. Everytime a report is refreshed, the user has to re-enter the parameter values. What's worse, the viewer doesn't remember what the user previously entered and makes them enter it all over again. For reports with multiple parameters, if the user just wants to change a single parameter, they still have to enter every parameter each time. To fix this, you have to write code that handles the viewer's ReportRefresh() event and manually populate the parameters. Chapter 16 has sample code that illustrates how to do this.

Binding Reports to the Web Viewer

After adding a viewer to the web page and setting its properties, the report needs to be bound to the viewer. As mentioned earlier, the easiest way to do this is by using the Smart Tasks panel. But if you wish, you can manually add a CrystalReportSource component to your web page and set its properties manually. This works equally well with both non-embedded and embedded reports.

Using the CrystalReportSource Component on the Viewer

The CrystalReportSource component makes it easy to specify which report the viewer is supposed to display. Add a CrystalReportSource component to the web page by double-clicking on it from the Toolbox (under the Reporting tab). When you add a CrystalReportSource component to your form, it adds it below the viewer. It also has a SmartTasks button which, when clicked, lets you open the Configure Report Source dialog box. This lets you select which report will be displayed. The dropdown control lists all the reports that are part of your project and it lets you create a new report or browse for an existing report.

After adding a CrystalReportSource component and setting the report to print, assign it to the viewer using the viewer's ReportSourceID property. When you click on it, there is a drop-down box listing the name of the CrystalReportSource in it.

As a short-cut, you can modify the ReportSourceID property directly and specify the report to print. This automatically creates a new CrystalReportSource component on your web page and attaches it to the viewer.

In Chapter 2, you saw how to build a report using the different report objects and tie it into a database. For creating simple reports this is all you need to know. But you will quickly find yourself developing reports that require more effort than listing records one by one. For reports that consist of dozens, if not hundreds, of pages, providing a meaningful format that groups the data into logical units will go a long way towards making your reports easier to read. Crystal Reports .NET makes this possible by giving you the ability to sort and group data. Grouping reports also gives you the ability to create drill-down reports and summarize data. All of these features are covered in this chapter.

Sorting Records

Being able to sort records in either ascending or descending order is a reporting fundamental. Sorting makes it easy for a user to quickly find a particular piece of data buried inside many pages of data.

Reports can be sorted on a single field or on multiple fields. When sorting on multiple fields, you have to specify which field gets sorted first. When there are duplicate values for the first field, the next field is used to resolve which record gets listed first. An example of this type of report is an employee report that sorts by name. The primary sort field is the last name. When there are duplicate last names, the secondary sort field (first name) is used.

Using the Record Sort Expert dialog box makes sorting records easy (shown in Figure 4-1). To use this dialog box, select the menu options Crystal Reports > Report > Record Sort Expert. On the left is the standard tree-view control listing the available fields. You can sort on fields from the report's data sources or your own custom formulas.

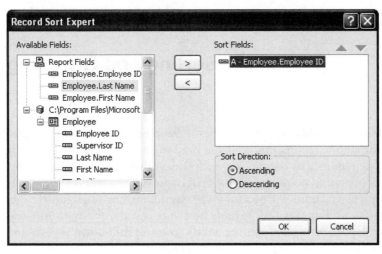

Figure 4-1. The record sort dialog box.

To select a field, either drag and drop it to the Sort Fields window on the right or click on the arrow buttons to move it over. The order in which you add the fields determines which one gets priority in the sort order. The first field listed becomes the primary sort field. The next field is the secondary field, and so on. When there are duplicate values in one of the fields, the next field on the list is used to resolve the conflict. This continues through all the sort fields as long as there are duplicates at each level.

If you wish to change the order that the fields are listed in, use the arrow keys in the top right corner. First, click the field you want to move, then click the appropriate arrow keys.

At the bottom of the dialog box is where you set whether the field is sorted in ascending or descending order. Each field is treated individually. First click on the field name and then click on the sort order.

As an example, let's look at the report shown in Figure 4-2. The primary sort field is the country. The secondary field is the region and this is followed by the customer name.

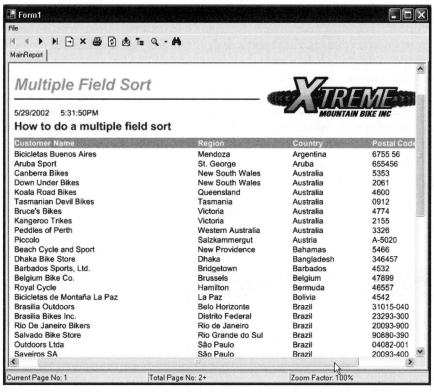

Figure 4-2. The multiple field sort report.

The report first lists all the countries that start with the letter "A". The country Australia has multiple records, so the report performs a secondary sort on the Region field.

If you later determine that you need to change the sorting order, you can modify it by using the same steps mentioned earlier. Just right-click on the report and select Report > Record Sort Expert.

Grouping Records

When a report has a lot of pages, it is hard to quickly find information as well as get a general idea of what the report is telling you. Sorting the data helps you find a specific record, but it doesn't give you high-level summary of what the data means. Grouping records lets you summarize data in a way that the reader can quickly grasp what the report is trying to say.

Grouping records is an advanced form of sorting. It lets you create categories to visually organize the records. You can summarize the data on critical fields and perform summing operations on the data within each group. If you need to see more information, you can explore the detail records that make up the group.

Sorting records in a report results in the records being ordered differently than their natural order, but it doesn't have any effect on how the report is structured. Grouping is different because it creates new sections in the report's design. For every group added to a report there is a corresponding group header and group footer added. This lets you add formatting to designate when a new group starts and when the group ends. Within each section you can show report fields, formula fields or summary fields. It's common to make fields in the group header be a different font (possibly bold) and in the footer it's common to show subtotals. The footer gives you a summary of the data within a group without having to read every line. If you don't need to display the group header or footer, each can be hidden.

Adding and Customizing Groups

Adding and customizing groups is very similar to working with the other sections of a report. Add a new group by right-clicking on the report and selecting Insert > Group. This displays the dialog box shown in Figure 4-3.

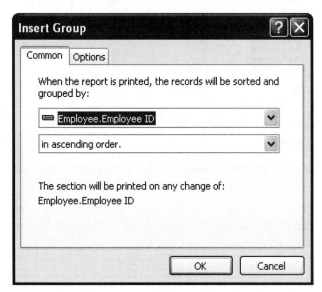

Figure 4-3. The Insert Group dialog box.

The Insert Group dialog box has two tabs. The Common tab sets which field the group is based on and the sorting order of the group values. The Options tab, shown in Figure 4-4, lets you customize the group name field and set whether the group data stays together and whether the group header should repeat on each page.

Figure 4-4. The Options tab of the Insert Group dialog box.

Selecting the Grouping Field

The first dropdown box at the top of the Common tab selects the field that the group is based on. You can choose from a current field on the report, any fields in the current data source, or a formula field. When selecting a group field that is a data type of Date, Time or DateTime, you have more options on how to group. A new dropdown box appears that lets you group on the specific part of the date or time (e.g. month, quarter, hour, etc.)

Setting the Sorting Order

The second dropdown box at the top selects the sorting order of how the groups are listed. With one exception, the sorting options are what you would expect and don't need any explanation. You can choose a sort order that is Ascending, Descending, Original Order (no sorting) or Specified Order.

Specified Order is the option that is not completely intuitive. Specified Order means that you specify the exact order to display every possible data value in that field. Once you select this option, two new tabs appear in the dialog box: Specified Order and Others. This is shown in Figure 4-5.

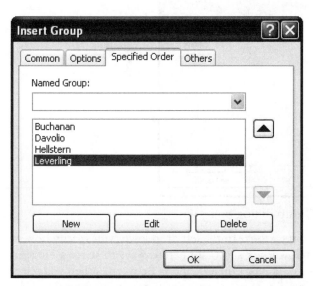

Figure 4-5. The Specified Order tab of the Insert Group dialog box.

The Specified Order tab is where you build the list of how the values are to be sorted. There are two controls in this dialog box. The top control is a dropdown box that lists all the possible values for the group field. The lower control is a listbox which shows the order that each value is to be listed in. Take values from the dropdown box and add them to the listbox in the appropriate order.

The order of the items in the listbox can be changed. Select the item to move and click on either the up or down arrows located to the right of the listbox.

There are two ways of adding items to the list box: adding individual items or adding named groups (a sub-group). Adding individual items is the easiest method because you simply click on one of the values from the dropdown box and it gets added to the list. Unfortunately, if you have a lot of possible values, this could be very time consuming. To make this a little easier, there is a second way of adding items to the list.

The second way of adding items is by creating named groups that specify a range of values. Specifying a group is done in the typical fashion of specifying a lower and upper bounds for the range or building a formula using Boolean logic. It may be easier to think of this as a sub-group. Any value that falls within this range gets put into the named group. This is obviously a faster way of adding the items because you don't have to specify individual values. Named groups also give you a lot of flexibility because the formulas can be quite complex.

To create a named group, click on the New button located below the list. This brings up the dialog box called Define Named Group. You can see in Figure 4-6 that this is a fairly simple dialog box.

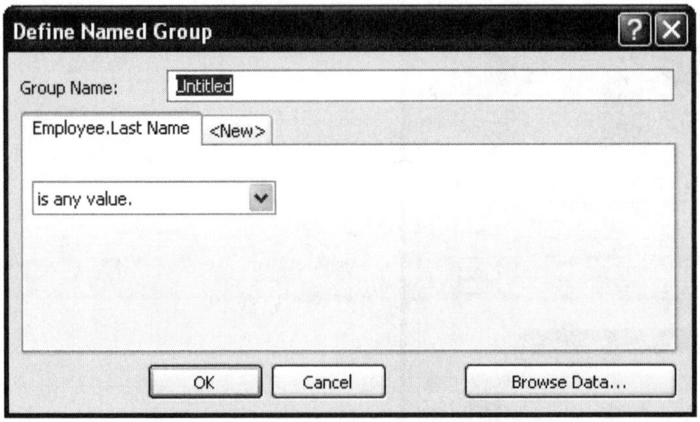

Figure 4-6. The Define Named Group dialog box.

Assign a name to the group in the top textbox. In the left dropdown, you specify how to filter the range of values. The dropdown box shows numerous ways to select a range of values. A few of these are: Is Equal To, Is Not One Of, and Is Between. When you select one of these operators, the proper input controls automatically appear to the right of the dropdown box. The input controls change depending upon the information needed to complete the filter. There are so many different variations of filtering options and their associated input controls, that they won't be explained here. They are all very intuitive and you shouldn't have any problem entering the proper data.

Within a named group, you have the option of using more than one filter. By clicking on the <New> tab, you are shown the same filtering options as on the first tab. But now you can make new selections and the resulting values are also associated with the current named group. From a Boolean logic standpoint, these filters are linked together using an OR operand. Thus, any of them can be true and the record will be included in the named group.

The last tab in the Change Group Options dialog box is the Others tab. Since it is very possible that some reports won't need to specify how every value will be grouped, this tab is used to accumulate all the remaining values that didn't get included in one of the named groups.

This is also useful for reports that group on fields where the data is dynamic and new values are being added. If the new values don't fall within the current named groups, they get associated with the group called Other.

Values in the Other group can either be excluded from the report or included in the report. If they are included in the report, they are always listed as the last group.

Customizing the Group Name

In most circumstances, the group name that is displayed on the report is the current value. For example, if you are grouping by country, then the group name is the country name. If you don't want to display the current value as the group name, you have the option of displaying another value instead. For example, a report group that lists how many products were sold for each day of the month is typically based on the inventory number. If the report is intended for users who recognize a product's name, but not its inventory number, then the group header won't mean anything to the reader. You want the group header to show the product's common name.

Under the Options tab, you can set another value to be displayed for a group's name. Click the option button Customize Group Field Name to use another field for the group name. Select that field from the dropdown box below it. When the report runs, the value from the other field is displayed.

There are times when the group name you want to display isn't a field in the table. It could be a custom formatting field that is derived from a formula. To make the group name display a formula instead, click the option button Use a Formula as Group Name and click the formula expert button.

Organizing the Group

The remaining two checkboxes on the Common tab affect how the group data is displayed on the report. The first checkbox controls whether the report should try to keep the entire group on the same page. The second checkbox controls whether the group header should be repeated on each page.

Setting the Keep Group Together checkbox is important if you want to prevent having only a few records of a group appearing at the bottom of a page. When this option is on, the entire group is analyzed before it is printed. If it can't fit on the rest of the page, then the remainder of the page is left blank and the group is started at the top of the next page.

The second checkbox, Repeat Group Header on Each Page, forces the group header to print at the top of every page. This is important for groups that can span multiple pages. By default, if a group extends to a second page, its header is not printed at the top of the second page. It might not be obvious how the detail records are related to each other. If you feel that showing the group header at the top of the page makes your report easier to read, you should click this checkbox.

Sorting the Group Data

After creating the groups and running a test report, you may notice that although your groups are fine, the individual rows within the group are out of order. If this happens, it is because you still need to add sort fields to your report. Telling the report how to group data doesn't imply that it knows which fields to use for sorting the detail records within the group. When using groups, the data within the group gets sorted according to how you set up the sort fields. If no sort fields are used, the records appear in their natural order (which still may not be what you expect because the grouping process reorders the records as well). Look at the earlier section Setting the Sorting Order for instructions on adding sort fields.

Changing the Field to Group On

Once the report is finished, you might decide that the records need to be grouped differently or you might create a new report that looks the same but has different groups. For example, the original design of the sales report groups by region and it works fine. But you also need a similar report that groups by salesperson. Rather than redo the report from scratch, you can make a copy of the report and modify the group fields that need to change. Changing the group field is done via the Group Expert dialog box.

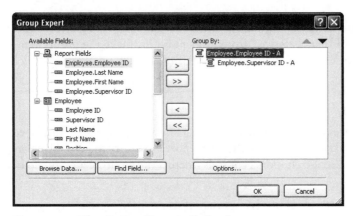

Figure 4-7. The Group Expert dialog box.

This dialog box can be accessed in two ways. The first way is to right-click on the group header bar and select Group Expert. The other way is to click the menu options Crystal Reports > Report > Group Expert.

The groups are listed in their current order. You can use the arrow buttons to the right to rearrange their order. To modify a group field, click on the group and then click on the Options button. This brings up the Change Group Options dialog box mentioned earlier. Since this is the same dialog box you used to create the group, you can also change any of the other group properties as well.

Note

The Group Expert dialog box lets you modify the existing groups, but you can't add new groups with it. To do that, you have to exit the report and select the menu options Crystal Reports > Insert > Group (as mentioned at the beginning of this section).

Displaying Top N Reports

An alternative to the standard grouping is to create reports that show the first or last set of records in a certain group. For example, rather than showing all the sales people for the company, you could show the 5 sales people that have the best sales for the month. Or you can do the opposite and show the 5 sales people with the worst sales for the month. The first report shows who deserves a bonus and the second report shows who should be talked to about improving their performance.

Generating a Top N report has a couple of requirements. The first is that your report must have at least one group in it. The second requirement is that the group must have a summary field in it (a sub-total, average, etc). The summary field is required because a Top N report needs this numeric value to calculate how to rank the groups.

To create a Top N report, select the menu options Crystal Reports > Report > Group Sort Expert. If it is grayed out, that means that you either don't have a group section or you don't have a summary field within the group. Correct this and it won't be grayed out any more.

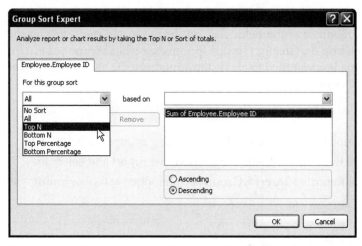

Figure 4-8. The Group Sort Expert dialog box.

When the Group Sort Expert dialog box opens, it defaults to a setting of All, for displaying all values. By clicking on this dropdown box, you can choose from a Top N or Bottom N selection basing it on a certain quantity or a percentage of the total records. It lets you select which field to base the comparison on (this must be a summary field), how many groups to show and whether all the remaining groups should be lumped into a final group called Others (or another name that you specify). If you want to select the number of groups based on the percentage of the total groups, select that in the dropdown box and the dialog box will stay the same with the exception that the number now represents a percentage.

The Group Sort Expert dialog box shows a separate tab for every group on your report that uses a summary field. This lets you create different Top N selections for each group.

Normally, you would use the Change Group dialog box (discussed in the previous section) to set the sort order, the group can only be sorted by the base value of a field in your data source. The Group Sort Expert dialog box shown in Figure 4-8 actually has a dual purpose. If you leave it at the default setting of All, you can have the group sort on its summary values, selecting a summary field in the right-most dropdown box to add it to the listbox below. You can have the group sorted on one or more summary values. By using summary fields to sort your groups, you get a lot more flexibility with how the groups get displayed.

Displaying Hierarchical Reports

A hierarchical report displays data to show relationships between records in the same table using a tree format. This is similar to having a self-join SQL statement that needs to join a table to itself using a common field. For example, when printing a supervisor list, you will show which employee reports to which supervisor. Ideally, you would link the Supervisor table to the Employee table. But in this circumstance, a supervisor is an employee as well. So you have to link the Employee table to the Employee table, thus creating a self-join SQL statement. Rather than do this work, let Crystal Reports do it by opening the Hierarchical

Group Options dialog box. In this dialog box, you specify which field is the parent and it will do all the linking for you. In this case, the Supervisor ID field is the parent of the Employee ID field. This is shown in Figure 4-9.

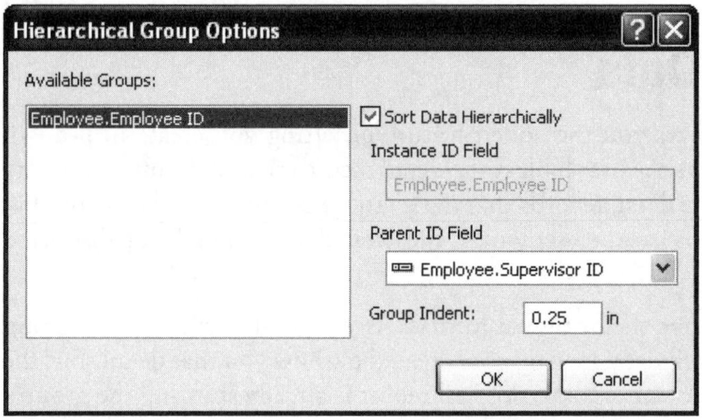

Figure 4-9. The Hierarchical Group Options dialog box.

The Available Groups listbox shows the current groups in your report. To use it for hierarchical grouping, click on it and check the Sort Data Hierarchically checkbox. The field for that group will be the subordinate field. In the dropdown box below the checkbox, select the field that will be the parent field. Since the parent field and employee field are going to be linked together, and the parent field will be listed in the group header field, both of these fields must be the same data type. The default indentation is 0.25 inches. You can change that if you wish.

Figure 4-10 shows what the supervisor report looks like. This is the Hierarchical Grouping report that is installed in the Samples directory with Crystal Reports.

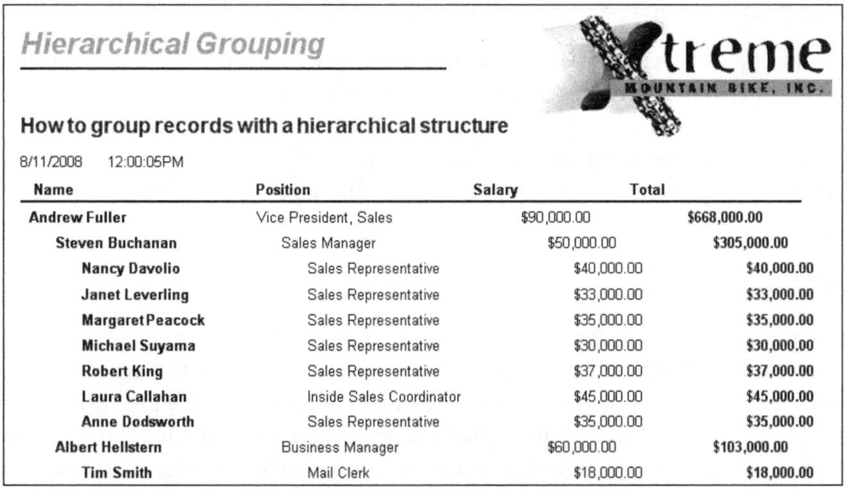

Hierarchical Grouping

Xtreme MOUNTAIN BIKE, INC.

How to group records with a hierarchical structure

8/11/2008 12:00:05PM

Name	Position	Salary	Total
Andrew Fuller	Vice President, Sales	$90,000.00	**$668,000.00**
Steven Buchanan	Sales Manager	$50,000.00	**$305,000.00**
Nancy Davolio	Sales Representative	$40,000.00	**$40,000.00**
Janet Leverling	Sales Representative	$33,000.00	**$33,000.00**
Margaret Peacock	Sales Representative	$35,000.00	**$35,000.00**
Michael Suyama	Sales Representative	$30,000.00	**$30,000.00**
Robert King	Sales Representative	$37,000.00	**$37,000.00**
Laura Callahan	Inside Sales Coordinator	$45,000.00	**$45,000.00**
Anne Dodsworth	Sales Representative	$35,000.00	**$35,000.00**
Albert Hellstern	Business Manager	$60,000.00	**$103,000.00**
Tim Smith	Mail Clerk	$18,000.00	**$18,000.00**

Figure 4-10. The Hierarchical Grouping report.

You might notice one small problem with hierarchical reports: when the rows are shifted to the right to represent a subordinate level, the columns no longer line up with the column header. Unfortunately, this can't be prevented and you must compensate for it with wider than normal column header widths.

Drilling Down on Data

Grouping data on a report gives you the added feature of letting you create drill-down reports. A drill-down report lets the user look at the detail records that make up a summary value. It takes a snapshot of the detail records that make up the summary and displays that snapshot on a separate tab. This lets the user look at the detail data without being distracted by the rest of the report.

Drill-down reports never change their original format. As you double-click on the group data to drill down into the detail data, new tabs are created to show you that detail. But the original report format stays the same. If the original report is already showing the group's detail, you can still double-click on it to open the detail in another tab on the viewer.

Since drill-down reports are designed with the purpose of having a user navigate through the data, they can only be used with the CrystalReportViewer control. Obviously, this wouldn't work on a report that has been printed because paper doesn't have a user interface.

The viewer shows you which groups can be drilled down into by changing the cursor into a magnifying glass as it passes over the group data. Perform the drill-down by double-clicking on the field.

By default, the group details are shown on a report and the drill-down feature is also turned on for every group. This just means that the details will be shown on the report and the user can click on the group header to display the details in a separate tab. If you want to hide the details, but still allow someone to drill-down into the details, right-click on the report and select Hide. If you don't want the details viewed at all, select Suppress.

An advanced example is a report that has secure data that can only be viewed by the appropriate level of personnel (e.g. an employee payroll report), but you want all other users to be able to view the group summary data. To implement this behavior, modify the group's object during runtime to either turn Suppress on or off depending upon the user. Modifying the group objects during runtime is covered in Part II of this book.

Summarizing Data

The purpose of grouping data is to make the report easier to read by creating categories that the detail records fit into. Within these categories you perform various summary functions on fields so that the user can get an overview of the information within the group without having to read all the data. Crystal Reports has a large variety of summary functions to display for a group. Examples of these summary functions are sub-totals, averages, and maximum values. Table 4-1 shows a complete list of the summary functions available.

Table 4-1. Summary functions for groups.

Function	Description
Average	Calculates the average value. (2)
Correlation	Calculates the correlation of two fields. (1) (2)
Count	Counts the number of detail records. Fields with NULL values are not included in the calculation. (3)
Covariance	Calculates the measure of the linear relation between paired variables. (1)
DistinctCount	Calculates the number of unique values for that field.
Maximum	Finds the maximum value of all the fields.
Median	Returns the middle value if all the fields were sorted. (1)
Minimum	Finds the minimum value of all the fields.
Mode	Returns the value with the most duplicates.
NthLargest	Finds the largest value of all the fields with a ranking of N. For example, if N were 6, it would return the sixth largest value.
NthMostFrequent	Finds the Nth ranking field with the most duplicate values. For example, if N were 6, it would return the value with the 6th most duplicates.
NthSmallest	Finds the smallest value of all the fields with a ranking of N. For example, if N were 6, it would return the sixth smallest value.
Percentage	Returns a percentage of the grand-total for the selected field. (2)
Percentile	Returns the value for the specified percentile of the field. (2)
PopStandard Deviation	Calculates how much a field deviates from the mean value. (1) (2)
SampleStandard Deviation	Returns the sample standard deviation for the field. (1) (2)
SampleVariance	Returns the sample variance for the field. (1) (2)
Sum	Returns the total of all the detail fields.(2)

WeightedAverage	Returns the weighted average of all the detail fields. (2)

Chart Notes:

1. See a statistics book for more information.

2. Can only be used for numeric data.

3. NULL values can be included if you set them to return their default values. To do this, select the menu options Crystal Reports > Report > Report Options. Then check the box for converting NULL field values to their default.

To summarize a field within the groups, right-click on the field that you want to summarize and select Insert > Summary.

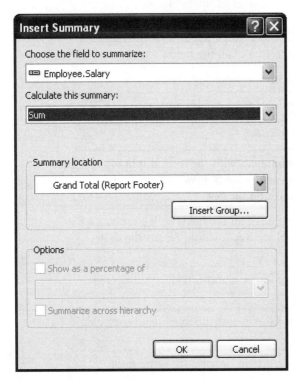

Figure 4-11. The Insert Subtotal dialog box.

Inserting a Grand Total displays a dialog box that lets you choose which function should be performed on the field. As the report is run, this function is calculated for each field and its total is displayed. After selecting the OK button, the grand total field is added in the Report Footer section and aligned directly below the original field.

Inserting a summary field brings up the dialog box in Figure 4-10. The top dropdown box lets you select which field to summarize. The next dropdown box sets which calculation to perform on the field. After that, you can select which group to put this summary into, or you can put it in the report footer as a grand total. If you want to insert the summary field into a group that you haven't created yet, you can click the Insert Group button.

By default, the summary field is automatically placed in the footer section. You can move this field to the group header by dragging and dropping it in design mode. This summary field has the same value, but now it prints before the detail records are printed.

You also have the option of showing the summary value as a percentage or summarize it across the hierarchy.

To change the summary function after it has been created, right-click on the summary field and select Change Summary Operation. That brings up a dialog box which lets you change the field to summarize and the summary calculation. Select the one you want to change and click on the OK button.

Using Parameters and Formulas

As Crystal Reports has become increasingly advanced over the years, the number of ways to customize reports has also increased. However, passing data to a report hasn't changed much. Parameters are still the preferred method of passing data to a report. This chapter explores how to create parameters, query the user for input, and use parameters to customize a report.

Inputting Parameters

A parameter is like any other field on the report: it can be displayed on the report, used in filters, and used to change the formatting of report objects. Crystal Reports considers parameters to be the programming language equivalent of a constant data type. The parameter is assigned a value when the report loads and that value never changes.

In their simplest form, parameters are used as an easy way to let the user enter a value. At another level, they can be thought of as a way of creating advanced input boxes. Parameters can have default values defined in such a way that the user is able to enter the value by selecting it from a predefined list in the combobox. The programmer controls how many options a user has in the combobox. The section on default values details the setting up of parameters in this way.

When a report loads, parameters get their values by displaying a dialog box to the user. This dialog box prompts the user for information and it has input fields for the user to enter one or more values. Once the user closes the dialog box, the report uses the user input to generate the report. An example of this is a report that prints records between a valid data range. Parameters confine the beginning and ending date ranges.

Adding Parameters

Parameters are another type of report object. The steps to add and modify them are similar to what you've already been doing. Add a parameter by clicking on the Field Explorer tab (on the left side of the IDE by default) and right-clicking on Parameter Fields. Then, select the New menu option. Clicking on an existing item allows the option to edit, delete or rename the item. Figure 5-1 shows this menu.

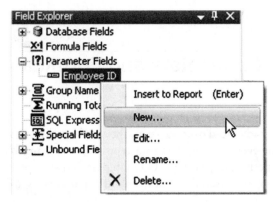

Figure 5-1. Menu option for adding a new parameter.

Once you select New, the Create Parameter Field dialog box appears, shown in Figure 5-2.

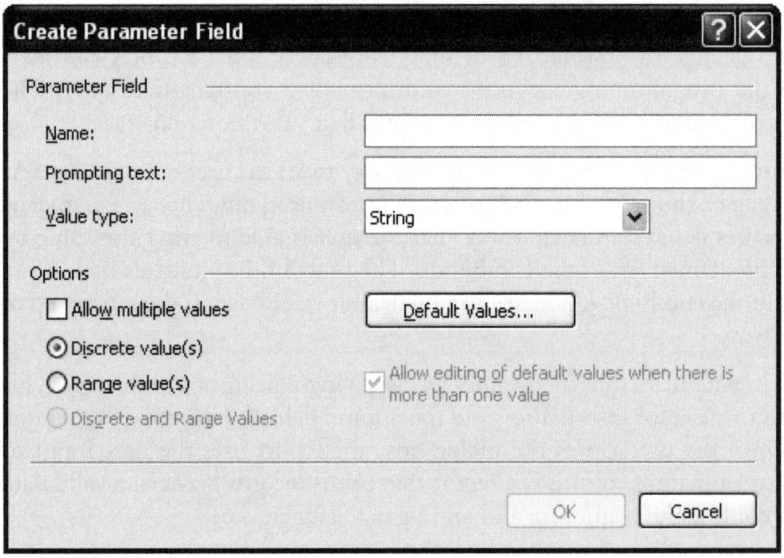

Figure 5-2. The Create Parameter Field dialog box.

This dialog box has two textboxes and one dropdown box at the top. This is for entering the necessary properties: the parameter's name, the prompting text, and the value type. The Name property is how the parameter is referenced in the report. Running the report triggers the display of the Prompting Text, which should describe what the user is asked to enter. The Value Type property selects the data type for the parameter field. All the available data types are listed in this dropdown box.

The lower half of the dialog box lets you set the options for the data that the parameter can store. Table 5-1 describes four options.

Table 5-1. Options for parameter fields

Option	Description
Discrete value(s)	The user must enter a single value.
Range value(s)	The user enters two values that are the beginning and ending points of a range. The range includes the values entered. For example, if you entered a range of 1,000 and 1,999, it would include all numbers from 1,000 up to and including 1,999.
Discrete and Range values	The user can enter both discrete and range values.
Allow multiple values	Allow a parameter to accept more than one value.

The option to allow multiple values is used with discrete values and range values. For discrete values, the user can enter multiple single values and they are each treated individually. For range values, the user can enter multiple sets of ranges and each range is treated separately from the other ranges entered. A parameter can also have a collection of both discrete values and range values.

The Create Parameter Field dialog box for Boolean data types has different options. When you change the Value Type property to Boolean, the lower half of the dialog box changes to reflect the new options (see Figure 5-3).

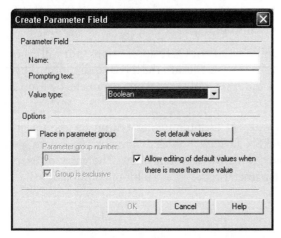

Figure 5-3. The Create Parameter Field dialog box for Boolean data.

Boolean parameters can be thought of as being similar to checkboxes or option buttons. With checkboxes, each value is independent of the other. That is, selecting or changing one checkbox has no effect on other checkboxes. This is the default behavior of Boolean parameters. Option buttons are used in groups and each is mutually exclusive of the other.

Selecting one will automatically turn off all others in the same group. The Place in Parameter Group option lets you place a Boolean parameter in a parameter group. Give it a group number and set whether the parameters in that group are mutually exclusive to each other. If the parameters are mutually exclusive, only one Boolean parameter can be assigned to True at a time. If the user sets two or more parameters to True, only the most recent will keep its value; the others are reset to False.

Setting the Default Values

Default values give the user a list of values to choose from, which saves the user from the chore of memorizing all the available values that could be entered. Default values also restrict what can be entered. This prevents a user from making a typographical error.

One drawback of using default values is that they create additional overhead and increase the risk of error because it goes against the methodology of Object Oriented Programming (OOP). The goal of writing applications using OOP techniques is to consolidate all the information about a business object within its respective classes. This gives you encapsulation and makes it easier to maintain your code. Setting default values within a report breaks this rule because you are storing information about an object outside of its classes. In fact, this data is being stored in a separate file entirely. This requires additional documentation stating that all rules regarding an object's default values must also be replicated to the related reports. If there is a bug in the report, both the report and the business objects would have to be debugged. This creates additional work during testing.

The best method is to not set default values within the report; instead use the .NET application to maintain this. Since the .NET front end is used to getting input from the user before printing the report, logic can be added here to pre-populate the front end with the appropriate default values that are derived from the class.

Of course, not everyone is going to write fully compliant OOP applications, nor will every report warrant the extra time required to fully integrate it into the .NET application. That being the case, this chapter explains how to create and use default parameters within a report.

Default values are added by clicking on the Set Default Values button on the Create Parameter dialog box. This brings up the Set Default Values dialog box. As Figure 5-4 shows, this is a fairly complex dialog box. This is because it allows the entry of every possible combination of values for each parameter type. That's a lot of combinations!

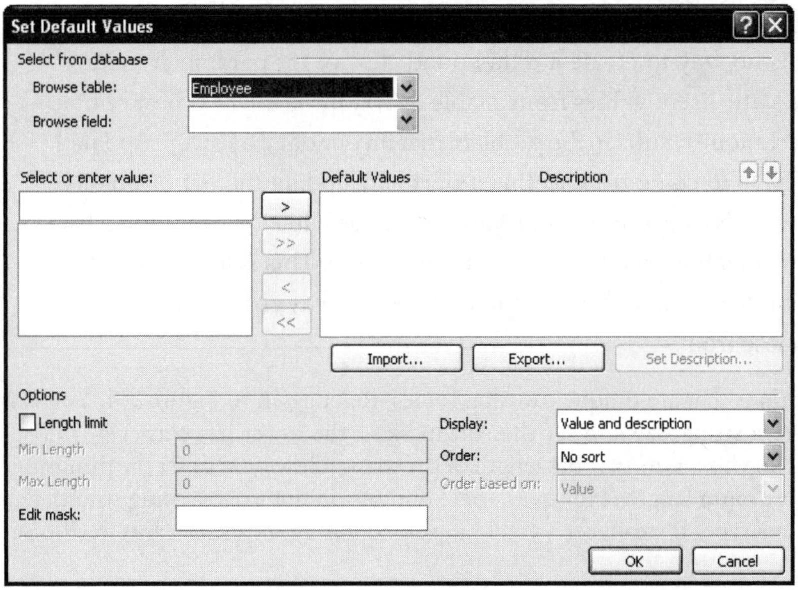

Figure 5-4. The Set Default Values dialog box for string data types.

It was mentioned earlier that default values can be designed so that the user is presented with a listbox showing all the possible values. The Set Default Values dialog box is where this is done. Within this dialog box, one can create either a single default value or a list of default values. If a single default value, the input box is pre-populated with that value. If you create a list of default values, the user, when entering a value for the particular parameter, can select one of those values from a combobox.

The middle of the dialog box is the central part of setting default values. The left side is the place to enter a default value in the textbox. Click on the right arrow to move it to the list of possible default values. There is no limit to the number of values added to the right listbox.

If entering a lot of default values, an alternative to manually typing all the default values by hand, is to pull them from existing tables. This neat trick is performed by selecting from the top two dropdown boxes, a table and a field to get the values from. Once the two items are selected, the values are pulled from the field and put into the listbox on the left. Clicking on the arrow keys allows one to select and transfer to the default value list any number of these items. Alternately, to import a list of default values from a text file, click on the Import Pick List button.

Tip

The options to pull a list of values from a table or from a text file are better served by creating your own interface using .NET. Both of these options are just a mediocre attempt at creating a data-bound combobox. In Crystal Reports .NET, there is no way to create a data-bound control for parameter values.[12] Presenting a static list of values from a table or text file is the next best option. Using this technique results in the problem that if your database were updated, you would have to come back to this report and update the list of possible values. But with .NET report integration, you can provide the user with a true data-bound combobox on a form in your application. This is a more practical solution to implement and it insures that the user always has a current list of values to choose from.

There are two options that are unique to string values. Refer again to Figure 5-4. You can limit the length of a string size and set the edit mask in the lower left corner of the Set Default Values dialog box. Limiting the length of the string allows you to set the minimum length and the maximum length. However, these options do not exist if using parameters with a numeric data type. Instead, set a valid range by entering minimum and maximum values.

The bottom right corner of the dialog box is the place to go for setting a description for each value, as well as the sorting order. This is similar to the functionality of a data-bound combobox because of the option to show a description rather then the actual value. This is useful for having the user select a table's primary key by clicking on the description rather than the numeric ID. The values can be sorted in ascending, descending and natural order.

Closing the Set Default Value dialog box brings back the Create Parameter Field dialog box. Now that the parameter has a stored default value, the checkbox Allow Editing of Default Values is no longer grayed out (it is checked by default). When this is checked, the user can enter a new value in addition to selecting an item in the list of default values. Un-checking this option requires the user to select an item from the list of values, which prevents him or her from entering an invalid value.

Entering Parameters when Running Reports

When a report has parameters, the user is prompted to enter values when the report is loaded, but before it is printed. After the user enters the values, the report is shown in the viewer or sent to the printer. Figure 5-5 is the Enter Parameter Values dialog box.

---

[12] Crystal Reports 2008 does have the feature to tie a list of default values to your data source.

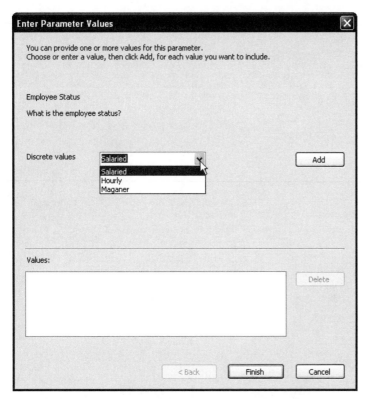

Figure 5-5. The Enter Parameter Values dialog box.

At the top is a description of what information can be entered. Below that is the prompt that is assigned to the parameter. The bottom of the dialog box is where the user enters the value(s) for the parameter field. Click on the Next button to go to the next field. Clicking on the Cancel button at any time cancels the report. Nor will it be displayed in the viewer. If the user refreshes the report, this dialog box gets displayed again.

Each parameter is shown separate from the others. If you select True for more than one parameter, only the most recent one will be True. The others will be reset back to False. Unfortunately, .NET doesn't tell you that this is happening nor does it give any indication that the parameter is part of a mutually exclusive group. Once again, this is just another reason to manage default values within your .NET application and not rely upon the report.

Caution

If you run a report and get the error "Operation illegal on linked parameter" it is because a formula references a parameter, but that parameter isn't used on the report. To fix this error, make sure that the parameter appears on the report.

Customizing Reports

You've had the opportunity to create basic report formats, including sorting, grouping and adding parameters. This chapter takes that knowledge a little further by showing you how to add more customization to your report. This customization consists of filtering records, using report sections for advanced formatting techniques, and creating running totals. Once you are finished with this chapter, you will have the foundation needed to generate the majority of reports you need on a daily basis.

Selecting Records

Until now, all the reports have printed all selected records from a table without regard to filtering the data. It was assumed that you wanted to display every record in the table. While this is true some of the time, you frequently want to filter the data so that only a subset of records gets printed. This lets you customize a report to only show the information that pertains to the current user. For example, you can design a sales report so that it selects data based upon the region, the sales person, or even on a sales person for just the last month. Almost any way that you can imagine to filter data can be done for a report.

Crystal Reports makes selecting records easy. It provides a Select Expert dialog box that lets you pick one or more fields and set the selection formula. The Select Expert dialog box is similar to other Crystal Report experts and is easy to learn.

Using the Select Expert

To open the Select Expert, select the menu options Crystal Reports > Report > Select Expert. If this is the first time the Select Expert has been run for the report, it shows the Choose Field dialog box. As you can see in Figure 6-1, it simply lists all the fields available, including report fields as well as database fields.

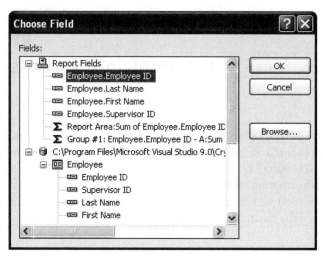

Figure 6-1. The Choose Field dialog box.

Once you select a field from this dialog box and click the Ok button, the dialog box is not shown again. Instead, you are always taken to the Select Expert dialog box shown in Figure 6-2.

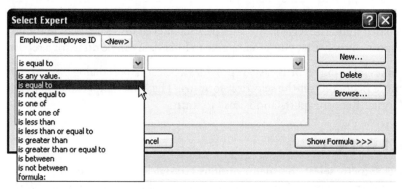

Figure 6-2. The Select Expert dialog box.

There are two tabs in this dialog box. The first is titled with the field that was selected in the Choose Field dialog box and the second is titled <New>. The tab with the field name has a dropdown box for selecting the filter criteria. By default, reports don't have any filters turned on and every record gets selected. This is set to is any value. Click the dropdown box to view available filtering options and select the one you want. The dialog box in Figure 6-2 shows all the options in this combobox. This list is the textual equivalent of the basic comparison operators that you would normally use in your programming code (e.g. =, >, <=, etc.). Except for the formula: option (discussed later), these are all standard comparisons and require no explanation.

Selecting a field that is of the DateTime data type gives you additional options listed with the comparison operators. These options include selecting dates that are within a certain fiscal quarter, within the past month, or even aging dates according to how many days ago they occurred. These advanced filtering options demonstrate the power of Crystal Reports for working with dates. See Chapter 9 for more information on how these date functions work.

After selecting a comparison method, the right side of the dialog box changes so that you can enter the value to compare the field to. With the majority of the comparisons, only a single combobox is shown. A very helpful feature is that all the current values for the field are listed in the dropdown box. Crystal Reports populates the list with the current data for that field from all the records. In fact, you will probably notice a short delay as it opens and reads in the records from the table. You can either select one of these fields from the list or enter a new value that isn't in the list.

If the report uses a connection to the database on the server, make sure you have an active connection to it. Otherwise, Crystal Reports temporarily freezes up while it pings the server waiting for a response.

Although most comparison operators only have a single dropdown box for entering values, there are a couple of exceptions. The is between and is not between comparisons give you two dropdown boxes. This lets you enter a beginning and ending range. The is between comparison is inclusive. The is not between comparison is exclusive. The other exception is when choosing a comparison of is one of or is not one of; the dialog box looks like Figure 6-3. This lets you build a list of items where the field should either be in the list or not in the list. As you select items from the combobox, they are added to the listbox below it. If you type in a value manually, add it by clicking on the Add button. If you add an item by mistake, delete it from the list by clicking the Remove button.

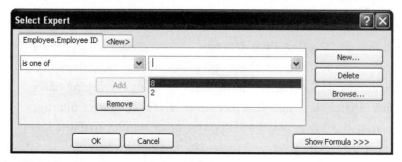

Figure 6-3. Building a list of items.

You are not limited to selecting records based on a single field. The <New> tab lets you select additional fields for record selection. Clicking on this tab shows the same Choose Field dialog box that you saw when you first opened the Select Expert. After selecting a field, you are brought back to this tab and that field is now in the tab header. The rest of the selection process is the same as what was just discussed.

When selecting multiple fields, Crystal Reports treats each field as being part of a Boolean **AND** statement. For a record to be selected by the report, it must successfully meet the criteria specified for each field listed in the dialog box. If there were four fields listed, and a record only matched three of the fields, the record wouldn't be selected.

From what you have seen so far, the Select Expert is a very helpful tool for selecting one or more fields using the basic comparison operators. This is probably adequate for many of the reports you write. But what about the other reports, where you need to build more complex filtering criteria? For those reports, there is the Formula Editor. The Formula Editor is described in complete detail in Chapter 7, but here is a summary of how to use it.

The Formula Editor lets you use Crystal syntax, the built-in programming language, to create sophisticated selection formulas. There is a large library of functions to choose from for building a selection formula. A simple example is when you don't want to use the Select Expert's default of requiring a field to match all the criteria selected. You can change the formula so that rather than use the default Boolean **AND** to join the conditions, it uses Boolean **OR**. Another example is rather than selecting a range of records based upon customer name, select the records based upon the first character of the customer name. This would let you choose all the customers with names starting with the letter "B".

Caution

When opening the Formula Editor from within the Select Expert, you are only given the option of using Crystal syntax as the programming language. As you will see in Chapter 7, Crystal Reports also gives you the option of using Basic syntax, which is very similar to VB.NET. Unfortunately, the Formula Editor for the Select Expert requires using Crystal syntax.

There are two ways to enter a custom formula. The first way is to click on the Show Formula button. This shows the existing formula built using the fields already selected. You can change this formula directly so that it matches the selection criteria you need. If you can't remember the different built-in functions well enough to type them in directly, click on the Formula Editor button. This brings up the Formula Editor dialog box (discussed in Chapter 7) and you can use it as a reference tool to build the formula. The second way to enter a formula is to click on the comparison list dropdown box and at the very bottom is an item called formula:. Clicking on this item changes the right side to a multi-line text box that lets you type a formula from scratch.

Caution

Crystal Reports raises the error "Failed to open rowset" when a record selection formula performs an empty string comparison on a field with a null value. Here is an example in Basic syntax.

Formula = {table.field} <> ""

To correct this you also have to check for null values.

Formula = Not(IsNull({table.field})) AND {table.field} <> ""

Selecting Records for Grouping

Setting a filter on summary data isn't done with the regular selection formula. Selecting records has the limitation that you can only set filters for raw data or basic formulas. You can't set filters that operate on summary fields or on formulas built with summary fields. You also can't use any fields that use second-pass data. As mentioned in Chapter 1, second-pass data includes summaries and subtotals. The reason for these restrictions is that filtering is done during a report's first pass. Second-pass data hasn't been calculated yet and consequently you can't filter on something that doesn't exist.

To get around this problem, you have to perform a grouping selection. Crystal Reports performs grouping selections during the second-pass when summary data is available.

There are two ways to add a grouping selection. The first way to add a grouping selection is to select the menu options Crystal Reports > Report > Selection Formula > Group. This brings up the Formula Editor dialog box where you can enter the necessary formula.

The second way is using the standard Select Expert dialog box and entering the filter as you normally would. The expert automatically recognizes that the formula entered is only valid as a grouping filter and will flag it as such. You can see this by clicking on the Show Formula button, and the Grouping option button will be selected.

Sections

Sections are used to determine where report objects will appear on a report. Each section has a different purpose and different rules that it follows to determine when and where it should appear on a report. For example, the Report Header section only appears at the top of the first page of a report. It does not appear on any other pages in the report. Although each section follows certain rules, there are many options available for customizing a section so that the report comes out just right. This section of the book shows you the different formatting options available as well as how to add sub-sections to a report for greater customization.

Formatting Sections

Report sections have many formatting options. You can hide a section, force it to print at the bottom of the page, force a page break afterwards and many other options. Creative use of these formatting options gives you control over how the report looks.

The formatting of each section is controlled by a single dialog box. The Section Expert, shown in Figure 6-4, is accessed by right-clicking on the report designer and selecting Section Expert.

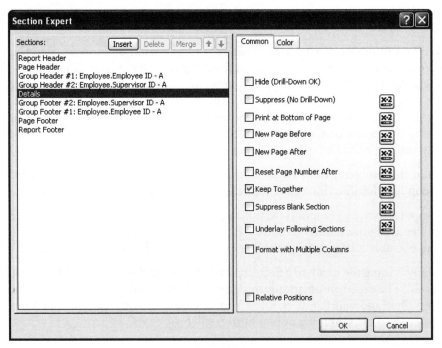

Figure 6-4. The Section Expert dialog box.

The Section Expert lists every section in the report and the formatting options available. The formatting options are represented by checkboxes because they are either enabled or disabled. Beside each option is a formula button that sets whether the option is enabled or disabled. This gives you flexibility for setting when a formatting option is turned on because the formula can use data from the currently printing record. Every time a section is printed, the formula is evaluated and its result determines whether the formatting option should be applied. This is described in more detail in Chapter 7.

When selecting the section from the list on the left, the formatting options on the right that are applicable to that section are enabled and the other options are grayed out. The list of formatting options doesn't change, but you are prevented from choosing the ones that don't apply.

With .NET, you can also access section properties via the Properties Window of the IDE. When you click on a section header, the properties in the window change to match the section selected. Each option shows whether it is enabled (True) or disabled (False). The drawback of using the Properties Window is that it has the limitation of not being able to use the advanced functionality of the Formula Editor. Table 6-1 lists the different formatting options for sections.

Table 6-1. The formatting options for sections.

Formatting Option	Description
Hide (Drill-Down OK)	Don't show the section, but allow the user the drill-down into the data.
Suppress (No Drill-Down)	Don't show the section. Drill-down is not allowed.
Print at Bottom of Page	Force the section to always print at the bottom of the page.
New Page Before	Force a page break before the section prints.
New Page After	Force a page break after the section prints.
Reset Page Number After	Reset the page number counter back to 1 after the section prints.
Keep Together	Keep the section together on the same page.
Suppress Blank Section	If there is no data in the section, do not print it.
Underlay Following Sections	Print the current section on top of the following sections. Proper alignment is critical so that objects don't overlap each other.
Format with Multiple Columns	Creates mailing labels and newspaper column style reports. This is only listed for the Details section.

Hiding and Suppressing Sections

Hiding sections is used for drilling-down on detail records. As discussed in Chapter 4, you can design your report so that groups only display summary information. This presents the user with a much smaller report. If they are previewing the report with the CrystalReportViewer, they can look at the detail information by double clicking on the group header. This creates a new tab in the viewer with the detail information being displayed inside.

Suppressing a section is done when you don't want the user to see the information in it. Of course, this leads to the question that if you don't want the user to see the information, why did you add the section? Suppressing sections is usually used in conjunction with conditional formatting. The Formula Editor is used to turn this option on or off depending upon other data that the report has access to. For example, if this is sensitive data, you would only let administrators see the detail information. All other users would have the detail section suppressed and they would only be able to see the summary information. This effectively lets you use one report for different users and different purposes.

Printing Sections at the Bottom of a Page

Printing sections at the bottom of the page is useful when printing reports that are one page long and have summary data listed at the bottom. Add a group to the report and set the group footer to print at the bottom of the page. An example is an invoice where the bottom of the page prints the total amount due. Invoices also print the aging schedule of past due balances at the bottom of the page. Another example is a form letter that requires authorized signatures of certain parties. Just put the signature lines in the group footer and set it to always print at the bottom of the page.

Note

Although you can set the Details section to print at the bottom of the page, this will have no effect. The detail records always print one after the other from top to bottom.

Forcing a Page Break

Page breaks are useful when you want groups to appear on their own pages. It is very common to want groups to appear by themselves so that data is listed separately from the other groups. An example is a report that has to be broken apart and distributed to multiple people. The group is used to identify where one report ends and the next one starts. Use the page breaks so that it is easy to separate the report pages and distribute them to the appropriate people.

Page breaks can be forced to occur either before or after a section. Unfortunately, each option has the problem of causing one blank page to be printed. If you force a page break before a group header, the first page of the report will be blank. If you force a page break after the group footer, the last page will be blank. The way around this is to use one of two built-in functions in the conditional formula: OnFirstRecord or OnLastRecord. By doing a Boolean Not in the formula, it temporarily turns suppression off for the section. For example, if you wanted to force a page break after the group footer, use the following formula (using Basic syntax) in the New Page After format option:

Formula = Not OnLastRecord

This formula returns True for every record leading up to the last record. Thus, there is always a page break after the group footer. Once the last record is printed, this formula returns False and the option to force a page break is turned off. The last page will not have a page break printed after it.

Resetting the Page Number

Resetting a page number back to Page 1 makes the page appear as if it is the first page in the report. This is good to use in combination with forcing a page break after a section. When you distribute the pages of the report to different people, each person will have a report that starts on page 1.

Keeping Sections Together

Since it is very hard to control exactly where a section is printed on a page, it is common for sections to be split across pages. A report can start printing a section at the bottom of the page but not have enough room to print all of it and will print the remaining portion of the section on the next page. If it is important that all the information within a section be printed together, turn this option on. Before the section is printed, it is analyzed to see whether it fits on the page. If it doesn't fit, a page break is forced and the section prints on the next page.

As discussed in Chapter 4, when using this formatting option with groups, the report will try to fit the entire group (including the footer) onto the page. If the group is larger than one page, a page break is forced and the group gets printed on the next page.

Suppressing Blank Sections

Printing sections that don't have any data leaves blank rows in the report. This makes a report look unprofessional because of the gaps that seem to randomly occur. To fix this, set the option Suppress Blank Section. The report skips over any sections that don't have any data and goes to the next record. This option is used most frequently in conjunction with creating multiple report sections. This is covered in section Adding Multiple Sections.

Underlaying the Following Sections

When formatting a section so that it underlays the following sections, the following sections print on top of it. This has the effect of superimposing one or more sections on top of another section.

Underlaying sections is useful when working with images or charts and the related information is printed beside the image. This concept might be tough to grasp at first, so let's look at two examples. The first example is an employee report which shows the employee's picture on the left and the employee detail listed next to it. The example in Figure 6-5 is from the Xtreme database.

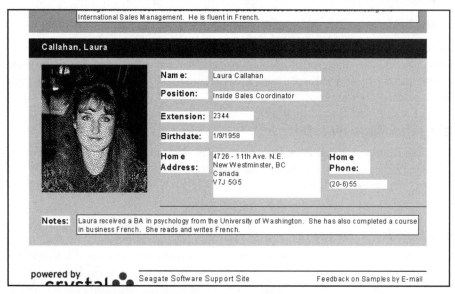

Figure 6-5. Employee Profile report with photo.

The data listed next to the employee picture is from the Employee table. It shows the different fields from a single employee record. There is a one-to-one relationship between the employee photo and the employee data.

This example is limited in that the photo can only be printed next to the data within a single employee record. If you wanted to print a photo with multiple detail records next to it, this approach wouldn't work. The next example shows how to fix this problem by underlaying sections.

Let's look at an inventory report which lists how many products are on-hand for each inventory item. These items are grouped together by category and a generic picture of each category is displayed.

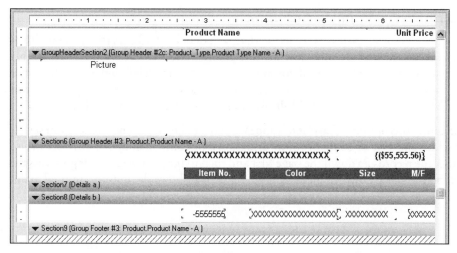

Figure 6-6. The Inventory report with pictures for each category.

To create this report, put the photo in the group header on the left most portion of the page. Put the detail fields in the detail section and make sure that all the fields are to the right of the picture. Lastly, turn on the Underlay format option for the group header.

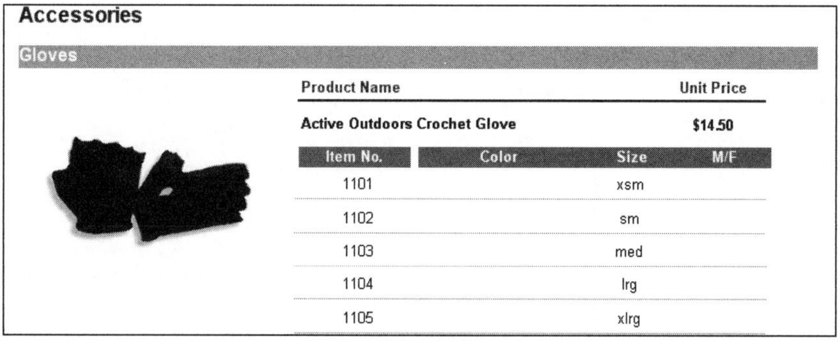

Figure 6-7. Inventory report with Underlay turned on.

This causes all the group's detail records to be printed on top of the group header. Since the image and the records aren't on the same part of the page, this gives the effect of printing multiple detail records beside a single image.

Printing a Watermark

Using the underlay feature is also useful when you want your report to have a watermark image on each page. Put the image in the page header and set the Underlay option on. Everything after the header is printed on top of it. Be sure to test the image to make sure it isn't too dark. A faint image works best as a watermark because it allows the rest of the report to be easily read.

Formatting with Multiple Columns

The default layout of a report is designed so that each detail record uses the entire width of the page and each row is printed below the one before it. Sections aren't designed to only use a partial page width. However, if you want to print mailing labels or a newspaper style report, you need to use sections that are small enough so that they can be repeated across the page. Setting the Format With Multiple Columns option lets you do that.

When selecting this option, a Layout tab appears in the dialog box. This tab lets you set the column width and spacing so that your information is put onto mailing labels. You can also set whether the records go down the page first and then to the next column, or go across the page first before going down to the next row. Figure 6-8 shows the options on the Layout tab.

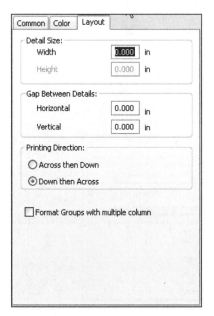

Figure 6-8. The Layout tab of the Section Editor.

The only problem with using the Layout tab is that it takes a little experimentation to get the formatting perfect. Precision is a necessity when printing labels and making a mailing list could take some work. You are much better off by using the Report Expert dialog box to create mailing labels. As Figure 6-9 shows, using the Report Expert lets you pick from a list of standard Avery numbers for the label format. Unless you are using a custom designed label, you can let Crystal Reports do all the work of formatting the label. This makes it easy to create mailing labels that print perfectly the first time!

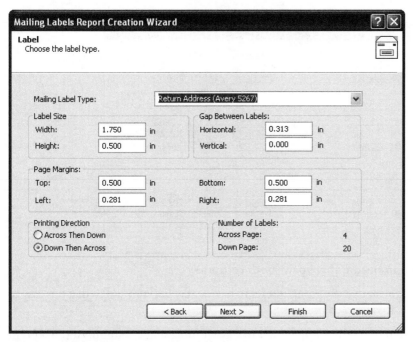

Figure 6-9. The Mailing Labels Report Expert.

Caution

Once you create a report using the Mailing Label Report Expert, you cannot go back and pick a new type of Avery label template. Instead, you have to use the Section Expert to manually change the label size.

Group Headers with Multi-Columns Reports

Crystal Reports has an interesting way of printing group headers on multi-column reports. By default, it formats a group header so that it spans across the entire page. For example, if a multi-column report has three columns, the group header will span across all three columns. This is shown in figure 6-10.

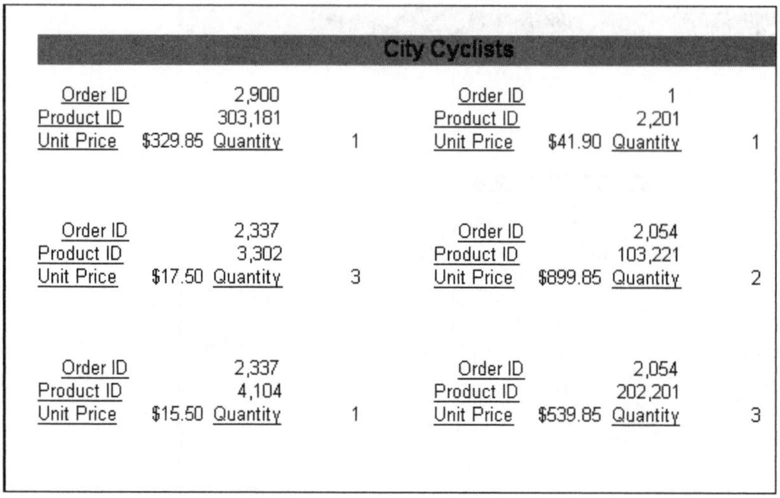

City Cyclists

Order ID	2,900			Order ID	1		
Product ID	303,181			Product ID	2,201		
Unit Price	$329.85	Quantity	1	Unit Price	$41.90	Quantity	1
Order ID	2,337			Order ID	2,054		
Product ID	3,302			Product ID	103,221		
Unit Price	$17.50	Quantity	3	Unit Price	$899.85	Quantity	2
Order ID	2,337			Order ID	2,054		
Product ID	4,104			Product ID	202,201		
Unit Price	$15.50	Quantity	1	Unit Price	$539.85	Quantity	3

Figure 6-10. Group header that spans both columns.

In this example, I formatted the group header to have a gray background so that it is easy to see that it spans across both columns.

You have the option to set the group header to stay within a single column. At the bottom of the Layout tab (see Figure 6-8), click on the Format Group With Multiple Column checkbox. When this is checked, it tells Crystal Reports to not let the group header span multiple columns, and only span a single column. This is shown in Figure 6-11.

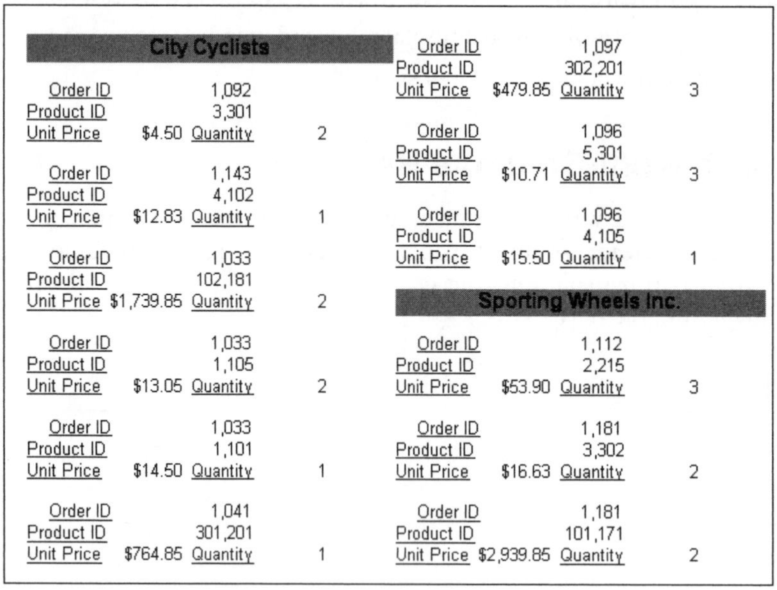

City Cyclists				Order ID	1,097		
				Product ID	302,201		
Order ID	1,092			Unit Price	$479.85	Quantity	3
Product ID	3,301						
Unit Price	$4.50	Quantity	2	Order ID	1,096		
				Product ID	5,301		
Order ID	1,143			Unit Price	$10.71	Quantity	3
Product ID	4,102						
Unit Price	$12.83	Quantity	1	Order ID	1,096		
				Product ID	4,105		
Order ID	1,033			Unit Price	$15.50	Quantity	1
Product ID	102,181						
Unit Price	$1,739.85	Quantity	2	Sporting Wheels Inc.			
Order ID	1,033			Order ID	1,112		
Product ID	1,105			Product ID	2,215		
Unit Price	$13.05	Quantity	2	Unit Price	$53.90	Quantity	3
Order ID	1,033			Order ID	1,181		
Product ID	1,101			Product ID	3,302		
Unit Price	$14.50	Quantity	1	Unit Price	$16.63	Quantity	2
Order ID	1,041			Order ID	1,181		
Product ID	301,201			Product ID	101,171		
Unit Price	$764.85	Quantity	1	Unit Price	$2,939.85	Quantity	2

Figure 6-11. Group header only spans one column.

You can see in this example that there are two group headers on the page. Each group header is the width of a single column and the next group header starts immediately following the last label in the previous group.

What makes this feature interesting is that it isn't available if you created the report using the Mailing Label Report Expert. For some reason, when using the report expert, Crystal Reports doesn't put Format Group With Multiple Column option on the layout tab. This is only available when creating a standard report and later changing it to multiple columns. When printing group headers on a mailing label report, the group header always spans across the entire page width.

Adding Multiple Sections

Throughout this book, when different parts of a report were discussed, they were referred to by their section name. For example, the part at the top of a group is called the Group Header section. However, reports also have Areas. By default, when you create a new report each area is composed of a single section, and every section is only in one area. In fact, an area is the container for a section. This gives you a one to one relationship between areas and sections. Thus, there is an area for the Report Header, Page Header, Details section, etc.

Crystal Reports lets you create dynamic reports by adding multiple sections to an area and formatting each section differently. This changes the relationship between Areas and Sections to a one-to-many relationship. One area can have multiple sections within it. All sections can be displayed or formulas can be used to determine which section to show and which ones to suppress.

Note

An area can have more sections added to it, but the sections must be of the same type. For example, the Details area can have two Detail sections in it, but it can't have a Group Footer section in it.

An example of multiple sections is shown in Figure 6-12.

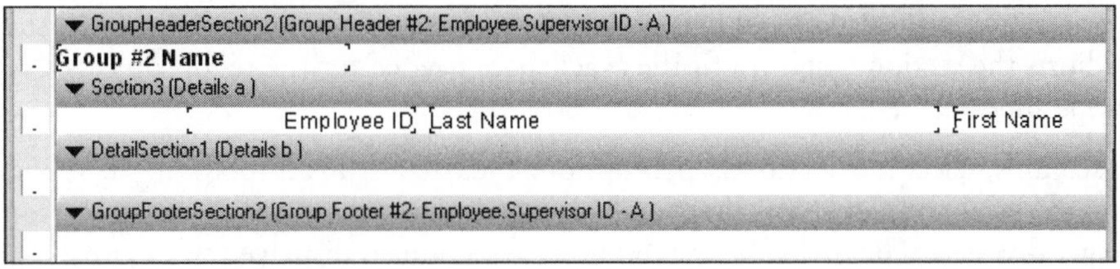

Figure 6-12. Multiple detail sections.

In this example, there are two sections between the group header and footer: Details a and Details b[13]. Each section is part of the Details area. The benefit of having two sections within the same area is that it gives you a lot of flexibility for formatting the report. Creative use of multiple sections solves many reporting problems.

You first have to understand a couple of rules for working with multiple sections. The first rule is that multiple sections are printed consecutively. The first section (labeled with the 'a') is printed first. The 'b' section is printed second, and so on. The second rule is that you can change the formatting of any section and it doesn't effect the formatting of the other sections. For example, a section can be suppressed or have its background color changed and this has no effect on the other sections within that area.

Multiple sections can be inserted, deleted, and merged with other sections. When you right-click on a section header, you get the menu shown in Figure 6-13.

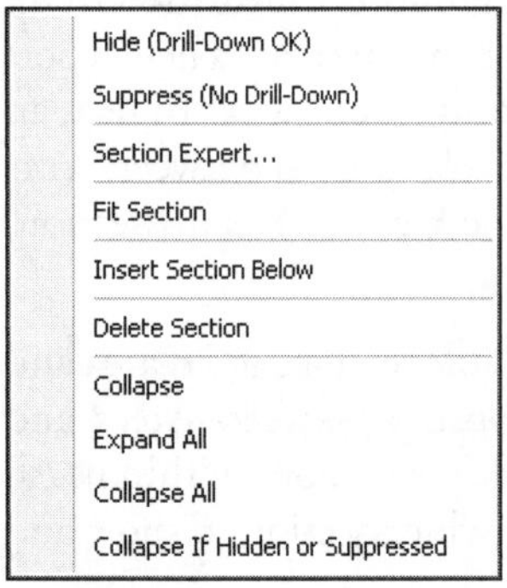

```
Hide (Drill-Down OK)
Suppress (No Drill-Down)
Section Expert...
Fit Section
Insert Section Below
Delete Section
Collapse
Expand All
Collapse All
Collapse If Hidden or Suppressed
```

Figure 6-13. Multiple section menu.

When selecting Insert Section Below, it inserts a new section below the section that was clicked on. Select Merge Section Below to combine the current section with the one below it. Crystal Reports merges the two by taking all the objects in the lowest section and copying them to the section above it. All the new objects go underneath the existing objects. Select Delete Section to delete a section from the report.

If a section has too much white space underneath the report objects, make the space tighter by placing your cursor at the top of the section below it and dragging it higher. An easier, and more accurate, way of doing this is to select the Fit Section menu option. Crystal Reports adjusts the section height to fit the exact space needed for the report objects. No extra space is allocated.

To move sections, select the Section Expert option. This dialog box displays all the report sections on the left-hand side. Now that you have multiple sections, the tabs along the top are no longer disabled. The dialog box with multiple sections is displayed in Figure 6-14. Use the arrow keys shown at the top to move the sections up or down.

---

[13] Adding additional sections automatically gets the next letter of the alphabet assigned to it.

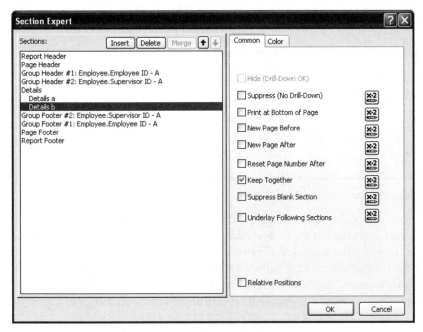

Figure 6-14. The Section Expert for multiple sections.

When looking at the menu options along the top of this dialog box, you see that it also has the options to Insert, Delete and Merge sections. If you are working in the report designer, you can also go to this dialog box by right-clicking on a section header and selecting Section Expert.

The key to making multiple sections work is to use formatting in combination with formulas. Although formulas are discussed in complete detail in Chapter 7, it is easy to understand the basic concepts before reading that chapter. Formulas are used to turn formatting options on and off using built-in functions with other data in the report. The best way to understand this is to see examples. Here are some common uses of formulas with multiple sections that you can start using right away.

Example 6-1. Eliminating blank address lines.

A common problem with printing addresses is that each one can have a different number of lines. Every address has a line allocated for the street address, but some addresses need a second line for other miscellaneous information. This could be an "Attention:" comment or the suite number. If an address doesn't use this second line, it appears as a blank line and messes up the formatting of the address. An example of these labels is shown in Figure 6-15.

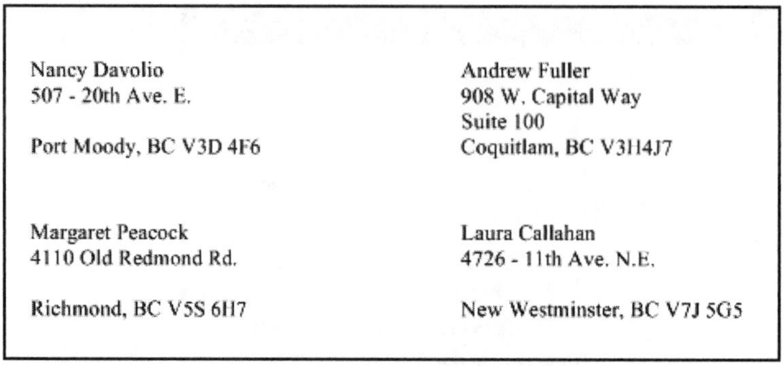

Nancy Davolio   Andrew Fuller
507 - 20th Ave. E.   908 W. Capital Way
                                        Suite 100
Port Moody, BC V3D 4F6   Coquitlam, BC V3l14J7

Margaret Peacock   Laura Callahan
4110 Old Redmond Rd.   4726 - 11th Ave. N.E.

Richmond, BC V5S 6H7   New Westminster, BC V7J 5G5

Figure 6-15. Address labels with blank lines.

To fix this problem, create three sections. The first section has the addressee's name and street. The second section only has the second address line. The third section has the rest of the address fields. To make the second section only appear when there is data in the second address line, set the formatting options Suppress Blank Section. If the second address line doesn't have any information, the section isn't printed and the blank line is eliminated. The labels in design mode are shown in Figure 6-16. The printed labels are shown in Figure 6-17.

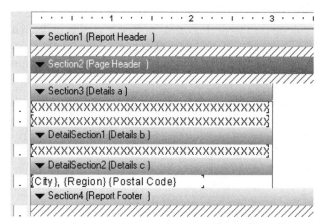

Figure 16-16. Address labels in design mode.

```
Nancy Davolio                    Andrew Fuller
507 - 20th Ave. E.               908 W. Capital Way
Port Moody, BC V3D 4F6           Suite 100
                                 Coquitlam, BC V3H4J7



Margaret Peacock                 Laura Callahan
4110 Old Redmond Rd.             4726 - 11th Ave. N.E.
Richmond, BC V5S 6H7             New Westminster, BC V7J 5G5
```

Figure 6-17. Address labels that suppress blank sections.

Example 6-2. Adding non-blank sections.

If you can use sections to suppress blank lines, you can do just the opposite: use sections to show special information. For example, you may want a report to only print a section for unique circumstances. There are a multitude of examples on how to use this feature. An employee report could print a special note if an employee's birthday falls within the current month. Invoices can print reminders to late customers that they need to pay or else penalties will be incurred. A recipe listing can print additional notes for favorite recipes. Each example benefits from using multiple sections because if the section doesn't have any data to print, additional room isn't allocated on the report.

Example 6-3. Suppressing sections for repeated fields.

Individual report objects have a Suppress If Duplicated property which suppresses the object if its data is the same as the previous record. This prevents the report from duplicating the same information multiple times. But sections don't have this property because Crystal Reports would have to analyze every field within the report section to make this decision. But you can write your own formula to do this and only base it on the fields that are important.

Crystal Reports gives you two formulas for comparing the current record to an adjacent record. In the Function Window under the Print State category, it lists the functions PreviousValue() and NextValue()[14]. The PreviousValue() function compares the current record's value to the previous record's value. The NextValue() function does just the opposite by comparing it to the following record's value. It returns True if the values match. You can use these functions to suppress an entire section if certain fields don't change from one record to the next.

The following Basic syntax code is the conditional formatting for the Suppress property of the Details section. It tests if the Orders.CustomerId field is the same as the previous record, and if so, the section is suppressed.

```
If ({Orders.Customer Id} = PreviousValue ((({Orders.Customer Id}) Then
```

---

[14] In Crystal syntax, these functions are called Previous() and Next().

```
    Formula = True
Else
    Formula = False
End If
```

Question: Is it possible to use a function such as NextValue (NextValue (field))? This would let me print out the value of the next two or three records.

Answer: No, you can't nest multiple NextValue() functions inside each other. You can only get the value of one record at a time.

Example 6-4. Swapping sections with each other.

Dynamic formatting is implemented using multiple sections. They can be used so that they both have similar information, but they are formatted completely different. Only one section is printed at any given time and the other section is hidden. Set each section to print using the opposite logic of the other. For example, a company could have a large client that gets the rules bent for them since they generate a large percentage of the revenue. This client requires their invoices to be in a certain format that simplifies their internal record keeping. Although the data is the same as all the other invoices being printed, the format is customized.

To solve this problem, create duplicate sections for each part of the invoice. In the Suppress formatting option, set the formula to only display the special sections for that customer. The other sections will have the opposite logic so that they get printed when it isn't that customer.

Another example is when printing multi-national reports that are grouped by country. Countries have data that is unique and doesn't need to get printed for the other countries. People reading the report would get distracted if there were a lot of blank fields allocated for data that doesn't apply to the current country. To fix this, create a different section for each country. Set the formula in the Suppress format property to only display the section when the data relates to that country.

Example 6-5. Alternating the background color.

A common reason for alternating the background color of sections is to make the report easier to read. It can be hard to visually move your eyes across a report and stay on the same row. To make this easier to do, reports often alternate the background color of each row. This is similar to the green-bar report paper that was frequently used at corporations.

This is done by creating two detail sections with different background colors. Using Basic syntax, the Suppress formatting formula for each section would be either

Formula = Remainder(RecordNumber, 2) = 0

Or

Formula = Remainder(RecordNumber, 2) = 1

Once you become familiar with all the different formatting options available within Crystal Reports, you will find that there are many ways to do the same thing. For example, if you want to change the background color of a section to red when a salesperson's quota isn't met, there are two ways you could do it. One solution would be to have two different sections as just discussed. Another solution would be to use only one section and put that same formula in the Background Color property. This will only turn the background color to red when the formula is true. Both solutions work equally well, although in this example, using a single section would require less work. The more you work with Crystal Reports, the more you will learn different tricks. The ones you use will depend upon what you think best fits the situation at the time.

Running Totals

Running totals are built-in fields that accumulate the total of another field. These fields save you the trouble of creating and maintaining a set of formulas that do the same thing. Since they are part of Crystal Reports, you have to do very little effort to use them in a report.

A running total takes a field on a report, performs a calculation on it, and adds the result to a report-wide variable that keeps track of the total amount so far. There are various calculations that can be used with running totals so that they can be customized to your exact needs. For example, you can calculate a running total that sums all the amounts, calculates the current average of all the amounts, or calculates the maximum amount. You can also set the interval for when to perform the calculation. You can do it on every field or whenever the field changes values.

To add a running total field to your report, right click on a numeric field that you want to track and select Insert Running Total. This presents you with the dialog box in Figure 6-18.

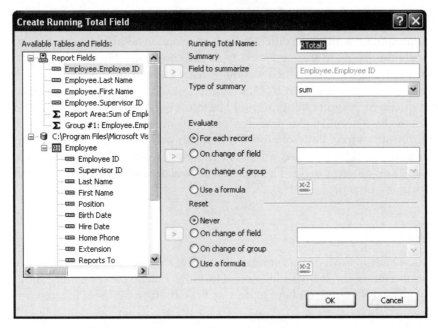

Figure 6-18. The Create Running Total dialog box.

When the dialog box opens, a default name and the field to summarize is already filled in. You should immediately change the name to something descriptive. There are also three options that can be set with a running total field: what type of calculation to perform, when to perform the calculation, and when to reset the total back to zero.

Just because the field is called Running Total doesn't mean that you are limited to calculations that only sum numbers. There are over a dozen different calculations available. It could calculate the average of all the numbers printed so far, or it can print the largest of all the numbers. The most simple, and the default, is the Sum operation. It sums a value as it is printed.

The value of the running total field is affected by when it is evaluated. You can have a value recalculated every time a detail record is printed, or if you have a group level field, then you can calculate it on every new group. You could also calculate it only when the summary field changes value.

Just as important as setting when to calculate the field is setting when to reset its value back to zero. If you want a running total to accumulate throughout the life of the report so that the last record shows the grand total, you don't want the value to ever get reset. But if you are tracking the running total for individual groups, you want it to reset every time the group changes. The dialog box also gives you the option to reset the running total when a field's value changes or by using a formula to trigger the reset. Clicking the formula button brings up the Formula Editor dialog box so that you can write more advanced formulas for determining when the running total is reset.

Where you place the running total is very important. It is only as accurate as the most recent record printed. If you want to keep a running total of the detail records, you would put the field in the detail section. If you put the field in the group summary section, it will calculate the total as of the last record in the group.

You might recall from Chapter 4 that when printing a subtotal on a group, you can put that field in either the group footer or group header and it still prints the same result. The location of a subtotal doesn't affect its value. This isn't the case with running totals. If you put a running total in the group header, it will only show the calculation for the first record. Since the other records haven't been printed yet, they aren't calculated. An example report showing this behavior is shown in Figure 6-19.

6/14/2002 3:17:33PM			
How to maintain running totals for a group			
Customer Name	Order ID	Order Amount	RunningTotal
Tienda de Bicicletas El Pardo			**5,219.55**
Tienda de Bicicletas El Pardo	1323	5,219.55	5,219.55
Tienda de Bicicletas El Pardo	1332	5,219.55	10,439.10
			10,439.10
Mad Mountain Bikes			**8,897.31**
Mad Mountain Bikes	1339	8,897.31	8,897.31
			8,897.31
Bikes, Bikes, and More Bikes			**8,819.55**
Bikes, Bikes, and More Bikes	1317	8,819.55	8,819.55
			8,819.55
Piccolo			**5,895.20**
Piccolo	1348	5,895.20	5,895.20
			5,895.20
Whistler Rentals			**16.50**
Whistler Rentals	1330	16.50	16.50
Whistler Rentals	1319	5,219.55	5,236.05
			5,236.05

Figure 6-19. The results of a running total field with a grouping report.

This is a Top N report that shows a running total column and there are three identical running totals fields. The running total field calculates the sum of each order amount, and it is reset when a group changes. There is a copy of it in the header, the detail, and the footer. You can see that the field in the detail section changes for every record and that the footer matches the value of the last record printed. But the header record doesn't match the footer value. Instead, it is equal to the first record printed in the group.

Running totals have similar functionality to summary fields, and they can also be duplicated with formula fields. This can cause some confusion as to when you should use a running total, a summary field, or a custom formula field. Each of these options has its unique characteristics.

Summary fields are useful for summarizing data outside of the detail section. For example, you can put subtotals in a group footer and put a grand total in the report footer. But you wouldn't want to put either of these fields in the Details section. Summary fields also have a limitation that if your report suppresses data, the summary calculation will include the records that don't get printed. This is because the summary fields are calculated during the first-pass, and this occurs before the fields are suppressed. They can't take into account which fields don't get printed. But the running total fields are calculated as each record is printed. If a record is suppressed, it doesn't get included in the calculation. As an example of this, the report in Figure 6-20 is the same Top-N report as the last example, but this report has two grand total fields added. The grand total in the right-most column is a running total field and it is a copy of the fields above it. The grand total field in the left column is a summary field that was added by right-clicking on the Order Amount field and selecting Insert Grand Total.

| How to maintain running totals for a group | | | MOUNTAIN BIKE INC |
Customer Name	Order ID	Order Amount	RunningTotal
Tienda de Bicicletas El Pardo			5,219.55
Tienda de Bicicletas El Pardo	1323	5,219.55	5,219.55
Tienda de Bicicletas El Pardo	1332	5,219.55	10,439.10
			10,439.10
Mad Mountain Bikes			8,897.31
Mad Mountain Bikes	1339	8,897.31	8,897.31
			8,897.31
Bikes, Bikes, and More Bikes			8,819.55
Bikes, Bikes, and More Bikes	1317	8,819.55	8,819.55
			8,819.55
Piccolo			5,895.20
Piccolo	1348	5,895.20	5,895.20
			5,895.20
Whistler Rentals			16.50
Whistler Rentals	1330	16.50	16.50
Whistler Rentals	1319	5,219.55	5,236.05
			5,236.05
		89,615.16	39,287.21

Figure 6-20. Summary field incorrectly calculates the grand total.

You can see that the grand total that is calculated with the summary field is much larger than it should be. It is including records that weren't printed on the report (they were filtered out). The running total field is correct because it only totals fields that were printed.

A formula should only be used when there isn't any other alternative. Not only does it incur more overhead when the report runs, but it requires more work on your part. If the previous two options are sufficient for your needs, you should use them first. Having said that, there are times when a running total is limited and using a formula will give you the results you are looking for. An example is a report that tracks how many records are printed on each page. It shows the row number next to each record and it resets the counter to zero for every new page. Since there isn't an option with running totals to reset at the top of a page, a formula is required. To implement this report, you need two formulas. The first increments a global variable by 1 for each record. This Basic syntax formula is put in the detail section.

WhilePrintingRecords

```
Global LineNumber  As Number
LineNumber = LineNumber + 1
Formula = LineNumber
```

The second formula resets the counter back to zero. It goes in the page footer so that it only gets called when a page is finished. It also has its Suppress format set so that the user can't see it on the report.

```
WhilePrintingRecords
Global LineNumber  As Number
LineNumber = 0
Formula = LineNumber
```

When this report is run, the first record will always show a line number of 1 at the top of each page. The last record will show how many total records were printed on the page.

Best Of The Forum

Question: I have a report that should only print 15 records per page. Any advice on how to do this?

Answer: You can use the MOD function to do this. The MOD function divides two numbers and returns the remainder. When you divide the current record number by 15 and it returns 0, then you know that it should print a new page. Right-click on the Details section and select Section Expert. Add the following formula for the Details' property New Page After:

```
Formula = (RecordNumber MOD 15) = 0
```

Using the Formula Editor

Formulas enable you to customize report output by analyzing the data in the report as it is being printed. There are two circumstances when you need to use formulas. The first is performing calculations based on the raw data. For example, when printing the monthly sales for a product, you can calculate the percent of total sales. Storing this in the database isn't practical because it is more efficient to calculate that value on an as needed basis rather than waste space storing the number in the database. The second circumstance where formulas are needed is dynamically modifying the formatting of fields or sections on the report. For example, you can simulate a "green bar" report by using a formula that alternates the background color of every other row. The flexibility and power of formulas make them one of the most useful features of Crystal Reports.

This chapter is the first of three that show you how to use formulas to make reports vibrant. It shows you when and how to use the Formula Editor. The next chapter is a syntax primer for both Basic syntax and Crystal syntax. These are the two languages that Crystal Reports uses. Chapter 9 is a reference for the common functions that are built into Crystal Reports.

Writing Formulas in the Formula Editor

The Formula Editor shown in Figure 7-1 is where you create and edit formulas. It consists of four separate windows. The three windows along the top of the dialog box present the entire set of tools to write a formula. Within these three windows is every available field, syntax construct, and built-in formula. The bottom window is the formula window where you write and edit the formula.

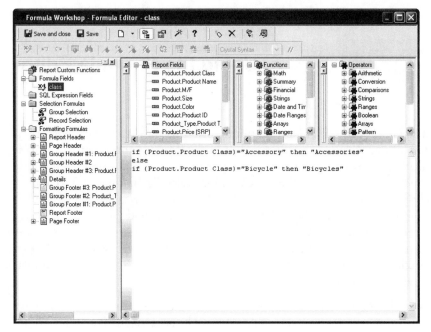

Figure 7-1. The Formula Editor window.

The top three windows assist you with writing formulas. Rather than having to use other tools to find out the names of the database fields and function names, they are listed in one of the windows at the top. When you double-click any of the items, that item appears in the code window at the current cursor position. You can also drag and drop the item into the code window. Effectively, you could write most of your formulas without doing any typing. Just double click the appropriate functions and insert the report fields and let the formula be built for you. Personally, as a programmer, I don't find this very practical. Scrolling through a hierarchy of syntax trees isn't nearly as efficient as just typing it in. However, it is very useful to have these trees available when you can't remember something because they are almost like having a mini-help file available. If there is a built-in function that you haven't used in a while, you can browse through the tree structure to look for it. You can also look at it just to find out all the parameters a function requires.

 In the top right corner of this dialog box is the drop-down list for whether you want to use Crystal syntax or Basic syntax. The individual windows are discussed in more detail in Chapter 5, but the following are brief descriptions.

The leftmost window is the Field Tree. It shows all the fields on the report. This consists of formulas, group fields, and data fields. Below that it shows every field in the current data source (whether they are in the report or not). You can use any report field in your formula as well as any database field. The database field doesn't need to be displayed on the report for it to be used in a formula.

The Function Tree is the middle window. It shows all the functions available. At first, this tree is a nice crutch to lean on as you learn the Crystal syntax or Basic syntax language. If you are a VB.NET programmer, you will find Basic syntax to be so similar that you will quickly learn the language and not rely on the Function Tree.

The Operator Tree shows the different operators grouped by category. Some of these categories are Arithmetic, Boolean, Comparisons, etc. It is similar to the Function Tree in that it is a nice crutch when you are new to formulas, but you will quickly outgrow it.

The Formula window is where you write the formulas. The font is color-coded so that reserved words use a blue font. Comments are in green. Variables and value constants are in black.

As you write formulas, you need to save and check the syntax of the formula. The left most portion of the toolbar has buttons that provide this functionality. Figure 7-2 shows that portion of the toolbar.

Figure 7-2. Formula buttons.

The buttons shown in Figure 7-2 are described here:

The first button, a disk with an "x", checks the syntax, saves the formula and closes the Formula Editor. It returns you to the report designer. You will probably use this one most of the time.

A disk, the second button, saves the formula and checks the syntax. You can continue working on the existing formula.

A blank sheet, the third button, creates a new formula. It first saves the current one and checks its syntax before creating a new formula.

The first button on the second row, the formula icon with a checkmark, checks the syntax of the formula. It gives you a message box telling you whether the formula is okay and then lets you go back to working on the formula. Use this to verify the syntax with a function you aren't familiar with.

Whenever you save a formula, the syntax is always verified. This ensures that if there is something wrong with the formula, it will be corrected right away. When a syntax error is found, a message box appears informing you of the problem. Unfortunately, the error messages that appear are usually not very helpful. You frequently have to decipher this yourself. If you find that there is a syntax error in your formula, you are not required to fix it right away. You can save it as is, and then come back later to fix the errors. Just don't forget to fix it or else your report won't run properly.

Using Formulas for Calculations

A report gets the majority of its data from a data source. This could be a table in a database, an XML data feed or a proprietary data source. Data usually consists of raw data that doesn't have extraneous information that can be derived by other means (e.g. calculations). It is more efficient to perform calculations on an as-needed basis than to save the results within the database. A formula can be calculated and displayed directly on the report or it can be used by other formulas.

Crystal Reports lets you add and edit formulas via the Field Explorer window in the report designer. Within the Field Explorer window, right click on any of the formula fields and select Edit or New to open the Formula Editor. You can also right click on the tree node Formula Fields. The Field Explorer window is shown in Figure 7-3.

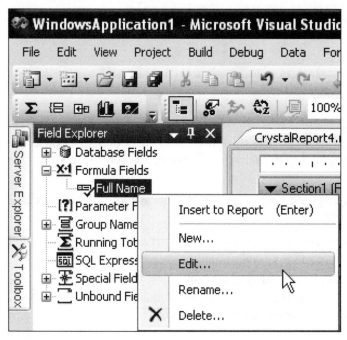

Figure 7-3. The field explorer window.

Once you've added a formula to the Field Explorer, you can display it on a report by dragging and dropping it to the report. You can tell the difference between database fields versus formulas because the formula fields are prefixed with a @. If you want to edit a formula field on the report, right click on it within the report layout and select Edit.

Dynamic Formatting with Formulas

Reports by their very nature are static. Although the printed data changes and the running totals are different every time, the report format stays the same. For example, if the first field in a column has a font of Arial and is black, every field in that column is also going to have a font of Arial and be black. After all, if every field in the same column had a different font, it would be very hard to read and people would question the abilities of the report designer. But, wouldn't it be nice to use visual cues to highlight important data? For example, you could change the color of an inventory quantity to red when it is below the minimum. The reader immediately knows that the item needs to be reordered. There might even be a special note to the side of the report stating whom to notify. In this circumstance, making a report dynamic increases its usefulness to the reader without adding clutter.

Crystal Reports gives you the ability to use formulas that dynamically modify the visual properties of fields and sections on a report. For example, you can use a formula that returns either True or False with the Suppress property of a section to either show or hide a section. You could also use a formula that returns a string and this can be used to add a special message at the end of each row.

Adding Formulas

When modifying a property in the designer, the changes you make to that property stay the same as the report runs. Most properties, but not all, can have a formula attached to them so that their value can be modified based upon other fields in the report. Clicking on the formula button next to a property lets you add a formula to do this. The formula button is shown in Figure 7-4. It has a blue "X-2" and there is a horizontal pencil underneath it. Once you add a formula to a property the "X-2" turns red and the pencil is at an angle. This is shown in Figure 7-5. Only properties with a formula button next to them can use a formula to make the values dynamic.

Figure 7-4. A button with no formula associated with it.

Figure 7-5. A button with a formula associated with it.

When assigning a formula to a property, you have to determine the data type that the property uses. This can be anything from Boolean, string, number, or Crystal pre-defined constants. The formula must return the proper data type to the property. If the formula returns the wrong data type, the Formula Editor returns an error when you try to save it.

As an example of using the proper data type, Figure 7-6 shows the Section Editor dialog box. All the properties displayed here use checkboxes. These properties are either on or off. Formulas that are associated with these properties have to return **True** or **False**. As expected, returning **True** is the same as a checked box, and returning **False** is the same as an unchecked box.

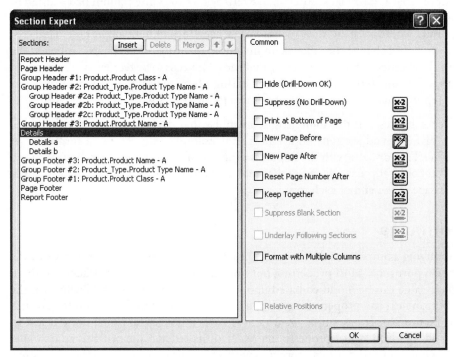

Figure 7-6. The section expert window.

As a more varied example, Figure 7-7 shows the Border tab of the Format Editor dialog box. This dialog box uses checkboxes, line styles and colors.

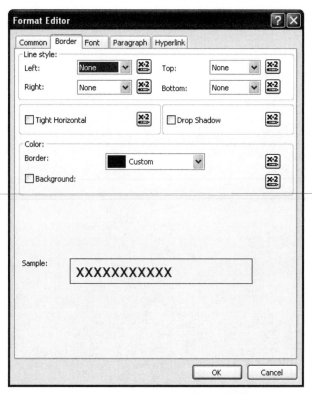

Figure 7-7. The Format Editor's border tab.

The values for the line style and color are predefined constants within Basic syntax. It can have values such as DashedLine, NoLine, etc. The color property can have values such as Aqua, Yellow, etc.

When you open the Formula Editor, the predefined constants for the current property are listed in the Function Tree. This list is dynamic and won't show predefined constants that don't apply to the current property. For example, if you are modifying a line style property, the Function Tree will show the different line styles, but won't list any colors. If you are modifying a color property, it will show the available colors, but no line styles. This is illustrated in Figure 7-8.

Figure 7-8. The Function Tree for line styles.

Printing Checkboxes

Displaying checkboxes on a report presents a new challenge. Checkboxes represent when a Boolean value is either true or false. But Crystal Reports doesn't have a way to print checkboxes. There are other ways to display a Boolean constant. For example, you can display the words Yes/No or True/False by right-clicking on the field and selecting Format field. The dialog box displays a drop-down box that lets you select how you want the data to be displayed (Yes/No, True/False, etc.).

Displaying Boolean values as a checkbox requires a little more creativity. You have to trick Crystal Reports into printing checkboxes by switching to the Wingdings font. There are a variety of interesting characters in the Wingdings font. But five of them can be used for displaying checkboxes. Figure 7-9 shows some of the Wingdings characters available.

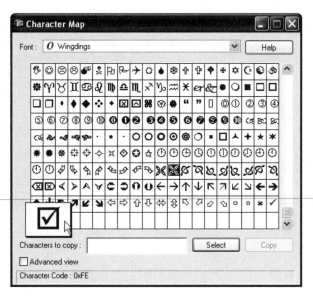

Figure 7-9. Wingdings control characters.

In the last two rows are the checkboxes. There are four types to choose from as well as an empty checkbox. To use these characters in your report you have to create a formula that uses the ASCII code for the checkbox you want to display and return the appropriate character. The only problem with this idea is that it is very difficult to determine the correct ASCII code. In previous versions of MS Windows, you could open the Character Map and it showed you the ASCII code at the bottom. You could easily type this number into your formulas. But with Windows XP, they stopped showing the ASCII code and now they only show the Hexadecimal equivalent. I don't know why Microsoft implemented this "feature" because it's very difficult to convert the hexadecimal number to a decimal. So rather than make you figure out the math, I'm going to give you a cheat-sheet to use for your reports. Table 7-1 shows each checkbox and its ASCII equivalent.

Table 7-1. The Wingdings checkboxes and their ASCII equivalents.

Checkbox	ASCII Value
☐	168
✘	251
✔	252
☒	253
☑	254

To display a checkbox on the report, create a new formula field and insert the following Basic syntax formula.

```
If {Table.Field} = True Then
    'Display the checkbox of your choice here
    Formula = Chr(254)
Else
    'Display empty checkbox
    Formula = Chr(168)
End If
```

This formula tests a field to see if it is true. If so, it returns the control character 254 (a checked box). If it is false, it returns the control character 168 (an empty checkbox). Save the formula and close the Formula Workshop.

Drag this formula from the Field Explorer onto the report. Finally, change the font to be Wingdings by right-clicking on the field and selecting Format Object. Click on the Font tab and use the dropdown box to select the Wingdings font. Save the report and preview it to see the checkbox displayed.

I recommend using a font that is two point sizes larger than the font size of the rest of the report text. The Wingdings font is slightly smaller than regular text and increasing its size makes it easier to see. You should experiment with the font size to see what suits your tastes.

Note

The Wingdings font has lots of unusual characters in it. You can use any of these characters in your report to print interesting graphics. For example, you might want to print a telephone graphic in the header of the phone number column and an envelope in the email column. You could print a time bomb on a row that requires immediate attention. Getting creative with the Wingdings font lets you have a little fun with a report and still keep a professional image.

Using the Default Attribute and Current Field Value

The value assigned to a property in design mode is called the property's default attribute. When assigning a formula to that property, the default value is overridden by what is in the formula. There are many times when a formula is only used to specify what happens in a unique circumstance (e.g. an inventory item being out of stock) and you don't want the formula to override the default value every time. The rest of the time you want the default value to be left unchanged. There are two ways of doing this: not specifying a value in the formula or using the keyword DefaultAttribute.

When you don't specify a value, you are letting Crystal Reports use what was specified in the Format Editor. For example, you may want a field to be the color red if its value is less than the minimum quantity, otherwise use the attribute specified in the Format Editor. You can use a Basic syntax formula like the following:

```
If {Inventory.OnHand} < {InventoryItems.MinimumQty} Then
    Formula = crRed
End If
```

If the condition is true, then the color becomes red. If it is false, then the color is left unchanged.

Although this is acceptable, it isn't perfectly clear what the color will be if the condition isn't true. As a second alternative you can use an Else statement and specify the result to be DefaultAttribute. By doing this, you are telling someone reading your code that the color will either be crRed or the attribute that is specified on the Format Editor. The new code would look like the following:

```
If {Inventory.OnHand} < {InventoryItems.MinimumQty} Then
    Formula = crRed
Else
    Formula = DefaultAttribute
End If
```

Formulas can be made generic so that they can be used on different fields. By replacing the field name with the keyword CurrentFieldValue, the formula can be called in various places on the report. This keyword returns the current value of the field that is being formatted. The CurrentFieldValue is seen in Chapter 11 which discusses Cross-Tab reports.

Use the Highlighting Expert?

The Highlighting Expert is a simplified version of the Format Editor. It gives you a wizard interface for creating rules that modify the font and border of a field. Figure 7-10 shows an example of using the Highlighting Expert for drawing a double box border around a field when its value is equal to "USA". The Sample column shows the result of what the field looks like after the rule has been applied. The Condition column shows the rule that is being applied. There can be multiple rules applied.

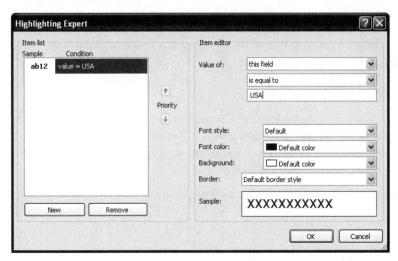

Figure 7-10. The Highlighting Expert window.

I don't recommend using the Highlighting Expert. There are two reasons for this. The primary reason is that it can create confusion when maintaining a report. There are now two places where the formatting of an object can be modified. If you inherited this report from another programmer and you want to determine if a field is going to have its format modified, you have to check the Format Editor and the Highlighting Expert. For a large report, this adds additional work. The second reason is that the rules in the Highlighting Expert always override the rules in the Format Editor. For example, if you create a formula in the Format Editor for the font and also use the Highlight Expert to modify the font, the formula is ignored and only the Highlighting Expert is used. This is most likely to happen when inheriting a report from another programmer who used the Highlighting Expert. You might add a formula with the Format Editor and spend a lot of time trying to debug it. But you won't be able to fix it until you remember to check the Highlighting Expert. All in all, this tool has the potential to do more harm than good.

The Highlighting Expert was originally designed as an easy way for end users to modify the format of a field without having to know how to program. It let them create formulas by pointing and clicking. Once an end user felt comfortable with programming logic, they would graduate to adding formulas with the Format Editor. As a .NET programmer, programming is what you do and you don't have to rely on a simplified tool for assistance. I recommend that you ignore it altogether and keep all the functionality within the Format Editor.

Evaluation Time Defaults

Chapter 1 discussed the Two-Pass Processing Model. Knowing how this model works is especially important when writing formulas. The type of formula determines when it is processed. Where you place a formula on a report and the functionality within that formula affects when the formula is evaluated and whether it returns the expected value or not. A formula can be placed on any section of your report, but you should plan this in advance so that you can guarantee the proper results. To determine where to place a formula, you need to know the rules that Crystal Reports uses to evaluate functions. In the following list are the rules that are applied.

- A formula that only references variables (it doesn't use group/summary fields or database fields) is evaluated before any records are read.

- Formulas using database fields are evaluated while records are being read.

- Formulas using group fields, summary fields, or page related fields (e.g. the page number) are evaluated after the records are read and while the report is being printed.

- You can't determine which formula within a section will be called first. This is because formulas within the same section are not evaluated in any particular order.

There are times when the default rules listed above will not give you the results you desire. For example, there may be a situation where you have two formulas in the same section and one formula relies upon the other to be called first. According to the default rules listed above, you know that there is no way to determine which one will be called first. You need some way to force one formula to be called before the other. Fortunately, Crystal Reports lets you override the default rules to fit your particular situation. There are four keywords that let you set when a formula is evaluated: BeforeReadingRecords, WhileReadingRecords, WhilePrintingRecords, and EvaluateAfter. Each keyword is added to the beginning of a formula to set when it gets evaluated. These keywords are listed in Table 7-2.

Table 7-2. Evaluation Time Keywords

Evaluation Time Keyword	Description
BeforeReadingRecords	Evaluate the formula before any database records are read.
WhileReadingRecords	Evaluate the formula while reading the database records.

WhilePrintingRecords	Evaluate the formula while printing the database records.
EvaluateAfter(formula)	Evaluate after another formula has been evaluated.

If a formula isn't returning the expected results, there is a good chance it's because of when the formula is being evaluated. If you are trying to debug a formula, you have to take many things into consideration: does the formula only use variables; should the formula be put in a different section; is the formula being evaluated while reading records or while printing records; does the report use a grouping section that may be affecting the order of evaluation. This is a lot to think about. You can cut down on the amount of time spent debugging formulas if you start out by following some general guidelines. The remainder of this section gives guidelines and examples for you to think about when writing your formulas.

Place formulas that reset variables to their default value in the Report Header or Group Header section. This insures that they are called before the formulas in the detail section are evaluated.

Be careful when using formulas that only have variables in them without any database fields. They will only get calculated one time prior to reading the records. If the formula is cumulative in nature, you need to force the evaluation time to be **WhileReadingRecords**. If the report uses groups then you should use the **WhilePrintingRecords** keyword.

The keyword **BeforeReadingRecords** can't be used with formulas that have database fields or grouping/summary fields in them.

When you place multiple formulas within the same section, you can't assume the order that they are executed in. If you need one formula to be evaluated before another formula (its result is used in other formulas) then put the **EvaluateAfter** keyword in the dependent formula. The following example shows how this is used. This formula relies upon the formula **ParseName** to take the {Customer.Name} field and parse the first name and last name out of it. The values are put into the global variables **FirstName** and **LastName**. This Basic syntax formula returns the **LastName** variable so that it can be displayed on the report. The **@ParseName** formula isn't shown here.

```
EvaluateAfter({@ParseName})
Global LastName As String
Formula = LastName
```

Summary calculations are performed while printing records. They can only do calculations on formulas that were evaluated beforehand (i.e. while reading records). Thus, a formula that uses **WhilePrintingRecords** can't have summary functions performed on it.

Of course, these guidelines won't be able to prevent every problem from happening, but they are here to help give you a start in the right direction.

To illustrate the importance of using the proper keyword in a formula, let's look at a final example that shows you each stage of writing a formula and how the output is affected by the evaluation time keyword.

The example report is a customer report that uses the Xtreme.mdb database. The report has the first column as the row number. The row number is tracked using a variable called RowNumber. The formula is as follows:

```
Global RowNumber As Number   'Don't use Local b/c that resets the variable
RowNumber = RowNumber + 1
Formula = RowNumber
```

Figures 7-11 shows the output of this report.

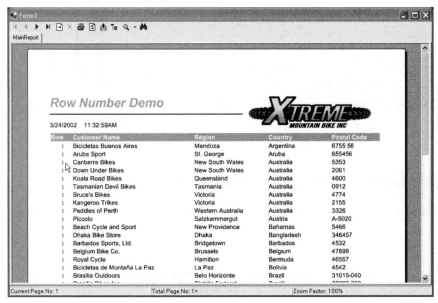

Figure 7-11. Row Number example output with same row number.

Notice that all the row numbers are 1. This is because the default rule states if a formula only has variables in it, it will be evaluated before any records are read. Even though this formula is placed in the detail section, it only gets evaluated once and the value variable never increases.

To fix this problem, use the keyword WhileReadingRecords in the formula.

```
WhileReadingRecords
Global RowNumber As Number   'Don't use Local b/c that resets the variable
RowNumber = RowNumber + 1
Formula = RowNumber
```

Figure 7-12 shows that the row number is now accurate because the formula is evaluated every time a record is read.

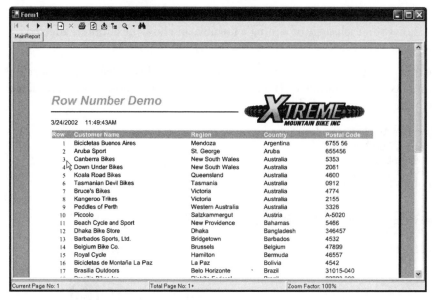

Figure 7-12. Row Number example output with correct row numbers.

Let's modify the example so that the report uses a grouping section based on the country name.

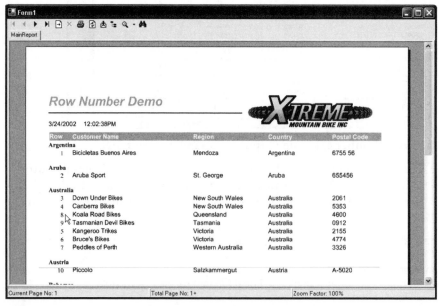

Figure 7-13. Row Number example output with grouping.

Figure 7-13 shows that the report now groups by country and uses a group header. Unfortunately, this change has introduced a bug in the report because the row numbers are now out of order (see the Australia group). This is because the row number is being calculated while the records are being read. After being read, the rows get resorted based upon their group. The row numbers get resorted as well. To fix this, change the formula so that the row number is being evaluated while the records are being printed and not while being read.

```
WhilePrintingRecords
Global RowNumber As Number   'Don't use Local b/c that resets the variable
RowNumber = RowNumber + 1
Formula = RowNumber
```

Figure 7-14 shows that the row number is now accurate.

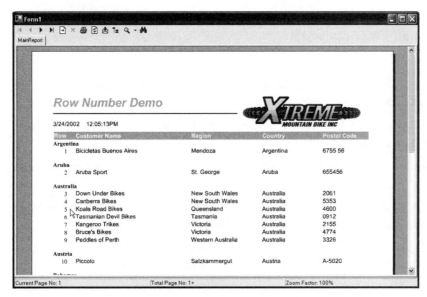

Figure 7-14. Row numbers are correct with grouping.

This series of examples shows that putting an Evaluation Time keyword at the beginning of a formula has a dramatic effect on the formula's value.

.NET User Function Library

Crystal syntax gives you many built-in functions and even lets you write custom functions, but what if your project has an existing library of business logic that needs to be used in your reports? Will you need to rewrite these rules from scratch using Crystal syntax? Fortunately, the answer is no. Crystal Reports lets you create user function libraries in .NET.

A user function library (UFL) is a set of custom functions developed in another language and accessible with the Crystal Reports designer. Your report can call those functions and display the return values on the report or use them in formulas.

Creating a UFL for Crystal Reports requires following certain rules. They are as follows:

- The project name has to be prefixed with "CRUFL".

- The project has to have both an interface class and implementation class. Both of which will have Com and GUID attributes.

- The assembly is added to the Global Assembly Cache so that it can be visible to Crystal Reports.

Let's walk through the steps to create a UFL. We'll create a custom function that is passed a month and it returns the company's fiscal month.[15] We'll call the function GetFiscalMonth().

Open Visual Studio .NET and create a new project. Use the Class Library template. Name the project **CRUFL_CorpFiscalMonth**.

Delete the Class1.cs file that is created by default.

Right-click on the **CRUFL_CorpFiscalMonth** project name and select Properties. Click the Signing tab and click the option Sign the Assembly.

Click on the drop-down list below the checkbox and select New. For the Key File Name property, enter any unique name. For this example, I'll use "uniquekey".

Uncheck the option Protect My Key File With a Password and click the OK button to save your changes.

If you're using VB.NET, click on the Compile tab. If you're using C#, click on the Build tab. Scroll down to select the Register For COM Interop option.

Right-click on the **CRUFL_ CorpFiscalMonth** project name and select Add > Class. Name the class **IFiscalMonth** and click the Add button. This will be the interface that defines the function's signature.

Copy the code from Listing 7-1.

Listing 7-1. IFiscalMonth code.

[VB.NET]

```
Imports System
Imports System.Collections.Generic
Imports System.Text
Imports System.Runtime.InteropServices

<ComVisible(True), InterfaceType(ComInterfaceType.InterfaceIsDual), Guid("C8DCF44C-853C-41d1-
    A85B-2E2E4D160779")> _
```

---

[15] A company uses a fiscal year to mark the beginning of their corporate earnings when they don't follow the typical calendar year that has January as the starting month. In financial reports the first month listed is the first month of the fiscal year and not the calendar year. For example, if a company has a fiscal year starting in July, then on the financial reports the month defined as "1" is actually July and "2" would be August.

```
Public Interface IFiscalMonth
    Function GetFiscalMonth(ByVal month As Integer) As Integer
End Interface
```

[C#]

```
using System;
using System.Collections.Generic;
using System.Text;
using System.Runtime.InteropServices;
namespace CRUFL_CorpFiscalMonth
{
    [ComVisible(true), InterfaceType(ComInterfaceType.InterfaceIsDual), Guid("ABBBB510-D2A0-4cab-
BAA8-73040F4056FA")]
    public interface IFiscalMonth
    {
      int GetFiscalMonth(int month);
    }
}
```

The key element of this code is that it adds a reference to the System.Runtime.InteropServices library. Secondly, it adds the COM and GUID attributes to the class.

Note

In the code, I specify a GUID that you can use. You should always create a new GUID string using Visual Studio .NET. Click the menu options Tools > Create Guid. This opens the Create GUID dialog box. Click the Registry Format option and select Copy. This copies the GUID to the clipboard. You can then copy and paste it to your programming code. Remember to remove the curly brackets at the beginning and end of the GUID. If you're using VS.NET 2005, you don't have the Create GUID program installed by default. You can run it by going to the Tools folder within the Visual Studio installation directory and running GuidGen.exe.

After entering the code in Listing 7-1, right-click on the CRUFL_ CorpFiscalMonth project name and select Add > Class. Name the class FiscalMonth and click the Add button.

Copy the code from Listing 7-2.

Listing 7-2. FiscalMonth code.

[VB.NET]

```
Imports System
Imports System.Collections.Generic
Imports System.Text
Imports System.Runtime.InteropServices
```

```
<ComVisible(True), ClassInterface(ClassInterfaceType.None), Guid("197222DE-FD22-4eb2-8B16-
C82B9C620FA7")> _
Public Class FiscalMonth
   Implements IFiscalMonth
Private FirstFiscalMonth As Integer = 7
Public Function GetFiscalMonth(ByVal month As Integer) As Integer Implements
IFiscalMonth.GetFiscalMonth
   Dim fiscalMonth As Integer = 0
   If month > FirstFiscalMonth Then
      fiscalMonth = month - fiscalMonth + 1
   Else
      fiscalMonth = month + fiscalMonth - 1
   End If
   Return fiscalMonth
End Function
End Class
```

[C#]

```
using System;
using System.Collections.Generic;
using System.Text;
using System.Runtime.InteropServices;

namespace CRUFL_CorpFiscalMonth
{
   [ComVisible(true), ClassInterface(ClassInterfaceType.None), Guid("FF7EBBE2-BB1D-4959-9779-
7A0ABFC7A643")]

   public class FiscalMonth : IFiscalMonth
   {
      private int FirstFiscalMonth = 7;
      public int GetFiscalMonth(int month)
      {
         int fiscalMonth = 0;
         if (month > FirstFiscalMonth)
         {
            fiscalMonth = month - fiscalMonth + 1;
         }
         else
         {
            fiscalMonth = month + fiscalMonth - 1;
         }
         return fiscalMonth;
      }
   }
}
```

This code defines the FiscalMonth class and inherits the IFiscalMonth interface. It adds code to the GetFiscalMonth() method to calculate the fiscal month based on the FirstFiscalMonth constant.

Save your project and build it using the menu items Build > Build Solution. This compiles a DLL and creates a type library file (.TLB) with the class signature in it. If you navigate to the project's Bin/Debug folder, you should see three files with these extensions: .DLL, .TLB, and .PDB.

For Crystal Reports to know that the library exists, you need to put the DLL into the Global Assembly Cache (GAC). To do this, go to the Visual Studio command prompt by clicking the Windows Start button and then selecting All Programs > Microsoft Visual Studio 2008 > Visual Studio Tools > Visual Studio Command Prompt.

Change the directory to where the DLL is located (using the 'C:\CD foldername' command).

Once in the directory enter the following command: gacutil /if CRUFL_CorpFiscalMonth.dll and press the Enter key.

You will get a confirmation message that the assembly has been added to the cache. You are now ready to go into Crystal Reports and call it from the Formula Workshop.

Open any existing project that uses Crystal Reports and open the report in design mode.

Right-click on the Formula Fields node and select New. Enter a formula name and click the Use Editor button. This opens the Formula Workshop.

Within the Formulas Workshop editor is the Functions window. Scroll down to the Additional Functions node and open it. Within it you'll see a new tab called Visual Basic UFLs.[16] Open it and you will see any custom functions that you've created. This is shown in Figure 7-15.

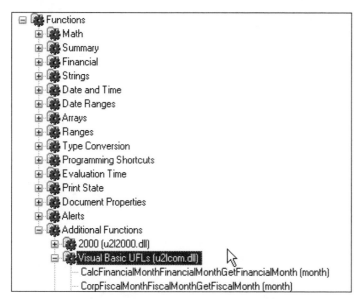

Figure 7-15. The list of custom user functions.

---

[16] Even though it has "Visual Basic" in the name, it lists both VB.NET and C# functions.

Notice that the name for each function is a combination of the project name, class name and the function name. It also lists the arguments that should be passed to the function.

You can now use this function in your reports and it will call the DLL that you built with Visual Studio .NET. This lets you take the business logic in your .NET application and implement it directly within your reports.

Programming with Basic Syntax

Formulas are used in Crystal Reports as a way to have enhanced control over a report as it prints. For example, if you want to have the rows on the report alternate colors, you can use a formula to change the background color of every other row. Another example would be using a field value in a row to determine when to hide a row.

Crystal Reports gives you the option to program formulas in either Crystal syntax or Basic syntax. This chapter teaches you how to program with Basic syntax. A reference for learning Crystal syntax is provided in Appendix A. You should read this chapter first before reading the Appendix.

Basic syntax is very similar (and in many ways identical) to the VB .NET syntax. Crystal syntax is similar to the C# syntax. If you are a C# programmer, you will probably be more comfortable programming with Crystal syntax.

When creating formulas, Crystal Reports defaults to Crystal syntax so you need to select Basic syntax. It is very tedious to specify Basic syntax every time you create a new formula. To change the default language to Basic syntax, right click on the report in design mode and select Designer | Default Settings. Go to the Reporting tab and at the bottom you can specify Basic syntax as the default language.

After you switch to Basic syntax, you'll notice that the syntax trees are refreshed so that they reflect the language you chose. Figure 8-1 shows how to choose Basic syntax from the Formula Editor.

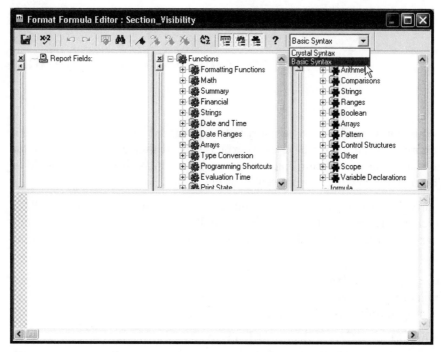

Figure 8-1. Language Selection

Since Basic syntax is so similar to VB .NET, this chapter gives an overview of the language and focuses on the areas where they are different. I assume that since you are already programming with Visual Studio .NET you don't want to be bored with elementary programming concepts. Throughout this chapter, Basic syntax will be compared to VB .NET syntax to bring noteworthy differences to your attention. Detailed examples will be shown when it is deemed to be helpful.

Formula Fundamentals

This section on fundamentals of writing formulas covers Case Sensitivity, Writing Comments, Returning a Value, Using Data Fields, Declaring Variables, Simple Data Types, Array Data Types, and Range Data Types. Each topic has its own section.

Case Sensitivity

Basic syntax is not case sensitive. The variable FirstName is the same as the variable firstname. Although these two variables are syntactically equivalent, it is recommended that you keep the case consistent so that your program is easier to read. If you always capitalize the first letter of a word in a variable, you should do so for all variables.

Writing Comments

Comments are designated by using a single apostrophe. You can also use the familiar REM keyword

```
'This is a comment
REM This is also a comment
```

Line Terminators

Basic syntax assumes that each programming statement only takes a single line of text. The carriage return (hidden) marks the end of the line. If a statement needs more than one line, the line continuation character _ is used.

```
X = 5 'This is a single line
Y = "This takes " _
& "two lines"
```

Returning a Value

Formulas are always used to return a value. The data types of these return values can be Number, Currency, String, Boolean, Date, Time, and DateTime. You cannot return data types of range and array.

Formulas return values by assigning the value to the Formula variable. Formulas have to always return a value. The following code simply returns the value True.

```
Formula = True
```

If a formula has multiple statements that return a value, all the assignments must be of the same data type. Although there is no way to specifically state what that data type is, the compiler will compare all the assignments and check them for consistency.

```
'The following IS NOT VALID due to the different data types returned
If Age > 65 Then
  Formula = "Retired"
Else
  Formula = Age
End If
```

Referencing Report Fields

Writing formulas requires referencing all types of data from your report and the databases that the report uses. The types of data that can be referenced consist of running total fields, the results of other formulas, and table fields. The syntax for referencing fields in a formula is to surround the field name with curly brackets. The syntax for referencing the field name is dependent upon the type of field it is.

Formulas are referenced by putting @ in front of the name.

{@Formula}

Parameters are referenced with a ? in front of the name.

{?Parameter}

Running total fields are referenced by putting # in front of the name.

{#RunningTotal}

Table fields are referenced by separating the table name and the field name with a period between the two. Spaces are allowed.

{Customer.First Name}

Group fields use the field name with the GroupName() formula.

GroupName({Table.GroupField})

Summary fields pass the field name and the group field to the summary function.

Sum({Table.FieldName}, {Table.GroupName})

Declaring Variables

Declaring a variable follows the standard format of declaring the variable using the As keyword and then its data type.

Dim var As datatype

Crystal doesn't reset its variables because of the way formulas and report sections work together. Formulas are usually added to sections of a report and a report section is repeatedly entered and exited as records are processed. If a variable lost its value every time a new record was processed, you wouldn't be able to track what happened with the last record. Making it easy for variables to retain their values while different records are processed is one reason why Crystal Reports is so powerful. If you want to make sure that a variable is reset to its default value every time, do so manually.

The first time a formula is called, all of the variables are automatically assigned their default values. See Table 8-1 for a list of the default values. Once you declare a variable and assign a value to it, that variable retains its value for the life of the report. Any future calls to that same formula will not initialize the variable back to its default value. This is the opposite of .NET. In .NET, a variable goes out of scope and its memory is released when the function exits. Every time the function is called, the variables are automatically reset to their default value.

Table 8-1. Data Type Default Values

Basic Data Type	Crystal Data Type	Default Value
Number	NumberVar	0
Currency	CurrencyVar	$0
Boolean	BooleanVar	False
String	StringVar	""
Date	DateVar	Date(0,0,0) – The Null Date value00/00/00
Time	TimeVar	No default valueNull
DateTime	DateTimeVar	No default valueNull

A variable's scope determines which formulas have access to that variable. There are three operators that you use to declare scope:

1. Local (Dim for Basic syntax): The variable can only be seen within the current formula. In a sense, a variable declared using the Dim keyword effectively defaults to Local scope.
2. Global: The variable can be seen within any formula inside the same report. Sub-reports do not have access to the variable.
3. Shared: Similar to Global, but the variable can also be seen within sub-reports.

Here are a couple of examples:

```
Local HireDate As Date
Shared AffiliateCities() As String
```

An unusual aspect of the Global/Shared variables is that even though their scope says that they can be seen by other formulas, you still have to declare them in each formula that wants to use them. This is unique because in VB .NET if a variable is declared as Public, and another procedure re-declares that variable, the new variable is created local to the procedure that declared it and the public variable is no longer accessible within the current procedure. When you re-declare the variable in Basic syntax, that means you now have access to the Global/Shared variable's memory space. If you don't re-declare the variable, it will give you an error stating that the variable doesn't exist. So no matter what the scope of a variable is, every formula must declare every variable that it uses.

Variable Assignment

To assign a value constant to a variable use the equal sign.

X = 5

Simple Data Types

Basic syntax supports the standard simple data types that we expect in a language: Boolean, Number, Currency, String, DateTime, Date, and Time.

Notice that rather than have a large number of numeric data types such as integer, double, etc., there is simply a single data type called Number. There is no need to worry about whether the number will use a decimal point or what its largest value is.

The Currency data type is treated the same as a Number data type with a few exceptions. They are listed below:

Currency can only have two decimal places. If assigned a number with more than two decimal places, it will round up to the nearest penny.

Currency automatically gets formatted as a monetary value. This eliminates the overhead of you always having to format the variable whenever it gets printed.

Since Currency is a different data type, it must be converted to a number to be used in mathematical assignments using non-currency variables. See the section "Converting Data Types" for more information.

Strings use the double quote, ", to specify a string literal. A character is represented by a string of length one. Referencing a position within a string is Base 1. Thus, if you want to refer to the first character in a string, you would use an index of 1. The maximum length of a string constant is 65,534 characters. Information on using the Basic syntax built-in string functions is in the next chapter.

```
'Demonstrate assigning a string constant to a variable
Dim Var As String
Var = "This is a string"
```

Dates are a little unusual in that there are three different data types available. The Date type can only store a date and the Time type can only store a time. It's preferable to use these data types if you don't need both values stored in a variable. If you do need both types in the same variable, use the DateTime type. Designate a DateTime constant by surrounding it with the # sign.

```
Dim MyBirthday As DateTime
MyBirthday = #5/23/1968#
```

Null Values

The Null value isn't a data type, but a type of data. It is a non-value used to mark when a field doesn't have a specific value stored in it. For example, if you are filling out a data entry form, there might be certain personal questions that you skip because you aren't comfortable answering them. When the program saves your answers to the database, it might put a null value in the questions you skipped to mark that you didn't answer them. Unfortunately, databases are meant to have data in them and using the null value can wreak havoc on your reports and formulas. If there is a chance that you are reporting from a database that has null values in it, you need to account for that so that your report runs smoothly.

In most cases you want to convert nulls to their default values. The default value is determined by the data type of the field being used. These values are shown in Table 8-1. There are two settings that control this and they are both found by selecting the menu options Crystal Reports > Report > Report Options. The first option, Convert Database NULL Values to Default, converts nulls when reading data from the database. The second option, Convert Other NULL Values to Default, applies to non-database null values (such as formulas). Check both of these options to keep null values from impacting your report.

There are times when you don't want to convert nulls to their default values because you want to know whether the data field is empty or if no value was saved at all. In this circumstance you have to be careful when using conditional statements that involve fields with null values. Crystal Reports will stop the evaluation and return no results. You need to test for this using the IsNull() function and handle the results correctly.

The IsNull() function returns true when the field is null and returns false for any other value. The following example tests whether the ID field is null or not. If so, it returns the dummy value of 9999.

```
If IsNull({Sales.PersonID}) Then
   9999
Else
   {Sales.PersonID};
```

If you want to use the IsNull() function in conjunction with another test, you have to perform the IsNull() test first. Otherwise, the report could error out. The next example tests whether a valid ID was entered.

```
If IsNull({Sales.PersonID}) OR {Sales.PersonID}=0 Then
   "This ID is not valid"
Else
   "The ID is valid";
```

In this example, if a field has a null value, the IsNull() function returns true and the test for zero doesn't need to be evaluated. But if the test for zero was performed first, the test would fail immediately when the null value was encountered.

Many times, a report will want to look ahead one record and see what a field's upcoming value is. Again, you need to test for null values. This is done with the NextIsNull() function.

```
If NextIsNull({SalesOrders.ShipDate} Then
   "This is the last order shipped.";
```

The PreviousIsNull() function performs the same test as the NextIsNull() function. But it looks at the previous record.

Question: I am trying to show a text field that says, "NONE", if no records are selected. Has anyone done this before?

Answer: To determine if a report doesn't have any records, use the IsNull() function to test if the total number of records is null. Right-click the text field that has "NONE" in it, and select Format Text Object. Add this conditional formula to the Suppress property:

formula = Not(IsNull(Count({Employee.Last Name})))

Array Data Types

Arrays provide a means of storing a collection of data in a single variable and accessing each element of the array using an index. Unlike .NET arrays which are Base 0, an array in Basic syntax is Base 1. Thus, the first element is referenced using 1 as the index. The maximum size of an array is 1,000 elements.

Basic syntax uses rounded parentheses to specify the array bounds.

X(1) = 5

When you declare an array, specifying the number of elements is optional. If you don't specify the number of elements in the declaration, before you use the array you have to either re-dimension it using the ReDim statement or assign an existing array to it.

```
Dim X() As Number 'Declare a non-dimensioned array
Dim Y(10) As Number  'Declare an array with 10 elements
```

The ReDim statement is the same as in VB.NET. It will change the number of elements in the array and reset their values. If you want to keep the existing values intact, also use the Preserve keyword.

```
Redim var(number)           'Redimension an array and reset all values
Redim Preserve var(number) 'Redim an array and preserve existing values
```

Assigning values to an array is done in different ways. If you know what the values of an array are during the development process, you can initialize the array with these values using the Array() function. Pass the Array() function all the elements as a comma delimited list and it returns an array that is fully populated with these elements. When using the Array() function you don't have to specify the array size. The compiler figures that out for you.

As expected, if you want to simply assign a value to an individual element in the array, the index must be within the array's bounds. But if you are assigning an entire array to another array variable and they are different sizes, you do not have to re-dimension the target array. The target array will be overwritten and it will have the size of the existing array.

```
'Demonstrate initializing an array and then overwriting it
Dim MonthsInSeason() As String
MonthsInSeason = Array("May", "June")
If LongWinter = True Then
    MonthsInSeason = Array("June", "July", "August")
End If
```

If you don't know the array values during the development process, you will probably assign the initial values to the array by looping through it. A common way of doing this is using a For Next loop where the range of the loop is the lower and upper bounds of the array. Another common method of assigning values to each element is to do so as the report is looping through its detail records. For each pass through the detail section you assign one of the fields to the array.

```
'Sample code within the detail section to track customer sales
Dim RecordCounter As Number
Dim SalesDetail() As Number
RecordCounter = RecordCounter + 1
SalesDetail(RecordCounter) = {Customer.Sales}
```

Once the array is populated, you can test to see if a certain value already exists in the array by using the In operator. Using the In operator saves you the trouble of looping through the entire array searching for a particular value. If the value already exists, the In operator returns True.

```
'Sample code to fill an array with the unique zip codes for all customers being printed
Dim RecordCounter As Number
Dim ZipCodes(100) As Number
If Not {Customer.ZipCode} In ZipCodes Then
    RecordCounter = RecordCounter + 1
    ZipCodes(RecordCounter) = {Customer.ZipCodes}
End If
```

Basic syntax has many predefined functions for summarizing the values in an array. These functions range from summing the total of all the values in the array to getting the maximum value in the array. Table 8-2 lists the array functions.

Table 8-2. Array Summary Functions

Basic Function	Description
Average(array)	Calculate the average of all numbers.
Count(array)	Count how many numbers there are.
DistinctCount(array)	Count how many numbers there are without including duplicates.

Maximum(array)	Return the maximum number.
Minimum(array)	Return the minimum number.
PopulationStdDev(array)	Return the Population Standard Deviation calculation.
PopulationVariance(array)	Return the PopulationVariance calculation.
StdDev(array)	Return the Standard Deviation calculation.
Variance(array)	Return the Variance calculation.

Although the functions are designed to only work with arrays, you can use them with table fields as well. This is done by creating a new array with the **Array()** function and passing it the fields to work with.

```
'Sample code for getting the maximum value of three fields
Dim MaxSales1stQtr As Number
MaxSales1stQtr = Max(Array({Sales.Jan}, {Sales.Feb}, {Sales.Mar}))
```

Best Of The Forum

Question: I only want to display the record with the most recent date. Is there a formula that does this?

Answer: You can compare the date of each record to the maximum date in the entire report. If they aren't equal, suppress the record. To implement this, right-click on the Details section and select Section Expert. In the Suppress property, enter the following Basic syntax conditional formula. Remember to replace the dummy field with your report's date field:

Formula = {Table.YourDate} <> Maximum ({Table.YourDate})

Range Data Types

The **Range** data type is a very useful data type that doesn't exist in .NET. It allows you to store multiple values within a single variable. In .NET, if you want to be able to store a range of values that have a definite start and end, you have to declare two variables where each variable represents an endpoint. If you want to see whether a field falls within this range, you have to compare the field to both variables. Crystal Reports greatly simplifies this with the **Range** data type. It stores a range within one variable and performs tests to see if another variable falls within that range. However, you can't just store any values in this variable. It must be a group of values with a definite starting and ending. All values in between are included. Of course, it should go without saying that the starting point and end point must be of the same data type.

To declare a variable as a Range data type, declare it as one of the standard data types and put the Range keyword at the end. The data types that are allowed to have a related Range data type are Number, Currency, String, DateTime, Date, and Time.

```
Dim var As datatype Range
```

Defining a range uses a variety of different operators. These operators specify the beginning and end of the range. The most basic operator is the To operator. It is placed between the start and end values. Using the To operator means that you want the start and end values to be included as valid members of the range.

```
'Demonstrate creating a range of all the days in a year.
Dim DaysInYear as Date Range
DaysInYear = #1/1/2002# To #12/31/2002#
```

A variation of the To operator is to use it with the underscore character. Placing the underscore on one side of the To operator states that you want all values leading up to that constant to be included, but you don't want the constant specified to be included. The underscore can be placed on either side, or both sides.

The following example demonstrates creating a range with all the days in the month. However, we only want to do so using the first day of the month in our range. The date 2/1/2002 won't be included in our range. Instead, the last day of the month just prior to it will be included.

```
Dim DaysInMonth As Date Range
DaysInMonth = #1/1/2002# To_ #2/1/2002#
```

When you want to find out if a field or variable is included within a specified range, use the In operator. This is useful when writing If statement and Select Case statements (described in the next section).

```
'Demonstrate calculating a volume price discount
Select Case UnitsSold
Case In (1 To_ 1000)
   Formula = Price
Case In (1000 To_ 5000)
   Formula = Price * .95
Case >= 5000
   Formula = Price * .90
End Select
```

Basic syntax has many predefined date range constants that can be used in your report. These are commonly used to filter out records that have dates that don't fall within the specified range. Table 8-3 lists the predefined date ranges and specifies which dates are considered to be included. Many of these constants use today's date to determine one of the end points of the range. You can tell the report to use a date other than the system date by setting the PrintDate property. This is done by right clicking on the Field Explorer, selecting Report, and selecting Set Print Date. This is saved with the report.

Table 8-3. Predefined Date Range Constants

Name	Description
AllDatesToToday	Includes any date prior to, and including, today.
AllDatesToYesterday	Includes any date prior to today. Today is not included.
AllDatesFromToday	Start: Today. End: Last date in field.
AllDatesFromTomorrow	Start: Tomorrow. End: Last date in field.
Aged0To30Days, Aged31To60Days, Aged61To90Days	Groups dates in 4 blocks of 30 days prior to today. Today's date is included in the Aged0To30Days range.
Calendar1stQtr, Calendar2ndQtr, Calendar3rdQtr, Calendar4thQtr	Groups dates in blocks of 3 months each. The first date is Jan 1 of the current year.
Calendar1stHalf, Calendar2ndHalf	Start: Jan 1 of the current year thru June 30. End: July 1 of the current year thru December 31.
Last7Days	Start: The six days prior to today. End: Today.
Last4WeeksToSun	Start: The first Monday of the four weeks prior to last Sunday. End: Last Sunday. Note: Does not include the days after the last Sunday thru today.
LastFullWeek	Start: The Sunday of the last full week. End: The Saturday of the last full week. Note: Does not include the days after Saturday thru today.
LastFullMonth	Start: The first day of last month. End: The last day of last month.
MonthToDate	Start: The first day of this month. End: Today.
Next30Days,	Groups dates in 4 blocks of 30 days after today. Today's date is

Next31To60Days, Next61To90Days, Next91To365Days	included in the Next30Days range.
Over90Days	Includes all days that come before 90 days prior to today.
WeekToDateFromSun	Start: Last Sunday. End: Today.
YearToDate	Start: Jan 1 of the current year. End: Today.

Conditional Structures

Conditional structures provide you with a way of testing one or more variables to see if they are equal to a value or are within a range of values. If the test succeeds, a code block is executed. If the test fails, then a different code block is executed. Since there are many different circumstances where you will want to do this, Basic syntax provides you with a lot of options to match your circumstance. Each has its own benefits and drawbacks that you need to consider when deciding which to use. The conditional structures are: If, and Select Case. The standard comparison operators are =, >, <, >=, <=, <>.

The If statement uses the standard VB .NET syntax of testing a condition and performing one action if it's true and another action if it's false. The code in the Else block is executed if the test returns false. Basic syntax also supports the Else If statement. Finish an If block with End If.

```
If condition1 Then
    ...code...
ElseIf condition2 Then
    ...code...
Else
    ...code...
End If
```

The Select Case statement uses the standard VB .NET syntax of putting the variable to be tested at the end of the Select Case statement. After the Select Case statement, list the test conditions and the related code blocks using the Case statement. You can list multiple conditions for a single Case statement by separating the conditions with a comma. If none of the Case statements return True, the code in the Case Else block is executed. Finish a Select Case block with End Select.

```
Select Case var
    Case condition1
        ...code...
    Case condition1, condition2
        ...code...
```

```
     Case Else
        ...code...
     End Select
```

See the previous section for a complete example of the Select Case statement.

Conditional Functions

Conditional functions let you evaluate different conditions and return a value based upon the result. These are very similar to the conditional structures If Then and Case because both allow you to evaluate different conditions and perform some action. However, conditional functions are different in that they can evaluate all the conditions in one line of code and they return a value when finished. Conditional structures require multiple lines of code. If a conditional structure needs to return a value, it must do so by storing it in a temporary variable for use after it finishes executing. Since conditional functions return the value themselves, and don't need a temporary variable, they can be used within another function! This gives you the ability to create a function that performs its operations using a number that changes depending upon certain conditions.

As an example, let's say you have an If statement that evaluates a condition and returns the result. This number is later used in another calculation. To make this work, there would have to be a function just for the If statement and this function would be called elsewhere in the report. You can replace this code with a single IIF() function (discussed next) that evaluates those conditions within the function and returns the value for use in the function. Everything is cleanly written with one line of code. An example that demonstrates how this works is within the discussion of the IIF() function.

Although conditional functions sound pretty good, they do have a drawback. If you get carried away with their use, your code will be harder to read and maintain. For example, an IIF() function is good at replacing a single IF statement. But if you want to replace a nested If statement, you will have to write nested IIF() functions. Although this will compile and run, it can be pretty hard for you or another programmer to read and understand. Use caution when deciding what is appropriate for the task at hand.

Being able to test conditions and return a result within a single function is very powerful. This section describes three conditional functions: IIF(), Choose(), and Switch().

The IIF() Function

The IIF() function is unique to Crystal reports. It is a shortcut for the standard If statement. Its purpose is to put both the True and False actions on the same line. It consists of three parameters. The first parameter is the test condition. If the test condition is True, the function returns whatever is in the second parameter. If the test condition is False, the function returns whatever is in the third parameter. This function can return any data type except for an array.

Although this is convenient because you can condense a multi-line If statement into one line, there are two restrictions. The first is that the second and third parameters can only be a constant, variable or a function. You can't put a statement or code block within these parameters. The second restriction is that both parameters must be the same data type.

The syntax for the IIF() function is as follows:

```
var = IIF(condition, true_result, false_result)
```

I frequently use the IIF() function when concatenating strings together and a certain string may or may not be needed. Since it is a function, I make it return a string. The following example creates a person's full name. If the middle initial wasn't entered into the database, we want to make sure we don't insert a "." inappropriately. The IIF() function tests whether the middle name exists, and if it does it adds it to the string with the proper formatting.

```
'Demonstrate using the IIF() function to create a user's full name
Dim FullName As String
FullName = {Person.FirstName} & " " & IIF({Person.MI}<>"",  {Person.MI} & ". ", "") &
{Person.LastName)
```

For purposes of comparing conditional functions with conditional structures, the following example is the same except that it uses an If Then statement.

```
'Demonstrate using the If Then statement to create a user's full name
Dim FullName As String
Dim MI As String
If {Person.MI}<>"" Then
    MI = {Person.MI} & ". "
End If
FullName = {Person.FirstName} & " " & MI & " " & {Person.LastName}
```

This example shows that using the If statement requires more coding. However, it does have the benefit of being easier to understand. It's a matter of personal preference as far as which one you choose to use. Personally, I always choose the IIF() function because it is an easy function to read. However, if the If statement were a lot more complicated, then using an IIF() function instead (or the other functions that are mentioned next) might make your code worse off.

The Choose() Function

The Choose() function returns a value chosen from a list of values. The value returned is determined by an index that is passed to the function. This function is like a shortcut for the If statement and the Select Case statement. You can use it when the range of possible values is relatively small and sequential.

The first parameter is an index representing which item to return. The remaining parameters are the items to choose from. The index range starts at 1 (it's not zero based). If the index is a value that is greater than the number of items passed, the default value for the appropriate data type is returned (e.g. zero for numbers, "" for strings). This function can return any data type except for an array. As expected, each item in the list must be of the same data type.

The syntax for the **Choose()** function is as follows:

```
Var = Choose(index, value1, value2, value3, ...)
```

The Switch() Function

The **Switch()** function is also like a shortcut for the If statement and the Select Case statement. The parameters are grouped in pairs. The first parameter is an expression to test and the second parameter is a result value that is returned if the expression is true.

The syntax for the **Switch()** function is as follows:

```
Var = Switch(condition1, result1, condition2, result2, ....)
```

What makes this unique from the If and **Select Case** statements is that every parameter is evaluated before a result is returned from the function. This can have good or bad results depending upon your needs. The result can be bad because there could be a performance issue if you are passing time-intensive functions as parameters or it could result in an error being raised. It can be good if you want to force various functions to be called prior to returning a value. This function can return any data type except for an array. The data types of each result must be the same.

Looping Structures

Looping structures let you execute a block of code multiple times. The number of times this code block is executed depends upon the type of loop used and what happens within the code block. The looping structures covered are: **For Next**, **While**, and the various **Do** loops.

For Next Loop

The **For Next** loop uses the standard VB .NET syntax of using the **For** statement followed by a variable and the start and ending range. You have to decide in advance how many times the code block gets executed.

The default loop increment is 1. Use the **Step** keyword to define a new increment. Terminate the **For** block using the **Next** statement. Putting the variable name after the **Next** statement is optional. You can prematurely exit the loop by using the **Exit For** statement.

```
For var = start To end Step increment
    ...code...
    If condition Then
        Exit For
    End If
Next
```

While and Do Loops

The While and Do loops all follow the standard VB .NET syntax. The While block is terminated with a Wend statement. The Do loops are terminated with a Loop statement. The While keyword is used to continue looping as long as the condition evaluates to True. The Until keyword is used to continue looping when a condition evaluates to False. You can exit a Do loop with an Exit Do statement.

Code template for While ... Wend:

```
While true_condition
    ...code...
Wend
```

Code template for Do While ... Loop:

```
Do While true_condition
    ...code...
Loop
```

Code template for Do Until ... Loop:

```
Do Until false_condition
    ...code...
Loop
```

Code template for Do ... Loop While:

```
Do
    ...code...
Loop While true_condition
```

Code template for Do ... Loop Until:

```
Do
    ...code...
Loop Until false_condition
```

Conditional Expressions

When performing actions based upon how a condition evaluates, there are numerous ways to build the condition. For example, when writing an If statement, you can compare a field to a constant using a variety of relational operators and you can join multiple conditions using Boolean operators. This section shows you all the ways you can evaluate fields and variables to see whether they match a certain value or a range of values.

You can test against a single constant or variable using the standard relational operators: <, >, <=, >=, =, <>.

You can also compare multiple expressions using the standard Boolean operators: And, Or, Not. A few operators that might be new to you are Xor, Eqv and Imp.

Eqv is for logical equivalence. It determines when the two expressions are the same. It returns True when both are true or both are false. If they are not the same, it returns False. The syntax is as follows:

exp1 Eqv exp2

Xor is for logical exclusion. It determines when the two expressions are different. It returns True if one is true and the other false. If both expressions are either true or false, then it returns False. The syntax is as follows:

exp1 Xor exp2

Imp is for logical implication. If the first expression is true, it implies that the second expression will also be true. If the second expression is also true, Imp returns True. If the second expression is False, Imp returns False because it didn't meet what was implied. On the other hand, if the first expression is False, nothing is implied and the result will be always be True. Thus, there is only one instance where Imp returns False: when the first expression is True and the second expression is False. The syntax is as follows:

exp1 Imp exp2

The Is operator is used with the Select Case statement when you want to use the relational operators (e.g. >, <, etc.). An example demonstrating this was already shown in the discussion on the Select Case statement.

The In operator is used for testing if a field or variable exists as an element in an array or if it falls within a range of values. For more information, see the previous sections Array Data Types and Range Data Types.

Using Built-In Functions

The Formula Editor in Crystal Reports gives you the ability to write very powerful functions. As you saw in Chapter 8, Crystal Reports lets you write functions to manipulate and analyze variables so that you can report on data specific to your business. In addition to writing your own formulas, Crystal Reports has dozens of built-in functions that decrease the amount of work you have to do. After all, why re-invent the wheel when you don't have too? This chapter shows you the different functions that come with Basic syntax. The functions are grouped by task so you can quickly find the ones you want. If you prefer to have an alphabetical list, just reference the Index at the back of the book to see the page number of the one you are looking for. This chapter has a section for each of these categories: String Functions, Converting Data Types, Formatting Values for Output, Math Functions, Generating Random Numbers, and Date and Time Functions,

String Functions

The ability to modify and concatenate strings is a powerful feature of many programming languages, and Basic syntax doesn't disappoint. This section breaks out the different categories of string functions and summarizes how they work. The categories are: Analyzing a String, Parsing Strings, and Manipulating Strings.

Throughout this section, many functions are listed that use one or both of the parameters called **compare** and **start**. Rather than repeat a description of those parameters for each function, they are explained here for your reference.

The **compare** parameter determines when string comparisons are supposed to be case sensitive. If **compare** is **0**, the search is case-sensitive. If it is 1, the search is not case-sensitive. This parameter is optional. If it is left out, the comparison defaults to 0, case sensitive.

The **start** parameter tells the function to process characters starting at the specified index.[17] Any characters that are prior to that index are ignored. This parameter is optional. If it is left out, the function will be performed for the entire string.

Analyzing a String

Strings are used to store a variety of data that are displayed in a report. They can come from a variety of sources such as database tables, user input or even XML. Most of the time you

---

[17] Remember from Chapter 8 that the first character of a string is at index 1.

will want to output the string directly to the report. But there are times when the information you want is stored as part of a larger string and you need to extract that data. To do this, it is necessary to analyze and parse a string's contents. Basic syntax gives you many functions for doing this. Table 9-1 shows the functions for analyzing a string's contents. Table 9-3 shows the functions for extracting sub-strings from a string. As a .NET programmer, you are already familiar with this functionality. Descriptions of each function are listed next to its name. Unless otherwise noted, the functions act the same as their .NET equivalents.

Table 9-1. String Analysis Functions

Function Name	Description
AscW(str)	Returns the ASCII value of a character.
ChrW(val)	Returns a character equivalent of an ASCII value.
Len(str)	Gets the number of characters in the string.
IsNumeric(str)	Tells if it can be properly converted to a number.
InStr(start, str1, str2, compare)	Determines if str2 is a sub-string of str1. The **start** and **compare** parameters are both optional.
InStrRev(start, str1, str2, compare)	Same as **InStr()**, but it starts at the end of the string and searches towards the beginning.
StrCmp(str1, str2, compare)	Compares two strings to each other. The **compare** parameter is optional.
Val(str)	Returns the numeric equivalent

The **StrCmp()** function returns a value based upon how the two strings compare to each other. Table 9-2 summarizes what these results mean. Just like the **Instr()** functions, you can pass a **compare** parameter to set case sensitivity.

Table 9-2. StrCmp(str1, str2) Return Values

Return Value	Description
-1	str1 < str2
0	str1 = str2
1	str1 > str2

Table 9-3. String Parsing Functions

Function Name	Description
Trim(str)	Trim the spaces from both sides of a string.
LTrim(str)	Trim the spaces from the left side of a string.
RTrim(str)	Trim the spaces from the right side of a string.
Mid(str, start, length)	Return a given number of characters starting at a specified position. The start and length parameters are optional.
Left(str, length)	Return a given number of characters starting with the leftmost character.
Right(str, length)	Return a given number of characters starting with the rightmost character.

The Trim() functions will delete all extraneous spaces from either side of the string, depending on which function you call.

The Mid(), Left(), and Right() functions return a partial string whose size is based upon the number of characters you pass to the function. If you don't pass a length to the Mid() function, it returns all characters starting with the first one you specified.

Manipulating Strings

It is common for a string to be modified before it is displayed on a report. This can consist of simple reformatting or even joining the different elements of an array into a single string. Basic syntax has many functions for manipulating string data. Table 9-4 shows the functions for manipulating strings. Descriptions of each function are listed next to its name. The functions Filter(), Split(), and Picture() are different from .NET and are defined in more detail after the table.

Table 9-4. String Manipulation Functions

Function Name	Description
Filter(str, find, include, compare)	Search an array of strings for a sub-string and return an array matching the criteria.
Replace(str, find, replace, start, count, compare)	Find a string and replace it with another string. The parameters start, count and compare are all optional.
StrReverse(str)	Reverse the order of all characters in the string.
ReplicateString(str, copies)	Returns multiple copies of a string.

Space(val)	Returns the specified number of spaces as a single string.
Join(list, delimiter)	Join an array of strings into one string and separate them with the specified delimiter.
Split(str, delimiter, count, compare)	Split a single string into an array of strings based upon the specified delimiter. The parameters count and compare are optional.
Picture(str, template)	Formats the characters in a string onto a template.

The Filter() function searches an array of strings for a matching sub-string. It returns an array of all the strings that have that sub-string in them. The first parameter is the string array and the second parameter is the sub-string to search for. Essentially, this function calls the InStr() function for every string in the array. If the InStr() doesn't return a zero, the string is added to the result array.

The Filter() function has an optional include parameter that tells the function to return an array of strings that don't match the sub-string. Essentially, this would be the same as saying that it returns all strings where the InStr() function returns a zero. Pass the include parameter the value False to get an array of the strings that don't have the sub-string in them. If you don't pass a value for this parameter, the default value of True is used. Listing 9-1 demonstrates using the Filter() function with different parameters.

Listing 9-1. Using the Filter() function

```
'Demonstrate the Filter() function
Dim StringArray() As String
Dim ResultArray() As String
StringArray = Array("abcd", "bcde", "cdef")
'This will return an array with two elements: "abcd", "bcde"
ResultArray = Filter(StringArray, "bc")
'This will return an array with one element: "cdef"
'This is because it is the only element that doesn't have the sub-string
ResultArray = Filter(StringArray, "bc", False)
```

The Replace() function searches for a sub-string within another string, and if it finds it, it will replace it.

The Replace() function has two optional parameters that are important: start and count. The count parameter lets you limit how many string replacements are done. If you pass a number for this parameter, the number of replacements done cannot exceed that value. If you don't pass a value for this parameter, all the sub-strings are replaced.

```
'Change the addresses so that they use abbreviations
Dim Streets As String
Streets = "123 Main Street, 456 Cherry Avenue, 999 Brook Street"
Streets = Replace(Streets, "Street", "St.")
```

```
Streets = Replace(Streets, "Avenue", "Ave.")
'Streets is now "123 Main St., 456 Cherry Ave., 999 Brook St."
Formula = Streets
```

The Split() and Join() functions work together nicely. The Split() function takes a string and splits it into a string array. This makes it easy to work on the individual strings. After you get done making any necessary changes to the individual strings, you can combine them back into one string using the Join() function. How convenient!

This example demonstrates combining the functionality of the Split() and Join() functions. A string with the names of customers is available. We want the string to only have names with a prefix of "Mr." This is done by splitting the names into an array of strings. Then the Filter() function is used to return an array with only the strings that match our criteria. This array is combined back into a comma-delimited string using the Join() function.

```
'Demonstrate the Split() and Join() functions
Dim Names As String
Dim NamesArray() as String
Names = "Mr. Jones, Sir Alfred, Ms. Bee, Mr. Smith"
NamesArray = Split(Names, ",")
'Get the names that only use Mr.
NamesArray = Filter(NamesArray,"Mr.")
'RJoin the array back into a comma-delimited string
Names = Join(NamesArray, ",")
'Names is now "Mr. Jones, Mr. Smith"
Formula = Names
```

The Picture() function maps a string onto a template. The first parameter is the source string and the second parameter is the template.

The template consists of a series of "x"s with other characters around it. Each character in the source string gets mapped onto each of the "x"s in the template. The source string can use any character and it will get mapped. If the source string has more characters than can fit in the template, all remaining characters are added to the end. If the template has any non-"x" characters, they stay as they are.

```
'Demonstrate mapping a string with non-alphanumeric characters
Formula = Picture("ab&[{1234", "xxx..xx..x..")
'The result is "ab&..[{..1..234"
```

This example illustrates that all characters in the source string were mapped onto the "x"s. It also shows that since the source string has nine characters and the template has six "x"s, the extra three characters are added to the end.

Best Of The Forum

Question: I have a formula that concatenates strings together. I want each string to print on a new line. How do I force a string to start on the next line?

Answer: You can insert a carriage return and line feed before a string to print it on a new line. Here is an example in Basic syntax. Remember to replace the variables and field with the appropriate names from your report.

```
Shared BigString As String
BigString = BigString + ChrW(13) + ChrW(10) + {Table.SomeField}
```

Converting Data Types

Basic syntax is a type safe language that requires all constants and variables in the same formula to be of the same data type. It also requires you to pass constants and variables as parameters using the exact data type that the formula expects. Even though the data types in Basic syntax are fairly simple, you still have to make sure that they are compatible. Fortunately, all the necessary type conversion formulas are available. Table 9-5 lists the conversion functions.

Table 9-5. Conversion Functions

Conversion Function	Description
CBool(number), CBool(currency)	Convert to **Boolean**.
CCur(number), CCur(string)	Convert to **Currency**.
CDbl(currency), CDbl(string), CDbl(boolean)	Convert to **Number**. Equivalent to **ToNumber()**. See the section "Formatting Values for Output".
CStr()	Convert to **String**. Equivalent to **ToText()**.
CDate(string), CDate(year, month, day), CDate(DateTime)	Convert to **Date**.
CTime(string), CTime(hour, min, sec), CDate(DateTime)	Convert to **Time**.
CDateTime(string), CDateTime(date), CDateTime(date, time), CDateTime(year, month, day)	Convert to **DateTime**
CDateTime(year, month, day, hour, min, sec)	Convert to **DateTime**.
ToNumber(string), ToNumber(boolean)	Convert to a **Number**.
ToText()	Convert to **String**. Same as **CStr()**.

IsDate(string), IsTIme(), IsDateTime()	Test a string for being a valid date/time.
IsNumber(string)	Test a string for being a valid number.
ToWords(number),	Convert a number to its word equivalent.
ToWords(number, decimals)	

Most of the above functions work the same as the similarly named .NET functions. The **CBool()** function takes a number or currency value and converts it to Boolean **True** or **False**. Any non-zero value is converted to **True** and zero is converted to **False**. When it is displayed on a report, it prints the words "True" or "False".

The **CCur()** function takes a number or string and converts it to the **Currency** data type. When converting a string, it can have formatting characters in it ("$", ",", etc.) and it will still be converted properly.

The **CDbl()** and **ToNumber()** functions are equivalent. Pass them a value and it gets converted to a number.

The **CDate()**, **CTime()** and **CDateTime()** are all similar. Pass all of them a string and it gets converted to the proper data type. The string parser for this function is very sophisticated. It will let you type in strings as diverse as "Jan 19, 1991", "5/26/1998" and "2002, Feb 04". You can also pass numbers as individual parameters for representing the different parts of a date and time. See Table 9-5 for the various parameter options.

When converting a string to a date or number, you run the risk of raising an error if the string isn't in the expected format. You can avoid this by testing the strings validity before converting it. The **IsDate()** and **IsNumber()** functions do this for you. They return **True** if the string can be properly converted. If not, they return **False**.

The **ToWords()** function takes a number and converts it to its equivalent in words. This is similar to writing an amount on a check and then spelling out the full amount in words. It will print the decimal portion as a being the "##/100". You can set the number of decimals it displays by passing a number to the second parameter, which is optional. Notice in the following example how the decimals are rounded up.

```
'Demonstrate the ToWords() formula
Formula = ToWords(123.45) 'Result is "one hundred twenty-three 45 / 100"
Formula = ToWords(123.45,1) 'Result is "one hundred twenty-three and 5 / 100"
```

Formatting Values for Output

When formatting output to be displayed in a report, the output is usually a combination of string data variables. As the last section stated, Basic syntax is a type safe language. As a result, you can't concatenate strings with numbers or dates. To build an output string with a combination of data types, you have to convert everything to a string using the **CStr()** method. This method takes all data types and converts them to a string.

The CStr() function is usually passed the value to format as the first parameter and the formatting string as the second parameter. The formatting string is used as a template that describes how the value should look when it gets converted as a string. Table 9-6 shows the different formatting characters that can be used. Table 9-7 shows examples of how different values will look after being formatted.

Table 9-6. CStr() Formatting Characters

Format	Description
#	Use with formatting numbers. If the number isn't large enough, spaces will be used instead. If the number is too large, the integer part will still be fully displayed. Unused digits after the decimal are zero filled.
0	Use with formatting numbers. If the number isn't large enough, it will be padded with zeros. If the number is too large, the integer part will still be fully displayed. Unused digits after the decimal are zero filled.
,	Use with formatting numbers to designate the thousand separators.
.	Use with formatting numbers to designate the decimal separator.
d, M	Day and month as a number (without a leading zero).
dd, MM, yy	Day, month and year as a two digit number (with a leading zero when necessary).
ddd, MMM	Day and month as a three letter abbreviation.
dddd, MMMM, yyyy	Day, month and year fully spelled out.
h, m, s	Time portions as a number without a leading zero.
hh, mm, ss	Time portions as a two digit number (with a leading zero when necessary).
HH	Show hours using a 24 hour clock (military time).
T	Single character representation of AM/PM.
TT	Two character representation of AM/PM.

Table 9-7. CStr() Example Output

#	CStr()	Output
1	CStr(1234, 2)	1,234.00

2	CStr(1234.567, 2)	1,234.57
3	CStr(1234.567, "#")	1234
4	CStr(1234.567, "0")	1234
5	CStr(1234, "0.##")	1234.00
6	CStr(1234, "0.00")	1234.00
7	CStr(1234.567, "#.##")	1234.57
8	CStr(1234.567, "0.00")	1234.57
9	CStr(1234.567, "#####")	1234
10	CStr(1234.567, "00000")	01234
11	CStr(1234.567, "#", 2)	1234
12	CStr(1234.567, "#.##", 2)	1234.57
13	CStr(1234.567, "#.###", 2)	1234.57
14	CStr(1234.567, "#.##", 2, ",")	1234.57
15	CStr(1234.567, "#.##", 2, ".", ",")	1234,57
16	CStr(1234.567, 2, ".", ",")	1.234,57
17	CStr(1234.567, "###,###.##")	1,234.57
17	CStr(#1/2/2003 04:05:06 am", "d/M/yy H/m/s t")	1/2/03 4: 5: 6 A
18	CStr(#1/2/2003 04:05:06 am", "dd/MM/yyyy HH/mm/ss tt")	01/02/2003 04:05:06 AM
19	CStr(#1/2/2003 04:05:06 am", "dd/MM/yyyy hh/mm/ss tt")	01/02/2003 04:05:06 AM
20	CStr(#3:20 PM#, "HH:mm")	15:20

Table 9-7 shows examples of many different **CStr()** function calls and the associated output. On the surface, this looks very straightforward and everything matches what was stated in Table 9-6. However, we know that in the world of software when you look below the surface things aren't always what they seem. You'll soon see that the simple **CStr()** function can get very complicated.[18]

---

[18] Who would have thought that a technical book would have foreshadowing in it?

Examples 1 and 2 are easy. The first parameter is the number to format and the second parameter is the number of decimals to display. If the number to format doesn't have any decimals, they are zero filled. Notice that in these examples as well as all the others, the decimals are rounded up.

With one exception, examples 3 through 10 are easy as well. The exception is that unlike the first two examples, the second parameter is the format string. Using this format string lets you be very specific about how to format the number.

Stop for a moment and look at examples 1 and 5. Do you notice one thing different between them? The difference is that the output in example 5 doesn't have a thousands separator. In both example 1 and example 5, no thousands separator is specified, but example 1 has it by default. This isn't the case when you use a format string. The documentation says that the format string needs to use an optional parameter to specify the thousands separator. But example 14 shows that Basic syntax has a bug that keeps this from working.[19]

Examples 5 and 6 show that if there aren't enough decimals, both the "#" and the "0" will zero fill their positions.

Examples 9 and 10 show that if there aren't enough digits to fill the whole number, the "#" fills it with a space and the "0" fills it with a zero.

Examples 11 through 13 are where things really get interesting. These examples show that you can use the format string and also specify how many decimals to display. If you think about this for a minute, it may not make sense why you would do this. After all, if you were using a format string, you shouldn't have to specify the number of decimals because it is already part of the format string. The only time you will do this is when you pass the optional parameters that specify the thousands separator and decimal character. Then you are forced to list all optional parameters and this means also specifying the number of decimals.

When you do specify the number of decimals, you should specify the same number that your format string allows. If you specify a number different than what is in this string, it uses the lesser of the two. Example 11 shows that the format string doesn't allow any decimals and that is how it is displayed. Example 13 shows that the number of decimals is two, and the format string allows three decimals. Thus, two decimals are displayed.

Example 14 shows that you can have a third optional parameter that specifies the thousands separator. Unfortunately, the output shows you that it doesn't have any effect. Example 15 tries to illustrate how to show a number using the European format of using a period for the thousands separator and a comma for the decimal. The output shows that the comma is now the decimal, which is correct. But again, no thousands separator is shown.

Example 16 shows that if you don't use a format string, everything works out perfectly.

---

[19] The suspense keeps building...

Does this mean that if you use the format string you can't have a thousands separator? No. It just means you have to do it manually. Example 17 shows a working example where everything is typed in. The proper characters are entered exactly where they belong in the string. If you use this method, be sure that you specify enough characters for the largest number that could be displayed.

The good news is that these problems only happen when you are formatting numbers for international display. By default, Basic syntax uses the computers international settings to determine how to format the number and you don't have to specify the format string. If you must use a format string, you will have to do it all manually like example 17.

All these variations on how to use the format string and remember where the bugs are can be pretty confusing. Just remember that if your format string doesn't act the way you think it should, then come back to this section for a quick refresher.

Unfortunately, the preformatted date strings that are in .NET (e.g. LongDate, ShortDateTime, etc.) are not in Crystal Reports. You have to write the entire format string manually. Although this certainly isn't difficult, the .NET feature has me spoiled.

The dates that are illustrated in examples 18 and 19 are much easier to look at, but far from perfect. First of all, you need to be very careful about capitalization. The compiler is case sensitive when formatting date strings. When entering a format string, refer back to Table 9-6 so that you get it right.

Now let's look at a couple of problems with formatting dates. According to the documentation, using a single "h", "m" or "s" will not put leading zeros in front of the hour, minute or second. This is shown to be true in Example 17. However, you can also see that it does insert a leading space. Even though we specified that all the characters are to be adjacent, it inserts spaces anyway. This is not what we wanted and there is not an easy way to fix it. To get around this, you have to concatenate the values together using the Hour(), Minute() and Second() functions. Unfortunately, these functions return two decimal places so you have to work a little harder than expected. The solution is shown in Listing 9-2.

Listing 9-2. Displaying a time with no leading spaces

```
'Demonstrate displaying a time with no leading spaces
Dim Now As Time
Now = CTime("1:2:3 AM")
Formula = CStr(Hour(Now), 0) & ":" & CStr(Minute(Now), 0) & ":" & _
   CStr(Second(Now), "0") & " " & CStr(Now, "tt")
'Now is formatted as "1:5:4 AM"
```

Math Functions

Table 9-8. Math Functions

Function Name	Description
Abs(number)	Return the absolute value.
Fix(number, decimals)	Return a number with a specified number of significant digits.
Int(number), numerator \ denominator	Return the integer portion of a fractional number.
Pi	3.14...
Remainder(numerator, denominator),	Return the remainder of dividing the numerator by the denominator.
numerator Mod denominator	Return the remainder of dividing the numerator by the denominator.
Round(number, decimals)	Round up a number with a specified number of significant digits.
Sgn(number)	Return number's sign.
Sqr(number), Exp(number), Log(number)	The standard arithmetic functions.
Cos(number), Sin(number), Tan(number), Atn(number)	The standard scientific functions.

The math functions listed in Table 9-8 are similar to the corresponding functions in .NET. There are only a couple of interesting points to notice.

Working with whole numbers and decimals is done in numerous ways. The Fix() and Round() functions take a fractional number and truncate it to a specified number of digits. The Round() function will round up to the nearest decimal. The number of decimals to display is optional and the default is zero. The Int() function is similar to the Round() function except that it only returns the whole number and will round down to the nearest whole number. Table 9-9 shows how the three functions will return a different number depending upon the decimal portion and whether the number is positive or negative.

Table 9-9. Examples of Truncating Decimals

Function	1.9	-1.9
Fix()	1	-1
Round()	2	-1
Int()	1	-2

If you want to get the whole number and you have the numerator and denominator available, you can use the \ operator to perform integer division. This does the division and only returns the integer portion of the result. The Mod operator and Remainder() function return the remainder after doing the division.

```
'Demonstrate the integer division and the Mod operator
Formula = 10 \ 3              'Returns 3
Formula = 10 mod 3           'Returns 1
Formula = Remainder(10, 3)   'Returns 1
```

Generating Random Numbers

Generating random numbers using the Rnd() function. When you use random numbers, you normally want to tell the computer to generate a new random number sequence based upon some internal method (usually using the system clock). This still applies with Basic syntax. The Rnd() function has an optional parameter that lets you tell the computer to generate a new random number sequence. With Basic syntax, you can pass your own random number seed value to generate the sequence. This is beneficial if you are writing a report that uses random numbers and want to test it using the same random number sequence each time. If you pass the Rnd() function a positive number, it does just that. However, if you want your sequence to be different every time, and thus your report will have different numbers every time, pass the Rnd() function a negative number. This tells it to use the system clock to generate the random number sequence. This results in a pseudo-random sequence of numbers each time you call it. Once you have called Rnd() with a seed, call the Rnd() function without a seed to get the next random number in the sequence.

Date and Time Functions

Table 9-10. Date and Time Functions

Function Name	Description
CurrentDate, CurrentTime, CurrentDateTime	Returns the current date and/or time.
DateSerial(year, month, day),	Returns a date or time.

DateTime(hour, minute, second)	
DateAdd(interval, number, date)	Increases the date by a certain interval.
DateDiff(interval, startdate, enddate, firstdayofweek)	Finds the difference between two dates.
DatePart(interval, date, firstdayofweek, firstweekofyear)	Returns a number representing the current interval of a date.
MonthName(integer, abbreviate)	Returns the full month name. Return the 3-letter abbreviation if the second parameter is True.
Timer	The number of seconds that have elapsed since midnight.
WeekDay(date, firstdayofweek)	Returns a number representing the day of the week.
WeekdayName(weekday, abbreviate, firstdayofweek)	Returns the full month name. Return the 3-letter abbreviation if the second parameter is True.

Table 9-11. Interval Strings for DateAdd(), DateDiff() and DatePart()

String	Description
"yyyy"	Year
"q"	Quarter
"m"	Month (1 through 12)
"ww"	Week of the year (1 through 53)
"w"	Day of the week (1 through 7)
"y"	Day of year (1 through 366)
"d"	Day part of the date (1 through 31)
"h"	Hour
"n"	Minute
"s"	Second

The date and time functions that come with .NET pale in comparison to what you can do with Crystal Reports. Although many of the Basic syntax functions are similar to their .NET counterparts, they give you more functionality. You can also combine different functions together to create very powerful date calculations. There are a lot of new concepts to learn.

DateAdd( )

For adding and subtracting dates and times, the easiest function to use is the DateAdd() function. This is very similar to the functions AddDays(), AddMonths(), etc. found in the .NET DateTime class. Using the DateAdd() function requires passing a string representing the type of interval to modify, the number of units to add or subtract, and the date to modify. There are a number of different strings that designate the interval to modify. The interval strings are listed in Table 9-11. To subtract a date interval pass a negative number of units. The DateAdd() function returns a DateTime value and this may need to be converted to either a Date or a Time depending on how you intend to use the result.

Using one q interval unit is the same as using three m intervals. The benefit of using the q interval is that many financial reports are printed on a quarterly basis. After the user is prompted for how many quarters they wish to print, you can take their input and use it to calculate a final date. Although multiplying their input by 3 is fairly trivial, having a shortcut is nice and it helps makes your code self-documenting.

Rather than using the DateAdd() function to add and subtract days, it is just as acceptable to directly add a number to the Date variable. Since the date is stored as a number, adding another number to it will increase the date by that number of days. The following examples both produce the same result.

```
Formula = DateAdd("d", 10, #1/1/2002#)        'Returns 1/11/2002
Formula = #1/1/2002# + 10          'Returns 1/11/2002
```

The benefit of using the DateAdd() function is that it takes into account how many days are in each month and it checks for valid dates. As an example, say that you want to find out the last day of the next month. To do this with the addition operator, you need to know how many days are in the next month so you will probably store that information in an array. You also need to track which years are leap years. Using the DateAdd() function is much easier because if you add one month to the current date, it will check that this returns a valid date. If there aren't enough days in the month, it will return the last valid day of the month. The same applies to using the quarter interval. The function adds three months to the current date and makes sure that this is a valid date. If not, it returns the last valid date of the quarter.

DateDiff( )

The DateDiff() function returns the difference between two dates or times. It can return the difference in different intervals. These intervals can be days, months, years or any of the intervals listed in Table 9-11.

Be careful when using the DateDiff() function for calculating an interval other than the number of days. When performing a difference calculation, it counts any interval less than a single unit as zero. For example, if you want to find out how many months have elapsed between two dates, and the two dates are the first day of the month and the last day of the month, the result is 0. This is because the interval is only a partial month and doesn't constitute a full month. The fact that the dates are 30 days apart is irrelevant. If you change this example so that rather than use the last day of the month, you use the first day of the next month, the result is 1. Even though the two examples had final dates that only differed by one day, the result is different. This applies to all the intervals including dates and times.

There is an optional parameter that lets you specify the first day of the week. This is only used by the DateDiff() function when the interval is ww. This counts the number of times a particular day of the week appears within a date range. To pass this parameter to the function, prefix the day by cr. For example, Friday is crFriday. The start date does not get counted when doing the calculation, but the end date does. Thus, if you pass the function a start date that falls on a Friday, and the parameter is crFriday, the result will not include this date.

```
'Demonstrate counting the number of paydays
Dim StartDate as Date
Dim NumberOfFridays As Number
StartDate = DateSerial(Year(CurrentDate), 1,1)   'First day of year
NumberOfFridays = DateDiff("ww", #1/1/2002#, CurrentDate, crFriday)
'If the first date was a Friday, add it back
If WeekDay(StartDate) = 6 Then
   NumberOfFridays = NumberOfFridays + 1
End If
Formula = NumberOfFridays \ 2          'Paid on every other Friday
```

The DateDiff() function treats the w and ww intervals differently than the DateAdd() and DatePart() functions. In both the DateAdd() and DatePart() functions, the w interval represents a single weekday and the ww interval represents a seven day period. However, the DateDiff() function treats the w interval as the number of weeks between two dates and the ww interval counts the number of times a certain weekday appears. Thus, the ww interval counts the number of times a seven-day period occurs and the w interval counts the number of times a single day occurs. This is the exact opposite of how the other two functions treat these intervals.

DatePart( )

The DatePart() function returns a number representing the part of the date that you specify using the interval parameter. These intervals are listed in Table 9-11. Pass the interval as the first parameter and the date as the second parameter.

```
'Get the current quarter
Formula = DatePart("q", CurrentDate)   'Returns a number 1 – 4
```

Use interval "w" to display the weekday and it returns a number from 1 to 7. By default, Sunday is represented by a 1. The optional third parameter designates which day of the week is considered the first day of the week. If you passed this parameter crMonday, Sunday is represented by a 7.

Use "ww" to display the week and it returns a number from 1 to 53. By default, the first week is the week that has January 1st in it. Use the optional fourth parameter to designate a different way of determining the first week of the year. There are two other methods to do this. The first method specifies that the first week is the one with at least four days in it. The second method specifies the first week as the first one to have seven full days in it. Table 9-12 lists the different constants that are used to specify the first week of the year parameter.

What happens if you specify the first week to be the first one with seven full days, and you pass it a date of 2/1/2002 that only has five days in the week? Does DatePart() return a 0? No, it returns 53 to let you know that the date falls before the first official week of the year.

Since the third and fourth parameters are both optional, if you want to specify the fourth parameter, you are also required to specify the third parameter (the first day of the week). Although by default this is crSunday, you must still pass it to the function in order to be able to use the fourth parameter. In this circumstance, the third parameter is ignored and the DatePart() function always assumes Sunday to be the first day of the week.

Table 9-12. First Week of the Year Constants

Constant	Description
crFirstJan1	The week that has January 1st.
crFirstFourDays	The first week that has at least four days in it.
crFirstFullWeek	The first week that has seven days in it.

MonthName( ), WeekdayName( ) and WeekDay( )

Just like the DatePart() function, these functions are given a date value and they return part of the date. The difference is that these functions are more specialized than the DatePart() function.

The MonthName() function is passed a number representing the month and it returns the name of the month fully spelled out. There is an optional second parameter that lets you specify whether it should be abbreviated to three letters. Pass True to the second parameter to get the abbreviated name. By default, this is False and it returns the full name.

The WeekdayName() function is passed a number representing the day of the week and it returns the name of the day fully spelled out. Just like MonthName(), you can pass True to the optional second parameter to get the 3 letter abbreviation.

The WeekDay() function is passed a date and it returns a number.

Both the WeekdayName() and WeekDay() functions use a number to represent the day of the week. By default, this number is a 1 for Sunday and a 7 for Saturday. As discussed for the DatePart() function, you can shift this number by specifying a different first day of the week. If you passed crMonday to the function, Sunday is represented by a 7. You pass this as the third parameter for the WeekdayName() function and as the second parameter for the WeekDay() function.

```
'Demonstrate using the first day of the week parameter
Formula = WeekdayName(2, True, crMonday)    'Returns "Tue" for Tuesday
Formula = WeekDay(#1/6/2002#, crMonday)     'Returns 7 b/c it is a Sunday
```

DateSerial( ) and TimeSerial( )

The DateSerial() and TimeSerial() functions can be used to create a date or time by passing the parts of the value as separate parameters to the function. The DateSerial() parameters are the year, month and day. The DateTime() parameters are the hour, minute, and seconds.

In the simplest form, these functions create a date or time using three parameters. But these functions are also very powerful for adding and subtracting values to a Date and Time. They are different from the DateAdd() function in that they perform the calculations using a cumulative process. They start by calculating a partial date (or time) value and build upon it and modify it each step of the way. It starts by calculating the year, then it calculates the month and finally the day. This is easiest to see by looking at a simple example first and a more complex example second. All of the examples use the following statements to declare and initialize the variable MyDate.

This code snippet shows the variable declaration that is used for the remaining examples.

```
'Declare the variable for use in the examples
Dim MyDate as Date
MyDate = CDate("2/4/2002")
```

This example gets the current year and month from the current date and passes them to the DateSerial() function. It passes the value 1 as the day parameter to force it to return the first day of the current month.

```
Formula = DateSerial(Year(MyDate), Month(MyDate), 1) 'Returns 2/1/2002
```

The next function calculates the last day of the prior month by using each parameter to create the next part of the date in sequence and modifying the result according to the arithmetic.

```
Formula = DateSerial(Year(MyDate), Month(MyDate), 1 - 1)      'Returns 1/31/2002
```

How it calculates the result is best shown using the steps listed here.

- Calculate the year. This returns a date with the year of 2002.

- Calculate the month. This returns a date of 02/2002.

- Calculate the day. The first part of the parameter is 1 and this returns a date of 02/01/2002.

- • The subtract operator tells it to subtract one day from the date as it has been calculated to this point. Thus, it subtracts one day from 02/01/2002 to give a date of 1/31/2002.

The next example is the most complex, but uses the same rules as the last example. It calculates the last day of the current month.

Formula = DateSerial(Year(MyDate), Month(MyDate) + 1, 1 - 1)   'Returns 2/28/2002

1) Calculate the year. This returns a date with the year of 2002.

2) Calculate the month. This returns a date of 02/2002

3) The addition operator tells it to add one month. This returns a date of 03/2002.

4) Calculate the day. The first part of the parameter is 1 and this returns a date of 03/01/2002.

5) The subtract operator tells it to subtract one day from the date as it has been calculated to this point. Thus, it subtracts one day from 03/01/2002 to give a date of 2/28/2002.

You can see from the three previous examples that using a cumulative approach to calculating the date is very powerful. It's almost like using a single function to write a simplified macro.

Timer

The Timer function returns the number of seconds that have elapsed since midnight. This can be used for doing performance evaluations. Unfortunately, it is only significant to the nearest second. So it is only useful for analyzing reports that have lengthy run times. The following code demonstrates timing how long it takes a report to run.

In the report Header put the following formula:

```
BeforeReadingRecords
Global StartTime as Number
StartTime = Timer
Formula = ""          'A necessary evil that won't affect the calculation
```

In the report Footer put the following formula:

```
WhilePrintingRecords
Global StartTime as Number
Formula = Timer – StartTime
'This returns the number of seconds it took to run the report
```

Other Functions

Although this chapter and the last two have listed many useful functions, Basic syntax still has many more to choose from. You've seen all the primary ones and I'm going to leave the remaining ones for you to explore on your own.

Visualizing data can have a tremendous impact compared to just printing raw numerical data. Adding a chart to a report makes it possible for readers to quickly grasp the important relationships between data. Many times reports are used with proposals to sell a reader on an idea or plan. Adding a colorful chart can sell your idea more effectively than a dry report filled with endless numbers. This chapter shows you what types of charts are available as well as how to modify their appearance so that they can make your report more appealing and quickly get your message across.

Choosing the Proper Chart

Charts are used to make it easy to compare sets of data. The visual aspect of a chart lets the reader immediately recognize things such as the differences in quantity, percentage of the whole or numerical trending. Depending upon the information you are trying to convey, certain chart styles are more effective at presenting this information than others. Table 10-1 lists different chart styles and what they are effective at presenting. This table gets you started in the right direction for choosing the proper chart.

Table 10-1. Effectiveness of different chart styles.

Chart Style	Effective at ...
Bar Chart	Comparing the differences between items and events.
	Comparing items and events against the same scale without relation to time.
	Showing relationships between sets of data using grouping.
	Note: The X-axis is generally non-numeric. When it is numeric, the interval isn't relevant.
Line Chart/Area Chart	Comparing continuous data over a period of time against a common scale.
	Tracking movement over time.
	Examining trends between two or more sets of data.
	Note: The X-axis represents a unit of time.
X-Y Scatter Chart	Charting a large quantity of values without relation to time.
	Finding groups of data where there is a large percentage of similar data points.
Bubble Chart	Similar to the X-Y chart, but with a third data point. The third data point determines the bubble's diameter. It is proportional to the value of this data point.
Pie/Doughnut Chart	Visualizing the percent of the whole.
	Examining relationships as part-to-whole.
	Note: There is only a single axis being represented. Thus, only one value is being charted.
Radar Chart	Comparing data sets in a star pattern. The importance/relationship of each data set is determined by having the target value start at either the center of the axis or the outside.
Stock Chart	Analyzing stock values. Shows the trading range for the day as well as first trade and last trade amounts.
3D Surface Chart	Showing trends with relationship to time.
	Note: It uses a three dimensional surface to make it easy to analyze a large quantity of data.

To use Table 10-1, think about why you are using a chart to present your data, ask yourself, "What is the message I am trying to convey to the reader?" Scan the list of reasons of why one chart is more effective than the other charts. Once you see a description that best matches your purpose, select that type of chart.

For example, assume that you have a report that prints the annual sales for each division in a corporation. The message you are conveying is which division had the largest sales volume as well as which division had the lowest sales. Three charts that are good at comparing different data sets are the bar chart, the line chart and the X-Y chart. The bar chart immediately looks good because it is effective at comparing differences between items. The line chart also compares data, but it does so over a period of time. This doesn't apply here because the data is within the same time period (i.e. the same year). So the line chart is not a good choice. The X-Y chart compares data, but it is done with respect to two data points. In other words, both the X and Y axis must represent numerical data. The sales report is charted with the sales volume and the division name. Since the division name isn't numerical data, it can't be used with the X-Y chart. The best choice for the division annual sales report is the bar chart.

Let's build on this example by saying that you are given a new requirement where the report has to be modified so that it is now a drill-down report. It currently shows the annual sales per division and it needs to be modified so that you can drill-down on a division and see its monthly sales. This helps the reader determine if the division had a particular month that was exceptionally better than the other months or if the division was consistently improving. The purpose of this chart is very similar to the first chart. You want to tell the reader how the total sales compare to each other. But this example has a slight variation: you are now charting for a single division and the individual months are being compared to each other. You are working with data that changes over a period of time and looking for the trend. The only reason we didn't use a line chart in the first example was because the data didn't relate to time. This example does relate to time and it is also looking at the sales trend. So the line chart is an excellent choice for presenting the monthly sales figures.

Adding a Chart

There are two ways to add a chart to a report: with the Report Expert and with the Add Chart Expert. If you are creating a report and you know in advance that it will use a chart, you can use the Report Expert to build the chart while performing the initial report design. If you decide to add a chart later in the report creation process, select the menu options Crystal Reports > Insert > Chart. This brings up the Chart Expert. Both methods show the same dialog box (Figure 10-1) for creating a chart. The Report Expert displays it on the Chart tab.

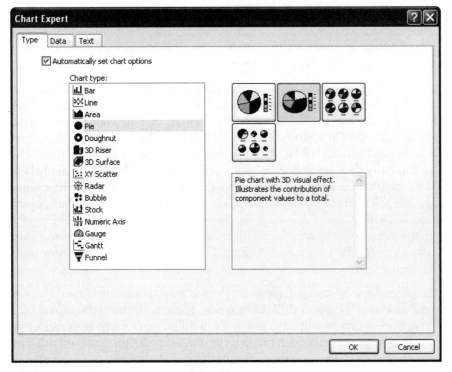

Figure 10-1. Chart Expert dialog box.

This dialog box has three tabs that are shown by default: Type, Data, and Text. There is also a checkbox on the Type tab titled Automatically Set Chart Options. It is checked by default. If you uncheck this option, two additional tabs appear on the dialog box: Axes and Options.

Selecting a Chart with the Type Tab

Use the Type tab to select the type of chart to display. A sample of each chart is shown in Table 10-2. The Chart Expert shows many examples of each chart to the right of the list. As you click on each chart type in the list, the variations will change to reflect the available options. Charts that use an X-Y axis format have an option button that selects whether it is a vertical or horizontal chart. Vertical is chosen by default.

Table 10-2. Example chart types.

Chart Type	Sample	Chart Type	Sample
Bar Chart		Doughnut Chart	
Line Chart		3D Riser Chart	
Area Chart		3D Surface Chart	
Pie Chart		XY Scatter Chart	
Bubble Chart		Radar Chart	
Stock Chart		Gauge Chart	
Funnel Chart		Gantt Chart	
Numeric Axis Chart			

Setting Data Points with the Data tab

The Data tab is the primary interface for configuring the chart and it is fairly complex. It sets the location of the chart and the fields that determine the coordinates of each axis as well as map the data points. It also has three buttons for setting the properties of specialized charts.[20] The Advanced button shows the default layout and is available for every report. The Group button is enabled when your report has a grouping section and the Cross-Tab

---

[20] There is actually a fourth button labeled OLAP. This isn't used with Visual Studio .NET and is always disabled.

button is enabled when there is a cross-tab object on the report. The default layout, Advanced, is shown in Figure 10-2.

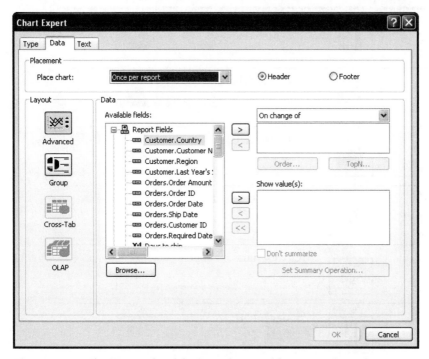

Figure 10-2. The Data tab with the Advanced button selected.

Note

The Advanced, Group, and Cross-Tab buttons each create a different type of chart. Although they are all on the same Data tab and appear to work together, they are mutually exclusive. Only the last one selected will be used to create the chart. For example, say that you set some properties for the Advanced tab. You decide that you would rather use a Group chart instead. So you click on the Group button and change the settings. When you run the report, the chart displayed on the report will be a group chart and reflect those settings. The settings you made with the Advanced button are ignored. In fact, when you close this dialog box and save your settings, only the settings for the current button are saved and any settings that were made with the other buttons are discarded.

The Placement frame controls which section the chart is placed in on the report. It is automatically placed there when you close the dialog box. The dropdown box sets whether the chart appears in the Report Header/Footer or whether it appears in the Group

Header/Footer. When you click on it, it displays the options Once Per Report or For Each xxx. The Once Per Report option always puts the chart in the Report Header/Footer. There is one For Each xxx option listed for each group on your report. If there aren't any groups on your report then the only option listed will be Once Per Report. To the right of the dropdown are the options to select placement in either the Header or the Footer.

The Data frame lets you choose the fields to plot onto the chart. The Available Fields list shows all the fields that the chart can use. To the right of this list is an Evaluate option[21] and below that is the Show Value(s) list. Use the Available Fields list to select the fields to put in the two options on the right.

Setting the Evaluate Option

The Evaluate option determines when a new element is shown on the chart. On a standard vertical chart, they would be the elements listed on the X-axis. For example, this determines when a new bar is drawn on a bar chart. There are three options to choose from and they are listed in Table 10-3.

Table 10-3. The Evaluate options.

Evaluate Option	Description
On Change Of	A new element is created when the value of the field changes. The value plotted on the other axis is the sum of all fields that are in each group.
For Each Record	A new element is created for each detail record in the table. Check the number of detail records because too many records will over-crowd the chart.
For All Records	Shows a single element on the chart. The value plotted on the other axis is the grand total of each field selected in the Show Value(s) list.

The On Change Of option requires a little more explanation than the other two options, which are fairly straightforward. The On Change Of option is used in conjunction with one or more report fields. It creates chart-only groups and summarizes the values within the group. The groups in the chart have no effect on the rest of the report.

When selecting the On Change Of option, you add the field(s) to group onto the listbox below the option. The number of fields you add determines how many groups are in the report. If you only have one field, each group name is listed as a single element on the chart. For example, Figure 10-3 shows a chart with an Evaluate field of Customer Name and the

---

[21] The label "Evaluate" is assumed and isn't actually shown in the dialog box. It is the dropdown box at the top.

Show Value field (discussed later) is Order Amount. This creates an element for each customer and it charts the total amount of all the orders in the report.

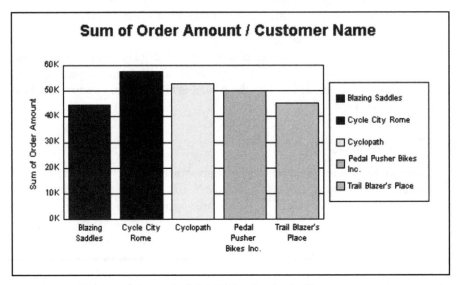

Figure 10-3. A chart with one field in the Evaluate list.

Having more than one field in the Evaluate list creates sets of data. Each set has the same number of elements in it and they are compared to each other as a group. The first element is the primary group and the second element is the sub-group. The primary group determines the sets that are charted. The sub-group charts each individual element within the primary group.

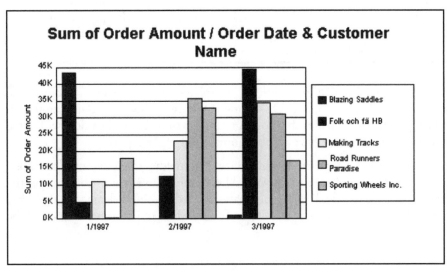

Figure 10-4. A chart with two fields in the Evaluate list.

The chart in Figure 10-4 also shows the total customer order amounts, but it does it per the month the order was placed. Putting two fields in the Evaluate list does this: The Order Date, by month, and the Customer Name. The Order Date is listed first so that the data sets are charted by month. The Customer Name is listed second so that it gets listed as a separate element on the chart.

For each field listed as an element, there are a few ways to customize it. Directly below the list are two buttons: TopN and Order. These are only enabled when you select one of the fields. These two buttons bring up the same dialog boxes that are used with formatting groups. The TopN button lets you filter the groups according to their overall ranking. The Order button lets you select whether the groups are sorted by Ascending, Descending, or Natural Order. You can also tell it to sort in a specified order. Please reference Chapter 4 if you need a refresher on how these dialog boxes work.

Setting the Show Value Fields

The Show Value list determines the fields that are plotted on the chart. On a standard vertical chart, this is where an element is plotted along the Y-axis. For example, this determines how high a bar is drawn on a bar chart. For each field listed, another element is drawn on the chart at each interval. If there is a line chart with three fields, each field would have a separate line plotting its values.

The Show Value fields are charted using either their actual value or using a summary function. This is determined by what is selected for the Evaluate option. If this option is set to For Each Record, each record gets charted according to its actual value. Thus, no summary calculation is performed. If the option selected is On Change Of or For All Records, a summary calculation is performed to determine what value to plot. The On Change Of setting calculates a summary value for each group. The For All Records setting plots a single summary value for the entire report. This has the effect of plotting one element for each field listed.

The default summary calculation is the Sum() function. If you had selected a text field for the Show Value field, the summary function would be Count(). You can change this by selecting the field and clicking on the Set Summary Operation button. This brings up the standard Change Summary dialog box where you click on the dropdown box to select a different summary function.

Meeting the Minimum Field Requirements

The Evaluate setting and Show Value setting work together to determine the X, Y and Z axis on each chart. Due to the fact that each type of chart can be unique in how it uses the fields in these settings to create the chart, it is important to know how many fields to put in each setting.

Charts have different requirements for the number of data values it needs to plot each point. For example, a line chart needs two values. The first value marks the time interval and the second value marks where on the chart the point will appear. A slightly more complicated chart, the X-Y Scatter chart, has different requirements. It needs a single value to set the intervals along the X-axis of the chart and it needs two values to mark where the point should appear on the chart. Table 10-4 shows the minimum number of fields required by each chart type.

Table 10-4. Required minimum number of fields for each type of chart.

Chart Type	# On Change Of	# Show Value
Bar/Line/Area	1	1
Pie/Doughnut	1	1
Pie/Doughnut multiple	1	Many
3D Riser	1	1
3D Surface	2	1
	1	Many
XY Scatter	1	2
Bubble	1	3
Stock	1	2
Stock with open/close marks	1	4

The middle column, # of On Change Of fields, tells you how many fields are required when you have selected the On Change Of option in the drop-down box. This doesn't apply if you selected either For Each Record or For All Records. This is because these selections automatically set the interval along the X-axis and you aren't allowed to add new fields. However, if a chart type has a requirement of two fields, you won't be able to use the For Each Record or For All Records options.

The last column, # of Show Value fields, tells you how many fields are required in the Show Values list. Each chart type requires at least one field and some charts allow you to add an unlimited number of fields. The only restriction is that it is limited to how many reasonably can fit on the chart.

Adding Group Charts

Below the Advanced button, on the Data tab of the Chart Expert, is the Group button. It is used to create a chart that shows each group and one of its summary fields. It can only appear within the Report Header/Footer. When you click on the button, the dialog interface changes to reflect options specific to grouping. This is shown in Figure 10-5.

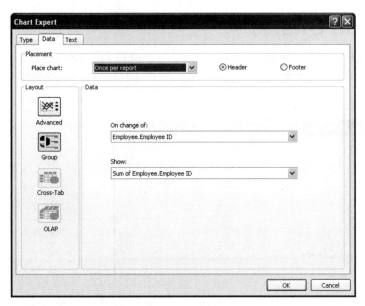

Figure 10-5. The grouping options of the Data tab.

The Group button presents a very simple interface when compared to the Advanced button. This is because the Group button is used for creating a simple chart. Whereas the Advanced button allows you a lot of variations on how many fields are charted on each axis, the Group button only lets you select a single group and a single summary field to chart.

There are two requirements for having the Group button enabled. The first requirement is that there is a group section. Of course, if your report doesn't have a group section, you certainly can't chart group values. The second requirement is that the group must use at least one summary field. This is because the group chart only plots summary fields. If you want to create a chart based on a group and your report doesn't meet these two requirements, you can choose to place the chart within a Group Header/Footer and set the options using the Advanced button.

The top dropdown box lists the groups on your report. The groups that are listed here change depending upon where you place the chart. No matter how many groups are on your report, only two groups will be listed. These are the top two groups below the location where you are placing the chart. For example, if you place the chart in the Report Header/Footer section, the first and second outermost groups are listed. However, if you place the chart in the first group's header/footer, the next two groups directly below it will be listed in the dropdown box. If there is only one group below where the chart is located, it will be the only one listed.

When you select the group, the lower dropdown box will show the summary fields for the group selected. From these summary fields, select which field to chart.

Adding Cross-Tab Charts

The Cross-Tab chart is similar to the Group chart because it takes one of the fields that the cross-tab object is grouped on and plots one of its summary fields. The related dialog box is shown in Figure 10-6.

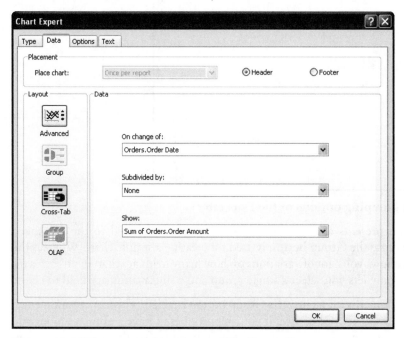

Figure 10-6. The cross-tab options of the Data tab.

The On Change Of dropdown box lists the two outermost group fields for the cross-tab object. If you have multiple fields listed for either the row or column setting, then the second and later fields are ignored and can't be used. The field selected in the dropdown box determines when a new element is drawn. Thus, the cross-tab chart can have either one element per row or per column.

The Show dropdown box, lets you select the summary field to plot. This serves the same purpose as the Show Value setting with the Advanced button. However, the Advanced setting lets you select multiple fields and the Cross-Tab settings only let you select one field.

The middle dropdown box, titled Subdivided By, lets you create a data set that is similar to having multiple fields in the Evaluate setting of the Advanced options.

Setting Captions with the Text tab

Use the Text tab to set the captions that appear on the chart as well as their fonts. This tab is shown in Figure 10-7. It is only visible when the Type tab option to automatically set chart options is unchecked.

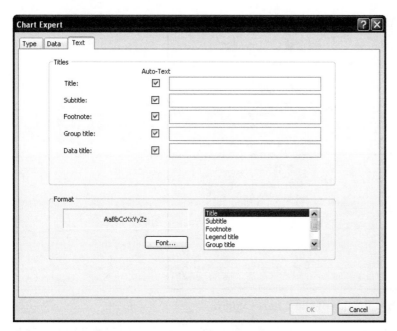

Figure 10-7. The Text tab of the Chart Expert.

The Text tab is very easy to understand and modify. It consists of two halves. The top half shows a checkbox for each title that appears on the chart. By default, each caption is set to Auto-Text. This means that the chart will set the caption when you print the report. It uses the chart's field names to determine what to print. For each caption, you can uncheck Auto-Text and enter your own caption. What you enter will override whatever the chart would have printed on its own. If you uncheck it, and leave the text blank, nothing is printed for that caption.

The lower half sets the font for each caption. To change the font, select the caption name from the list on the right and click on the Font button. This brings up the standard Font dialog box and you can set the properties as you wish. When you click OK, you are brought back to the Chart Expert. An example of how the new font settings look are shown above the Font button.

Using the Options Tab

The Options tab, shown in Figure 10-8, has a few miscellaneous options for customizing the layout of the chart. Like the Text tab, it is only visible when the Type tab option to automatically set chart options is unchecked.

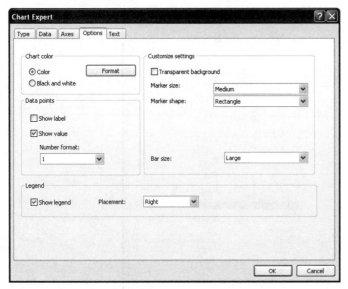

Figure 10-8. The Options tab of the Chart Expert.

There are four main areas on the Options tab. The Color Chart frame lets you set the chart to be in color or black and white. Black and white can be helpful when you are sending the report to the printer. The Data Points frame is used to toggle displaying the data point on or off. A data point is an identifier on a chart's element telling what the element represents. This can be its text value or its coordinate on the chart. Figure 10-9 shows a chart with the data points turned on.

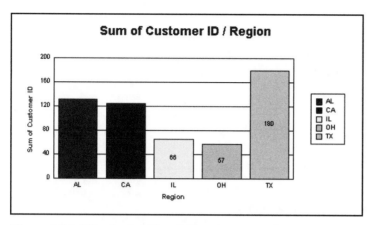

Figure 10-9. Displaying the data points on a chart.

The Customize Settings frame sets whether the chart background has a transparent background, how large the markers are and what shape the markers are. The Legend frame sets whether the legend is displayed, and where it is displayed. It can be displayed to the right or left of the chart or at the bottom.

Using the Format Menus

Once a chart is finished and the Chart Expert is closed, two new menu items become available. By right-clicking on the chart object in design mode, you are given two formatting specific menu options: Format and Format Chart. The Format menu gives you the standard formatting dialog box that you've already seen with the other report objects. It lets you select options such as suppressing the object and changing the border. These have already been discussed in detail in Chapter 4 and you can reference that chapter if you need more information.

The Format Chart menu item is specific to the chart object and it gives you four new menu items: Template, General, Titles, and Grid. Each of these menu items opens a new dialog box with options that provide you with the ability to add a finer amount of customization to your chart. This menu is shown in Figure 10-10.

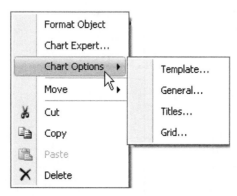

Figure 10-10. The Format Chart menu items.

You probably won't need to use these menu options with the majority of your reports. The formatting options provided by the Chart Expert will serve most of your needs on a daily basis. But there will be times when you want to take one of the options in the Chart Expert and fine tune it to a greater degree. That is when you will use these menu options.

A lot of the functionality in the Chart Expert is duplicated by these menu options. But in addition to that, they also give you many more selections to choose from. It's the multitude of selections that make these menu items powerful. Since you won't need to reference them very often and they are easy to understand, you are left to explore them in more detail on your own.

Cross-tab reports are a powerful way to create summaries of data in a spreadsheet style format. They generate summary data in a grid where the rows and columns represent groups of data. This provides the user with a report format that is easy to read and uses a small footprint.

Ask a programmer how he or she feels about cross-tab reports and you will probably get a variety of answers - both good and bad. I think that programmers can be put into three general categories about their experiences with cross-tab reports. Some programmers have tried using cross-tab reports and found them to be too confusing. They shrug them off as being unworthy of the effort to learn. Other programmers have successfully used cross-tab reports, but found a variety of problems in getting the data that they wanted. This group uses cross-tab reports only when absolutely necessary. And last, but not least, is the programmer who has successfully mastered the cross-tab report and found it to be a great way of producing reports that quickly summarize groups of data. They gladly use cross-tab reports whenever appropriate. The goal of this chapter is to take you from being a beginner in writing cross-tab reports to the level of an expert.

Understanding Cross-Tab Reports

Cross-tab reports are a way of reformatting a report that groups data into a grid format. This grid format is very similar to the way a spreadsheet represents data. It lets the user visually analyze the data in a way that makes it easy to compare values in one group against the values in another group. Let's look at the grouping report in Figure 11-1 and we'll see it reformatted as a cross-tab report.

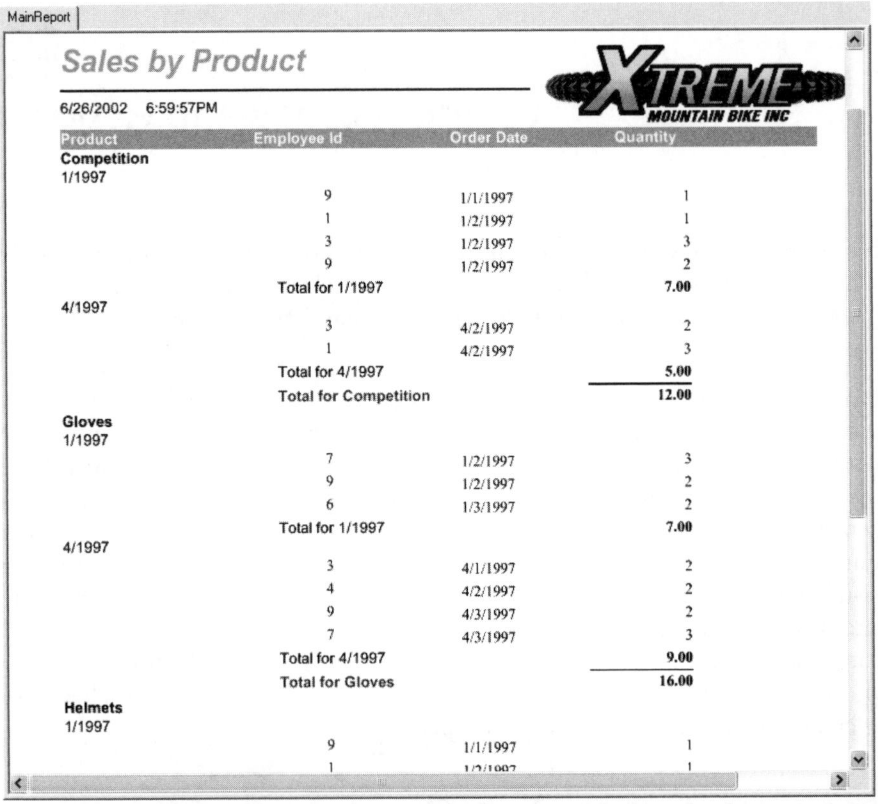

Figure 11-1. Grouping by Product and Quarter.

This report has two grouping fields. The outermost group is by Product Type and the innermost group is the Order Date grouped quarterly. The group header for the Order Date is the first date in the period. The detail records show you the Employee ID, Order Date, and Quantity. There are two sub-totals of the quantity. The first occurs on the change of quarter and the next is on the change of product type.

This is a pretty standard grouping report and it shares a common problem with other grouping reports: the sub-total amounts are spread out across multiple pages. This makes it hard to compare numbers because they aren't consolidated into a single page.[22] A user reading this report will find that they are continuously flipping pages to see how the sales of one product compare to the sales of another product.

Re-writing this report as a cross-tab report eliminates this problem. Figure 11-2 shows the same report in cross-tab format.

---

[22] Normally, the details for each group would span a page or more. To make the report small enough to fit onto a single page I had to filter the records down to just a few days in each month.

Quarterly Sales by Product

6/26/2002   7:24:09PM

	1/1997	4/1997	Total
Competition	7.00	5.00	12.00
Gloves	7.00	9.00	16.00
Helmets	2.00	3.00	5.00
Locks	11.00	0.00	11.00
Mountain	5.00	2.00	7.00
Saddles	3.00	3.00	6.00
Total	35.00	22.00	57.00

Figure 11-2. Cross-tab report by Product and Quarter.

The cross-tab is much easier on the eyes. The outermost group field, Product Type, is represented on each row of the grid. The innermost group field is Order Date grouped by quarter, and makes each quarter a separate column. These columns span horizontally along the page. Although there are many detail records in the original report, these are ignored when generating the rows and columns. Only the values of the grouping fields are listed. The cross-tab report took two grouping fields and made them the X-axis and Y-axis of the grid.

The data inside the grid corresponds to the subtotals on the grouping report. The first row is for the Competition product type. It shows values of 7, 5 and a total of 12. When you look at the grouping report in Figure 11-1 you see that these match the subtotals for the Competition product type. Each row in the cross-tab report shows the same subtotals that are displayed in the grouping report for the product type groups. Thus, the cross-tab report took the sub-totals of a grouping report and formatted them as a grid. All the data is summarized into a very compact space and it doesn't span many pages like the grouping report would.

Note

It might help to think of a cross-tab report as taking a multi-group report and just copying the group footers into a grid.

The benefits of using a cross-tab report can be offset by the drawbacks. As powerful as the cross-tab report is for summarizing data, it has a limitation that it can't show any detail records. For example, the cross-tab report doesn't show the fields for Employee ID or the Shipping Date. Although these fields are very important, they aren't printed because a cross-tab report can only show summary calculations.

A standard grouping report is great for showing as much information as necessary and having control over the format. But the data could span many pages and this makes it hard to do analysis with. The cross-tab report gives you the ability to quickly analyze summary data, but you have to give up looking at the detail records that make up the data.

Tip

If you have a report that needs to benefit from both types of reports, a solution is to combine the two reports. Create a grouping report that prints all the necessary detail information. Then add a cross-tab object to the report header or group header. This lets a user see a summary of the critical information on the first page of the report and dive into the details printed on the remaining pages.

Creating a Cross-Tab Object

The name "Cross-Tab Report" is a little misleading. It makes it sound like the whole report only shows the cross-tab grid and that no other data is printed. This isn't true. A cross-tab report refers to a report that has a cross-tab object in one of its sections. This object is similar to the other report objects on a report. It has properties that let you modify its fields and how it's formatted.

There are two ways to add a cross-tab object to your report. The first way is to add a new report to your application from the Project menu and choose the Cross-Tab Expert from the Crystal Report Gallery dialog box. This is shown in Figure 11-3.

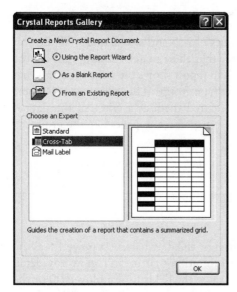

Figure 11-3. Choosing the Cross-Tab Expert from the Gallery.

You can also add a cross-tab object to an existing report by selecting the menu option Crystal Reports > Insert > Cross-Tab. Both methods of adding a cross-tab object to your report gives you the dialog box shown in Figure 11-4.

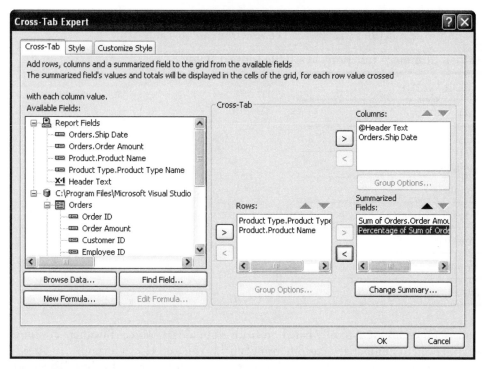

Figure 11-4. The Cross-Tab Expert dialog box.

There are three primary input areas on this dialog box: Rows, Columns, and Summarized Fields. Below these three sections is the list of fields selected for printing. Add fields from the list of available fields on the left into the appropriate sections to the right. Do this by either dragging and dropping the fields or by selecting a field and clicking one of the arrow buttons next to the appropriate section. If you want to see an example of the data that a field contains, click on the Browse Data button in the bottom left corner.

All three windows require you to add a minimum of one field to each before the cross-tab is functional. For example, you can't specify fields for the Rows and Summary Fields windows and not put a field in the Columns window. You can also add multiple fields to each window to make the cross-tab print additional data.

When you add a field to the Summarized Fields window, by default it assigns one of two different summary functions to the field. If the field is numeric, then the Sum() function is used. If the field is text, the Count() function is used. You can change the default summary function after it has been added to the Summary Fields window by clicking on the Change Summary button.

When changing the summary function for a numeric field, all the summary functions in Crystal Reports are available. Summarizing on a text field is more restrictive. You have to choose from a list of text compatible summary functions because not every function works with a text field. For example, it isn't possible to calculate the average value of a text field.

However, you can determine the 5th largest item of all available items and print that. The text compatible functions that you can choose from are in Table 11-1.

Table 11-1. Summary functions available for text fields.

Function Name
Count()
DistinctCount()
Nth Largest()
Nth Smallest()
Nth Most Frequent()
Minimum()
Maximum()
Mode()

Summary functions are typically based on fields from a data source. But there are times when you need to summarize a custom formula field. You can select a formula that already exists or you can create a new formula from the Cross-tab Expert dialog box. When you click the New Formula button, it brings up the Formula Editor dialog box.[23] This is the same dialog box discussed in Chapter 7. After you save and close this dialog box, that formula is added to the list of available fields at the bottom of the dialog box. You can drag and drop the formula field into the Summary Fields window. Although this formula was created via the Cross-tab Expert, it will now be listed along with all the other formulas in your report. Thus, it can be placed on your report just like any other report object.

Caution

Cross-tab summary functions can't perform many tasks that you take for granted with other types of reports. For example, it is a common error to attempt to devise formulas for a cross-tab report that calculates a value depending upon the value of another cell in the cross-tab or the sum of a group of cells in another row or column. You expect this to be possible because it is easy to do for a standard report. But a cross-tab report can't do this because it is built around the premise that each summary value is calculated independently of the other cells. Cross-tab summary fields are calculated during the report's

---

[23] The New Formula button is only visible when the Cross-Tab Expert is shown with an existing cross-tab object. It doesn't appear when creating a new report using the Cross-Tab Expert.

first-pass and there is no mechanism to reference the value of any other field in the cross-tab. You can try to get creative and write a formula to emulate these tasks, but you will find that each formula relies upon having information about the other fields in the cross-tab. Thus, it won't succeed. The tasks that a cross-tab report can't perform are as follows: calculating second-pass formulas, calculating running sums, calculating percentages of the subtotal/grand total and sorting rows according to the row totals.

Once you are finished adding the fields, click the OK button. The cross-tab object is added to your report and you are put back at the report designer.

Adding additional summary fields to the cross-tab object results in the values being placed in the same cell. Each is stacked vertically on top of the other. The first field added is placed at the top. You also have the option of placing them side-by-side by going to the Customize Style tab and selecting the Vertical option.

Adding additional grouping fields for either the rows or columns creates a sub-group format. This is very similar to a standard report that uses multiple groups. The first field becomes the outermost group and the remaining fields are grouped based upon the subset of data. If you preview the report and find that the fields are not in the proper order, you can rearrange them by opening the Cross-tab Expert again and using the mouse to drag and drop the fields to the correct position in the list.

Figure 11-5 shows a cross-tab object in design mode that has two grouping fields in the row and two summary fields.

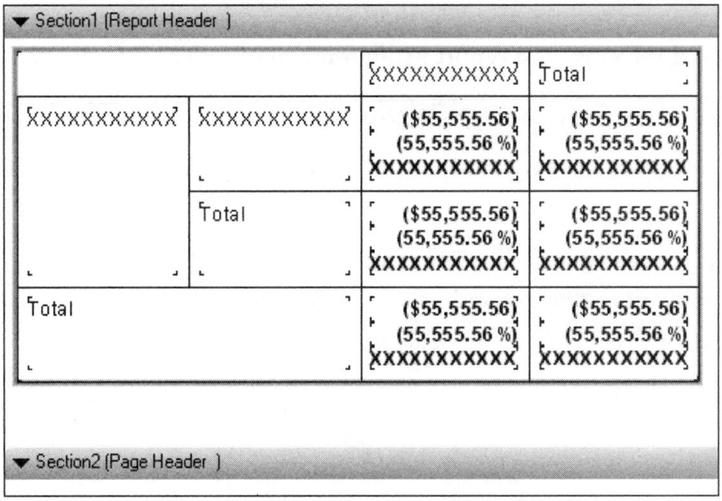

Figure 11-5. The cross-tab object using multiple fields.

The large, left-most block in the cross-tab object represents the outermost group. The innermost group is represented by the two thinner blocks just to the right of it. Both groups have a subtotal field associated with them. This is similar to a standard multi-group report because when it prints there will be a group footer showing the subtotal for the group. The two summary fields are visually represented by the multiple fields filled with the number five. The top-most field is the first summary field that was added to the Summary Fields window. Running the report generates the output shown in Figure 11-6.

		2/2000	3/2000	12/2000	1/2001	2/2001		3/2001
Competition	Descent	$17,716.86 45.83%	$5,895.20 33.74%	$96,033.66 74.64%	$86,341.44 49.10%	$178,548.46 70.77%		$105,5 7:
	Endorphin	$1,799.70 4.66%	$1,851.38 10.60%	$9,786.51 7.61%	$26,190.91 14.89%	$43,406.31 17.21%		$4,9 :
	Mozzie	$19,138.35 49.51%	$9,723.33 55.66%	$22,842.13 17.75%	$63,328.23 36.01%	$30,329.80 12.02%		$32,6 2:
	Total	$38,654.91 100.00%	$17,469.91 100.00%	$128,662.30 100.00%	$175,860.58 100.00%	$252,284.57 100.00%		$143,1 10(
Gloves	Active Outdoors Crochet Glove	$221.00 5.55%	$87.00 1.42%	$9,736.57 48.66%	$4,863.84 12.26%	$8,318.52 22.10%		$3 :
	Active Outdoors Lycra Glove	$1,188.30 29.83%	$77.85 1.27%	$6,279.49 31.38%	$25,632.28 64.63%	$23,184.69 61.59%		$9,5 8
	InFlux Crochet Glove	$0.00 0.00%	$0.00 0.00%	$106.30 0.53%	$6,225.95 15.70%	$6,041.40 16.05%		$4 :
	InFlux Lycra Glove	$2,574.55 64.62%	$5,956.55 97.31%	$3,886.69 19.42%	$2,935.19 7.40%	$100.40 0.27%		$1,0 !
	Total	$3,983.85 100.00%	$6,121.40 100.00%	$20,009.05 100.00%	$39,657.26 100.00%	$37,645.01 100.00%		$11,3 10(
Helmets	Triumph Pro Helmet	$939.01 18.77%	$4,618.81 51.76%	$6,694.18 27.14%	$32,404.99 34.35%	$5,033.75 9.62%		$27,0 6(
	Triumph Vertigo Helmet	$3,052.41 61.03%	$1,067.50 11.96%	$5,686.48 23.05%	$47,237.73 50.08%	$28,648.44 54.76%		$17,6 3!
	Xtreme Adult Helmet	$0.00 0.00%	$3,134.73 35.13%	$11,722.02 47.52%	$13,385.80 14.19%	$12,723.28 24.32%		$1 (

Figure 11-6. The output of the cross-tab report using multiple fields.

Best Of The Forum

Question: My data is a range of numbers between 1 and 100. I want my cross-tab to group the data in intervals of 10. How can I do that?

Answer: This can be accomplished by creating a formula that returns the grouping names you want to display and using that formula in the cross-tab object. Here is an example formula using Basic syntax:

```
Select Case {table.yourfield}
   Case 0 to 10
      Formula = "0 to 10"
   Case 11 to 20
      Formula = "11 to 20"
   ....
End Select
```

Placing the Cross-Tab Object

If you look back at the cross-tab report example from earlier in the chapter, you might realize that the cross-tab object as it appears in the report designer doesn't look like the cross-tab grid as it appears when printed on the report. This is because the report designer's cross-tab object is a template for showing you what fields are used and how the cross-tab grid will be formatted. When the report is run, the cross-tab object expands vertically and horizontally so that it can print as many columns and rows as necessary to show each group. If you expect your report to have a lot of columns, make sure it is placed along the left side of the report to account for all the columns.

Tip
When you put a cross-tab object in a section, it will grow as large as necessary to print all the data. If you place other report objects below the cross-tab component, and in the same section, the cross-tab grid will probably overwrite them when it expands during the print process. Fix this by creating a second section in that area and place the lower data in the new section. This will let it appear just below the cross-tab grid without any overlapping.

The cross-tab object can only be placed in certain sections: the Report Header/Footer and the Group Header/Footer. It can't be placed in the detail section because it can't print detail records. It also can't be placed in the Page Header because it would be duplicated on each page without any of its data changing. This would create redundant information that wastes space.

Be careful about where you put the cross-tab object. Placing the cross-tab in the Report Header/Footer produces different results than putting it in the Group Header/Footer. It prints out whatever information is available to it. When placed in the Report Header, it has access to every record in your report, and it summarizes all the data that is printed. When placed in the Group Header, it only has access to the data for that group. The cross-tab will be much smaller because it only prints a subset of all the report data.

Formatting the Cross-Tab Grid

As with every report object in Crystal Reports, the cross-tab object has many formatting options to make it look just the way you want. These changes can be categorized according to whether they affect the grid and its layout or whether they affect the individual fields within the grid.

Since the number of rows and columns of the cross-tab is dynamic, you can't control its final size on the report. But you can control the individual row and column widths. This has a direct effect on the total size of the cross-tab grid when it prints. When you select a field in the cross-tab object and resize it, the entire row and column changes to reflect this change. Changing the width changes the width of the entire column. Changing the height changes the height of the entire row. Thus, a change to one field affects all the fields that are in the same column and row.

To set the standard formatting properties of the overall cross-tab object, right-click on the cross-tab object and select Format Object. Be careful when doing this because if your cursor is positioned above one of the fields in the cross-tab, you will get the format dialog boxes for that field. To set the formatting for the cross-tab object, position your cursor in the top left-hand corner of the object. This is where there are no other fields that could be selected by mistake.

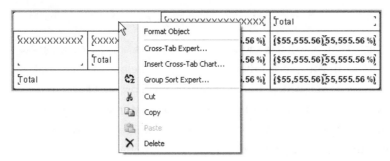

Figure 11-7. Selecting the Format menu item of the cross-tab object.

Both the grid and the fields within the grid can be formatted using the standard formatting properties. Some examples of these properties are suppressing the object, setting the font properties, changing the border, etc. Most of these properties have a formula button so that their value can be the result of a formula that you program.

There are two formatting related functions that can be used with cross-tab cells. As stated earlier, each cell has to display the output of the same formula. However, you can make each cell stand out by using the formulas with the formatting properties. Since each cell is identical, there are two formulas that let you identify what value is being displayed as well as identifying the current row and column values. The CurrentFieldValue() function returns the cell's current value. Use this to highlight values that fall within or outside of a certain range. The function GridRowColumnValue() returns the value of the row or column that the cell is in. Pass it the name of the group field, either the row's field name or the column's field name, and it returns the current value. For example, if the column groups by months of the year, a cell in the third column will return the month name "March". If you want to refer to the row or column field as a different name, assign it an alias to make it easier to reference it. This is done via the style options in the Format Cross-Tab expert. That expert is shown next.

Formatting the Style Properties

The grid has some unique formatting properties that don't appear with other objects. These are called the Style properties. Right-click on the cross-tab and select Cross-Tab Expert.

The Cross-Tab tab is shown by default and this has already been discussed. Click on the Style tab, the second tab, to choose from a list of more than a dozen predefined styles. As you click on each style, the right window shows a template of how your cross-tab object will be formatted.

Click on the Customize Style tab to make your own changes to the style. If you selected a predefined style in the previous tab, you will be prompted about whether you want to save that style. If you choose Yes, the new style will be reflected on the Customize Style tab. If you choose No, the Customize Style tab will reflect the formatting of the cross-tab object before you opened the Cross-Tab Expert.

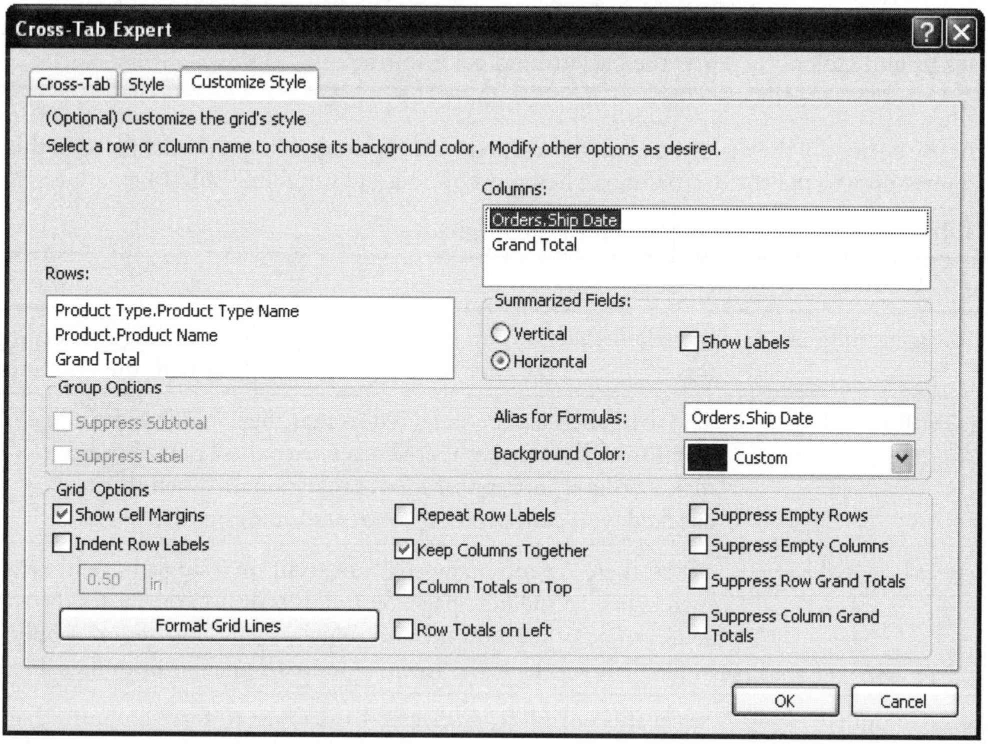

Figure 11-8. The CustomizeStyle tab of the Format Cross-Tab expert.

The Customize Style tab has numerous properties that you can use to format the cross-tab grid to look exactly like you want. There is a Rows window and a Columns window and within each window are the names of the grouping fields. Click on the field you want to format to change its properties. The properties and their descriptions are listed in the Group Options frame directly below those windows. Each of these properties only affects the group field that is currently selected. These style properties are listed in Table 11-2.

Table 11-2. Style formatting properties for cross-tab group options.

Style Property	Description
Suppress Subtotal	When you have multiple groups for a row or column, the cross-tab grid shows a subtotal for the top-most groups. This suppresses that subtotal from printing.
Suppress Label	This suppresses all data for that field from appearing in the cross-tab grid.
Alias for Formula	This changes the name that you use to reference the group in the conditional formatting formulas.
Background Color	Sets the background color for the cell.

At the bottom of the dialog box is a frame titled Grid Options. The properties listed in this frame apply to the entire cross-tab. These grid options are listed in Table 11-3.

Table 11-3. Grid options for the cross-tab object.

Grid Option	Description
Show Cell Margins	By default, each group field has a margin surrounding it. Turning this off makes the edge of the group field flush with the grid lines.
Indent Row Labels	The row labels can be indented so that they are offset from the Total row. This makes it easier to notice the Total row and it makes your report appear more professional. When this is checked, you can specify the indentation in inches.
Repeat Row Labels	When there are too many columns to fit on a single page, they will span across to the next page. Setting this option on causes the row values to be printed on the additional pages. This option is only available if you have the Keep Columns Together option enabled.
Keep Columns Together	Select this option (it is selected by default) to force columns that span multiple pages to stay intact. Unselecting this option could cause a column to be split in half.
Row/Column Totals on Top	Forces totals to be switched from their default position. Row totals will be at the top-most row and column totals will be left-most column.
Suppress Empty Rows/Columns	Don't print rows/columns with no data.
Suppress Row/Column Grand Totals	Don't print the grand-totals for rows and/or columns.

The Format Grid Lines button is used to set the line styles for the grid. Clicking on this button brings up the Format Grid Lines dialog box shown in Figure 11-9. For each grid line in the cross-tab object, you can set the color, style, and width properties. You can also suppress a line by unchecking both Draw options. If you don't want any grid lines to be shown then uncheck the Show Grid Lines option.

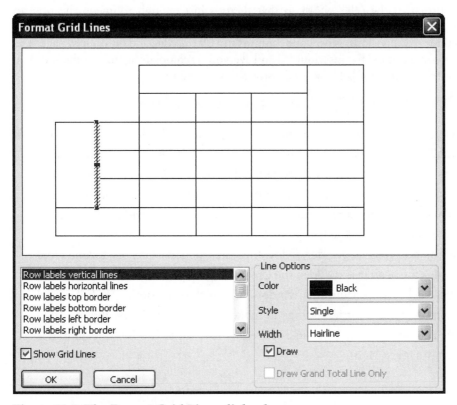

Figure 11-9. The Format Grid Lines dialog box.

Managing the Columns

One of the most interesting features of the cross-tab object is that it is dynamic. The number of columns changes according to the data being displayed. As an example, assume that you have a cross-tab report where the columns represent the historical sales figures per year. If a company has been in existence for five years, there will be five columns printed. Once a new year starts, a new column is automatically added to the cross-tab. Columns are created on an as needed basis without requiring any additional work on your part.

Dynamic columns are a blessing and a curse. The fact that you can even have dynamic columns is great. Being able to have the number of columns grow and shrink according to the data in a table is very powerful. You can't do this with standard reports objects.[24] The drawback is that you can't control how many columns are created and you can't insert additional columns.

Having columns dynamically added to your report is a problem when you get more columns than you expected. For example, your company has twenty divisions world-wide and you formatted the cell's width so that there is just enough room on the page to represent each division. The report runs fine until six months later when your company acquires three new divisions. Now your columns run off the edge and onto a new page. The number of pages printed has just doubled and everyone is complaining to you about it. You have to watch out for this behavior and correct it, if necessary.

Tip

When a cross-tab object spans multiple pages, the only data printed on the "virtual" pages is what is generated by the cross-tab report. The other report objects on the report do not get printed. If there is a header value that should be printed above the cross-tab, it will not appear after the first page. You can simulate a report header by adding an additional column field to the cross-tab object that only prints the header text.

To simulate a cross-tab header, follow these instructions. Create a formula that generates the header text. Open the Cross-Tab Expert and add the formula as the first field in the Columns window. Go to the Customize Style tab and experiment with the grid settings to make the report look just the way you want. You will have to turn on Suppress Row Grand Totals. An example is shown in Figure 11-10.

		Corporate Sales Totals					
		2/2000	3/2000	12/2000	1/2001	2/2001	3/2001
Competition	Descent	$17,716.86 45.83%	$5,895.20 33.74%	$96,033.66 74.64%	$86,341.44 49.10%	$178,548.46 70.77%	$105,565.52 73.74%
	Endorphin	$1,799.70 4.66%	$1,851.38 10.60%	$9,786.51 7.61%	$26,190.91 14.89%	$43,406.31 17.21%	$4,960.69 3.47%
	Mozzie	$19,138.35 49.51%	$9,723.33 55.66%	$22,842.13 17.75%	$63,328.23 36.01%	$30,329.80 12.02%	$32,630.03 22.79%
	Total	$38,654.91 100.00%	$17,469.91 100.00%	$128,662.30 100.00%	$175,860.58 100.00%	$252,284.57 100.00%	$143,156.24 100.00%

Figure 11-10. Adding a heading to the cross-tab object.

---

[24] Actually, you can create dynamic columns. But it requires writing some very advanced formulas and associating them to the columns. You also have to write formulas for the formatting properties of each column so that they are suppressed when necessary.

Another problem with dynamic columns is that you can't insert additional columns in the grid. This is a common problem with reports that use the month of the year as the column. When the report is run at the end of the year there are twelve columns, and this is what you would expect. But when the report is run in February, only two columns are printed: January and February. Some people want their reports to show all twelve months even if they haven't occurred yet. Cross-tab reports won't do this. A similar problem is a report that uses the weeks of the year as the column heading. Assume a company is a production plant and they want to see the volume of units produced every week. Occasionally, the plant builds up too much inventory and is shut down for a week. The report should show a zero balance for the week that was shutdown. But since there wasn't any activity, no records exist for that week and a column won't be printed. The cross-tab report can't print a zero-filled column for that week because it doesn't have any data to even know that the week exists.

There really isn't an easy solution for this. The best advice is to write an SQL query that uses a creative Outer Join statement to generate zero value data for the missing records. Another option is to create a zero filled table with a record for each column. Use an SQL Union statement to join it with the live data. Each situation is unique and presents a new challenge.

Caution

The SQL Outer Join functionality doesn't work in .NET 2005. It only works in .NET 2008. Hopefully, this will be fixed in a future service pack.

Incorporating Subreports

A limitation of the standard report is that only a single view of the data can be displayed. Subreports are used to create multiple views of data on a single report. Rather than create one or more reports to present additional views of the data, subreports are used to present data that is independent of the main report or present multiple parent-child relationships.

From a functional and design standpoint, a subreport is virtually identical to a standard report. It has the same layout as a standard report and it uses the same report objects. The subreport differs from a standard report in that it is an object on a report. Thus, it is part of another report.

Adding subreports to a main report requires knowledge of three things: the options for linking subreports to the main report, how to add and edit a subreport object and whether it should be bound to the main report.

Linking Options

The most important aspect of a subreport is the various options for linking them to the main report. Subreports are either linked or unlinked to the main report. A linked subreport relies upon the main report to tell it what to print. An unlinked subreport doesn't use any data from the main report to determine what to print.

If the subreport is linked to the main report, the subreport's data is dependent upon the data in the main report. For example, let's say that a subreport is linked to the main report via the Customer ID. The subreport's data will only display records related to the current Customer ID on the main report. When the Customer ID on the main report changes, so will the detail data displayed in the subreport. The main report effectively acts as a filter for the subreport.

When the subreport is unlinked, it is independent from the main report. For example, assume that the main report is an employee sales report. It is grouped by sales person and it is broken apart to be distributed to each sales person. Within the group header is a chart showing the company's overall sales for the month. This chart will be added to the main report as an unlinked subreport. The chart prints the same data no matter which sales person is currently being printed.

For subreports that are linked to the main report, the main report needs a method of telling the subreport what data to print. One way of doing this is using a parameter field that is populated with information from the main report. Another way is to use shared variables. Shared variables are not normally used for filtering data, but they are used in formulas in the report. Table 12-1 is a summary of the different linking options between a main report and its subreports. A more thorough description of these options and related examples are listed after the table.

Table 12-1. Subreport linking options

Linking Option	Description
Linked with a data field	A field from the main report is passed to the subreport and this is used for filtering records. If the field is from a PC database (e.g. MS Access), it must be indexed.
Linked with a formula field	A formula's value from the main report is passed to the subreport and this is used to filter records. Used to link to non-indexed fields in PC databases (e.g. MS Access, Excel).
Unlinked	The subreport is not connected to the main report. There is no data passed between the main report and the subreport. The subreport uses a data source that is independent of the parent report. This is used for combining unrelated reports into a single report.
Unlinked and using a formula field	A formula's value from the main report is passed to the subreport, but it doesn't affect record selection. It can be used for displaying non-critical data on the subreport.
Unlinked and using global variables	Multiple variables are used to pass data back and forth between the parent report and the subreport. This lets the parent report keep track of what the subreport is printing.

Linking with a Data Field

Linking subreports with a data field lets you filter the data in the subreport based upon the data that is in the main report. This is useful when you are printing data derived from tables that have a parent-child relationship.

First let's look at when a subreport isn't the best option. A good example is a simple report that links multiple tables together that have a one-to-one relationship or when two tables have a parent-child relationship. When tables have a one-to-one relationship, it is easy to match up the detail records and print them together. When two tables have a parent-child relationship, it is easy to group the records based on the parent data and print the associated child records within the detail section of each group.

Subreports become practical when there is a single parent table with more than one child table. If you tried to use a single report to print this data and you link the tables using the default inner join, it is possible that not every record will print when there isn't a matching primary key in both child tables. If you use an outer join to link the tables, you could get some records printed multiple times depending upon how many times the primary key appears in each child table.

Using a subreport with multiple child tables corrects these problems. Within the main report, print the records from only one of the child tables in the detail table. For the other child tables, create a subreport for each one and use the main report's primary key to link them together. The subreports are placed in their own Details section so that their records are independent of the other sections and they print sequentially after the main report's detail records.

The drawback to linking with a data field is that if you are using a PC database (e.g. MS Access), the fields must be indexed. You must create an index for each linking field before running the report.

An example of linking with a data field is shown in Figure 12-1. This report shows the sales detail for each customer. Below the detail records is a list of all the credits that have been issued to this customer. Since there are two listings of detail records, the second list must be printed as a subreport. In this example, the subreport is added to the main report's Group Footer section. It is linked via the Customer ID.

Customer Sales

ID	Customer Name	Order	Order Date	Ship Date	Amount
1	City Cyclists				
		1,143	06-Jan-1997	08-Jan-1997	$62.33
		1,246	30-Jan-1997	30-Jan-1997	$3,884.25
		1,296	16-Feb-1997	16-Feb-1997	$6,682.98
		1,387	01-Mar-1997	01-Mar-1997	$1,515.35
		1,717	14-Jun-1997	15-Jun-1997	$70.50
		1,763	24-Jun-1997	30-Jun-1997	$2,378.35
					$14,593.76

Credits Issued For City Cyclists

Credit Authorization Number	Amount
CR1608	($1,792.91)
CR5241	($951.33)
CR6321	($1,484.68)
CR6592	($1,237.54)
CR6798	($727.56)

ID	Customer Name	Order	Order Date	Ship Date	Amount
2	Pathfinders				
		1,145	06-Jan-1997	17-Jan-1997	$27.00
		1,171	14-Jan-1997	14-Jan-1997	$479.85
		1,233	27-Jan-1997	29-Jan-1997	$139.48
		1,254	03-Feb-1997	04-Feb-1997	$2,497.05
		1,256	04-Feb-1997	04-Feb-1997	$70.50
		1,288	12-Feb-1997	12-Feb-1997	$8,819.55

Figure 12-1. Linked subreport in the Details section.

Linking with a Formula Field

Filtering records in a subreport is also done using a formula field. There are two benefits to using formula fields: they give you more flexibility because formulas can be customized to parse or join multiple data fields, and they can link non-indexed fields from PC databases.

Being able to parse or join multiple data fields and use the results to link to a subreport is very helpful. It is a common task to have to link tables from two different programs together and the data isn't compatible. This can happen when the programs were developed by different teams in the same company or when one company acquires another company and they have to consolidate their data. Formulas give you the flexibility to massage the data from one table into a format compatible with the data in another table. This can consist of converting the field to a different data type, concatenating multiple fields together or parsing a field to extract the extraneous characters.

Subreports aren't restricted to using indexed fields for linking tables. Linking with formulas lets you use any field in the table to link the two reports together.

Using Unlinked Subreports

An unlinked subreport is used when you want to combine two or more reports onto one report and these reports don't have any common data to create a relationship between them. The unlinked subreport is completely independent of the main report and the main report's data doesn't affect the subreport.

Figure 12-2 shows an example of an unlinked subreport. It is a customer sales report that shows the prior year sales amount for each customer.

Customer Sales Detail By Country

Summary of Sales by Country

Country	Sales
Australia	$40,446.64
Austria	$201,000.00
Bahamas	$14,463.35
Bangladesh	$4,683.50
Barbados	$4,443.80
Belgium	$200,000.00

	ID	Customer Name	Last Year's Sales
Australia	149	Tasmanian Devil Bikes	$1,739.85
	148	Koala Road Bikes	$6,744.80
	147	Peddles of Perth	$8,945.25
	146	Bruce's Bikes	$1,138.09
	145	Kangeroo Trikes	$9,594.70
	144	Canberra Bikes	$10,662.75
	143	Down Under Bikes	$1,621.20
			$40,446.64
Austria	66	Piccolo	$201,000.00
			$201,000.00
Bahamas	156	Beach Cycle and Sport	$14,463.35
			$14,463.35

Figure 12-2. Unlinked subreport being used in the report header.

The report is grouped by country and within each group it shows the customers from that country and what their sales were last year. At the top of the report it shows a summary of the prior year sales for each country. This lets you analyze how each country compares to the other before looking at detail records within each customer. Since there isn't a field that can be linked between the summary report and the customer detail report, these two reports are unlinked. This is implemented by adding the summary report as a subreport in the main report's header section.

Let's look at an example of an unlinked subreport that at first may appear to be a linked report. This example is a form letter that has a variable number of standard attachments printed at the end of it. This could be a legal document where each client needs to have signature pages attached to the end of it.

Within the Report Footer area, there are multiple sections. Within each section is a subreport that represents a standard attachment. The conditional formatting suppresses the section if a field in the main report doesn't meet a certain value. In this case, the person receiving the form letter would have Boolean fields that are set to True for each attachment that should be included. If the proper field isn't set to True, the section is suppressed and the attachment isn't printed. Although this may appear to be a linked subreport because data in the main report determines whether to print the subreport, it isn't. It is an unlinked subreport because there is no data that is being passed to the subreport. The Boolean field in the main report determines which sections get suppressed or printed. But this is all done at the main report level and not at the subreport level. The Boolean field never gets passed to the subreport and its value doesn't affect the content of what is printed.

Using Formula Fields without Linking

Formula fields can also be used by a subreport without linking them. This is used when you want to pass data to a subreport without filtering the data. For example, the main report can pass a string to the subreport so that the string gets printed in the subreport's header.

Passing Data Via Shared Variables

Shared variables let you share data between a main report and its subreports. This lets you perform calculations, track subtotals and create strings in one report and pass this data to the other report.

Adding a Subreport

A subreport is added to the main report in the same way that the other report objects are added: using the Insert menu item. Select the menu options Crystal Reports > Insert > Subreport. This gives you the outline of a subreport object attached to the mouse cursor and you move the cursor around to position it in the proper place on the report. Click the mouse to drop the subreport onto the report.

Note

Subreports can only be one level deep. A subreport object can only be added to a main report and it can't be added to another subreport. If you right-click on a subreport and select Insert, the Subreport option will be disabled.

After placing the subreport object on the report, the Insert Subreport dialog box is opened. This dialog box, shown in Figure 12-3, gives you three ways of creating a subreport.

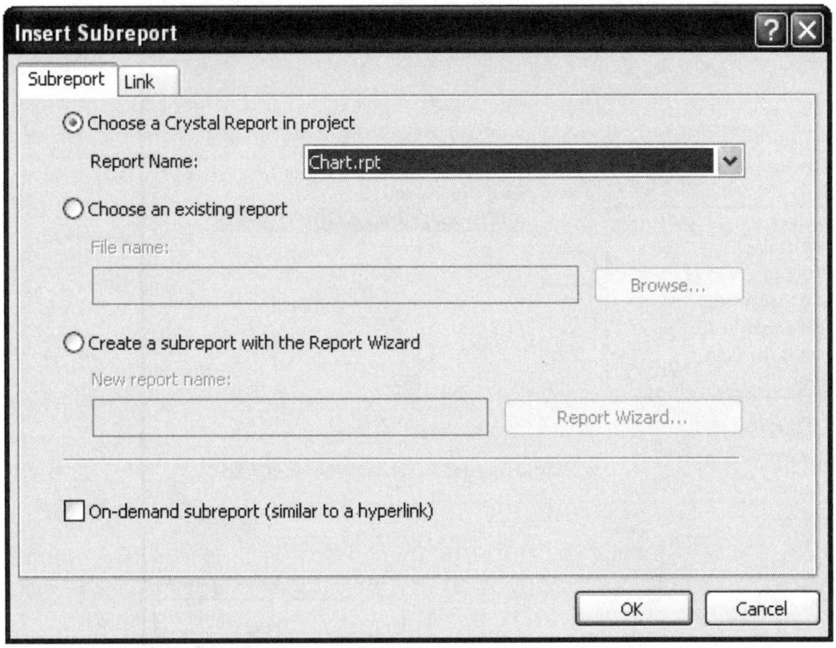

Figure 12-3. The Insert Subreport dialog box.

The first way is to select an existing report that is in the current project. Click on the dropdown box to see all the reports in your project. Select the one you want. The second way to create a subreport is to import one from outside the project file. The Browse button lets you find the report on your local computer or on the network. The third way is to create a report from scratch. When selecting this option, you also have to click on the Create Report button to open the Report Expert dialog box. If you don't click this button, the OK button will stay disabled until you do so. The Report Wizard button opens the Report Expert for a standard report. Once you are finished building your report template, click Finish and you are brought back to the Insert Subreport dialog box. The OK button is now enabled, but don't click on it until you decide how to link the subreport to the main report.

Note

When importing an existing report as a subreport, whether already in the project or external to the project, the subreport is a copy of the original report. When you make changes to the subreport, the original report is not modified. The subreport is saved within the same .rpt file as the main report.

After setting the report information on the main tab, go to the Links tab (shown in Figure 12-4) to set whether the report is linked or unlinked.

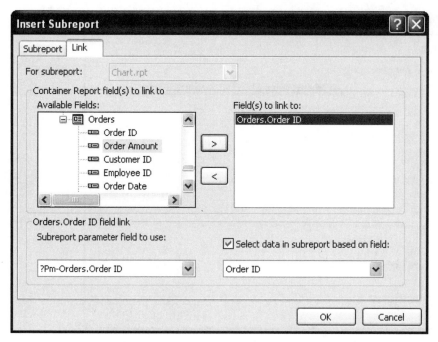

Figure 12-4. The Links tab of the Insert Subreport dialog box.

This dialog box is where you set the properties that determine how the subreport is linked to the main report. The Links tab has a list on the left side that shows the available report fields, formulas and data fields. The list on the right shows the fields from the main report that are selected to link to the subreport. At the bottom is a frame that shows the details of how the field(s) will be linked to the subreport. These linking options and how to set the properties for each are listed next.

Linked with a Data Field

Linking subreports with a data field lets you use a data field in the main report to filter the data in the subreport. The two fields must be of the same data type to link them together. If this is a PC database, both fields must have an index already set up in the database.

To create a linked subreport, select the data field from the listbox on the left and add it to the listbox on the right. Once the data field is added, the linking frame at the bottom appears and shows you the parameter field name and the field in the subreport's data field to link to. The parameter name is automatically filled in for you. This parameter is used internally to pass the main report's field value to the subreport. Normally, when you have a parameter field on a report, the user is prompted to enter a value for the parameter before the report can be run. This is not the case with subreports. Subreports populate the parameter with the value of the field from the main report behind the scenes. You do not have to worry about this implementation.

The checkbox on the right tells the subreport that the main report's data field is being linked to a field in the subreport. This will be checked by default. Below the checkbox is a dropdown box listing the fields in the subreport. Select the one that is used to filter the data in the subreport. It must be of the same data type as the field from the main report.

Linking with a Formula Field

Linking records in a subreport can also be done using a formula field. This gives you more creativity for how it is linked to the main report. There are many reasons for wanting to link with a formula field rather than a data field.

When using a formula to link to a subreport, you aren't restricted to using indexed fields. Linking with formulas lets you use any field in the table to link the two reports together. As long as the data in both tables match, you're good to go.

It is a common task to have to link tables from two different programs together when the data isn't compatible. Using formulas to parse or join multiple data fields and using the results to link to a subreport is perfect for this. This situation can happen when the programs were developed by different teams in the same company or when one company acquires another company and they have to consolidate their data. Formulas give you the flexibility to massage the data from one table into a format compatible with the data in another table. This can consist of converting the field to a different data type, concatenating multiple fields together or parsing a field to extract out the extraneous characters.

Telling Crystal Reports to link on a formula involves the same steps as linking on a data field, the key difference is that you have to make sure that the formula is already created prior to creating the subreport. When you create the subreport and click on the linking tab, the formula is shown in the Available Fields list on the left. Simply double-click on it to add it to the Fields to Link To list on the right.

Unlike other dialog boxes in Crystal Reports, the Link tab doesn't have a Formula button to create a new formula at that moment. That is why if you want to link your subreport using a formula, then you have to create it before the subreport. Otherwise, you have to close this dialog box, go back to the main report to create the formula, and then edit the subreport again to link on the formula. A little pre-planning makes your life easier!

Once the formula field has been added, the frame at the bottom of the dialog box appears and it works the same as adding a data field: the parameter name is automatically filled in and you pick a subreport field from the dropdown list to link to.

Here are some examples of useful formulas for linking subreports.

Linking on multiple fields

Formulas are often used for linking concatenated string fields together. It is common to have tables with similar information, but a slightly different structure.

For example, the part number for an inventory item is usually broken up into different groups of numbers and each group has a different meaning. The groups could be category, product grade, and item number. One table could list the inventory number as a single field with each group separated by dashes (e.g. 999-99-9999) and another table could list the number across three different fields (one field for each group). Normally, it isn't possible to link these two tables together because you can't link one field to three different fields. However, you can use a formula to combine the three fields so that they match the format of the field in the other table. For example, we can create a Basic syntax formula that combines the three fields together and link the formula to the other table.

Formula = {Inventory.Category} & '-' & {Inventory.Grade} & '-' & {Inventory.Item}

Linking on a non-indexed field

As we just mentioned, formulas can be used to link on non-indexed fields. This is a very simple process. Simply create a new formula and set it equal to the non-indexed field. Then use that formula as the linking field. In the example below, the field Customer Credit ID is not indexed, but you can link to it using a formula field.

Formula = {Customer.Customer Credit ID}

This formula simply repeats the name of the field in it. It's very simple, but that is all that is needed when the field isn't indexed.

Linking on a partial string

There are times when a field has too much information in it. You only need part of the string for linking to another table. Consider the previous inventory example where the table has all three groups of the inventory number in one field. The middle portion of the string is the product grade and you want to link to a subreport which summarizes the sales for all products with that specific grade. You can't link to the whole inventory number because it has the other grouping data in it as well. Instead, you have to pull out just the product grade portion and use that to link to the subreport.

Formula = Mid({Inventory.Inventory ID},5,2)

In this formula, the Inventory ID field stores the product grade as the middle portion of the Inventory ID. So the formula uses the Mid() function to extract the two middle characters from the string, starting at position five. Now the formula can be used to link to a subreport which summarizes data on product grade.

A very common report type is a directory listing. This report groups everything by the first letter of the person's name (or product name). So the first group is on the letter A and the second group is on the letter B, etc. When you put a subreport in the group header or footer, you want the subreport to also print by the same letter. The formula for doing this is easy enough. Use the Left() function to parse out the first letter of the product name.

Formula = Left({Inventory.Product Name},1)

What is good about this example is that the formula for grouping the data in the main report is also the same formula for linking to the subreport. The main report groups all its data on the first letter of the product name and so does the subreport. You don't have to create an extra formula for linking to the subreport. Use the same one that you used for creating the groups.

Linking with Memo Fields

Crystal Reports doesn't let you use a memo field to link reports together. Memo fields aren't displayed in the Subreport Links dialog box. However, you can use a formula field instead. Create a formula and make it equal to the memo field. Now when you go to link to the subreport you'll see the new formula in the Available Fields list.

Converting data types

A common problem with databases is that they can be developed over a long period of time and worked on by different people. This creates a situation where the same fields can have different data types in different tables. Ideally, there would be clear specifications on the data type that each field has. But unfortunately this doesn't happen often enough.

For example, a company could originally have their inventory IDs being a combination of strings and numbers. But at a later point in time, they decide to buy new inventory management software and it only uses numbers. It's easy enough to convert the original inventory IDs to numbers, but the problem comes when you try to build a report with the new tables and include a subreport that uses historical data from the archived tables. You can't link the tables together because the original table uses a string data type and the new inventory package uses a numeric data type. To fix this problem, you have to convert the field from the new inventory system into a string so that it can link to the subreport that uses the original data.

Formula = CStr({InventorySystem.InventoryID, 0})

This formula uses the CStr() function to convert the number to a string. It also specifies that we want zero decimal places so that it returns a whole number.

Linking to Subreport Parameters

If the subreport has parameter fields in it, when the user refreshes the report they are prompted to enter values for the subreport parameters. If you don't want the user to be prompted to enter a parameter value, you can link a field from the main report to the subreport parameter. This automatically populates the subreport parameter field with a value from the main report without prompting the user.

To link a field from the main report to a subreport parameter, right-click on the subreport in design mode and select Change Subreport Links. This opens the Subreport Links dialog box previously shown in Figure 12-4. In the Available Fields list, double-click the field from the main report that holds the value you want to pass to the subreport parameter. This adds the field to the Fields To Link To list on the right.

When you move a field to the Fields To Link To list, Crystal Reports' default behavior is to automatically create a matching parameter in the subreport which is passed the value from the main report. If you look in the bottom left hand corner of the dialog box, you'll see that there is a parameter name with a prefix of "?Pm-..." However, in this circumstance you don't need Crystal Reports to create a new parameter for you because the subreport already has a parameter that you want to link the data to. Instead of letting Crystal Reports create a new parameter, click on the dropdown list and select the existing parameter from the list. This links the field on the main report to the existing subreport parameter.

Tip

If you don't see the subreport parameter in the dropdown list, then there is a data type mismatch between the chosen field in the main report and the parameter. Cancel your changes and go back to make sure that both the main report field and the subreport parameter have the same data type. If not, create a formula in the main report which converts the field to the proper data type and use this formula to link to the subreport parameter.

After selecting the existing subreport parameter to link to, the option to the right, Select Data In Subreport Based On Field, becomes disabled. This option is no longer necessary since you are passing the data to an existing parameter.

Save your changes and refresh the report data. The subreport will get its data from the main report and you will no longer be prompted to enter a parameter value.

Linking to a Stored Procedure with Parameters

I recently saw two very similar questions about stored procedures posted to the book's online forum. I thought they were excellent questions and that many readers of this book would benefit from the details.

Both questions said that they had a main report and a subreport that were linked to an SQL database. The data sources were stored procedures and each had an input parameter associated with it. When they ran the report, they were prompted with two parameters instead of one. They wanted to only enter one parameter and have it passed to the stored procedure for both the main report and the subreport. However, they couldn't figure out how to get rid of the second parameter prompt for the subreport.

The key to fixing this problem is to understand what the previous section said about how to pass data to a subreport parameter. In the previous section, the parameter was created by the report designer (presumably you) and we learned how to pass a data field from the main report to it. This told Crystal Reports not to prompt the user for the subreport's parameter. The questions on the forum are very similar, but with a couple of differences.

The first difference being that in this case Crystal Reports created the subreport parameter automatically when you selected the stored procedure as the data source. The second difference is that instead of eliminating the parameter prompts altogether, you want to keep one parameter prompt and have its value shared between both reports.

You first have to understand that whenever you create a report whose data source is a stored procedure with an input parameter, Crystal Reports automatically creates a parameter with a similar name and the same data type.[25] When you run the report, you are prompted to enter a value for the parameter and that value gets passed to the stored procedure. In the previous section, we saw how to link a data field from the main report to the subreport parameter and this keeps the user from getting prompted to enter the parameter value. The same applies here except that we want be prompted for the first parameter only, and have its value passed to the subreport.

The key to making Crystal Reports pass the same data to both the main report and subreport is to link the two parameters together on the Subreport Links dialog box. Instead of double-clicking a data field in the Ava ilable Fields list, you want to double-click the parameter field from the main report's stored procedure. After that, at the bottom of the dialog box, select the parameter field for the subreport's stored procedure. For example, Figure 12-5 shows a Subreport Links dialog box which links the two reports based on the @NameParam parameter that was created for each stored procedure.

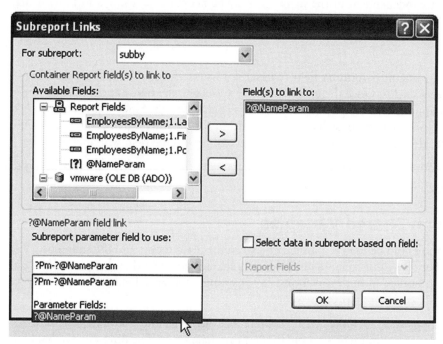

Figure 12-5. Linking two stored procedure parameters together.

---

[25] This is discussed in great detail in the Database Connectivity chapter.

When you preview the report, you are prompted to enter a value for the main report's parameter. Crystal Reports takes this value and passes it to the stored procedure for the main report. Crystal Reports also sees that the main report's parameter is the linking field for the subreport and passes the same value to the subreport's parameter field. Since this value gets passed to stored procedure for the subreport, there is no need to prompt you a second time.

Unlinked Subreports

An unlinked subreport doesn't have a connection to the main report. It is totally independent. To create an unlinked subreport, do not set any properties on this dialog box. If you had already added fields to the listbox on the right, remove them and this will remove any links between the main report and this subreport.

Unlinked with a Formula

Formulas are used with unlinked subreports so that information can be passed to the subreport without filtering any data. This is similar to the unlinked subreport because both subreports are independent of the main report. The benefit with using a formula is that although the subreport isn't linked, you can still pass information from the main report to the subreport. This information can be displayed on the report or used in the subreport's formulas.

To create an unlinked formula field, select the formula from the main report's list of available report fields. Once the formula has been selected, the frame at the bottom of the dialog box appears and the parameter name is already filled in. Since this is an unlinked report, uncheck the checkbox that is to the right of the parameter name. This causes the linking field dropdown box to become disabled and no linking field will be specified.

When the subreport runs, it can reference the parameter that is created by this dialog box to get the formula's value from the main report.

Unlinked with Shared Variables

Shared variables can be used to pass data between the main report and the subreport. The difference between using a parameter field and a shared variable is that shared variables can be used to pass data in both directions. When using parameter fields, data can only be passed from the main report to the subreport.

Since the subreport is not linked to the main report and no formulas are being passed to the subreport, you shouldn't set any properties on this dialog box. The difference is that both reports have to have a formula that declares and uses the shared variable.

To illustrate how this works, let's modify the example report shown earlier that lists the customer sales and any credits issued to the customer. The report is also going to show the net amount of adding the total sales with the total credits issued. This revised report is shown in Figure 12-6.

Customer Sales

ID	Customer Name	Order	Order Date	Ship Date	Amount
1	City Cyclists				
		1,143	06-Jan-1997	08-Jan-1997	$62.33
		1,246	30-Jan-1997	30-Jan-1997	$3,884.25
		1,296	16-Feb-1997	16-Feb-1997	$6,682.98
		1,387	01-Mar-1997	01-Mar-1997	$1,515.35
		1,717	14-Jun-1997	15-Jun-1997	$70.50
		1,763	24-Jun-1997	30-Jun-1997	$2,378.35
					$14,593.76

Credit Authorization Number	Amount
CR1608	($1,792.91)
CR5241	($951.33)
CR6321	($1,484.68)
CR6592	($1,237.54)
CR6798	($727.56)
	($6,194.02)

Sub-Total of Net Orders For City Cyclists Is $8,399.74

ID	Customer Name	Order	Order Date	Ship Date	Amount
2	Pathfinders				
		1,145	06-Jan-1997	17-Jan-1997	$27.00
		1,171	14-Jan-1997	14-Jan-1997	$479.85
		1,233	27-Jan-1997	29-Jan-1997	$139.48
		1,254	03-Feb-1997	04-Feb-1997	$2,497.05
		1,256	04-Feb-1997	04-Feb-1997	$70.50
		1,288	12-Feb-1997	12-Feb-1997	$8,819.55
		1,399	02-Mar-1997	02-Mar-1997	$53.90

Figure 12-6. Calculate net sales amount using a subreport.

Since the sales amount is on the main report and the credits are listed on the subreport, it needs to use a shared variable so that the two reports can share their data. A formula is added to the subreport to calculate the total credit amount for the customer. The formula is placed in the report header of the subreport so that it gets calculated when the report is first run. Note: these formulas use Basic syntax.

```
Shared TotalCredits as Currency
TotalCredits = Sum({Credits.Amount})
Formula = TotalCredits
```

The main report is modified so that it has a formula that declares the same shared variable and uses it in the calculation. If the main report didn't declare the variable as shared, it would always be zero. Notice in the formula that the **TotalCredits** variable is being added to the sum of the order amounts. It isn't being subtracted because it is already a negative number.

```
Shared TotalCredits as Currency
Formula = Sum({Orders.Order Amount}, {Customer.Customer ID}) + TotalCredits
```

A variation of using shared variables with subreports is to use a subreport to perform a particular calculation but not show the subreport on the report. The last example used a subreport to display and calculate the total credits given to a customer. However, you could have chosen to not show the details of the credits on the report and instead just use the total amount in the formula. If you try to do this by either hiding or suppressing the subreport or the section it is in, the subreport won't calculate the shared variable. This is because the subreport has to be printed in order for the formulas on the subreport to be calculated. One alternative is to make the subreport object very small so that it isn't visible on the report. Depending upon how the subreport is designed, this may or may not print any extraneous graphics on the page. A better alternative is to modify the subreport object in your .NET application so that its height is set to 0 and the object isn't allowed to grow. The designer doesn't let you set the height to 0 but setting it via code gets around this limitation.

```
Dim rpt As CrystalDecisions.CrystalReports.Engine.ReportDocument
Dim rptObjects As CrystalDecisions.CrystalReports.Engine.ReportObjects
rpt = New SuppressSubreportDemo()
rptObjects = rpt.ReportDefinition.ReportObjects
rptObjects.Item("Subreport").ObjectFormat.EnableCanGrow = False
rptObjects.Item("Subreport").Height = 0
CrystalReportViewer1.ReportSource = rpt
```

Best Of The Forum

Question: I'm using shared variables to pass data from the subreport back to the main report. But if the current record in the main report doesn't have data in the subreport, the shared variable's value doesn't change. It is the same as the previous record.

Answer: This is a common problem when you don't reset the shared variable back to zero (or whatever default value you want to use). Put the following Basic syntax formula in the Report Header section of your subreport (and remember to enter the proper variable name).

```
WhilePrintingRecords
Shared YourVariable As Number
YourVariable = 0
Formula = 0
```

Editing the Subreport

Once the subreport object has been added to the main report, you will probably need to edit it. Depending upon the types of changes you want to make to the subreport, there are different ways of editing it.

To edit the content of the subreport, from the main report either double-click on the subreport object or right-click on it and select Edit Subreport. This opens the subreport in the same design tab as the main report. The subreport is now treated the same as any other report. You can add new report objects, modify existing ones, or delete report objects.

When editing a subreport, the report designer changes so that it displays tabs at the bottom of the designer. Each tab lists the name of the main report and all open subreports. This lets you move back and forth between the main report and its subreports. This is shown in Figure 12-7.

Figure 12-7. The tabs that list the main report and open subreports.

If you have a main report that uses many subreports, you may find that you can't open them all and see their tabs listed at the bottom of the designer. At the bottom right-hand corner of the designer are two arrows. Click on them to scroll through the open subreports.

You can also modify other aspects of the subreport. When viewing the main report in design mode, right-click on the subreport object and there are two menu options called Format Object and Change Subreport Links. The Format Object menu item opens the standard format dialog box where you set properties such as Suppress, Keep Object Together, etc. The formatting options on the Border, Subreport and Font tabs control how on-demand subreports are displayed on the main report. This is discussed in the next section. The Change Subreport Links menu item opens the Subreport Links dialog box. This lets you change the fields that are used to link the main report to the subreport.

Best Of The Forum

Question: My subreport doesn't have any data in it, but it still prints the column headers on the report. Is there a way to hide subreports that don't have any data?

Answer: Yes, there is. Hiding an empty subreport is a two step process. First, in the main report, right-click on the subreport and select Format Object. On the subreport tab, check the option Suppress Blank Subreport and click the Ok button to close it. Second, put this subreport in its own section (it has to be isolated from all other report objects) and right-click on the section header to select Section Expert. On the Section Expert dialog box, select the option Suppress Blank Section. This hides the section if it is blank, and since the subreport is also suppress, then nothing will print on the report.

Using On-Demand Subreports

By default, subreports are run at the same time as the main report. When you view or print the main report, the subreport information is printed as well. This may result in a performance decrease because the subreport could require just as much time, if not more, to process as the main report. If performance becomes a problem, declare the subreport so that it isn't bound to the main report. This is called an on-demand subreport.

An on-demand subreport doesn't print at the same time as the main report. Instead, a hyperlink that describes the subreport is shown where the subreport should appear.[26] When the user clicks on the hyperlink the subreport is processed and shown to the user. The on-demand subreport is shown on a separate tab in the viewer.

Caution
On-demand subreports are for reports viewed with the CrystalReportViewer control. If you send the report directly to the printer, only the placeholders are printed and not the subreport. This doesn't give the reader the detail information they are looking for.

To define a subreport as being an on-demand subreport, use the Format Object menu option to open the Format Editor dialog box. On the subreport tab is an On-Demand Subreport checkbox. It is unchecked by default. Click on it to make the subreport an on-demand subreport.

By default, an on-demand subreport is shown as a hyperlink on the main report. The text is the name of the subreport.

---

[26] A placeholder can be displayed instead of the hyperlink.

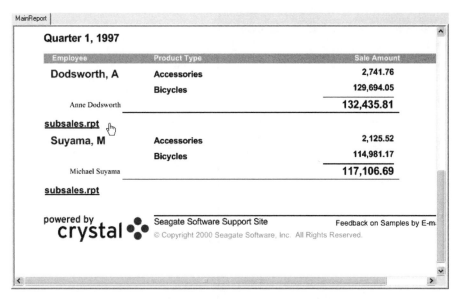

Figure 12-8. On-demand subreports shown as a hyperlink.

When you click on the hyperlink the subreport is processed and displayed on a new tab in the viewer. Each on-demand subreport is displayed on its own tab.

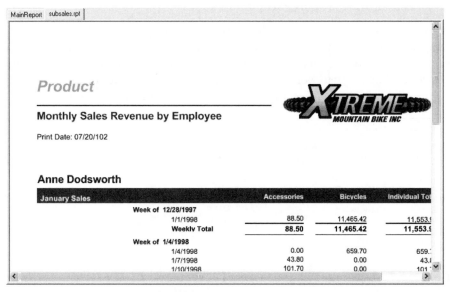

Figure 12-9. On-demand subreports shown on a separate tab.

If you feel that displaying a hyperlink isn't professional enough, you can display a customized placeholder instead. When you are in design mode, right-click on the subreport object and choose Format Object. Go to the Subreport tab that is shown in Figure 12-10.

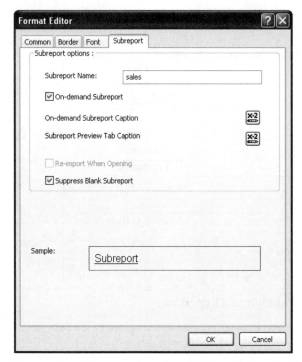

Figure 12-10. Formatting the subreport placeholder.

There is a formula button for modifying the caption that is displayed on the main report. You can enter a simple string in this formula or customize the string by concatenating data fields into it. The rest of the tabs on this dialog box can be used to format how the placeholder looks. For example, you can change the font, the background color and the border. Figure 12-11 shows the placeholder formatted with a border and a larger font size.

Employee	Product Type	Sale Amount
Dodsworth, A	Accessories	2,741.76
	Bicycles	129,694.05
Anne Dodsworth		132,435.81

Click here to view product sales by month for Anne Dodsworth

Suyama, M	Accessories	2,125.52
	Bicycles	114,981.17
Michael Suyama		117,106.69

Click here to view product sales by month for Michael Suyama

powered by crystal

Seagate Software Support Site
© Copyright 2000 Seagate Software, Inc. All Rights Reserved.

Feedback on Samples by E-mail
1

Figure 12-11. The subreport placeholder.

Data Connectivity

The backbone of every report is the data it prints. Large corporations merge data on servers into reports that consolidate and chart information from a dozen or more tables. Small businesses optimize their report distribution and expand their client base by providing their data in an XML format and letting companies from around the world generate reports on it. Home offices often do simple tasks such as tracking and printing monthly sales figures from an Access database or an Excel spreadsheet.

Crystal Reports is designed to work with many types of data. Reports can be generated regardless of where the data is stored; SQL Server, MS Access or even the Outlook email repository. Crystal Reports allows many ways to connect to databases, and learning each method can be quite an undertaking. This chapter sorts out these options and presents them in an easy to read format. You can determine which method best meets your needs and how to quickly implement it.

All database connectivity is built around one of two models: the Pull Model and the Push Model. The Pull Model is the simplest to implement and is very easy to learn because it doesn't require writing any programming code. Reports designed to use the Pull Model make everything automatic. Crystal Reports does all the dirty work: creates the connection, reads the data, populates the report and then closes the connection. The Pull Model is covered in this chapter. The Push Model, which is covered in Chapter 17, is just the opposite. You write the code to do all the work in your program. You have to open the connection, get the data into memory, pass the data to the report, and close the connection.

So why would anyone ever want to use the Push Model? Who would want to when they know that the Pull Model Crystal will do everything for them? The answer is no different from any other choice you make when writing software. Tasks that require more effort allow more functionality. Since the Pull Model is very simple, it's less flexible than the code intensive Push Model.

This chapter focuses on connecting to databases using the Visual Studio IDE. The IDE makes it easy to connect to a data source and generate reports without having to write any programming code. Chapter 17 in Part II of this book shows the how to's of solving more complex reporting problems by writing programming code that connects to data sources using the ReportDocument object.

Note

If you are using datasets in a report, this is part of the Push Model. See Chapter 17 for printing with datasets.

Implementing the Pull Model

The Report Expert uses the simplest form of the Pull Model to create reports. Within the Report Expert is the Database Expert, where the data source(s) that the report connects to and the tables that have the data are defined. The Report Expert generates a default report layout and builds, behind the scenes, all the data connections necessary. The only thing you have to do is call the proper method to either preview or print the report. All the examples in the book prior to this chapter used the Pull Model. This was done so that you could focus on report design and layout issues, unencumbered with worries about the intricacies of a database. As you can see, implementing the examples didn't require any knowledge about data connectivity.

However, there are more aspects to the Pull Model you need knowledge of. They are: adding a data source, linking tables, and using multiple data sources.

Adding Data Sources

The Pull Model uses the Database Expert dialog box as the interface for selecting data sources for your report. It is a visual expert for opening data sources, finding tables within the data sources, and linking their related fields together. To get to it, create a new report using the Report Expert, or select the menu options Crystal Reports > Database > Database Expert.

The Database Expert uses two dialog boxes: Data and Links. The Data dialog box, shown in Figure 13-1, is the way to add data sources to the report. It has two windows: Available Data Sources and Selected Tables.

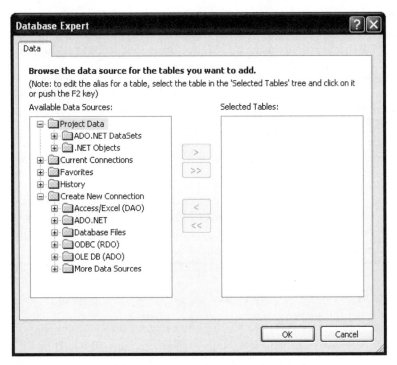

Figure 13-1. The Data Tab of the Database Expert.

The Available Data Sources window lists different categories of data sources. Table 13.1 lists these available data source categories.

Table 13-1. Available Data Sources

Data Source	Description
ADO.NET DataSets	These are the DataSet classes listed in the Visual Studio Project Explorer window. They give you the flexibility to tie your report to virtually any type of data.
.NET Objects	This is a list of all the classes in your .NET project. Note that since this is a comprehensive list for your project, most classes listed will not be acceptable as a Crystal Reports data source.
Current Connections	Select from any connections already established within the Server Explorer.
Favorites	Choose from commonly used data sources you added to your Favorites list. Existing items can be added to the favorites list by right-clicking on them and selecting Add To Favorites. A Favorite can be renamed by clicking on it and pressing the F2 key.
History	Choose from data sources that have been used for other reports

	within the current project.
Access/Excel (DAO)	Retrieve records using a DAO recordset that accesses a Microsoft Access database or Excel spreadsheet.
ADO.NET	Connect to XML data or an ADO.NET dataset that doesn't exist in your project.
Database Files	Select a PC database file using its file location.
ODBC (RDO)	Connect using an ODBC driver by selecting an existing System DSN[27].
OLE DB (ADO)	Builds a connection string to access data sources using an OLE DB driver. It gives you a two screen wizard which asks you for the data source to connect to and any relevant information regarding its location and logon information.

Tip

If you are connecting to SQL Server, it can sometimes be helpful to download and install the SQL Native Client. The SQL Native Client contains OLE DB and ODBC drivers that are optimized for SQL Server and the latest features. It can be found on the internet by Googling, "SQL Native Client". There is also a similar driver for the Oracle database.

To select the data source from the Database Expert dialog, click on the proper category node to expand it. This triggers a dialog box which asks for information about the data source. The dialog changes to match the needs of each data source. This information can range from a simple file path to a database server name and the appropriate logon credentials. Upon entering the information, the dialog box closes and the data source name is shown in the Database Expert and listed under its category. Under the data source name is the list of available tables, views and stored procedures.[28] Click on the plus signs next to the individual items to expand the list.

Add the tables you need to your report by selecting them and clicking on the Add Table button. Double-clicking on the table will also add it to the list. When all have been added, go to the Links tab to establish the relationship between the tables.

---

[27] You should only use System DSN's. File DSN's and User DSN's are buggy.
[28] If you don't see everything listed in the Database Expert (particularly stored procedures), right-click the report and select Crystal Reports > Design > Default Settings. Go to the Database tab and click on the items you want to see in Database Expert.

Tip

There is one small quirk about the Available Data Sources window you should be aware of. It occurs when you click on the plus sign to expand a node and a data source dialog pops up. Once you close the dialog box there is no option to open the dialog box again. You have to click on the minus sign to close the node and then click on the plus sign to expand it again. This triggers the dialog box to open again. After adding a data source to that node, this isn't an issue because there will now be an item listed as the first item and clicking on it lets you add another data source.

Linking Tables

Whenever there are two or more tables, they need to be linked so that Crystal Reports knows how they are related. For example, a pet store that wants to print a list of its products by Animal ID needs to build a report using an animal table and a product table. To match the product to the appropriate type of animal, both tables will be linked by the Animal ID. It would be impossible to determine which products are associated with which animal without this link. The Links dialog box, shown in Figure 13-2, sets the linking fields.

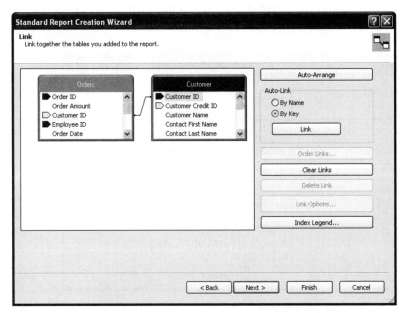

Figure 13-2. The Links tab.

When the Link dialog box is first displayed, it creates default links. This is the equivalent of Crystal's "best guess" for the relationships between the tables. In an effort to make it easier for you, Crystal Reports tries to figure out which fields in each table should be linked to each other. It does this based upon indexes and fields that have the same name and data type.

Tip

To get the most benefit out of the auto-arranged links, design your tables with field names that use a consistent naming convention and have well thought out indexes. This will result in a higher probability that Crystal Reports will create the appropriate default links.

The default links are not set in stone. You are free to delete or add more, according to your needs. To delete a link, simply click on it (to select it); click on the button labeled Delete Link. You can also just press the Delete key after selecting it. To add a new link, drag and drop the field from one table onto the matching field in the other table.

There are a couple of buttons that are helpful for managing links. The Auto-Arrange button rearranges the tables into an easier-to-read layout, which is useful when handling a report with many tables. A multitude of tables makes difficult the visualization of their relationship with one another and the overall structure. The Auto-Link button rebuilds the links based on whether you want to link by field name or by index. This comes in handy for undoing any new links you added, should you want to start from scratch. The Clear Links button removes all the links between the tables. The Link Options button opens the Link Options dialog box, shown in Figure 13-3.

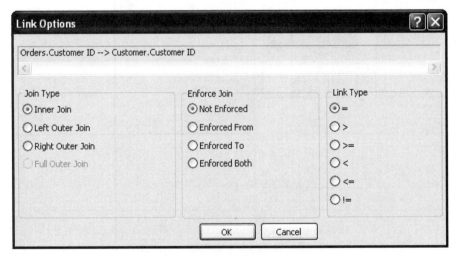

Figure 13-3. The Link Options dialog box.

The Link Options dialog box establishes the type of relationship between the two fields. It sets the type of join (Inner, Left Outer, Right Outer, or Full Outer) as well as how the fields are compared (equal to each other, less than, etc.). Table 13-2 shows a list of the different linking options and how they affect the resulting data.

Table 13-2. Join Options

Join Type	Resultset Description
Inner Join	Records from the left table are matched with records from the right table. Only records with an exact match are included.
Left Outer Join	All records from the left table are included. Field values are included if there is a matching record in the right table . NULL values are stored in the corresponding fields if there is no matching record in the right table..
Right Outer Join	All records from the right table are included. Field values are included if there is a matching record in the left table. NULL values are stored in the corresponding fields if there is no matching record in the left table.
Full Outer Join	Every record from both tables is included. When records from both tables match, the fields in the new recordset are filled in as normal. The other fields are set to NULL if there is no matching record for one of the tables.

The Enforce Join options let you determine whether a field is forced to be included in an SQL statement. For example, if you join together Table A and Table B, but you don't add any fields from Table B to the report, then Crystal Reports will drop Table B from the SELECT statement. In certain advanced circumstances you might still want Table B to be included to force the relationship between the two tables to be maintained. The default is Not Enforced and only tables that have data on the report are included in the SELECT statement. The other three options can force either the From, To or Both tables to be included even when their data isn't used.

The Order Links button sets the order in which the links between the tables are created. This is used only when there is more than one link shown. The tables will be linked automatically, in the order that they are shown in the dialog box. The default linking order processes the links on the left before the links on the right. Changing the default linking order is useful when there is a hierarchy of tables joined together and the order to which they are joined is important. This can happen when you are using a link to return a subset of records from two tables, and these records must therefore be linked to another table. Changing the order of the links changes the resulting data.

Best Of The Forum

Question: I'm using .NET 2005 and I can't get the left outer join to work. No matter what I do, it only prints parent records that have a matching child record. How do I fix this?

Answer: Unfortunately, this is a bug with .NET 2005. It still isn't fixed in Service Pack 1 either. The only way to get around it is to write your own SQL query in a Command object or write a stored procedure. However, left outer joins are working in .NET 2008.

Using Multiple Data Sources

Complex reports often require printing data of different origins. This can happen when you have tables in an SQL Server database and they need to be linked to tables in an Oracle database. There can also be SQL Server databases on different servers on the network. Although Crystal Reports is capable of printing such reports, it doesn't always run flawlessly. Using multiple data sources has the potential for a variety of problems. There is no easy fix.

Crystal Reports, by design, takes the data connectivity information that is saved with a report and generates SQL statements with it. The statements are then delivered to the database server. Although every major database vendor claims to be compliant with the SQL standard, they each have their own subtle differences that can cause them to reject the SQL language of another database. But Crystal Reports doesn't have the capability to, within a single report, generate SQL that is compatible with multiple variations of the SQL specification. It will inevitably create non-compatible SQL for one of the databases. You will have a compatibility issue.

That is not all. Different database servers manage their standard data types differently, chiefly in the way they store them internally. The way one database represents an Integer can be totally different from another database. When Crystal Reports tries to link these two fields together, it won't be able to because they look like different data types.

While it is true that Crystal Reports is designed to work with the majority of database servers, it doesn't imply that the database servers themselves will work with one another. Since every database tries to be better than the next database, companies are more concerned about performance than compatibility. There are limitations with reports using different databases.

Fortunately, there are some general rules you can follow to reduce the headaches caused by these problems. You should be able to generate the reports you need if you follow the following rules (with a little trial and error).

When linking tables together, only use fields that are of the String data type. String is the most consistent data type among different database servers and has the least likelihood of causing problems. This is no guarantee against all problems, however. For example, a string can be represented by variable and fixed length data type and this can create incompatibilities.

Rather than try to link tables from different data sources together, use subreports to print the same data. The benefit of using subreports is that they are treated individually. When Crystal Reports generates the SQL statements for the sub-report, it does so independently of the main report. Also, it has only to worry about working with a single database driver. This independence eliminates a lot of potential problems. Using subreports also allows for more flexible linking options between a main report and subreport. You aren't limited to linking with strings and you can also use formulas to perform data type conversions when necessary.

There are reports where using a subreport isn't an option. For example, if all the detail fields need to be printed side by side, you can't use subreports because the fields will have to be printed underneath the others. In this circumstance, find out if your database lets you create links to outside databases. Putting the links within the database server itself puts the responsibility of managing this data within the server. Crystal Reports benefits because now it only has to use one database driver to retrieve the data. You also get better performance because the database server maintains the additional connection and links.

Secured Databases

Most databases have security implemented in them. They require valid user credentials before accessing the data. This means that you have to pass a User ID and Password to the database prior to printing the report. Crystal Reports handles security differently, depending upon how the report is bound and the database used.

In most circumstances, a Windows application displays a login dialog box prompting the user to enter their user credentials. After entering the credentials, the user can login. However, this isn't always the case. If you are using an MS Access database with a database password or if you are printing from an Excel spreadsheet using OLE DB, the login dialog box isn't compatible. The user won't be able to print the report. Rectifying this problem requires passing the user credentials during runtime. See Chapter 17 for a thorough discussion of connecting to every type of data source during runtime.

Connecting with Stored Procedures

As mentioned earlier in the chapter, stored procedures can be used as a data source just like a table. Crystal Reports can open a stored procedure, retrieve the data and print it. The one thing that can make a stored procedure unique is if it has input parameters.

For a stored procedure to execute, it must have a value for every input parameter. Crystal Reports automatically creates report parameters when it sees that the stored procedure has one or more input parameters. There is one report parameter for every stored procedure parameter and they will have identical names and data types. When the report runs, the user is prompted to enter a value for each parameter. Internally, Crystal Reports passes these report parameters to the stored procedure.

The following code is a sample stored procedure from the Northwind database.

```
CREATE PROCEDURE CustOrderHist
@CustomerID nchar(5)
AS
SELECT ProductName, Total=SUM(Quantity)
FROM Products P, [Order Details] OD, Orders O, Customers C
WHERE C.CustomerID = @CustomerID
AND C.CustomerID = O.CustomerID
```

In this stored procedure, there is one input parameter called @CustomerId that is a 5 character string. When this report is selected as the data source for a report, Crystal Reports automatically creates a parameter called @CustomerID as a String data type. The report prompts the user to enter a Customer ID when it is run. The report passes this value to the stored procedure; the stored procedure only returns records with a matching ID.

Note

If you want your application to directly pass the parameters to the stored procedure, you have to set the parameter objects during runtime. The user won't be prompted with the parameter dialog boxes and the report will run seamlessly. See Chapter 17 for the steps to set report parameter values during runtime.

If you are using two stored procedures and linking them together, make sure that the parameters have different names. When Crystal Reports creates parameters for each stored procedure, it doesn't have the capability to create a new alias for the parameter names. Consequently, it will only create one report parameter with that name and it won't know which stored procedure to assign the parameter to. Make sure that parameters use unique names.

When working with stored procedures and non-SQL Server databases, things can sometimes get tricky. Crystal Reports is not 100% compatible with every type of database, nor the various data types supported by each database. If you find that you are having any problems with a database, it may be because you are connecting to it using OLE DB. Various knowledge base articles state that ODBC provides the strongest amount of compatibility across all the database vendors. Of course, this might not solve every problem you encounter, but it can be the best solution available.

Best Of The Forum

Question: I have a multi-value parameter and I want to pass it to my stored procedure. However, the SQL query shows that it receives NULL instead of a comma separated list. How do I fix this?

Answer: Unfortunately, Crystal Reports can't pass multi-value parameters to a stored procedure. You can only pass discrete parameters to a stored procedure.

Working with SQL Statements

Reports connect to databases, which in turn, return a set of records. The portion of the report's design that works with data is translated into an SQL statement that is syntactically valid for each specific data source.

Crystal Reports gives you many ways to customize the SQL statement that is passed to the database. This can be done while designing a report as well as during runtime. A few reasons for customizing the SQL is to create more sophisticated SQL queries, increase the database's performance, or to perform runtime customization according to a user's input.

Crystal Reports breaks an SQL statement into three distinct parts: table selection, filtering records, and sorting/grouping. Each of these parts is identified by an SQL keyword. The **SELECT** keyword specifies the tables and fields to use. The **WHERE** keyword specifies which records should be included and which should be filtered out. The **SORT BY** and **GROUP ON** keywords specify how to perform the sorting and grouping of the records. The following sections explain these three parts of the SQL statement and show the options for customizing them.

Selecting Tables and Fields

The Database Expert dialog box makes the selection of tables and fields a piece of cake. You get to select the tables to use, how the tables are linked, and the fields to print by nothing more than a mere point and click action. As to the final SQL statement that your report passes to the data source, this is the **SELECT** part of the SQL statement.

There are times when doing simple joins between tables isn't sufficient for your reporting needs. For example, Crystal Reports doesn't support the **UNION** statement for doing a non-linked merge of two tables. In these circumstances, you can specify your own SQL statement rather than use the one that Crystal creates.

Note

The **SELECT** portion of the SQL statement can only be customized while the report is being designed. There is no functionality in Crystal Reports to modify the **SELECT** statement during runtime.

When creating custom SQL statements for a report, it's critical that you are well versed in the proper syntax for the database you are using. Although most databases state that they are ANSI SQL-92 compliant, there are minor differences between each implementation as well as enhancements to the standards. You should, if you aren't familiar with these differences, familiarize yourself with the SQL language reference guide that came with the database.

A good way to learn how SQL works is to look at the SQL statements that Crystal creates for your reports. Select the menu options Crsytal Reports > Database > Show SQL Query. This opens the dialog box (Figure 13-4) that shows the **SELECT** portion of the SQL statement that is passed to the database.

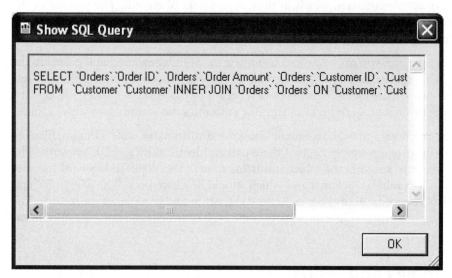

Figure 13-4. The Show SQL Query dialog box.

This dialog box displays the **SELECT** portion of the SQL statement, but it doesn't let you change it (it is read only). Writing a custom SQL statement for your report requires creating a new data source based on a Command object rather than modifying an existing connection.

Best Of The Forum

Question: I want to see a report's SQL query from within my .NET application during runtime. Which report property tells me this?

Answer: The Crystal Reports object model doesn't have a property that tells you the SQL query that a report uses. Consequently, you can't override it during runtime either. To learn more about how to create custom data sources during runtime, see Chapter 17.

Enter a custom SQL statement by opening the Database Expert and selecting the OLE DB (ADO) category and creating a new connection to the server. If the connection you want already exists, you can use it. Once the connection is created, double-click on the Add Command option to open the Add Command To Report dialog box. Enter an SQL statement and click OK.

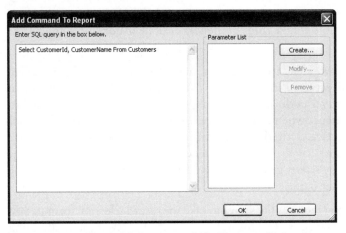

Figure 13-5. The Add Command To Report dialog box.

The new command is listed under the connection node, and the available fields are listed under the command node. At this point, the command is treated as a standard data source and you can select the fields you want to appear on the report.

Filtering Records

When printing records from one or more tables, you probably don't need to print every single record. It is common to print only a subset of the original records. For example, rather than print every customer in the database, the report prints customers that have been added within the past thirty days. SQL statements use the **WHERE** statement to filter out records that aren't relevant to your query.

Crystal Reports uses selection formulas for data filtering. Selection formulas can be created at two dialog boxes designed for just such a purpose: the Select Expert and the Record Selection Formula Editor. As explained before, the Select Expert sets the fields and criteria used in the selection formula. It automatically builds the selection formula in Crystal Syntax. This makes it easy for you to quickly create filters without having to know the programming syntax.

When a report is run, all the records that are returned from the database are processed by the report engine and tested against the selection formula. Records meeting the conditions in the selection formula are printed on the report. This method of processing records is reliable, but slow.

It is slow because the way the selection formulas are processed makes for three bottlenecks. First, the server passes all the records to the client computer. The speed at which these records are transferred is constrained by the physical limitations of the network design as well as the traffic already on the network. Secondly, the report engine has to process all the records through the selection formula. Depending on the complexity of the formula and the number of records being processed, this can be a very time intensive process. Lastly, the passing of all these records across the network can hinder the performance of other applications on the network. As the report designer, your goal is to design a report that is displayed as efficiently as possible. These three bottlenecks can be major stumbling blocks to that reality.

The solution is to transfer the workload from the client machine to the server. This is called "pushing down data" to the server. Pushing down data derives a big improvement in performance by having the server perform the filtering. Database servers are designed to provide the optimum performance when processing massive quantities of data. It can filter out records that don't meet a certain criteria in a fraction of the time that the report engine would take. Pushing down data has the secondary benefit of passing less data along the network back to the client. The report gets the data quicker and there is less traffic on the network that would affect other users.

Pushing down data to the server requires the server to take the record selection formula you created and test each record against it. The formula you created is saved internally using Crystal syntax. Since databases only understand SQL and not Crystal syntax, the Crystal formula gets converted to SQL. Crystal Reports tries to do this conversion with every selection formula because pushing down data gives the best performance.

Converting a formula involves the creation of the equivalent of a **WHERE** clause in SQL. The **WHERE** statement gets appended to the **SELECT** statement, which Crystal Reports always passes to the database server. Any one familiar with SQL would know that not only is it totally different from Crystal syntax, it also has a lot less functionality than Crystal syntax. The upshot: these differences can create problems when the formula is being converted to SQL. In fact, since Crystal Reports has a function library that is much more robust than the SQL language, it is very possible that the selection formula can't be converted into a valid **WHERE** clause.

When a formula can't be converted to a valid **WHERE** clause, it won't be included in the SQL string passed to the database server. Only the **SELECT** portion of the SQL statement is sent. This results in the database server passing all the records from the **SELECT** statement back to the client computer. The report has to manually process all the records with the selection formula to find those that ought to be printed. The result is a much slower performance than what would have been, had all the filtering been done on the server.

Now that you know that not every selection formula can be converted to SQL, let's look at how to make this happen as frequently as possible.

Before any formula can be converted to SQL, the report needs the feature to be turned on. The option "Use Indexes or Server for Speed" must be enabled for the report to push data down to the server. This option tells the report to use indexes when selecting records from a database and it tells it to use the server to improve performance whenever possible. You can set this option to be turned on by default for all reports or for just the current report. To make it the default setting, select the menu options Crystal Reports > Designer > Default Settings. Go to the database tab and look at whether it is checked or unchecked. If it is unchecked, click on it to select it. It will now be selected for every report. If you want to set it for just the current report, select the menu options Crystal Reports > Report > Report Options. The checkbox is listed near the bottom.

Note

PC databases (e.g. MS Access) have an additional restriction for pushing down data. The fields in the record selection formula must be indexed.

After enabling this option for the report, you want to create a selection formula that would deliver the best performance for your report. The optimum selection formula is one that can be converted to SQL completely. However, you may not have a choice in whether you can write a formula that can be converted to SQL or not. As mentioned earlier, Crystal syntax has a lot more functionality than SQL. Since the purpose of a formula is to carry out the requirements of the report's design, you don't have a lot of choice about what will be in the formula. You have to write it so that it performs the required functionality. Converting the selection formula to SQL is a great benefit, but it is secondary to generating the necessary data.

One way to ensure the selection formula gets converted into SQL is to write it using SQL Expressions. An SQL Expression is a formula that is built using only valid SQL functions. Since it only has valid SQL functions, Crystal Reports will always be able to convert it to a valid **WHERE** clause. SQL Expressions are explained in greater detail in a later section.

A general rule of thumb to follow is that if you use the Select Expert, it usually results in a valid **WHERE** clause that will be sent to the database server. This is because the Select Expert doesn't do anything complex. It uses basic comparison operators that can be easily converted into SQL. A good rule to follow when using the Select Expert is to only specify database fields in the criteria. Since formulas generally use functions that can't get translated into SQL, including them in the selection could result in it not being converted. Restricting the selection formula to only database fields ensures its convertibility.

When a formula uses multiple conditions, they can be joined with either the AND operator or the OR operator. Each affects performance differently. To understand how this works, you have to understand how each operator is used.

When two or more conditions are combined using the AND operator, Crystal looks at each condition independently. If a condition can be converted to SQL, it is appended to the **WHERE** clause and passed down to the server. Any conditions that can't be converted are left for the report engine to process. Crystal will pass as many conditions down to the server as it can and leave the rest for the client. The result is improved performance because, even though the client has to process some of the records, there will be fewer to process. Many records have already been filtered out by the server.

The OR operator works differently from the AND operator. When using the OR operator, Crystal Reports looks at all the conditions as a whole. Like the AND operator, it tries to convert each condition into SQL. But this time, if it finds that any of the conditions can't be converted, none of them will be converted. For example, assume a record selection formula has three conditions and they are joined using the OR operator. If the first two conditions can be converted to SQL, but the last one can't, none of them will be passed down to the server. The entire record selection formula will be processed by the client.

The reason for this is that when using the OR operator, all records are tested for each of the stated conditions. Only passing some of the conditions doesn't reduce the number of records that need to be passed to the client. For example, assume that there are two conditions and one of the two conditions was passed to the server. After the server processes the SELECT statement, it is left with 100 records. Even if the server performs the first test and 70 records fail, there is still a chance that these 70 records will pass the second test. However, the second test is on the client, which means the 70 records have to get passed to the client for testing. In effect, the server ends up passing all the records to the client. Using the OR operator didn't speed up the processing at all.

If you are using a PC database, those rules don't apply. Using a PC database means you can't use the OR operator at all. Whether the individual conditions can be converted to SQL or not won't have any effect.

Tip

If you want to find out whether a selection formula was converted into SQL, select the menu options Crystal Reports > Database > Show SQL Query. If you see that the query includes the WHERE clause, it was successfully converted. If the WHERE clause isn't included, one of the formulas or functions couldn't get converted.

Record Grouping and Sorting

When Crystal Reports generates a report that uses fields for grouping and sorting, it has to collect all the data within the client's computer and process each record. It takes a lot of resources to organize and sort each record as well as perform any necessary summary calculations. This section elaborates on the how-tos of enabling reports to optimize grouping and sorting, the restrictions of doing so, and how to customize the grouping formula during runtime.

Optimizing and modifying a report's grouping and sorting is very similar to working with the record selection formulas. You want to push down data to the server for processing. You learned in the last section, that for Crystal Reports to push data down to the server, you have to turn the feature on. The same goes for grouping records. Enable the option called "Perform Grouping on Server". This makes the server do as much of the grouping, summarizing and subtotaling as possible.

You can't select the option to perform grouping on the server unless the option to use the server for performance is also turned on. If it isn't selected, the grouping option is disabled.

To turn it on by default, select the menu options Crystal Reports > Designer > Default Settings. Go to the database tab and click on the "Perform Grouping on Server" option if it isn't already checked. If you want to set the options for just the current report, select the menu options Crystal Reports > Report > Report Options. Both options are listed near the bottom of the dialog box. There is also a short-cut just for the grouping option. Select the menu options Crystal Reports > Database > Perform Grouping On Server. This toggles the grouping option on or off. A check is shown next to the menu option so you can see its current value.

Restrictions on Grouping and Sorting

Having the server perform the grouping has certain restrictions associated with it. These restrictions are as follows:

- The goal of performing grouping and sorting on the server is to reduce the number of records passed back to the client and consequently reduce the amount of processing the client has to do. To make this possible, the report is restricted to printing only the group fields and summary fields. The Details section must be hidden and there can't be any detail fields in any of the header or footer sections.

- The report derives all its data from a single data source or stored procedure. You can't have two different data sources linked together.

- Grouping can't be performed on a formula, and formulas can't be used in summary fields. If either one of these is true, then all records will be passed back to the client for processing. This probably comes as a surprise since some formulas can be used in a record selection formula and can be passed to the server for processing. It is not the case with grouping.

- Sorting can't be done using specified order. It is impossible for Crystal Reports to convert the logic required to perform specified order sorting into valid SQL statements. This is always done on the client's machine.

- Running total fields must be based on summary fields. If a running total is based on a detail field, all the detail fields will be passed to the client to perform the calculation.

- The report cannot use summaries based on Average or Distinct Count.

- The fields that are being grouped must either be the actual database fields or SQL Expressions. SQL Expressions can always be sent to the server because they are built using valid SQL functions. This is discussed in the next section.

Using SQL Expressions

SQL Expressions are report formulas that only use SQL compatible functions. As mentioned in the last section, many formulas written with Crystal syntax don't have an SQL compliant equivalent. Thus, the report engine has to take the data returned from the server and process it on the client's computer. SQL Expressions alleviate this problem because they are passed directly to the server for processing. The data returned to the client computer has already been processed. SQL Expressions can be used as formulas that are used directly on the report output, or they can be included as part of the formulas.

Writing reports requires achieving a balance of functionality and performance. Many reports need to use custom formulas and functions to produce the proper output. But this can result in slower performance because it requires the report engine to do more work on the client computer. Thus, you would want to, whenever possible, push as much work as possible onto the database server. The drawback to using SQL Expressions is that they aren't as robust as formulas written with Crystal syntax or Basic syntax. Crystal Reports has an extensive library of functions that isn't matched in other programs. The functions found in the SQL language pale in comparison to Crystal Reports. Many formulas can't be rewritten using an SQL Expression.

When deciding when to use SQL Expressions instead of the standard formulas, you have to decide which gives you the best cost-benefit ratio. There are three places where formulas are used: as part of the report output, in the record selection formula, and as a sorting/grouping field. You should focus your attention on using SQL Expressions in formulas that are used for either record selection or sorting/grouping. Formulas that are used as part of the report output don't have a major effect on report performance because the report engine can quickly calculate these as it processes each record. The additional overhead incurred isn't significant. SQL Expressions should definitely be used to replace formulas that are used for record selection or sorting/grouping. Both of these tasks are very resource intensive and can affect the number of records that are passed from the server back to the client. The database server is optimized to perform record selection and sorting/grouping on a large number of records very quickly. Replacing these formulas with SQL Expressions can result in noticeable improvements in report performance.

To create an SQL Expression, look in the Field Explorer window for the SQL Expressions category.[29] Right-click on the SQL Expressions category and select New. An SQL Expression Name dialog box opens where you enter a name for the expression. Once you click the OK button, the SQL Expression Editor window opens. You can see that the SQL Expression Editor looks almost identical to the Formula Editor.

---

[29] If you don't see SQL Expressions, then you are either using a PC Database or another non-compatible database. In general, you have to be using SQL Server or an ODBC database to create an SQL Expression.

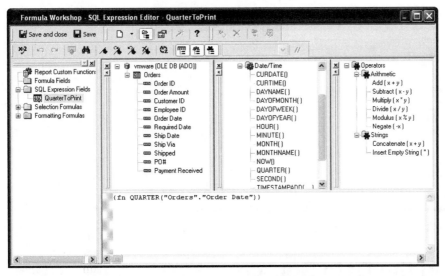

Figure 13-6. The SQL Expression Editor dialog box.

The process of creating an SQL Expression is the same as creating other formulas. You select the functions to use and apply them to the listed database fields. The important difference between regular formulas and SQL Expressions is that SQL Expressions have a more limited functionality. The only fields that you can use in an SQL Expression are database fields. You can't use other formulas, parameters or special fields. The available functions are also limited to SQL specific functions.

> ### Caution
>
> The list of available functions is specific to the database server you are connected to. If you create an SQL Expression and later change database servers, the expression may not be valid if the new database doesn't support one of the functions used.

After adding an SQL Expression to the report, the **SELECT** statement passed to the database server is modified to include the SQL Expression. It becomes an additional field that is requested from the server. If you also include the SQL Expression in a record selection formula, or sorting/grouping formula, this is also added to the query. Figure 13-7 shows how the formula is used as part of the **SELECT** portion of the query as well as the WHERE clause.

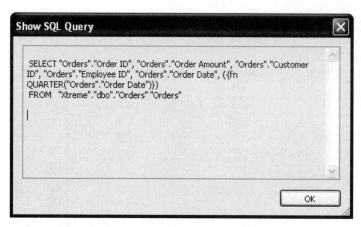

Figure 13-7. The SQL Query using an SQL Expression.

Changing the Data Source

Many reports are very simple and all the tables come from the same data source. The tables that are used when you designed the report are the same tables that will be used when the application is put into production. But this isn't always the case. It is common for the requirements to change and for a report to use a data source different from what it was designed with. Or, you may have a development server that is used for designing the application and a production server that is used when the application is finished.

Crystal Reports has a number of features that make it easier to change the location of the tables. It lets you set the location of a data source, change the name that a table is referenced by, and verify whether a database is valid.

Set Location Dialog Box

The Set Location dialog box, shown in Figure 13-8, is used to change the data source of an existing table. You might need to do this when the reporting requirements change, or when you find that, after having used one data source for coding and testing, you have to change to the production data source before releasing the program.

The Set Location dialog box lets you replace an existing data source with a new data source. You can switch the database server so that all the tables from one server are switched to a different server. You can also change the data source for just one table and it won't affect the other tables in that report. This includes changing the database server for that table or switching out the table for a totally different table.

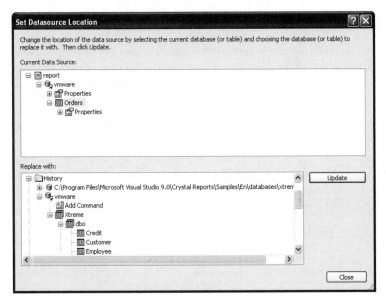

Figure 13-8. The Set Location dialog box.

Open the Set Location dialog box by selecting the menu options Crystal Reports > Database > Set Location. It has a window labeled "Current Data Source". This lists the current connections and any tables that are being used with that connection. The window at the bottom is labeled "Replace With". It lists the same data sources that are displayed in the Database Expert dialog box.

To replace the entire data source for all the tables, select the database server from the Current Data Source window on the left.

To replace a single table, drill down to select the specific table. The other window is refreshed to display the information about the table.

The Replace With window is where you select the data source that will replace what was selected in the combo box. Scroll through this window to find the new data source. If the Current Data Source combobox lists a database server, choose a database server within the Replace With window. If the Current Data Source is a table, you have to have a table selected within the Replace With window.

When both the current data source and the new data source are selected, click the Replace button. The existing data source gets replaced with the new data source.

If you find that the Replace button isn't enabled, you haven't selected data sources that are compatible with each other. For example, if you have a table selected, you have to have a table selected in the Replace With window. If there is a data source selected, the Replace With window can't have a table selected.

Verifying Changes to the Data Source

If you make changes to a table and its fields using the management console of the database, this will impact the reports that use that table. Modifying a field's data type can affect how the report formats the data. Changing a field's name causes the report to lose its reference to the field.

Crystal Reports has a Verify Database function that checks whether the fields in a report match the fields in the current data source. This should be done whenever you suspect that the tables have been modified. Access this function by selecting the menu options Crystal Reports > Database > Verify Database. It displays a confirmation box if the database is up to date. If Crystal Reports determines that the fields in your report do not match, it lets you re-map them to their equivalent fields in the new table structure.

Re-mapping Fields

When replacing one table with another table, it is possible that one or more of the fields on the report won't have exact matches in the new table. If the fields in a table are renamed or deleted, this can affect the existing fields on your report. When this happens, Crystal Reports gives you the option to remap the existing fields to the new fields in the database.

After using the Set Location dialog box or when using the Verify Database function, Crystal Reports checks if any changes have been made to the table. If it detects that a change has occurred that affects fields being used on the report, it opens the Map Fields dialog box shown in Figure 13-9. It shows the fields that don't have a matching field in the current table. It also shows you the new fields in the data source so that you can match the old fields to the new fields. Crystal replaces them accordingly.

Note

There is no way to open the Map Fields dialog box directly. It only opens in response to another action. For example, you have to open it indirectly by choosing the menu options Verify Database or Set Location.

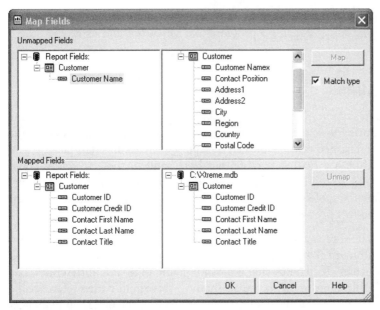

Figure 13-9. The Map Fields dialog box.

This dialog box is only displayed when necessary. If changes are made to fields that have not been added to the report yet, it isn't necessary to re-map these fields. Fields that only have their data types changed are not mapped either, but you should check their output when the report runs to make sure they are formatted properly.

The Map Fields dialog box is divided into two halves. The top half shows the unmapped fields. The left-most window shows the fields that are in the report but don't have a matching field in its assigned table. The right-most window shows all the fields from the currently selected tables. Select one of the unmapped fields in the left window and then select one of the available fields in the right window. Click on the Map button to replace the old field with the new field. You might notice that not all the fields are listed in the right-most window. This is because the checkbox to the right, labeled "Match type" is checked by default. This requires you to only match fields that have the same data type. It won't list the fields that don't have the same data type. If you uncheck this checkbox then all fields are displayed and you can replace a field with a field of a different data type. If you do this, you should go back to the report and make sure that the formatting and spacing of the new field is appropriate. The formatting of the old field may not have carried over properly.

If there are fields that are currently mapped, but you still want to replace them, use the window in the lower half of the dialog box. In the left-most window, click on the field to replace and then click the Unmap button. This moves the field to the Unmapped window in the top half and you can now follow the previous steps to re-map it with a new field.

After you accept the mapping changes, the report is automatically updated so that all report fields and formulas have the old field name replaced with the new field name. This saves you the trouble of going back through a report and modifying all formulas that referenced that field. This is the same effect as using a program like MS Word and using the Search and Replace function.

Setting a Table's Alias

When fields are added to a report, they are referenced by a combination of their table name and their field name. During the course of designing a report and making updates to it, the fields can have the table renamed or the table can be replaced with a different table. If you created formulas based upon a field in a table that has changed, these formulas could potentially become invalid. In this situation, you would expect to have to go back through the formulas and update the table names for each field. Fortunately, Crystal Reports has thought of a way around this problem.

In the prior discussion about re-mapping old field names to new field names, you learned that Crystal Reports automatically performs a search-and-replace to change the old field names with new field names. It handles changes to the name of a table differently. The report still uses the old table name in the formulas. But now these table names reference the new table name behind the scenes. On the surface, it appears that the table still references the old table because its name hasn't changed. This new table name is called an alias.

An alias is a name that is assigned to a database table that isn't the actual name of the table. If you replace a table with a new table, Crystal Reports refers to the new table using the same name as the original table. You can think of an alias as a variable that points to a table. You can change which table the variable points to, but the name of the variable never changes.

Every table in a report is referred to by an alias. When a table is first added to a report, an alias is created and its name matches the name of the table. Since they are the same, you don't even realize that an alias is being used. When you use the Set Location dialog box to change a data source's table to a new table, the alias name stays the same, but the table it refers to is now different.

As an example, consider a report that prints fields from a table called CustomerData. The table is later modified so that the name is now called Customer. You use the Set Location dialog box to change the CustomerData table to the Customer table. When you close the dialog box, you will see that the formulas still reference the table using CustomerData name. You might incorrectly think that the table name wasn't changed. But it was.

You can also use aliases to make it easier to design a report. For example, if you are using a table name that is extremely long, you can use an alias that is a shorter name. If you have a table name that uses a cryptic naming schema, you can use the alias to give the table a more useful name. For example, rather than referring to a table as "AR970EOY" you could refer to it as "Accts Receivable Year End". Everywhere in your report where this table is referenced, you will see the alias name that you assigned it rather than the actual name of the table used in the database.

The interesting thing about having an alias in a formula is that unlike re-mapping fields, aliases don't change anything on the surface. Since formulas reference the name of the alias and this name never changes, you don't have to worry about updating the formulas.

Tip

If you are going to rename a table's alias to make it easier to work with, make sure you do so before creating any formulas with that table. When you change a table's alias, the formulas are not updated. Your formulas will quit working until you modify them to use the new alias name.

Another reason to use an alias is when want to use a table for a self-join SQL statement. You need to rename the alias of one of the tables before linking them together. The alias that the table is named doesn't have any effect on the table's actual name in the database. When you give a table an alias, Crystal Reports modifies the **SELECT** statement so that it uses the new alias name.

To manually change the alias of a table, open the Database Expert dialog box. Click on the table that you want to assign an alias to and press the F2 key. This puts the name in edit mode and you can change it.

If you are using multiple data sources, it's possible that you will add two tables with the same name to your report. Crystal Reports forces you to give one of the tables an alias so that there isn't a naming conflict. Before it lets you add the table, it prompts you with the Database Warning dialog box in Figure 13-10. It tells you that there is already a table with that same alias and asks if you really want to add it to your current connections. If you click Yes, it prompts you to enter a new alias name. The table gets added to your current connections using the new alias name.

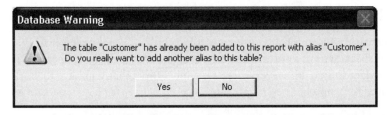

Figure 13-10. The Database Warning dialog box.

Tip

It isn't obvious when a table is using an alias that is different than the actual table name. If you are given a report that you didn't design, a table that uses an alias can make it difficult to determine what the actual table is. To find out which tables have aliases and which table is used, open the Set Location dialog box. When you click on the table name, the Properties node below the table shows you the details about the alias. The actual table name is shown in this information. The following figure shows that the alias CustomerData references the Customer table.

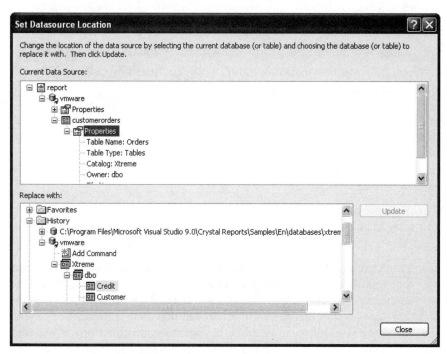

Figure 13-11. Finding a table's alias.

Printing with MS Excel Files

One of the data sources that you can print from is a MS Excel file. Crystal makes it simple to print using the worksheets within a spreadsheet file. It references each worksheet as if it were a table within the data source. However, there are a few quirks that you have to work around to make it function properly.

The most obvious way of printing from an Excel file is to use the Database Expert and go to the category called More Data Sources. Within this category, you find an option for connecting to MS Excel via DAO (data access objects). Select this option and find the Excel file you want to print from. It will list each worksheet that has data on it. Add the worksheets to print from into the Selected Tables window. Once the worksheets have been selected, proceed to design the report as normal.

PART II
Programming Reports

Advanced report designers aren't satisfied with using the built-in functions to customize reports. They want to integrate their .NET applications with Crystal Reports during runtime. Part II shows you how to seamlessly integrate your reports into .NET with runtime customization of report objects and modifying parameters. Dynamic data connections let you connect to virtually any data source. For the most advanced reporting functionality, develop Report Web Services or upgrade to the stand-alone version of Crystal Reports 2008 and use .NET to program with the RAS SDK. Part II shows you how to take your reporting skills to the expert level.

Part I of this book taught the details of how to use the Crystal Reports embedded designer to create professional reports. When a report is complete, its design and layout stays the same every time it is run. The data that it prints will change, but the report format is locked. With Crystal Reports .NET, reports have the flexibility to be dynamic. .NET programmers have full access to the properties of a report and the underlying report objects. These properties can be read and many of them can be overridden. You get the power to create a reporting solution that takes user input and customizes each report prior to printing it. This can range from changing the formatting of report objects, modifying the grouping and sorting, and changing the data source. The more you learn about runtime customization, the more you will find out what you can do. This chapter serves as the foundation for building your knowledge throughout the rest of this book.

The reason why you have so much power to modify reports is because .NET treats every report as an object-oriented class. The entire object model is exposed to your .NET program. Whether you program with VB.NET or C# isn't important. The object model can be accessed by any of the .NET languages.

There are three ways to use the Crystal Reports object model. The first is to use the **ReportDocument** class. It is the most powerful because it references virtually every class and property of the report. The second way is to use the methods and properties of the CrystalReportViewer control. When compared to the **ReportDocument** class, the viewer only has a small subset of properties and methods. The viewer lets you modify the properties that affect logging in to a data source, setting report parameters, and deciding which report to preview. The last way to work with the object model is to subscribe to the events that are triggered while the report is previewed and printed. These events are useful for knowing what part of the report is being looked at and what the user is doing. This chapter goes into detail on all three ways of customizing reports during runtime.

Basic Customization

No matter what type of runtime customization you want to perform, customizing reports always starts with the same premise: declare and instantiate a **ReportDocument** object, modify its properties, and print or preview it. These steps are discussed in more detail next.

Note

As discussed in Chapter 3, Windows applications allow you to use either embedded or non-embedded reports. ASP.NET applications only allow non-embedded reports. The code listings in this chapter will give examples of how to use both types of reports. In the majority of cases, non-embedded reports will be used since they are available for both Windows and ASP.NET applications, but you can always use embedded reports if you are developing a Windows application.

Step 1: Declare and instantiate the ReportDocument object variable.

When using non-embedded reports, you have to declare and instantiate an object variable derived from the ReportDocument class. The report is loaded into memory by calling the Load() method of this object.

If you are using an embedded report in a Windows application, a class that has the same name as your report was automatically created in your project when you created the report. You can instantiate this class directly and it loads the report into memory. There is no need to call the Load() method.

Note

In the examples throughout this chapter and the rest of the book, the report name being referenced is called CrystalReport1. This is the default report name that is given by the report wizard. When you implement the sample code in your applications, replace the name CrystalReport1 with the name of the report you want to print. I also name the report object variables 'myReport'. When using the code listings in your own application, replace this name with a variable name that best describes your report.

Step 2: Modify the properties of the report object.

After instantiating the report object, all the properties and methods of the ReportDocument object are available to you. Set the properties that need to be modified. The different properties of the report object are explained throughout all the chapters in Part II of this book.

If you only want to print the report without changing any of the report properties, you can skip this step. The following examples will skip this step because it is covered in extensive detail throughout the rest of this book.

Step 3: Preview or print the report.

To preview the report, assign the report object variable to the viewer's ReportSource property. This automatically displays it to the user and lets them use the toolbar to navigate through the pages, export the report to an external file, or send it to the printer. If you want to print a report without previewing it, call the PrintToPrinter() method, discussed in the next section.

The following sections are sample code for previewing reports using a Windows client.

All the reports in this chapter assume that the report is not connecting to a secure data source. Passing login credentials is much more involved and has an entire chapter dedicated to it. See Chapter 17 for more information.

Listing 14-1. Windows client, embedded report, Crystal viewer

[VB.NET]

```
Dim myReport As New CrystalReport1
CrystalReportViewer1.ReportSource = myReport
```

[C#]

```
CrystalReport1 myReport = new CrystalReport1;
CrystalReportViewer1.ReportSource = myReport;
```

In this code, the following assumptions are made: there is an embedded report called CrystalReport1, and that a viewer control has been added to the current form. The report was also created within the Windows project and automatically added to the Solution Explorer as a class.

The first line of code instantiates the class and assigns it to the myReport object variable. The second line of code assigns this object to the ReportSource property of the viewer control. This automatically shows the user a preview of the report within the viewer.

Listing 14-2. Windows client, non-embedded report, Crystal viewer

[VB.NET]

```
Dim myReport As New CrystalDecisions.CrystalReports.Engine.ReportDocument()
myReport.Load("CrystalReport1.rpt")
CrystalReportViewer1.ReportSource = myReport
```

[C#]

```
CrystalDecisions.CrystalReports.Engine.ReportDocument() myReport = new
CrystalDecisions.CrystalReports.Engine.ReportDocument();
myReport.Load("CrystalReport1.rpt");
CrystalReportViewer1.ReportSource = myReport;
```

In this code, it is assumed that there is a non-embedded report called "CrystalReports1.rpt" that is saved to the same directory where the project's executable is located. There is also a viewer control that has been added to the current form. The first line of code declares and instantiates the ReportDocument class and assigns it to the myReport object variable. The second line of code uses the Load() method to load the report from the hard drive into memory. The last line of code assigns the object to the ReportSource property of the viewer control. This automatically shows the user a preview of the report within the viewer.

Non-embedded reports can be a little confusing when you first start working with them because they are not located in the same path as your application's executable. Visual Studio compiles your executable into a sub-folder named \Bin\Debug (or \Bin\Production depending upon how you compile it), but your report file is located with the source code. Thus, it is two sub-folders back and the code in Listing 14-2 won't work. To make this work, you either have to copy the report file to the Debug folder or modify your code so that it references the subfolder. If you choose to do that, you would use the code in listing 14-3.

Listing 14-3. Windows client, non-embedded report, Crystal viewer

[VB.NET]
```
Private Sub Form1_Load(ByVal sender As System.Object, ByVal e As System.EventArgs) Handles yBase.Load
    CrystalReportViewer1.ReportSource = "..\..\CrystalReport1.rpt"
End Sub
```

[C#]
```
private void Form1_LOAD(object sender, EventArgs e)
{
    CrystalReportViewer1.ReportSource = @"..\..\CrystalReport1.rpt";
}
```

Sending Reports Directly to the Printer

If you want to send the report directly to the printer without previewing it, call the PrintToPrinter() method. When you call this method, the report is sent directly to the printer without any user interaction. This is useful when generating reports in a batch format or if you are creating a custom toolbar with a print button on it. The parameters of the PrintToPrinter() method are listed in Table 14-1.

Table 14-1. PrintToPrinter() parameters.

Parameter	Description
nCopies	The number of copies to print.
Collated	Set to True to collate the pages.
startPageN	The first page to print. Set to 0 to print all pages.
endPageN	The last page to print. Set to 0 to print all pages.

All the parameters listed in Table 14-1 are required. If you don't need to use one or more of them, pass it the default value. The first parameter, **nCopies**, sets how many copies of the report to print. If more than one copy of the report is being printed, the second property tells whether or not to collate the copies.[30] Passing **False** tells it to print each full report

---

[30] Collating copies of a report means that all the copies of each page are printed before the following page is printed. For example, all the copies of page 1 will print before page 2 gets printed.

prior to printing the next copy. The collated property is only used if nCopies is greater than 1. Otherwise it is ignored. The last two parameters, startPageN and endPageN, set the page range. Pass it the first page to print and the last page to print. To print the entire report, pass 0 to both parameters.

Listing 14-4. Windows client, non-embedded report, print to printer

[VB.NET]

```
Dim myReport As New CrystalDecisions.CrystalReports.Engine.ReportDocument()
myReport.Load("CrystalReport1.rpt")
myReport.PrintToPrinter(1, False, 0, 0)
```

[C#]

```
CrystalDecisions.CrystalReports.Engine.ReportDocument() myReport = new
CrystalDecisions.CrystalReports.Engine.ReportDocument();
myReport.Load("CrystalReport1.rpt");
myReport;.PrintToPrinter(2, True, 0, 0);
```

This code is similar to the previous listings with the exception that the report is sent directly to the printer. The VB.NET example prints one copy of the entire report. The C# example prints 2 copies and collates the report pages.

Locating the Report Code

The previous code listings only show you the steps for previewing/printing the reports in a Windows form. But they don't show you where you should put the code in your form. You can put this code anywhere in the form and it will work fine. For example, if you want to show the report when the form opens, put the code in the Load() event. There are times that you are going to call this code after the user has entered various data that specifies how the report should be customized. If that's the case, you could put the code in response to the click event of an OK button that confirms they are finished inputting data. The following code sample demonstrates putting it in the Load() event.

Listing 14-5. A template for modifying reports.

[VB.NET]

```
Private Sub Form1_Load(ByVal sender As System.Object, ByVal e As System.EventArgs) Handles MyBase.Load
    Dim myReport As New CrystalDecisions.CrystalReports.Engine.ReportDocument()
    myReport.Load("CrystalReport1.rpt")
    CrystalReportViewer1.ReportSource = myReport
End Sub
```

[C#]

```
private void Form1_Load(object sender, EventArgs e)
{
    CrystalDecisions.CrystalReports.Engine.ReportDocument() myReport = new
CrystalDecisions.CrystalReports.Engine.ReportDocument();
```

```
myReport.Load("CrystalReport1.rpt");
myReport;.PrintToPrinter(2, True, 0, 0);
}
```

Note

All report customization must be done prior to previewing or printing the report. No changes are allowed once the report is generated. For example, you can't use .NET to change the way a field is formatted depending upon the current group value. Making dynamic report changes while the report is running requires writing formulas and using conditional formatting (discussed in Chapters 7, 8, and 9).

Printing from ASP.NET Websites

Printing reports within an ASP.NET application requires a slightly different coding template than the previous listings. Reports shown on an ASP.NET page are unique in that each time the user moves to a new report page, the web page gets reloaded. If a report is resource intensive, this can slow performance or tie up resources. For example, a report that connects to SQL Server will open a new connection each time the page is loaded. In addition to wasting resources, reports will often 'forget' which page they were previously showing. I frequently see people posting questions on the book's forum asking why a page will jump from page 3 back to page 1.

Fixing this problem requires making two specific coding changes. The first requires loading the report in the web page's **Page_Init()** event. Normally, you would put your code in the **Page_Load()** event, but the **Page_Load()** event has timing issues of how the report viewer binds to the report and how it responds to mouse click events. Putting the report initialization code in the **Page_Init()** event solves this timing problem and the viewer will respond to mouse clicks correctly.

The second change you need to make is saving the report object to the Session collection. This lets you persist the report across page views. When the page loads it can pull the existing report from the Session and pass it to the report viewer. This saves resources because the report won't re-query the database or re-process the report each time the web page is loaded.

Saving the report to the Session collection adds a little complexity to your code because you have to determine if the report was already saved in the Session by the previous page. If so, load the existing report into a **ReportDocument** object variable. If the report isn't in the Session, you have to instantiate a new report object and save it to the Session collection.

In the following code sample, there are two procedures. The first, the **Page_Init()** event, determines if the report is already in the Session. If not, it calls the second procedure, **ConfigureReport()**, which loads the report into memory and saves it to the Session collection.

Listing 14-6. Template for ASP.NET pages.

[VB.NET]

```
Partial Class _yourWebPage
   Inherits System.Web.UI.Page
   'The myReport object varialble is local to the web page
   Dim myReport As CrystalDecisions.CrystalReports.Engine.ReportDocument
   Protected Sub Page_Init(ByVal sender As Object, ByVal e As System.EventArgs) Handles Me.Init
      If Session("myReport") Is Nothing Then
         'The report hasn't been created yet. Do so now.
         ConfigureReport()
      Else
         'The report has already been created, load it from the Session collection
         myReport = CType(Session("myReport"),
CrystalDecisions.CrystalReports.Engine.ReportDocument)
      End If
      CrystalReportViewer1.ReportSource = myReport
End Sub
Private Sub ConfigureReport()
   myReport.Load(Server.MapPath("CrystalReport1.rpt"))
      'custom report modifications would go here
   Session("myReport") = myReport
End Sub
```

[C#]

```
public partial class HealthInfo : System.Web.UI.Page
{
   //The myReport object varialble is local to the web page
   CrystalDecisions.CrystalReports.Engine.ReportDocument myReport = new
CrystalDecisions.CrystalReports.Engine.ReportDocument;
   protected void Page_Init(object sender, System.EventArgs e)
   {
      if (Session["myReport"]==null)
         {
            //The report hasn't been created yet. Do so now.
            ConfigureReport();
         } else {
            //The report has already been created. Load it from the Session collection
            myReport=(CrystalDecisions.CrystalReports.Engine.ReportDocument)Session["myReport"];
         }
         CrystalReportViewer1.ReportSource = myReport;
      }
   }
   private void ConfigureReport()
   {
      myReport.Load(Server.MapPath("CrystalReport1.rpt"));
      //custom report modifications would go here…
      Session["myReport"]=myReport;
   }
}
```

The myReport object variable is declared immediately after the class declaration for the web page (your Partial Class declaration will be named differently than the one I show in the code listing). This makes the myReport variable local to the web page and all the methods have access to it.

The Page_Init() event checks for two scenarios. The first scenario is that this is the first time the web page is loaded and the report hasn't been created yet. It calls the ConfigureReport() method and saves the report to the Session collection. If the report is already in the Session, it pulls it from the collection into the myReport object variable. Notice that it has to cast the Session object as a ReportDocument class. This is because the Session collection doesn't track a variable's data type and it stores everything as a generic object variable.

The ConfigureReport() method declares and instantiates a new ReportDocument object and loads it into memory using the Load() method. It also uses the Server.MapPath() method to map the virtual file to a physical path on the server. After loading the report, it saves it to the Session collection using the name "myReport". This name can be used to retrieve the report on the next page load. By creating a separate method to load the report into memory, you can call it from other places within the webpage if necessary (e.g. responding to a button click event).

Caution

The template modifies the report's properties after the ReportDocument is loaded into memory. If you later call the viewer's Refresh() method, the viewer loads the report back into memory again and loses all changes you made to the report. You will have to set the properties again.

Disposing of the Report's Memory

Web applications that produce a high volume of reports frequently have a problem with running out of memory. This is because reports require a lot of memory to process them as well as store the actual report object in memory. Properly disposing of a report's memory footprint on the server differs from how you dispose of other objects and it isn't very well understood by most programmers. This makes it easy to think that your reports are being removed from memory when in reality they aren't. Let's look at what is involved in properly disposing of reports from memory.

When you print a report, there are three ways that it uses resources on the server. As you saw in the previous section, the ReportDocument object is used to load a report onto the page, and it obviously consumes memory. In addition to that, the actual report as it is rendered requires memory. Lastly, the Session collection has a copy of the report in its memory. You have to dispose of the memory for each of these circumstances to completely optimize the web server's resources.

When a web page closes, the ReportDocument object variable falls out of scope. .NET keeps it in memory until it determines that it is necessary to perform garbage collection for the entire application. I've found in certain high-volume sites that garbage collection isn't as reliable as I would like it to be and I have to force garbage collection manually. In this circumstance, I'll call the Dispose() method of the report object to drop it out of scope, and then call the GC.Collect() method to force garbage collection.

The physical copy of the report is removed from memory by calling the Close() method of the ReportDocument object. I put this immediately before calling the Dispose() method. If you dispose of the report object before closing the report, it loses the internal link to the physical report and you won't be able to call the Close() method on it. It is essential that you do this in the proper order.

I put my cleanup code in the Page_Unload() event. This is the last event called when the web page finishes processing the page data and passes the HTML code to the browser. Many people are confused by the Page_Unload() event because they think that it is called when the user closes the page on the browser. But this isn't the case. Since the browser is stateless and doesn't have a direct connection back to the web server, there is no way to determine when the user has closed the browser window. Thus, the Page_Unload() event can't be called when the web page closes because the web server won't know when this happens. What really happens is that when the server has finished generating the entire page output and is ready to send the HTML code to the browser, it calls the Page_Unload() event. Since the HTML has been created, the web server no longer needs any of the data that was used to build the page. You can put code in the Page_Unload() event to clean up any orphaned objects that were created during the processing of the page (data connections, reports, etc.) Listing 14-7 is the sample code that closes the report and disposes of its memory.

Listing 14-7. Removing a report from an ASP.NET page.

[VB.NET]
```
Private Sub Page_Unload(ByVal sender As Object, ByVal e As System.EventArgs) Handles
MyBase.Unload
    MyReport.Close()
    MyReport.Dispose()
    GC.Collect()
End Sub
```

[C#]
```
private void Page_Unload(object sender, System.EventArgs e) Handles MyBase.Unload
{
    MyReport.Close();
    MyReport.Dispose();
    GC.Collect();
}
```

The third place where you need to clean up the report's memory is in the Session collection. Since the report is stored there between page loads, it also needs to be removed when the user is finished viewing the report. This is done automatically by the web server because, at some point, the user's session will time out and the objects in the Session collection get cleared. This works for the majority of web sites, but it won't be good enough for a high volume site that generates many reports. For this scenario, you have to remove the report from the Session collection manually. The code is pretty simple and it is shown in Listing 14-8.

Listing 14-8. Removing the report from the Session collection.

[VB.NET]

```
Session("myReport")=Nothing
```

[C#]

```
Session["myReport"] = null;
```

The next decision you have to make is where to put this code. We know that the report needs to be cleared from the Session collection when the web page is closed, but we learned earlier that it isn't possible to know when the user closes the page. So how do you know when to remove the report from the Session? You don't. What I do is put the code to clear the report from the Session collection on the main menu page for the web application. I know that the main menu is the page most frequently visited by every user. By putting the code there, I ensure that it will be removed in a relatively short period of time. Of course, this rule of thumb doesn't apply to every web application and you have to use your best judgment when determining where to put your code.

You might also notice that in this code I referred to the report name as "myReport". This brings up another potential problem because if your web application has many reports on it, the main menu page would need a lot of code to clear out all the potential reports that the application can generate. Every page that produces a report needs to have that report removed from the Session collection. To fix this problem, I use the same session name for all the reports in the web application. Since the web application can only display one report at a time, it's okay to re-use the same name without worrying about conflicts. In addition to that, since the report is cleared out on the main menu page, I know that it will be empty when the next page with a report loads.

The ReportDocument Object

The ReportDocument class is the base class for all reports. Its properties give an application the ability to thoroughly examine all the report objects. Many of these properties, but not all of them, have write capabilities so that you can modify their values.

Each report is a class that inherits from the ReportDocument class. Figure 14-1 shows the Object Browser window with the class for a blank report, CrystalReport1. You can see that ReportClass is the base class for the report. The members listed to the right of the figure belong to the ReportDocument class.

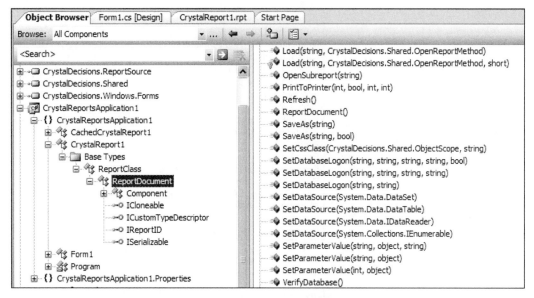

Figure 14-1. Object Browser view of the ReportDocument class.

The ReportDocument class has seven other classes that it references. Figure 14-2 shows the ReportDocument object model. The class thoroughly exposes all the objects of a report. Since the coverage is so broad and hits many topics covered in this book, the relevant classes are covered in different chapters. This chapter gives you an overview of all the classes and goes into detail on the two generic classes SummaryInfo class and ReportOptions class.

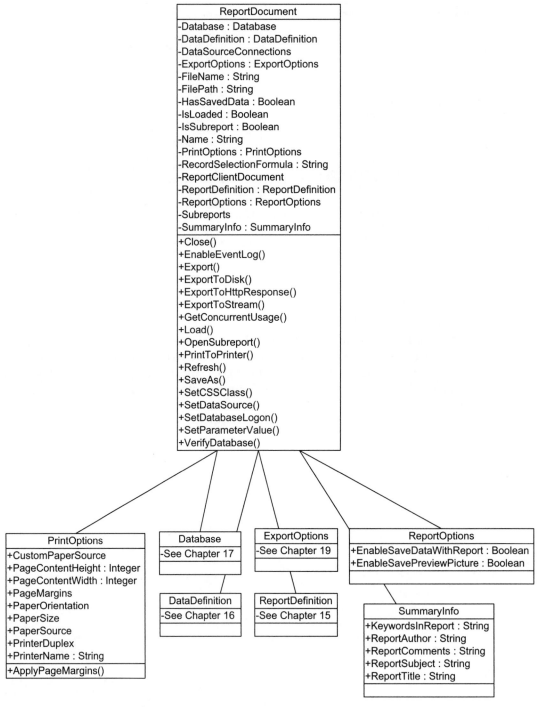

Figure 14-2. The ReportDocument object model.

Retrieving Summary Information

Every report has a variety of summary information saved with it. This information is set by the report designer and it usually consists of things such as the report author, the report title and report comments. This information is set during design mode by right-clicking on the report and selecting the menu options Crystal Reports > Report > Summary Info. The class that maintains this summary information is the SummaryInfo class. Although you can override the property values, more than likely, you will only want to read from these values. This information was set by the report designer and won't need to change during runtime. There are only a half dozen properties that this class exposes (see Table 14-2).

Table 14-2. Properties of the SummaryInfo class.

Property	Description
KeywordsInReport	The keywords in the report.
ReportAuthor	The author of the report.
ReportComments	Comments about the report.
ReportSubject	The subject of the report.
ReportTitle	The title of the report.

The following code in this example displays a message box showing the author of the CrystalReport1 report. You can see that accessing these properties is very simple.

```
Dim myReport As New CrystalReport1
MessageBox.Show(myReport.SummaryInfo.ReportAuthor)
```

Setting the Report Options

The ReportOptions class only has a few properties that can be set. They are listed in Table 14-3. This information is set during design mode by selecting the menu options Crystal Reports > Design > Default Settings and selecting the Reporting tab. These properties were discussed in Chapter 2.

Table 14-3. Properties of the ReportOptions class.

Property	Description
EnableSaveDataWithReport	Saves the latest data with the report. Allows report to be opened without a live data connection.
EnableSavePreviewPicture	Saves a thumbnail picture of the report.
EnableSaveSummariesWithReport	Saves data summaries with the report.

EnableUseDummyData	Uses dummy data when viewing the report.
InitialDataContext	The specific record or records that will become the initial data displayed in the CrystalReportsPartViewer.
InitialReportPartName	The name of the report part that will be displayed in the CrystalReportsPartViewer.[31]

The following example sets the **EnableSaveDataWithReport** property to **True**.

```
Dim myReport As New CrystalReport1
myReport.ReportOptions.EnableSaveDataWithReport = True
```

Modifying the Printing Options

The **PrintOptions** class stores the options for how a report is sent to the printer. This can consist of the destination printer, the paper orientation or the page margins. This is normally set during design mode. While the majority of an application's reports will use the same settings, you can override the default settings for specific reports. Table 14-4 lists the properties.

Table 14-4. PrintOptions properties.

Property	Description
ApplyPageMargins()	Sets new page margins.
CustomPaperSource	Sets the current printer paper source.
PageMargins	Gets the page margins.
PaperOrientation	Switches between Landscape and Portrait.
PaperSize	Sets the paper size using pre-defined size constants.
PaperSource	Sets the tray that the paper is printed from.
PrinterDuplex	Sets the current printer duplex option.
PrinterName	Change the printer by passing a string that exactly matches the printer name listed in the Printers Control Panel.

---

[31] See Chapter 19 for a discussion of the report parts viewer for ASP.NET sites.

Each of these properties is easy to modify. In some cases, you will have to use a predefined constant to set the property (e.g. PaperOrientation and PaperSize).

Caution

Changing the printer name can cause the report output to be scrambled. Each printer uses a unique printer language for producing output. If the new printer doesn't use the same printer language as the default printer that the report was designed to use, the report will not print correctly. For example, if a report was designed for use with an HP printer, it is okay to switch between similar models of an HP printer. But printing this report to Acrobat PDFWriter will result in an unreadable PDF file.

Listing 14-9. Change a report's printer settings.

[VB.NET]

```
Dim MyReport As New CrystalReport1
MyReport.PrintOptions.PaperOrientation = CrystalDecisions.[Shared].PaperOrientation.Landscape
MyReport.PrintOptions.PrinterName = "HP LaserJet510"
MyReport.PrintToPrinter(1, False, 0, 0)
```

[C#]

```
CrystalReport1 MyReport = new CrystalReport1();
MyReport.PrintOptions.PaperOrientation = CrystalDecisions.Shared.PaperOrientation.Landscape;
MyReport.PrintOptions.PrinterName = "HP LasterJet510";
MyReport.PrintToPrinter(1, false, 0, 0);
```

Best Of The Forum

Question: How do I set the report to use the "No Printer" option?

Answer: Set the PrinterName property to an empty string.

Connecting to the Data Sources

The Database class is used for examining the tables used in a report and their relationships with each other. It's also used for setting the login information before opening the report. This class is described in Chapter 17.

Exporting Reports

If your application only sends reports to the printer, it is lacking the functionality to make your data accessible to a variety of applications. Crystal Reports lets you export a report in many different formats so that different applications can read the data. For example, you can export report data to an Excel spreadsheet so that an end user can perform a statistical analysis on the data. The ExportOptions class has the properties that specify the exporting options. This is discussed in Chapter 19.

Referencing and Formatting the Report Objects

The ReportDefinition class is responsible for maintaining the collections of the basic report objects. These objects consist of the Areas collection, Sections collection and the ReportObjects collection. Each Section class contains the report objects that are within that section. You can modify the formatting properties of any of these objects. This is discussed in Chapter 15.

Changing Report Objects

Every report can have many types of fields that are used to generate the report, but don't have to appear directly on the report. Some examples are grouping fields, parameter fields, and formula fields. Even though these fields may not be shown directly on the report, they are updateable during runtime and can be used to change the report's appearance. For example, you can change the grouping field so that the report sorts and summarizes in a new way. The DataDefinition class manages the collections that control these aspects of the report. These collections are discussed in the appropriate chapters throughout this book.

CrystalReportViewer Object Model

From the user's perspective, the CrystalReportViewer control is only used to preview reports. But, from the programmer's perspective, it offers much more. The CrystalReportViewer object model, shown in Figure 14-3, has properties and methods that give you the ability to modify the report object, change the look and feel of the viewer, and respond to reporting events.

CrystalReportViewer (Windows)
+ActiveViewIndex : Integer
+BackColor
+BackgroundImage
+BackgroundImageLayout
+DisplayBackgroundEdge : boolean
+DisplayGroupTree : boolean
+DisplayStatusBar : boolean
+DisplayToolbar : boolean
+EnableDrillDown : boolean
+EnableToolTips : boolean
-LogOnInfo : TableLogonInfos
-ParameterFieldInfo : ParameterFields
+ReportSource
+RightToLeft
+SelectionFormula : String
+ShowCloseButton : boolean
+ShowExportButton : boolean
+ShowGotoPageButton : boolean
+ShowGroupTreeButton : boolean
+ShowPageNavigationButtons : boolean
+ShowPrintButton : boolean
+ShowRefreshButton : Border
+ShowTextSearchButton : boolean
+ShowZoomButton : boolean
-ViewCount : Integer
+CloseView()
+DrillDownOnGroup()
+ExportReport()
+GetCurrentPageNumber()
+PrintReport()
+RefreshReport()
+SearchForText()
+ShowFirstPage()
+ShowGroupTree()
+ShowLastPage()
+ShowNthPage()
+ShowPreviousPage()
+Zoom()

CrystalReportViewer (Web)
+AutoDataBind : boolean
+BestFitPage : boolean
+BorderStyle
+ClientTarget : String
+CssFileName : String
+DisplayGroupTree : boolean
+DisplayPage : Boolean
+DisplayToolbar : boolean
+EnableDatabaseLoginPrompt : boolean
+EnableDrillDown : boolean
-EnableParameterPrompt : Boolean
+EnableToolTips : boolean
+GroupTreeImagesFolderUrl : String
+GroupTreeStyle
+HasCrystalLogo : boolean
+HasDrillUpButton : boolean
+HasExportButton : boolean
+HasGotoPageButton : boolean
+HasPageNavigationButton : boolean
+HasPrintButton : boolean
+HasRefreshButton : boolean
+HasSearchButton : boolean
+HasToggleGroupButton : boolean
+HasViewList : boolean
+HasZoomFactorList : boolean
+HyperlinkTarget : String
-LogOnInfo : TableLogOnInfo
+PageToTreeRatio : double
+PageZoomFactor : int
-ParameterFieldInfo : ParameterFields
+ReportSource
+ReuseParameterValuesOnRefresh : boolean
+RightToLeft
+SelectionFormula : String
+ToolbarImagesFolderUrl : String
-SeparatePages : Boolean
+RefreshReport()
+SearchAndHighlightTest()
+SearchForText()
+ShowFirstPage()
+ShowLastPage()
+ShowNextPage()
+ShowNthPage()
+ShowPreviousPage()
+Zoom()

Figure 14-3. The CrystalReportViewer object model.

As you can see in Figure 14-3, there is a different object model for the Windows viewer and the web viewer. The web object model has more properties because web forms have options for how a page is displayed in a browser (e.g. CSS files, setting URL locations, etc.).

Although the viewer can be used to modify properties of the report object, it isn't recommended that you do so. It is a lightweight alternative for updating the report and only exposes a few properties. You can use it when you only need to perform basic tasks. The problem with using the viewer to modify the report is that it conflicts with changes made directly to the **ReportDocument** object. Crystal Reports can use changes made to either the viewer or the **ReportDocument** object, but not both, and it will not keep all the changes. It is best to always make changes using the **ReportDocument** class to prevent possible conflicts that will require debugging.

If you do wish to use the viewer to modify the report, there are three properties that you need to be aware of and they are covered throughout this book. The **RecordSelection** property filters the report data. The **ParameterFieldInfo** property is the **ParameterFields** collection (discussed in Chapter 16). The **LogOnInfo** property (discussed in Chapter 17) is a collection of **TableLogOnInfo** objects for setting the user credentials for each table.

You should use the properties of the viewer class to make changes to its visual layout. For example, you can customize the look so that it blends in with the formatting of the rest of your application. You can hide buttons that aren't necessary or replace their functionality with your own buttons. The custom properties were already discussed in detail in Chapter 1 and you can see that names used in the object model are self-explanatory.

Responding to Events

Report classes are built with events that let you respond to the actions that the user is doing as they preview a report. Your application can subscribe to these events and be alerted when they occur. Since a user can only preview a report using the CrystalReportViewer, the events are written for this class. Table 14-5 lists the reporting related events.

Note

The CrystalReportViewer also has the standard events associated with all controls (e.g. **Click**, **GotFocus**, etc.) However, these are not unique to Crystal Reports, so if you need more information about them, please consult MSDN.

Table 14-5. The primary events for reports.

Event	Description
AfterRender()	Fired after the HTML page is rendered.
AfterRenderContent()	Fired after the content on the HTML page is rendered.
AfterRenderObject()	Fired after each report object is rendered onto the report

BeforeRender()	Fired before the HTML page is rendered.
BeforeRenderContent()	Fired before the HTML content is rendered.
BeforeRenderObject()	Fired before each report object is rendered onto the report.
Drill()	Fired when the user drills down on a field.
DrillDownSubReport()	Fired when the user drills down on a subreport.
HandleException()	Fired when an exception occurs.
Navigate()	Fired when a user moves to another page on the report.
ReportBookmarkNavigation()	Fires after the user navigates to a report part in the same report or another report.
ReportRefresh()	Fired when the user refreshes the report data.
Search()	Fired when the user enters a search string.
ViewZoom()	Fired when the user changes the zoom percentage.

The Drill() event is fired whenever a user clicks on a field to drill down on it. It passes an object of type DrillEventArgs. This object can be examined to find the group level the user is currently looking at, as well as the new group level it's being moved to. Table 14-6 lists the properties of the DrillEventArgs event type.

Table 14-6. Properties of the DrillEventArgs event type.

Property	Description
CurrentGroupLevel	Returns an integer representing the current group level.
CurrentGroupName	Returns a string representing the name of the current group level.
CurrentGroupPath	A string representation of the group number and the current group level.
NewGroupLevel	Returns an integer representing the new group level.
NewGroupName	Returns a string representing the group level name.
NewGroupPath	A string representation of the group number and group level being drilled into.

The DrillDownSubReport() event is similar to the Drill() event and it is fired when the user drills down on a subreport. Although the functionality is similar, this event passes an object of the DrillDownSubreportEventArgs type. It gives you information such as the subreport name and the page number. Table 14-7 lists the properties of this event type.

Table 14-7. Properties of the DrillDownSubreportEventArgs event type.

Property	Description
CurrentSubreportName	The name of the current subreport.
CurrentSubreportPageNumber	The page number that the subreport is on.
CurrentSubreportPosition	Returns a Point object that tells the position of the subreport on the viewer.
Handled	Set to true if you do not want the subreport to be drilled down to.
NewSubreportName	The name of the new subreport.
NewSubreportPageNumber	Sets the page number to drill down into.
NewSubreportPosition	Returns a Point object that tells the position of the new subreport on the viewer.

The HandleException() event is used for capturing exceptions and handling them. This is discussed in detail in the section Handling Exceptions.

The Navigate() event is fired when the user moves to another page in the report. This can be done by paging forward through the report or jumping to the beginning or end of the report. Table 14-8 lists the properties for the NavigateEventArgs event type.

Table 14-8. Properties of the NavigateEventArgs event type.

Property	Description
CurrentPageNumber	The page number that the report is on.
GroupPath	A string representation of the group number and the current group level.
Handled	Set to True if you do not want to move to the new page.
NewPageNumber	The page number that the user is moving to.

The ReportRefresh() event is fired when the user refreshes the report data. The only property for this event is the Handled property. It is the same as the other events.

The Search() event is fired when the user searches for text within the report. Table 14-9 lists the properties for this event type.

Table 14-9. Properties of the SearchEventArgs event type.

Property	Description
Direction	Gets or sets the direction to be backward or forward. Use a variable of the SearchDirection type.
Handled	Set to True if you do not want to search for the text.
PageNumberToBeginSearch	Gets or sets the page number to start searching.
TextToSearch	Gets or sets the string to search for.

The ViewZoom() event is fired when the user changes the zoom level of the preview image. This event lets you find out the current zoom level and what the new zoom level will be. Table 14-10 lists the properties for this event type.

Table 14-10. Properties of the ZoomEventArgs event type.

Property	Description
CurrentZoomFactor	Gets the current zoom factor.
Handled	Set to true if you do not want to change the zoom factor.
NewZoomFactor	Gets the new zoom factor.

Runtime Report Rendering Events

The ASP.NET viewer has events that let you track the progress of the report's rendering process. This is useful when your application needs to know the exact moment a report is finished rendering. For example, you could write an entry to a report log file upon completion or queue up another report for processing on a high-volume site. To do this, you can add code to the AfterRender() event. The events, listed in Table 14-5, are triggered in the following order.

BeforeRender()

BeforeRenderContent()

BeforeRenderObject() – repeated for each report object

AfterRenderObject() – repeated for each report object

AfterRenderContent()

AfterRender()

I think that the most interesting event is the BeforeRenderObject() event. It is triggered before every report object is rendered to the report. This gives you the ability to evaluate every report object as it is printed and add javascript to different browser events. For example, you can add code to the OnClick() javascript event. By using the BeforeRender() event in conjunction with javascript events, you take report customization to a whole new level.

The following code sample demonstrates how to show a pop-up window to the user when they click on text object on the report. To simplify the example, the alert message only displays the text shown in the text box.

Listing 14-10. Adding an Alert() action to a text field's OnClick() event.

[VB.NET]

```
Protected Sub CrystalReportViewer1_BeforeRenderObject(ByVal source As Object, ByVal e As _
    CrystalDecisions.Web.HtmlReportRender.BeforeRenderObjectEvent) Handles
CrystalReportViewer1.BeforeRenderObject
    Dim myText As CrystalDecisions.CrystalReports.ViewerObjectModel.TextObjectInstance
    If TypeOf e.Object Is CrystalDecisions.CrystalReports.ViewerObjectModel.TextObjectInstance Then
        myText = CType(e.Object,
CrystalDecisions.CrystalReports.ViewerObjectModel.TextObjectInstance)
        e.OnClickHandler = "alert('" & myText.getObjectText & "');"
    End If
End Sub
```

[C#]

```
protected void CrystalReportViewer1_BeforeRenderObject(object source,
    CrystalDecisions.Web.HtmlReportRender.BeforeRenderObjectEvent e)
{
    CrystalDecisions.CrystalReports.ViewerObjectModel.TextObjectInstance myField;
    if (e.Object is CrystalDecisions.CrystalReports.ViewerObjectModel.TextObjectInstance)
    {
        myField = (CrystalDecisions.CrystalReports.ViewerObjectModel.TextObjectInstance)e.Object;
        e.OnClickHandler = "alert('" + myField.getObjectText() + "');";
    }
}
```

The code first declares an object variable of type TextObjectInstance. This is within the class CrystalDecisions.CrystalReports.ViewerObjectModel. This class has a data type defined for every possible report object that can be printed on the report. You can review the help file for an official list of all the type names.

Since the BeforeRender() event is called before every report object is rendered, the code first checks the data type of the current object being rendered. The current object being printed is stored in the argument e.Object. If the types match, e.Object is cast as a TextObjectInstance data type and assigned to the object variable myText.

The last step assigns the alert() JavaScript code to the OnClickHandler() object. You can assign any JavaScript here or you could even call JavaScript functions in a common library and pass the current object as a parameter.

Unfortunately, the render events cast report objects as classes derived from the ViewerObjectModel class. The properties of this class are primarily read-only and are only useful for determining which report object is currently being printed. If they were derived from the ReportDefinition class (see Chapter 15), you could modify the properties of the report object prior to it being printed and make your reports completely customizable. But this isn't the case.

Being able to add JavaScript to each report object is a every powerful feature to have. If you were really serious about modifying the report objects during runtime, you could write JavaScript functions which take the current object and modify its properties via the JavaScript DOM. Doing it this way lets you use the browser to update the HTML rather than setting properties of the report object.

Crystal Reports also gives you a class called ViewInfo for deriving more information about the report's status. It lets you find out if the user is viewing a page in the main page, a subreport, or a drill down view. You can also determine the current page number and the last page number (if it is known). The properties of the ViewInfo class are in Table 14-11.

Table 14-11. ViewInfo class properties.

Property	Description
IsLastPageNumberKnown	Is the last page number known for the report?
IsMainReportDrillDownView	Is the report in a main report drill down view?
IsMainReportView	Is the report in a main report view?
IsSubreportDrillDownView	Is the report in a subreport drill down view?
IsSubreportView	Is the report in a subreport view?
LastPageNumber	The reports last page number.
PageNumber	The current page number

Handling Exceptions

Crystal Reports gives you the ability to handle any errors that might occur while printing and previewing. The benefit to handling the error yourself is that you can customize the error handling process. For example, you could write the error to a log file or you can gracefully exit the process without throwing an error message at the user.

The CrystalReportViewer class has an Error() event that you can subscribe to. It is fired whenever an error occurs. This event has properties to tell you the exception information and give you the option to handle it yourself. Table 14-12 lists the properties for the ExceptionEventArgs() type.

Table 14-12. Properties of the ExceptionEventArgs event type.

Property	Description
Exception	The exception class for getting the error number and description.
Handled	Set to True if you do not want the standard error message shown.

Here is sample code for handling a report error.

Listing 14-11. Handling report exceptions.

```
Private Sub CrystalReportViewer1_Error(ByVal source As System.Object, _
    ByVal e As CrystalDecisions.Windows.Forms.ExceptionEventArgs) _
    Handles CrystalReportViewer1.Error
        'put your code to handle the error here – maybe save to a log file?
        '...
        'Tell the viewer that you handled the error and suppress the error message
        e.Handled = True
End Sub
```

If you aren't using the viewer control, e.g. exporting reports, the ReportDocument class doesn't have any error handling events associated with it. You will have to use the standard Try Catch method of trapping errors.

Runtime Customization

This chapter builds on the basic report customization shown in Chapter 14. It focuses on working with the DataDefinition and ReportDefinition classes. The DataDefinition class controls Record selection, Grouping and Sorting, and Parameters/Formulas. [32] The ReportDefinition class handles the functionality for report sections, grouping/sorting and running totals. With respect to the number of objects contained within it, an object variable of the ReportDefinition type is the largest report object by far. It manages the collection objects for all the areas, sections, and report objects within a report.

If you learn best by seeing sample code, this chapter is for you!

Modifying the Record Selection

There are two types of record selection formulas. The first type selects records based upon data that is available during the first-pass stage. This consists of raw data and fields/formulas that don't use summary information. The second type of formula is a group selection formula that is based on second-pass data (e.g. summary fields and subtotals). Selecting records during the first-pass is done with the RecordsSelectionFormula property. Figure 15-1 shows the properties that modify the record selection formulas.

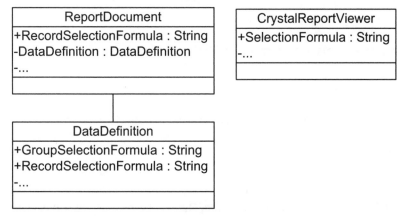

Figure 15-1. Properties used in selecting records.

The record selection formula is modified in two places: the ReportDocument class and the DataDefinition class. The properties are identical and you can use either class. Setting the

---

[32] Parameters are discussed in Chapter 16.

group selection is done with the GroupSelectionFormula and it is only found in the DataDefinition class.

The CrystalReportViewer class has a SelectionFormula property that is equivalent to the RecordSelectionFormula property. The viewer doesn't have a property for setting the group selection formula.

Modifying the record selection formulas is one of the easiest runtime changes to make to a report. The selection formula is a string and all you have to do is assign a new string to it. The formula syntax must be Crystal syntax. Basic syntax isn't allowed for selection formulas. The following code listings set the formulas to filter on records that are within a certain date range. The listings demonstrate making the change with the DataDefinition class as well as the CrystalReportViewer class.

Listing 15-1. Changing the selection formula via the ReportDocument.

[VB.NET]
```
Dim myReport As New CrystalReport1()
myReport.DataDefinition.RecordSelectionFormula = "{Orders.Order Date} in Date (1996, 02, 19) to Date (1996, 03, 28)"
CrystalReportViewer1.ReportSource = myReport
```

[C#]
```
CrystalReport1 myReport = new CrystalReport1();
myReport.DataDefinition.RecordSelectionFormula = "{Orders.Order Date} in Date (1996, 02, 19) to Date (1996, 03, 28)";
CrystalReportViewer1.ReportSource = myReport;
```

Listing 15-2. Changing the selection formula with the viewer control.

[VB.NET]
```
Dim myReport As New CrystalReport1()
CrystalReportViewer1.ReportSource = myReport
CrystalReportViewer1.SelectionFormula = "{Orders.Order Date} in Date (1996, 02, 19) to Date (1996, 03, 28)"
```

[C#]
```
CrystalReport1 myReport = new CrystalReport1();
CrystalReportViewer1.ReportSource = myReport;
CrystalReportViewer1.SelectionFormula = "{Orders.Order Date} in Date (1996, 02, 19) to Date (1996, 03, 28)"
```

I frequently see people mistake how to set the selection formula for string constants. You need to include quotes around any string data that is passed to the selection formula. Since the formula itself is a string, this makes it a little confusing. The easiest way to make this work is to either use single quotes within the string or use the ChrW(39) function. I prefer using ChrW(39) because putting a single quote next to a double quote makes your code hard to read. Here is an example.

Listing 15-3. Assigning a string constant via the ReportDocument object

[VB.NET]

```
Dim myReport As New CrystalReport1()
myReport.DataDefinition.RecordSelectionFormula = "{Customer.LastName}=" & ChrW(39) & Name & ChrW(39)
CrystalReportViewer1.ReportSource = myReport
```

 [C#]

```
CrystalReport1 myReport = new CrystalReport1();
myReport.DataDefinition.RecordSelectionFormula = "{Customer.LastName}=" + ChrW(39) & Name + ChrW(39);
CrystalReportViewer1.ReportSource = myReport;
```

Mapping the ReportDefinition Classes

The ReportDefinition class manages everything printed on a report. It has collection classes for storing each area, section, and object shown on the report. You can map out every detail about your report. Learning how to map these collections teaches you how they are organized. This is necessary for learning how to modify the individual report objects.

Figure 15-2 shows the object model for the ReportDefinition classes. It uses three collections for managing the objects: **Areas**, **Sections** and **ReportObjects**. You can see that the class tree is only a couple of levels deep and that each collection is similar to the others. This makes them easy to understand.

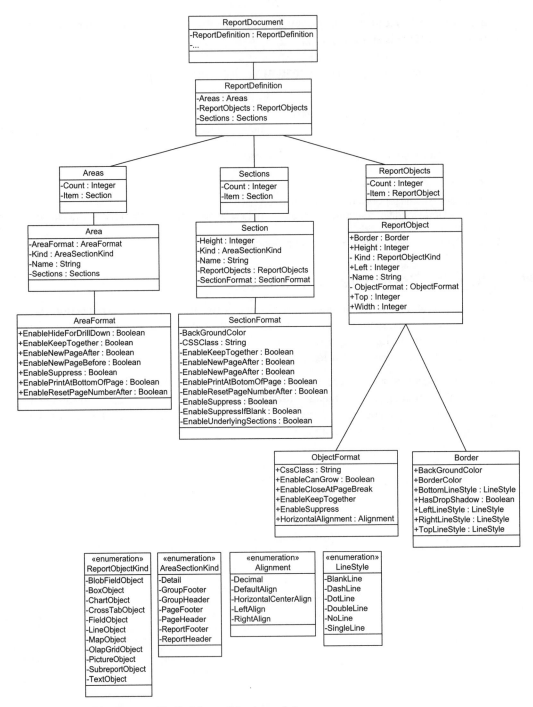

Figure 15-2. The ReportDefinition object model.

The **Areas** collection stores the **Area** object. This **Area** object has a property that lets you access its formatting properties. The **Sections** collection class stores the **Section** object. The **ReportObjects** collection manages the **ReportObject** object. It is the final object in the object model and it only has formatting properties.

Each of the collections can be referenced directly or through its parent collection. For example, you can go directly to each report object via the **ReportObjects** collection. You can also reference each report object via the section it is in. Each **Section** object has a **ReportObjects** collection that references just the report objects that are within that section.

Mapping out the report objects consists of looping through each collection and printing out the properties of each object. To be concise, this code only prints a few properties for each object. If you want to modify the code to print more properties, you can look at the object model to see the names of the additional properties and add them.

The sample program is a Windows program that uses a listbox, **lstMapping**, for the output. Each property is printed as a string in the listbox. Indentation is used to offset the object from its properties so that it is easier to read. Notice that all the parameters and variables are declared using the full namespace. You can see that this is quite lengthy and that the code could be shortened considerably by using the VB.NET **Imports** (or C# **using**) statement at the beginning of the program. However, in this book I always use the full namespace for learning purposes. The program also uses a generic **Output()** procedure for printing this information. This makes it easy for you to modify the program so that it can fit your needs. You could modify the code to save it an XML file or print to a console window.

Listing 15-4. Mapping the ReportDefinition object model.

[VB.NET]

```
Private Sub Form1_Load(ByVal sender As System.Object, _
    ByVal e As System.EventArgs) Handles MyBase.Load
    Dim myReport As CrystalDecisions.CrystalReports.Engine.ReportDocument
    myReport = New CrystalReport1()
    MapAreas(myReport.ReportDefinition.Areas, 0)
End Sub
Sub MapAreas(ByVal Areas As _
    CrystalDecisions.CrystalReports.Engine.Areas, ByVal Indent As Integer)
    Dim Area As CrystalDecisions.CrystalReports.Engine.Area
    For Each Area In Areas
        MapArea(Area, Indent)
    Next
End Sub
Sub MapSections(ByVal Sections As _
    CrystalDecisions.CrystalReports.Engine.Sections, ByVal Indent As Integer)
    Dim Section As CrystalDecisions.CrystalReports.Engine.Section
    For Each Section In Sections
        MapSection(Section, Indent)
    Next
End Sub
Sub MapReportObjects(ByVal ReportObjects As _
    CrystalDecisions.CrystalReports.Engine.ReportObjects, _
```

```
    ByVal Indent As Integer)
    Dim ReportObject As CrystalDecisions.CrystalReports.Engine.ReportObject
    For Each ReportObject In ReportObjects
        MapReportObject(ReportObject, Indent + 2)
    Next
End Sub
Sub MapArea(ByVal Area As CrystalDecisions.CrystalReports.Engine.Area, _
    ByVal Indent As Integer)
    Dim Section As CrystalDecisions.CrystalReports.Engine.Section
    'Print the Area properties
    Output("Area: " & Area.Name, Indent)
    Output("Kind: " & Area.Kind.ToString, Indent + 2)
    Output("Suppress: " & Area.AreaFormat.EnableSuppress.ToString, Indent + 2)
    Output("Keep Together: " & Area.AreaFormat.EnableKeepTogether.ToString, _
        Indent + 2)
    For Each Section In Area.Sections
        MapSection(Section, Indent + 2)
    Next
End Sub
Sub MapSection(ByVal Section As _
    CrystalDecisions.CrystalReports.Engine.Section, ByVal Indent As Integer)
    Dim ReportObject As CrystalDecisions.CrystalReports.Engine.ReportObject
    'Print the Section properties
    Output("Section: " & Section.Name, Indent)
    Output("Suppress: " & _
    Section.SectionFormat.EnableSuppress.ToString, Indent + 2)
    Output("Keep Together: " & _
    Section.SectionFormat.EnableKeepTogether.ToString, Indent + 2)
    For Each ReportObject In Section.ReportObjects
        MapReportObject(ReportObject, Indent + 2)
    Next
End Sub
Sub MapReportObject(ByVal ReportObject As _
    CrystalDecisions.CrystalReports.Engine.ReportObject, _
    ByVal Indent As Integer)
    'Explicitly cast the ReportObject as its native data type
    Select Case ReportObject.Kind
        Case CrystalDecisions.[Shared].ReportObjectKind.TextObject
            MapTextObject(CType(ReportObject, _
            CrystalDecisions.CrystalReports.Engine.TextObject), Indent)
        Case CrystalDecisions.[Shared].ReportObjectKind.FieldObject
            MapFieldObject(CType(ReportObject, _
            CrystalDecisions.CrystalReports.Engine.FieldObject), Indent)
    End Select
End Sub
Sub MapTextObject(ByVal TextObject As _
    CrystalDecisions.CrystalReports.Engine.TextObject, _
    ByVal Indent As Integer)
    Output("Name: " & TextObject.Name, Indent)
    Output("Kind: " & TextObject.Kind.ToString(), Indent + 2)
    Output("Text: " & TextObject.Text, Indent + 2)
End Sub
    Sub MapFieldObject(ByVal FieldObject As _
```

```
        CrystalDecisions.CrystalReports.Engine.FieldObject, _
        ByVal Indent As Integer)
        Output("Name: " & FieldObject.Name, Indent)
        Output("Kind: " & FieldObject.Kind.ToString(), Indent + 2)
        Output("DataSource.Name: " & FieldObject.DataSource.Name, Indent + 2)
        Output("DataSource.Formula: " & FieldObject.DataSource.FormulaName, _
        Indent + 2)
End Sub
Sub Output(ByVal Line As String, ByVal Indent As Integer)
        lstMapping.Items.Add(New String(" "c, Indent) & Line)
End Sub
```

[C#]

```
private void Form1_Load(object sender, System.EventArgs e)
{
    CrystalReport1 myReport = new CrystalReport1();
    MapAreas(myReport.ReportDefinition.Areas, 0);
}
public void MapAreas(CrystalDecisions.CrystalReports.Engine.Areas Areas, int Indent)
{
    foreach(CrystalDecisions.CrystalReports.Engine.Area Area in Areas)
    {
        MapArea(Area, Indent);
    }
}
public void MapSections(CrystalDecisions.CrystalReports.Engine.Sections Sections, int Indent)
{
    foreach(CrystalDecisions.CrystalReports.Engine.Section Section in Sections)
    {
        MapSection(Section, Indent);
    }
}
public void MapReportObjects(CrystalDecisions.CrystalReports.Engine.ReportObjects ReportObjects,
int Indent)
{
    foreach(CrystalDecisions.CrystalReports.Engine.ReportObject ReportObject in ReportObjects)
    {
        MapReportObject(ReportObject, Indent + 2);
    }
}
public void MapArea(CrystalDecisions.CrystalReports.Engine.Area Area, int Indent)
{
    Output("Area: " + Area.Name, Indent);
    Output("Kind: " + Area.Kind.ToString(), Indent+2);
    Output("Suppress: " + Area.AreaFormat.EnableSuppress.ToString(), Indent+2);
    Output("Keep Together: " + Area.AreaFormat.EnableKeepTogether.ToString(), Indent+2);
    foreach(CrystalDecisions.CrystalReports.Engine.Section Section in Area.Sections)
    {
        MapSection(Section, Indent + 2);
    }
}
public void MapSection(CrystalDecisions.CrystalReports.Engine.Section Section, int Indent)
```

```
{
   //Print the Section properties
   Output("Section: " + Section.Name, Indent);
   Output("Suppress: " + Section.SectionFormat.EnableSuppress.ToString(), Indent);
   Output("Keep Together: " + Section.SectionFormat.EnableKeepTogether.ToString(), Indent);
   foreach(CrystalDecisions.CrystalReports.Engine.ReportObject ReportObject in
Section.ReportObjects)
   {
      MapReportObject(ReportObject, Indent + 2);
   }
}
public void MapReportObject(CrystalDecisions.CrystalReports.Engine.ReportObject ReportObject, int
Indent)
{
   switch(ReportObject.Kind)
   {
      case CrystalDecisions.Shared.ReportObjectKind.TextObject:
      {
         MapTextObject(((CrystalDecisions.CrystalReports.Engine.TextObject)ReportObject), Indent);
         break;
      }
      case CrystalDecisions.Shared.ReportObjectKind.FieldObject:
      {
         MapFieldObject(((CrystalDecisions.CrystalReports.Engine.FieldObject)ReportObject), Indent);
         break;
      }
   }
}
public void MapTextObject(CrystalDecisions.CrystalReports.Engine.TextObject TextObject, int Indent)
{
   Output("Name: " + TextObject.Name, Indent);
   Output("Kind: " + TextObject.Kind.ToString(), Indent + 2);
   Output("Text: " + TextObject.Text, Indent + 2);
}
public void MapFieldObject(CrystalDecisions.CrystalReports.Engine.FieldObject FieldObject, int Indent)
{
   Output("Name: " + FieldObject.Name, Indent);
   Output("Kind: " + FieldObject.Kind.ToString(), Indent + 2);
   Output("DataSource.Name: " + FieldObject.DataSource.Name, Indent + 2);
   Output("DataSource.Formula: " + FieldObject.DataSource.FormulaName, Indent + 2);
}
public void Output(string Line, int Indent)
{
   lstMapping.Items.Add(new string(' ',Indent) + Line);
}
```

Most of this code is pretty simple. It consists of procedures that use For Each loops to traverse a collection. While traversing the collection, the object's properties are printed and if there is a sub-collection, it is traversed as well.

There are some interesting aspects of the code that need to be explored. Notice that there are three main mapping procedures: MapAreas, MapSections, and MapReportObjects.

These directly correspond to the three distinct collections of the ReportDefinition class. The top-most collection is the Areas collection. This collection can be used to reference the Sections collection, which is used to reference the ReportObjects collection. But when you look at the object model previously shown in Figure 15-2, these collections each have their own property in the ReportDefinition class. Thus, you can also go directly to the Sections or ReportObjects collections.

This example uses the form's Load() event to call the MapAreas() procedure so that you can see how the entire object hierarchy is mapped out. But you can isolate the individual collections by replacing the MapAreas() call with a call to either MapSections() or MapReportObjects().

The MapReportObject() procedure (near the end of the listing) also deserves mentioning. The ReportObject class isn't used to represent any actual objects on your report. Instead, it is the base class for those objects. You have to explicitly cast the object as the proper data type before working with it. The actual report objects are shown in Figure 15-3. They are all very similar to each other, and some properties are even repeated. But each one has at least a few properties that make it unique from the other classes.

FieldObject

```
+Border
+Color
-DataSource : FieldDefinition
-FieldFormat
+Font
+Height : Integer
-Kind : ReportObjectKind
+Left : Integer
-Name : String
+ObjectFormat : ObjectFormat
+Top : Integer
+Width : Integer
```
```
+ApplyFont()
```

FieldDefinition

```
-FormulaName : String
-Kind : FieldKind
-Name : String
-ValueType : FieldValueType
```

BlobFieldObject

```
+Border
-DataSource : FieldDefinition
+Height : Integer
-Kind : ReportObjectKind
+Left : Integer
-Name : String
+ObjectFormat : ObjectFormat
+Top : Integer
+Width : Integer
```

TextObject

```
+Border
+Color
- Font
+Height : Integer
- Kind : ReportObjectKind
+Left : Integer
-Name : String
+ObjectFormat : ObjectFormat
+Top : Integer
+Width : Integer
+Text : String
```
```
+ApplyFont()
```

SubreportObject

```
+Border
+EnableOnDemand : Boolean
+Height : Integer
-Kind : ReportObjectKind
+Left : Integer
-Name : String
+ObjectFormat : ObjectFormat
+Top : Integer
+Width : Integer
```
```
+OpenSubreport()
```

LineObject

```
+Border
+EnableExtendToBottomOfSection : Boolean
+EndSectionName : String
+Height : Integer
-Kind : ReportObjectKind
+Left : Integer
+LineColor
+LineStyle : LineStyle
+LineThickness : Integer
-Name : String
+ObjectFormat : ObjectFormat
+Top : Integer
+Width : Integer
```

PictureObject / ChartObject / CrossTabObject

```
+Border
+Height : Integer
-Kind : ReportObjectKind
+Left : Integer
-Name : String
+ObjectFormat : ObjectFormat
+Top : Integer
+Width : Integer
```

BoxObject

```
+Border
+EnableExtendToBottomOfSection : Boolean
+EndSectionName : String
+FillColor
+Height : Integer
-Kind : ReportObjectKind
+Left : Integer
+LineColor
+LineStyle : LineStyle
+LineThickness : Integer
-Name : String
+ObjectFormat : ObjectFormat
+Top : Integer
+Width : Integer
```

Figure 15-3. The report classes that inherit from the ReportObject class.

When mapping out the report objects, there is no immediate way to know what type of object is being referenced. Fortunately, the ReportObject class has a property that identifies this. The Kind property tells you what type of object it is. The MapReportObject() procedure uses a Select Case statement to determine what type of report object it is, and calls the proper mapping procedure. When it calls the mapping procedure, the report object variable is cast as the proper class within the parameter list. This listing only shows the code for mapping the TextObject and the FieldObject, but it is simple to add the other objects if you wish.

Let's run this program on a sample report. I made a few changes to the label report from Chapter 6. The names of the sections were changed so that they are descriptive. By default, when you create a report, the section names are given generic names such as Section1, Section2, etc. Since the Crystal Reports designer prints a section description next to the section name, this normally isn't a problem. But the mapping example prints out raw text and doesn't have the designer available, so the names were changed to make it easier to read the output. The changes to the section names are shown in Figure 15-4. The area names can't be changed, so they will always use the generic naming convention.

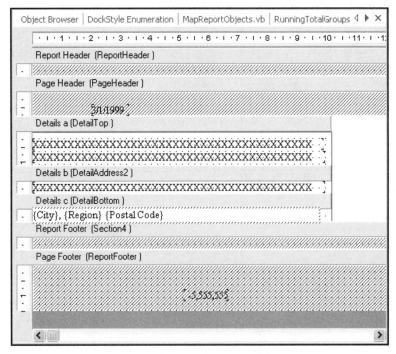

Figure 15-4. The report designer for the labels report.

This example is fairly simple so that most of the important output can be shown here. Most of the sections simply show a text box that represents a field of the customer's address. The different headers and footers are suppressed so that only the Detail sections are shown. There are three Detail sections and they are all part of the same area. Thus, the output should show a single Area object with three detail sections listed.

The section DetailBottom is a text field that is composed of three fields and a comma to separate the City from the Region[33]. When you look at this field in the example's output, it only shows a comma. Thus, the actual composition of the field is stored in an internal format that you can't access. This is shown near the bottom of the output.

---

[33] Normally, this is shown in the designer as "XXXXX". But for the illustration I double-clicked on it so that it would be placed in edit mode. This lets you see how the field is composed.

```
Area: Areal
  Kind: ReportHeader
  Suppress: False
  Keep Together: False
  Section: ReportHeader
    Suppress: True
    Keep Together: True
Area: Area2
  Kind: PageHeader
  Suppress: False
  Keep Together: True
  Section: PageHeader
    Suppress: True
    Keep Together: True
    Name: Field5
      Kind: FieldObject
      DataSource.Name: PrintDate
      DataSource.Formula: PrintDate
Area: Area3
  Kind: Detail
  Suppress: False
  Keep Together: False
  Section: DetailTop
    Suppress: False
    Keep Together: True
    Name: Field9
      Kind: FieldObject
      DataSource.Name: Name
      DataSource.Formula: {@Name}
    Name: Field10
      Kind: FieldObject
      DataSource.Name: Address1
      DataSource.Formula: {Employee_Addresses.Address
  Section: DetailAddress2
    Suppress: False
    Keep Together: True
    Name: Field11
      Kind: FieldObject
      DataSource.Name: Address2
      DataSource.Formula: {Employee_Addresses.Address
  Section: DetailBottom
    Suppress: False
    Keep Together: True
    Name: Text1
      Kind: TextObject
      Text: ,
Area: Area4
  Kind: ReportFooter
```

Figure 15-5. Mapping the objects of the label report.

Programming the ReportDefinition Objects

The ReportDefinition classes are used for modifying all the report objects. With every object, you can modify the formatting properties to change its appearance. Some of the objects, such as the TextObject and FieldObject, can have their content modified. This isn't the case for every report object. This section shows you how to get a reference to the report object and how to modify its properties.

Before learning the details of the ReportDefinition object, you need to understand the limitations. First of all, the object model is designed so that you can modify the objects, but not add new ones. In other words, none of the collections have an Add() method. For example, if your report has two text objects, you are free to change what they display, but you can't add any additional text objects.

Secondly, not all properties can be modified. Flip back at Figures 15-2 and 15-3. The properties with a + next to them are read-write. The properties with a - are read-only. As you can see, most properties are read-only. Although you can't modify everything, many important properties can be changed.

Referencing the Report Objects

To modify any of the objects, declare an object variable of the proper data type and have it reference the report object. Referencing the report object is done by passing the object name to the Item property of the collection and assigning this to the object variable. Of course, use the appropriate collection to get a reference to the object you want. Don't try to reference a Section object with the Areas() collection.

Listing 15-5. Get a reference to the ReportFooter section.

[VB.NET]

```
Dim myReport As New CrystalReport1()
Dim mySection As CrystalDecisions.CrystalReports.Engine.Section
mySection = myReport.ReportDefinition.Sections.Item("ReportFooter")
```

[C#]

```
CrystalReport1 myReport = new CrystalReport1();
CrystalDecisions.CrystalReports.Engine.Section mySection;
mySection = myReport.ReportDefinition.Sections["ReportFooter"];
```

Report object variables can be declared as either the ReportObject base class or the classes for the specific object (e.g. TextObject, BoxObject, etc.) The benefit to using the object's specific class is that you have access to its unique properties. The ReportObject class has generic properties that apply to all the report objects, but not to the specific ones.

Listing 15-6. Get a reference to the report object State using the ReportObject data type.

[VB.NET]

```
Dim myReport As New CrystalReport1()
Dim myObject As CrystalDecisions.CrystalReports.Engine.ReportObject
myObject = myReport.ReportDefinition.ReportObjects.Item("State")
```

[C#]

```
CrystalReport1 myReport = new CrystalReport1();
CrystalDecisions.CrystalReports.Engine.ReportObject myObject;
myObject = myReport.ReportDefinition.ReportObjects["State"];
```

Listing 15-7. Get a reference to the State object using the object's specific data type.

[VB.NET]

```
Dim myReport As New CrystalReport1()
Dim myField As CrystalDecisions.CrystalReports.Engine.FieldObject
myField = CType(myReport.ReportDefinition.ReportObjects.Item("State"), _
CrystalDecisions.CrystalReports.Engine.FieldObject)
```

[C#]

```
CrystalReport1 myReport = new CrystalReport1();
CrystalDecisions.CrystalReports.Engine.FieldObject myField;
myField = (CrystalDecisions.CrystalReports.Engine.FieldObject)
myReport.ReportDefinition.ReportObjects["State"];
```

Note

Referencing a section can be a little tricky because you might use the wrong name for it. When you look at the report in design mode, a section appears to have two names. The first name is a description of the section (e.g. Page Header, Details, etc.) but this isn't the name that it's referenced by. It's simply a description so that you know what the purpose of the section is. Right after the description is the name enclosed in parentheses: Page Header (Section2). In this example, Section2 is the name that you should use when referencing the section from the Sections collection. You will also see the section name listed in the properties window under the Name property.

Modifying the Report Object Properties

The Area class and Section class have similar properties to each other. You can enable or disable formatting properties such as suppressing the object, keeping the object on the same page, and printing it at the bottom of the page. The difference between the two is that every section has to be within an area. Any formatting done to the area will affect all the sections within the area. But formatting done to a section will not affect the area it is in. Nor will other sections in the area be affected.

The ReportObject class is the base class for the objects that are used in a report. It has some of the basic formatting options that are common to all objects. For example, there are properties in the class for changing the objects positioning on the report. You can modify the Top and Left properties as well as the Left and Width properties. You can also modify the object's border using the Border property and its various Enable related options (Suppress, KeepTogether, etc.) using the ObjectFormat property.

To modify the properties that are unique to an individual report object, the object variable must be declared as the proper data type. For example, declaring an object variable of the type LineObject lets you modify the LineThickness property. Assign the report object to the variable by explicitly casting it as the proper data type. The next few examples demonstrate modifying different objects on a report.

Listing 15-8. Modify properties of the ReportFooter section.

[VB.NET]

```
Dim myReport As New CrystalReport1()
Dim mySection As CrystalDecisions.CrystalReports.Engine.Section
```

```
mySection = myReport.ReportDefinition.Sections.Item("ReportFooter")
mySection.SectionFormat.EnableKeepTogether = True
mySection.SectionFormat.EnableSuppress = False
CrystalReportViewer1.ReportSource = myReport
```

[C#]

```
CrystalReport1 myReport = new CrystalReport1();
CrystalDecisions.CrystalReports.Engine.Section mySection;
mySection = myReport.ReportDefinition.Sections["ReportFooter"];
mySection.SectionFormat.EnableKeepTogether = true;
mySection.SectionFormat.EnableSuppress = false;
crystalReportViewer1.ReportSource = myReport;
```

Listing 15-9. Modify the border of the report object State using the ReportObject data type.

[VB.NET]

```
Dim myReport As New CrystalReport1()
Dim myObject As CrystalDecisions.CrystalReports.Engine.ReportObject
myObject = myReport.ReportDefinition.ReportObjects.Item("State")
myObject.Border.TopLineStyle = CrystalDecisions.[Shared].LineStyle.SingleLine
myObject.Border.BottomLineStyle = CrystalDecisions.[Shared].LineStyle.DoubleLine
CrystalReportViewer1.ReportSource = myReport
```

[C#]

```
CrystalReport1 myReport = new CrystalReport1();
CrystalDecisions.CrystalReports.Engine.ReportObject myObject;
myObject = myReport.ReportDefinition.ReportObjects["State"];
myObject.Border.TopLineStyle = CrystalDecisions.Shared.LineStyle.SingleLine;
myObject.Border.BottomLineStyle = CrystalDecisions.Shared.LineStyle.DoubleLine;
crystalReportViewer1.ReportSource = myReport;
```

Listing 15-10. Modify the line properties of the object Line using the object's specific data type.

[VB.NET]

```
Dim myReport As New CrystalReport1()
Dim myLine As CrystalDecisions.CrystalReports.Engine.LineObject
myLine = CType(myReport.ReportDefinition.ReportObjects.Item("Line1"), _
CrystalDecisions.CrystalReports.Engine.LineObject)
myLine.LineStyle = CrystalDecisions.[Shared].LineStyle.DashLine
CrystalReportViewer1.ReportSource = myReport
```

[C#]

```
CrystalReport1 myReport = new CrystalReport1();
CrystalDecisions.CrystalReports.Engine.LineObject myLine;
myLine = (CrystalDecisions.CrystalReports.Engine.LineObject)
myReport.ReportDefinition.ReportObjects["Line1"];
myLine.LineStyle = CrystalDecisions.Shared.LineStyle.DashLine;
crystalReportViewer1.ReportSource = myReport;
```

The TextObject lets you modify the content that an object displays on the report. It has a Text property that sets what is displayed. Simply assign a string to it to change its contents.

Listing 15-11. Modify the Text property of a TextObject located in ReportHeader.

[VB.NET]

```
Dim myReport As New CrystalReport1()
Dim myText As CrystalDecisions.CrystalReports.Engine.TextObject
myText = CType(myReport.ReportDefinition.ReportObjects.Item("HeaderText"), _
CrystalDecisions.CrystalReports.Engine.TextObject)
myText.Text = "New Report Header"
CrystalReportViewer1.ReportSource = myReport
```

[C#]

```
CrystalReport1 myReport = new CrystalReport1();
CrystalDecisions.CrystalReports.Engine.TextObject myText;
myText = (CrystalDecisions.CrystalReports.Engine.TextObject)
myReport.ReportDefinition.ReportObjects["HeaderText"];
myText.Text = "New Report Header";
crystalReportViewer1.ReportSource = myReport;
```

The FieldObject object is used to print fields from a data source. You can't modify it. The DataSource property is a FieldDefinition class and this is where the content is stored. Unfortunately, it is a read-only property and you aren't allowed to modify it. This applies to database fields, running totals, summary fields, etc. The only way to modify these fields is to base them off of a formula and modify that formula during runtime. This is discussed in Chapter 16.

Grouping and Sorting Data

The Crystal Reports object model lets you examine how a report is sorted, grouped and what type of data is summarized. You can change many of these properties prior to running the report.

Since the sorting and grouping features of a report are so closely related, it makes sense that their classes are also closely related. Within these classes there is overlap because grouping is an advanced form of sorting. Grouping has more features and within each group you have to sort the records that it prints. The respective classes for sorting and grouping are shown in Figure 15-6.

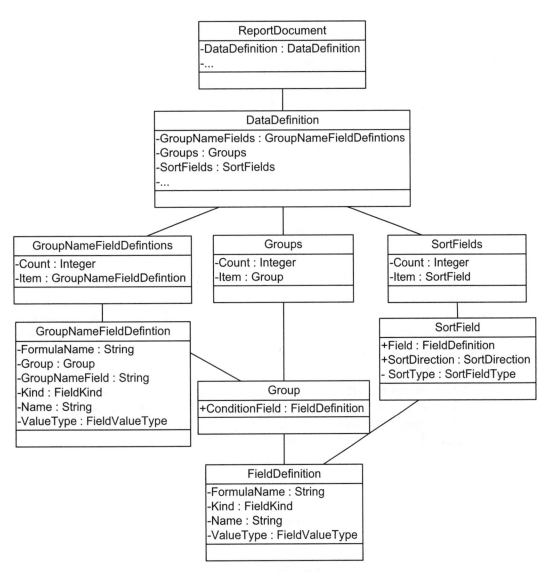

Figure 15-6. The Sorting and Grouping object model.

Many of the classes have properties that are enumeration constants. These are documented in Figure 15-7.

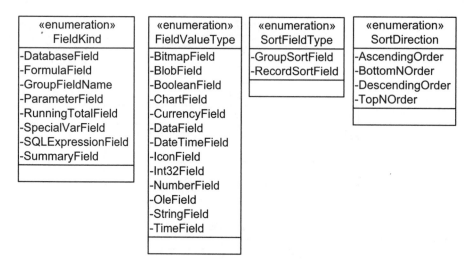

Figure 15-7. Sorting and Grouping enumeration constants.

Sorting and grouping are both based on one thing: a field. The field determines what the sort order is and how the records are grouped. Whether this field is a report field, database field or a formula field isn't important. But without a field you can't have sorting or grouping. Thus, the field classes are shared throughout the class diagram and you need to understand how they are organized before you can work with sorting and grouping.

The ReportDocument.DataDefinition class has the collections that manage the sorting and grouping fields. Groups are managed with the Groups collection and the GroupNameFieldDefinitions collection. The primary means of working with these collections is by using a For Each loop.

The sort fields are referenced using the SortFields collection. The SortFields collection is a property of the DataDefinition object. Navigate through this collection using a For Each loop.

The SortFields collection stores SortField objects. The SortField object has properties that determine the sort field, sort direction, and whether it represents a simple record sort or a group. The SortField class is defined in the namespace CrystalDecisions.CrystalReports.Engine.

An interesting aspect about the SortFields collection is that it assigns a SortField object for each group in the report. This is because group fields have to be sorted prior to determining what order the groups are printed in.

The grouping fields are referenced using two collections: Groups and GroupNameFieldDefinitions. These collections are a property of the DataDefinition object. Navigate through these collections using a For Each loop.

Both group collections have properties for storing the object's name, the formula, the data type and whether it is a report field, formula field, etc. Since both collections give you the same information, the one you decide to use is more of a personal preference than a hard and fast rule. Each collection has its own pros and cons.

The GroupNameFieldDefinitions collection gives you more direct access to the group properties (e.g. the name, field kind, etc.). However, this collection has a lot of redundancy in it because it also has a reference to the Group object. Within the Group object is the ConditionField object and this object gives you the same information already in the GroupFieldNameDefinition object.

The Groups collection is pretty simple because it only references the Group object. Each Group object has all the information that you need and there is no redundancy. Another benefit is that the FieldDefinition class is the same class used to map the report fields and formula fields. This lets you quickly change the fields that a group is based on. You can also do this with the GroupNameFieldDefinitions collection, but not as direct.

To keep things simple, I will only use the Groups collection to work with the group objects. If you prefer to use the GroupNameFieldDefinitions collection, it is easy to modify the sample code.

Mapping the Grouping and Sorting Objects

To learn how to use the different sorting and grouping classes, let's start with some generic procedures that traverse the collections in a report and print out the various properties. The code isn't very complicated because it primarily consists of For Each loops to traverse the collection objects and print out the properties of each object. The important part is to look at which collections manage which objects and see how the object variables are declared.

Listing 15-12. Mapping the sorting and grouping objects.[34]

[VB.NET]

```
Private Sub Form1_Load(ByVal sender As System.Object, _
    ByVal e As System.EventArgs) Handles myBase.Load
    Dim myReport As New CrystalReport1()
    MapSortFields(myReport.DataDefinition.SortFields, 0)
    Output("-----", 0)
    MapGroups(myReport.DataDefinition.Groups, 0)
End Sub
Sub MapSortFields(ByVal SortFields As _
    CrystalDecisions.CrystalReports.Engine.SortFields, _
    ByVal Indent As Integer)
    Dim SortField As CrystalDecisions.CrystalReports.Engine.SortField
    Output("Total SortFields: " & SortFields.Count, Indent)
    For Each SortField In SortFields
        MapSortField(SortField, Indent)
    Next
```

---

[34] The sample code only prints out a few of the properties for each object. This example is not meant to be comprehensive.

```
End Sub
Sub MapSortField(ByVal SortField As _
   CrystalDecisions.CrystalReports.Engine.SortField, _
   ByVal Indent As Integer)
   MapFieldDefinition(SortField.Field, Indent)
   Output("Direction:" & SortField.SortDirection.ToString, Indent + 2)
   Output("Type:      " & SortField.SortType.ToString(), Indent + 2)
End Sub
Sub MapGroups(ByVal Groups As _
   CrystalDecisions.CrystalReports.Engine.Groups, ByVal Indent As Integer)
   Dim Group As CrystalDecisions.CrystalReports.Engine.Group
   Output("Total Groups: " & Groups.Count, Indent)
   For Each Group In Groups
      MapGroup(Group, Indent)
   Next
End Sub
Sub MapGroup(ByVal Group As CrystalDecisions.CrystalReports.Engine.Group, _
   ByVal Indent As Integer)
   MapFieldDefinition(Group.ConditionField, Indent)
End Sub
Sub MapFieldDefinition(ByVal FieldDefintion As CrystalDecisions. _
   CrystalReports.Engine.FieldDefinition, ByVal Indent As Integer)
   Output("Field Name: " & FieldDefintion.Name, Indent)
   Output("Formula:" & FieldDefintion.FormulaName, Indent + 2)
   Output("Kind:      " & FieldDefintion.Kind.ToString(), Indent + 2)
   Output("Value Type: " & FieldDefintion.ValueType.ToString(), Indent + 2)
End Sub
Sub Output(ByVal Line As String, ByVal Indent As Integer)
   lstMapping.Items.Add(New String(" "c, Indent) & Line)
End Sub
```

[C#]

```
private void Form1_Load(object sender, System.EventArgs e)
{
   CrystalReport1 myReport = new CrystalReport1();
   MapSortFields(myReport.DataDefinition.SortFields, 0);
   Output("---",0);
   MapGroups(myReport.DataDefinition.Groups, 0);
}
public void MapSortFields(CrystalDecisions.CrystalReports.Engine.SortFields SortFields, int Indent)
{
   Output("Total SortFields: " + SortFields.Count, Indent);
   foreach(CrystalDecisions.CrystalReports.Engine.SortField SortField in SortFields)
   {
      MapSortField(SortField, Indent);
   }
}
public void MapSortField(CrystalDecisions.CrystalReports.Engine.SortField SortField, int Indent)
{
   MapFieldDefinition(SortField.Field, Indent);
   Output("Direction: " + SortField.SortDirection.ToString(), Indent + 2);
   Output("Type: " + SortField.SortType.ToString(), Indent + 2);
```

```
}
public void MapGroups(CrystalDecisions.CrystalReports.Engine.Groups Groups, int Indent)
{
    Output("Total Groups: " + Groups.Count, Indent);
    foreach(CrystalDecisions.CrystalReports.Engine.Group Group in Groups)
    {
        MapGroup(Group, Indent + 2);
    }
}
public void MapGroup(CrystalDecisions.CrystalReports.Engine.Group Group, int Indent)
{
    MapFieldDefinition(Group.ConditionField, Indent);
}
public void MapFieldDefinition(CrystalDecisions.CrystalReports.Engine.FieldDefinition FieldDefinition,
int Indent)
{
    Output("Field Name: " + FieldDefinition.Name, Indent);
    Output("Formula: " + FieldDefinition.FormulaName, Indent + 2);
    Output("Kind: " + FieldDefinition.Kind.ToString(), Indent + 2);
    Output("Value Type: " + FieldDefinition.ValueType.ToString(), Indent + 2);
}
public void Output(string Line, int Indent)
{
    lstMapping.Items.Add(new string(' ',Indent) + Line);
}
```

Mapping the properties of the sort objects is done by instantiating the report object and passing the DataDefinition.SortFields collection to the MapSortFields() procedure. This procedure prints the number of sort fields in the collection and traverses the collection. It calls MapSortFields() which calls MapSortField() for each object in the SortFields collection. The MapSortField() procedure calls the MapFieldDefinition() procedure to print out the details of the field object. It prints the sort direction and whether this is a group sort or a record sort.

Mapping the properties of the group classes is done by instantiating the report object and passing the DataDefinition.Groups collection to the MapGroups() procedure. This procedure prints the number of groups in the report and traverses the collection. The MapGroups() procedure calls the MapGroup() procedure for each group object. The Group object has one property, ConditionField, which is of type FieldDefinition. So the MapGroup() procedure only calls the MapFieldDefinition() procedure to print out the properties of the field.

To see the output created by this program, I created a simple report.[35] The report is a sales report that prints the order detail from the Extreme.mdb database. It prints all the orders for each month. The group field is the Order Date and it groups the date by month. The most recent month is printed first, so a descending sort order is used. Within each group,

---

[35] I'm not going into the details of how to create the sample report. The important part is to understand the general structure of the report so that the program's output makes sense.

the details of the order for each product are shown. These records are sorted by order date. Thus, the order date is being used in two different ways. The groups are sorted by month in a descending fashion and the detail records are sorted by the individual order date in an ascending order. Figure 15-8 shows the report designer and Figure 15-9 shows the report preview.

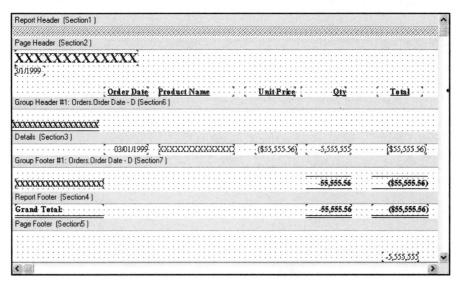

Figure 15-8. The Sales Report in the report designer.

MainReport					

Sales Report
6/2/2002

	Order Date	Product Name	Unit Price	Qty	Total
5/1998					
	05/01/1998	Triumph Pro Helmet	$39.81	2	$79.62
	05/01/1998	Triumph Pro Helmet	$41.90	3	$125.70
	05/01/1998	Triumph Vertigo	$51.21	1	$51.21
	05/01/1998	Triumph Vertigo	$53.90	2	$107.80
	05/01/1998	Triumph Vertigo	$53.90	1	$53.90
	05/01/1998	Guardian Chain Lock	$4.50	2	$9.00
	05/01/1998	InFlux Crochet Glove	$13.50	3	$40.50
	05/01/1998	InFlux Crochet Glove	$13.50	2	$27.00
	05/01/1998	InFlux Crochet Glove	$13.50	2	$27.00
	05/01/1998	Xtreme Youth Helmet	$33.90	2	$67.80
	05/01/1998	Xtreme Rhino Lock	$9.98	3	$29.94
	05/01/1998	Xtreme Titan Lock	$36.01	3	$108.03
	05/01/1998	Xtreme Anatomic	$14.50	3	$43.50
	05/01/1998	Descent	$2,939.85	1	$2,939.85
	05/01/1998	Descent	$2,792.86	3	$8,378.58
	05/01/1998	Mozzie	$1,739.85	1	$1,739.85
	05/01/1998	Nicros	$329.85	1	$329.85
	05/02/1998	Active Outdoors	$14.50	3	$43.50
	05/02/1998	Active Outdoors	$16.50	2	$33.00
	05/02/1998	Triumph Vertigo	$53.90	2	$107.80
	05/02/1998	Xtreme Wide MTB	$14.50	3	$43.50
	05/02/1998	Roadster Mini Mtn	$15.00	1	$15.00
	05/02/1998	Descent	$2,939.85	2	$5,879.70
	05/02/1998	Mozzie	$1,739.85	3	$5,219.55
	05/02/1998	Wheeler	$539.85	3	$1,619.55
	05/02/1998	Rapel	$479.85	2	$959.70
5/1998				**56.00**	**$28,080.43**
4/1998					
	04/01/1998	Active Outdoors	$14.50	3	$43.50
	04/01/1998	InFlux Crochet Glove	$13.50	1	$13.50
	04/02/1998	Active Outdoors	$14.50	2	$29.00
	04/02/1998	Active Outdoors	$14.50	3	$43.50

Figure 15-9. The preview of the Sales Report.

The sample application is run using this report and the output is shown in Figure 15-10. You can see that the SortFields collection has two items in it: the group field and the sort field. The last property listed for each field tells whether it belongs to a group or is an individual sort record. After listing the sort objects, the program lists the group objects. In this example, the report only has one group. You can see that there isn't as much information for the group field. Although it tells you about the field that is being grouped, it doesn't tell you what direction the sort is. You can only find this out by browsing the SortFields collection.

```
Total SortFields: 2
Field Name: Order Date
  Formula:    {Orders.Order Date}
  Kind:       DatabaseField
  Value Type: DateTimeField
  Direction:  DescendingOrder
  Type:       GroupSortField
Field Name: Order Date
  Formula:    {Orders.Order Date}
  Kind:       DatabaseField
  Value Type: DateTimeField
  Direction:  AscendingOrder
  Type:       RecordSortField
-----
Total Groups: 1
Field Name: Order Date
  Formula:    {Orders.Order Date}
  Kind:       DatabaseField
  Value Type: DateTimeField
```

Figure 15-10. The output of the mapping application.

Programming the Grouping and Sorting Objects

The sorting and grouping objects in a report can be modified during runtime. You can use a form to have the user enter criteria to modify the default properties of a report and your program can change the report to meet these criteria. Modifying the objects during runtime is very powerful, but it requires you to understand what the limitations are.

Just like you learned at the beginning of the chapter, you can't add new report objects to the report. Secondly, only certain properties can be modified. The properties with a + can be modified and the ones with a − are read-only.

The SortField class controls how the fields are sorted. You can modify the SortDirection property to set whether it is ascending or descending. Listing 15-13 shows how to modify the SortDirection property.

Although the Groups collection appears to give you complete access to the group objects, it is missing the sort direction. You can't use the Groups collection exclusively and find out whether the group is being sorted ascending or descending. You have to use the SortFields collection to modify a group's sort order.

Listing 15-13. Changing the sort direction of a field

[VB.NET]

```
Private Sub btnModifySorting_Click(ByVal sender As System.Object, _
    ByVal e As System.EventArgs) Handles btnModifySorting.Click
    Dim myReport As New CrystalReport1()
    Dim crSortFields As CrystalDecisions.CrystalReports.Engine.SortFields
    Dim crSortField As CrystalDecisions.CrystalReports.Engine.SortField
    'Modify the sort order of the OrderDate field to be Descending
    'Access the fields by traversing the sort fields collection
    crSortFields = myReport.DataDefinition.SortFields
```

```
      For Each crSortField In crSortFields
        If crSortField.Field.Name = "Order Date" Then
          'There are two differnt sorts with this field name.
          'Make sure its a record sort
          If crSortField.SortType = _
             CrystalDecisions.[Shared].SortFieldType.RecordSortField Then
             crSortField.SortDirection = _
             CrystalDecisions.[Shared].SortDirection.DescendingOrder
          End If
        End If
      Next
      CrystalReportViewer1.ReportSource = myReport
End Sub
```

[C#]

```
private void btnModifySorting_Click(object sender, System.EventArgs e)
{
   CrystalReport1 myReport = new CrystalReport1();
   //Modify the order of the OrderDate field to Descending
   //Reference the fields by traversing the sort fields collection
   foreach(CrystalDecisions.CrystalReports.Engine.SortField mySortField in
      myReport.DataDefinition.SortFields)
   {
      if (mySortField.Field.Name == "Last Name")
      {
         //There are two different sort objects with this name
         //Make sure its a record sort.
         if (mySortField.SortType ==
         CrystalDecisions.Shared.SortFieldType.RecordSortField)
         {
            mySortField.SortDirection =
            CrystalDecisions.Shared.SortDirection.DescendingOrder;
         }
      }
      crystalReportViewer1.ReportSource = myReport;
   }
}
```

This example uses a form with a button on it which changes the sorting order of the report used in the last example. When the user clicks on the button, it loads the report into the object variable **myReport**. The **SortFields** collection is traversed looking for the **SortField** with a name property of "Order Date". In this example report, there are two fields with this name. This is because the group section is based upon the order date's month, and within the group the individual records are sorted by the day of the order date.

Once it matches the name of the field, it has to check if this is the field for the group section or the individual record. When it is certain that it has the object for the individual record, it changes the sort order to descending. Once this is finished, the report object is assigned to the viewer. If you wanted to modify the sort order for the group section, you would do it here, but instead you would check if the field is of type **GroupSortField**. The report output is shown in Figure 15-11.

	Order Date	Product Name	Unit Price	Qty
5/1998				
	05/02/1998	Active Outdoors	$14.50	3
	05/02/1998	Active Outdoors	$16.50	2
	05/02/1998	Triumph Vertigo	$53.90	2
	05/02/1998	Xtreme Wide MTB	$14.50	3
	05/02/1998	Roadster Mini Mtn	$15.00	1
	05/02/1998	Descent	$2,939.85	2
	05/02/1998	Mozzie	$1,739.85	3
	05/02/1998	Wheeler	$539.85	3
	05/02/1998	Rapel	$479.85	2
	05/01/1998	Triumph Pro Helmet	$39.81	2
	05/01/1998	Triumph Pro Helmet	$41.90	3
	05/01/1998	Triumph Vertigo	$51.21	1
	05/01/1998	Triumph Vertigo	$53.90	2
	05/01/1998	Triumph Vertigo	$53.90	1
	05/01/1998	Guardian Chain Lock	$4.50	2
	05/01/1998	InFlux Crochet Glove	$13.50	3
	05/01/1998	InFlux Crochet Glove	$13.50	2
	05/01/1998	InFlux Crochet Glove	$13.50	2
	05/01/1998	Xtreme Youth Helmet	$33.90	2
	05/01/1998	Xtreme Rhino Lock	$9.98	3
	05/01/1998	Xtreme Titan Lock	$36.01	3
	05/01/1998	Xtreme Anatomic	$14.50	3
	05/01/1998	Descent	$2,939.85	1
	05/01/1998	Descent	$2,792.86	3
	05/01/1998	Mozzie	$1,739.85	1
	05/01/1998	Nicros	$329.85	1
5/1998				**56.00**
4/1998				

Figure 15-11. Report output after modifying the sort order.

Both the SortField class and Group class have a property that lets you modify the field they are based on. It is called Field in the Sort class and called ConditionField in the Group class. Both are of the type FieldDefinition. To modify this property, you have to set it to a reference of an existing field object. Thus, the field must already exist somewhere on the report. This field could be a field from one of the report tables or a formula field. Listing 15-14 demonstrates how to change the field by modifying the group object. This code works the same way for modifying a sort field.

Listing 15-14. Modifying a group's field

[VB.NET]

```
Private Sub btnModifyGrouping_Click(ByVal sender As System.Object, _
    ByVal e As System.EventArgs) Handles btnModifyGrouping.Click
    Dim myReport As New CrystalReport1()
    Dim crGroups As CrystalDecisions.CrystalReports.Engine.Groups
    Dim crGroup As CrystalDecisions.CrystalReports.Engine.Group
    Dim crField As CrystalDecisions.CrystalReports.Engine.DatabaseFieldDefinition
    'Modify the group to use CustomerName rather than OrderDate
```

```
'Get the field to base the group on
crField = myReport.Database.Tables("Customer").Fields("Customer Name")
'Access the group by traversing the groups collection
crGroups = myReport.DataDefinition.Groups
For Each crGroup In crGroups
   If crGroup.ConditionField.Name = "Order Date" Then
      crGroup.ConditionField = crField
   End If
Next
CrystalReportViewer1.ReportSource = myReport
End Sub
```

[C#]

```
private void btnModifyGrouping_Click(object sender, System.EventArgs e)
{
   CrystalReport1 myReport = new CrystalReport1();
   CrystalDecisions.CrystalReports.Engine.DatabaseFieldDefinition myField;
   //Modify the group to use CustomerName rather than Orderdate
   //Get the field to base the group on
   myField = myReport.Database.Tables["Employee"].Fields["First Name"];
   //Reference the group by traversing the Groups collection
   foreach(CrystalDecisions.CrystalReports.Engine.Group myGroup in
myReport.DataDefinition.Groups)
   {
      if (myGroup.ConditionField.Name == "Last Name")
      {
         myGroup.ConditionField = myField;
      }
   }
   crystalReportViewer1.ReportSource = myReport;
}
```

This example uses another button on the same form as the last example and it also modifies the original report example. It changes the group from being based on Order Date to using the Customer Name field.

It first uses the **Tables** collection to get a reference to the Customer Name field from the Customers table.[36] It loops through the Groups collection to find the correct **Group** object. The field is changed by setting the **ConditionField** to the field object variable. Once this is finished, the report object is assigned to the viewer and the viewer is refreshed. The output is shown in Figure 15-12.

---

[36] See Chapter 17 for a discussion of tables.

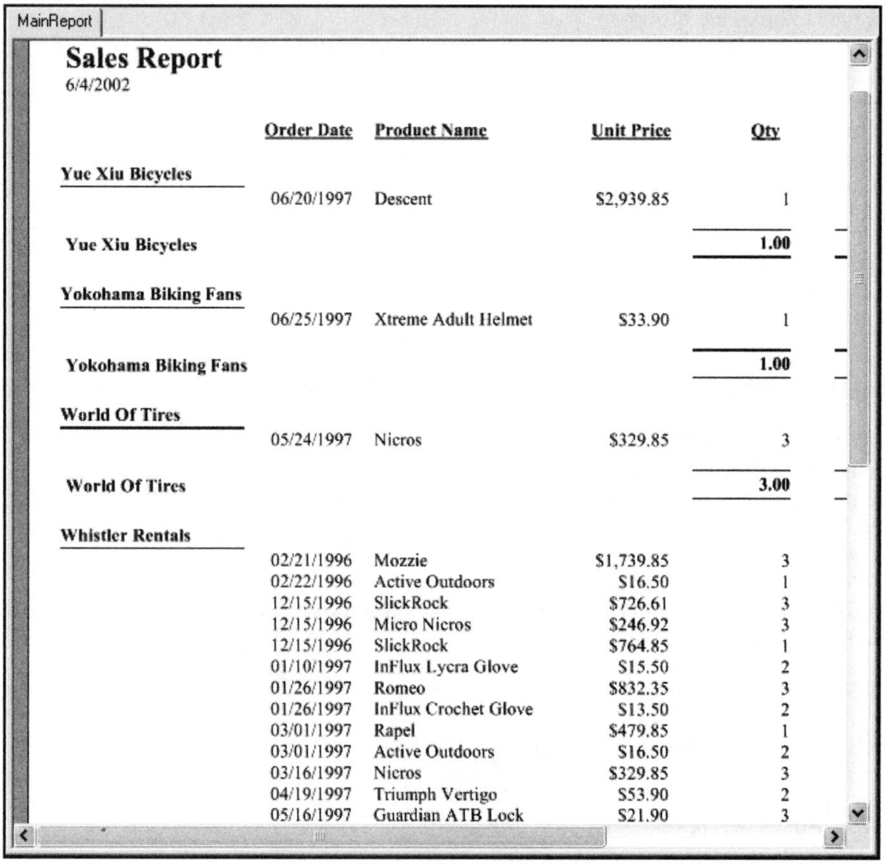

MainReport

Sales Report
6/4/2002

	Order Date	Product Name	Unit Price	Qty
Yue Xiu Bicycles				
	06/20/1997	Descent	$2,939.85	1
Yue Xiu Bicycles				**1.00**
Yokohama Biking Fans				
	06/25/1997	Xtreme Adult Helmet	$33.90	1
Yokohama Biking Fans				**1.00**
World Of Tires				
	05/24/1997	Nicros	$329.85	3
World Of Tires				**3.00**
Whistler Rentals				
	02/21/1996	Mozzie	$1,739.85	3
	02/22/1996	Active Outdoors	$16.50	1
	12/15/1996	SlickRock	$726.61	3
	12/15/1996	Micro Nicros	$246.92	3
	12/15/1996	SlickRock	$764.85	1
	01/10/1997	InFlux Lycra Glove	$15.50	2
	01/26/1997	Romeo	$832.35	3
	01/26/1997	InFlux Crochet Glove	$13.50	2
	03/01/1997	Rapel	$479.85	1
	03/01/1997	Active Outdoors	$16.50	2
	03/16/1997	Nicros	$329.85	3
	04/19/1997	Triumph Vertigo	$53.90	2
	05/16/1997	Guardian ATB Lock	$21.90	3

Figure 15-12. Report output after modifying the group field.

Understanding the Summary Field Classes

The summary field classes are referenced with the SummaryField property of the DataDefinition class.

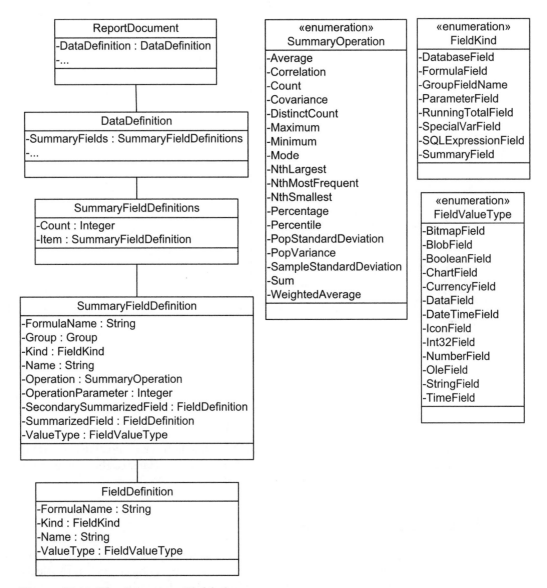

Figure 15-13. The Summary Field classes.

The SummaryField property is a collection of SummaryFieldDefinition objects. Each object contains all the information about each summary field: the field, the summary operation, etc. Unfortunately, it is missing one key piece of data: the section it is located in. There are no properties to tell you if it is a subtotal or a grand total. This is an important piece of information that you need to know about a field. To see how much information is provided to you, look at Figure 15-14. It is the output of the Mapping application for the SummaryField collection. You can see that there is no way to determine which fields are subtotals and which ones are grand totals.

```
Total SummaryFieldDefinitions: 4
Field Name: {Orders_Detail.Quantity}
  Formula:     {Orders_Detail.Quantity}
  Kind:        DatabaseField
  Value Type: Int32sField
  Operation:  Sum
  Parameter:  0
  Value Type: NumberField
Field Name: {@ItemTotalPrice}
  Formula:     {@ItemTotalPrice}
  Kind:        FormulaField
  Value Type: CurrencyField
  Operation:  Sum
  Parameter:  0
  Value Type: CurrencyField
Field Name: {Orders_Detail.Quantity}
  Formula:     {Orders_Detail.Quantity}
  Kind:        DatabaseField
  Value Type: Int32sField
  Operation:  Sum
  Parameter:  0
  Value Type: NumberField
Field Name: {@ItemTotalPrice}
  Formula:     {@ItemTotalPrice}
  Kind:        FormulaField
  Value Type: CurrencyField
  Operation:  Sum
  Parameter:  0
  Value Type: CurrencyField
```

Figure 15-14. The summary fields mapping output.

While accessing all the summary fields from the DataDefinition class is possible, you aren't given enough information to make it practical. It is better to reference these fields from within the sections they are located in.

Modifying Subreports

Modifying the properties of a subreport is the same as modifying the properties of any report. Throughout this book, there is code for modifying report objects such as the fields, groups and formatting, and there is code for setting login information. Every line of the code samples can be used on a subreport without making any changes. This is because subreports are also derived from the ReportDocument class just like the main report is.

The only difference with modifying subreports is how you get a reference to them. When you add a subreport to the main report, it is derived from the class **SubReportObject**. But the **SubreportObject** class doesn't let you modify the report objects. Instead, you have to instantiate the subreport as a new **ReportDocument** object variable. Use this object variable to modify all the properties and objects of the subreport.

There are two ways of getting a reference to subreport objects. The first way is to call the **ReportDocument.OpenSubreport()** method and pass it the subreport name. The second way is looping through the **ReportObjects** collection of the main report and finding each subreport. Referencing the subreport by name is much easier because you only have to call a single method. But that doesn't mean that looping through the **ReportObjects** collection is frivolous. There is a reason for using both methods.

Use the **OpenSubreport()** method when you want to modify the properties of only one of the subreports. For example, you could have a subreport with salary information and it gets suppressed if the user doesn't have permission to view it.

Looping through the **ReportObjects** collection is used when you want to apply the same modification to all the subreports. As each subreport is found, call a method which performs an operation on it and returns to look for more subreports. An example of this is setting the login credential for every subreport.

Let's look at a couple of examples to see how it all works. The first example opens a subreport using the subreport's name.

Listing 15-15. Open a subreport using the subreport name.

[VB.NET]

```
Dim myReport As New CrystalReport1
Dim mySubReport As CrystalDecisions.CrystalReports.Engine.ReportDocument
Dim myReportObject As CrystalDecisions.CrystalReports.Engine.ReportObject
Dim myTextObject As CrystalDecisions.CrystalReports.Engine.TextObject
mySubReport = myReport.OpenSubreport("Sales Subreport")
myReportObject = mySubReport.ReportDefinition.ReportObjects.Item("Text3")
myTextObject = CType(myReportObject, CrystalDecisions.CrystalReports.Engine.TextObject)
myTextObject.ObjectFormat.EnableSuppress = True
CrystalReportViewer1.ReportSource = myReport
```

[C#]

```
CrystalReport1 myReport = new CrystalReport1();
CrystalDecisions.CrystalReports.Engine.ReportDocument mySubReport;
CrystalDecisions.CrystalReports.Engine.ReportObject myReportObject;
CrystalDecisions.CrystalReports.Engine.TextObject myText;
mySubReport = myReport.OpenSubreport("Sales Subreport");
myText = (CrystalDecisions.CrystalReports.Engine.TextObject)
    myReport.ReportDefinition.ReportObjects["Text3"];
myText.ObjectFormat.EnableSuppress = true;
crystalReportViewer1.ReportSource = myReport;
```

After declaring the necessary variables, the first line of code calls the OpenSubreport() method of the report. This method takes the name of the subreport and instantiates a new ReportDocument object for the subreport. Notice that the variable mySubReport is declared as a ReportDocument class. In this example I used "Sales Subreport", but you should replace this with the name of your subreport.

At this point, the variable mySubReport is just like any ReportDocument object variable that is used throughout this book. Modify its properties as you normally would. For illustration purposes, I got a reference to the Text3 object and suppressed it. The last step is assigning the main report object variable to the viewer so that the user can preview it.

As you can see, using the OpenSubreport() method is very simple. But there is one part that could cause you some confusion: figuring out the report name. The subreport has multiple names depending upon what part of the report designer you are looking at. The most obvious way of getting the report name is to look at the report object on the designer.

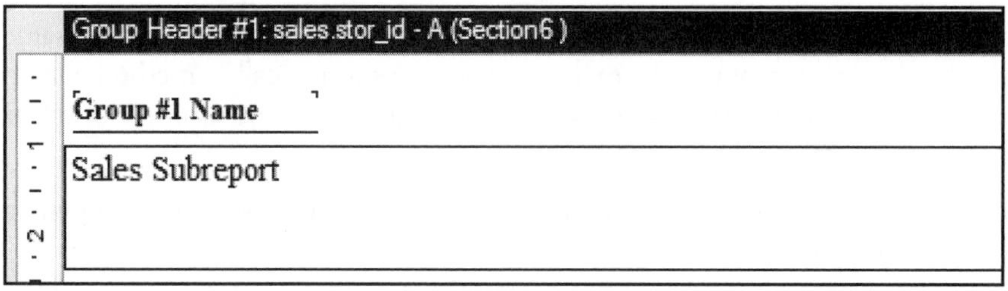

Figure 15-15. The subreport object in the designer.

In Figure 15-15 the subreport's name is Sales Subreport. Luckily, if you get the name in this way, you are correct. The tricky part is if you look in the Properties Window. The name is listed here as Subreportx (e.g. Subreport1). This is not the name that should be passed to the OpenSubreport() method. To make things even more unusual, try double-clicking on the subreport to open it in the designer. Look at the Properties Window under the Report property. The Report property for the subreport lists the main report's name, not its own name.

The second way of referencing a subreport is to loop through the ReportObjects collection and find each subreport. The next example uses this technique to clear the record selection formula of all subreports.

Listing 15-16. Find subreports using the ReportObjects collection.

[VB.NET]

```
Dim mySubReport As CrystalDecisions.CrystalReports.Engine.ReportDocument
Dim mySubReportObject As CrystalDecisions.CrystalReports.Engine.SubreportObject
Dim myReportObject As CrystalDecisions.CrystalReports.Engine.ReportObject
Dim myReport As New CrystalReport1
For Each myReportObject In myReport.ReportDefinition.ReportObjects
    If myReportObject.Kind = CrystalDecisions.[Shared].ReportObjectKind.SubreportObject Then
```

```
        mySubReportObject = CType(myReportObject,
CrystalDecisions.CrystalReports.Engine.SubreportObject)
        mySubReport = myReport.OpenSubreport(mySubReportObject.SubreportName)
        mySubReport.RecordSelectionFormula = ""
    End If
Next
CrystalReportViewer1.ReportSource = myReport
```

[C#]

```
CrystalReport1 myReport = new CrystalReport1();
CrystalDecisions.CrystalReports.Engine.SubreportObject mySubreportObject;
CrystalDecisions.CrystalReports.Engine.ReportDocument mySubreport;
foreach(CrystalDecisions.CrystalReports.Engine.ReportObject myReportObject in
myReport.ReportDefinition.ReportObjects)
{
    if (myReportObject.Kind == CrystalDecisions.Shared.ReportObjectKind.SubreportObject){
        mySubreportObject = (CrystalDecisions.CrystalReports.Engine.SubreportObject)myReportObject;
        mySubreport = mySubreportObject.OpenSubreport(mySubreportObject.SubreportName);
        mySubreport.RecordSelectionFormula = "";
    }
}
crystalReportViewer1.ReportSource = myReport;
```

Listing 15-16 gets a reference to each report object in the **ReportObjects** collection. It tests the **Kind** property to see if the object is a subreport. If it is, it assigns the report object to a variable by explicitly casting it as the **SubreportObject** class. You need to cast it as the **SubreportObject** class because this class has a property called **SubreportName**. Pass the **SubreportName** property to the main report's **OpenSubreport()** method. The object variable **mySubReport** is a **ReportDocument** object that holds the subreport. Just like the last listing, you can now modify the properties of the subreports using the properties and methods of the **ReportDocument** class. This example clears the record selection formula so that none of the subreports use any filtering. Once all the report objects have been examined and all the subreports have been modified, assign the main report object variable to the **ReportSource** property of the viewer so that the report can be previewed.

Modifying Formulas and Parameters

Formulas and parameters are the two primary ways of customizing reports. For example, formulas let you create new calculations using existing the report date as well as customizing the report's formatting. Parameters allow the user to specify the report criteria and customize each report according to their needs. This lets the report be tailored for each user printing it.

The Crystal Reports object model makes it easy for you to modify both formulas and parameters within your application. By calling a couple simple methods, you can use data from your application to override the report's existing formulas and parameter values. This makes it possible to apply an application's business rules across one or more reports with very little effort. The remainder of this chapter shows you the steps for overriding a report's functions and parameter values.

Modifying Formulas

To override a formula, pass the formula name to the **FormulaFields** collection and assign the new formula to the Text property. The tricky part is knowing the proper way to assign data to the formula. Formulas are always stored internally as a string and the syntax for storing each data type to the formula is slightly different.

When overriding the text of an existing formula, you must use Crystal syntax. The Crystal Reports object model doesn't let you use Basic syntax when overriding formulas from a .NET application. Oddly enough, it doesn't matter if the formula was originally written using Basic syntax. You always have to use Crystal syntax. The runtime engine only has access to the Crystal syntax compiler and it can't interpret Basic syntax.

Invalid Index Error

When referring to a formula name in your .NET application, don't put @ in front of the formula name. Although this is required when referencing formulas from within a report, it isn't used by .NET when referencing report objects via the object model. You'll get the error Invalid Index if you do so.

Numbers

To assign a number to a formula, simply use the text equivalent of that number. No special formatting is needed

Listing 16-1. Assigning numbers to formulas

[VB.NET]

```
'Assign the value 999 to the formula called CustomerId
myReport.DataDefinition.FormulaFields("CustomerId").Text = "999"
'Assign the integer variable UserId to the formula called UserId
myReport.DataDefinition.FormulaFields("UserId").Text = UserId.ToString()
```

[C#]

```
//Assign the value 999 to the formula called CustomerId
myReport.DataDefinition.FormulaFields["CustomerId"].Text = "999";
//Assign the integer variable UserId to the formula called UserId
myReport.DataDefinition.FormulaFields["UserId"].Text = UserId.ToString();
```

Strings

Programmers frequently use the wrong syntax when assigning a string variable to a formula. Since both the formula and the variable are the same data type, it's easy to think that you can just assign the variable to the **Text** property. Most people forget to put quotes around the variable so that Crystal Reports knows that you are passing it a string. Otherwise, it doesn't know how to interpret the data. You could be trying to pass a formula, a report field, etc. Putting quotes around the data makes it clear to Crystal Reports that it should interpret it as a string constant.

Listing 16-2. Assigning strings to formulas

[VB.NET]

```
'Assign the string variable NewName to the formula called Name
myReport.DataDefinition.FormulaFields("Name").Text = Chr(39) & NewName & Chr(39)
'Override the formula ReportTitle
myReport.DataDefinition.FormulaFields("ReportTitle").Text = "'New Report Title'"
'Override a formula with a string and data field concatenated together
myReport.DataDefinition.FormulaFields("InvoiceHeader").Text = _
Chr(39) & "Invoice Number:" & Chr(39) & "+Cstr({Invoices.InvoiceNumber})"
```

[C#]

```
//Assign the string variable NewName to the formula called Name
myReport.DataDefinition.FormulaFields["Name"].Text = (char)39 + NewName + (char)39;
//Override the formula ReportTitle
myReport.DataDefinition.FormulaFields["ReportTitle"].Text = "'New Report Title'";
//Override a formula with a string and data field concatenated together
myReport.DataDefinition.FormulaFields["InvoiceHeader"].Text =
(char)39 + "Invoice Number:" + (char)39 + "+Cstr({Invoices.InvoiceNumber})";
```

The first example assigns the variable **NewName** to the formula. Notice that it is surrounded by the function **Chr(39)** to hard-code a single quote around the value. You could also use **Chr(34)** to surround it with double-quotes because Crystal Reports uses them both interchangeably.[37] In the second example, rather than using the **Chr()** function, it uses

---

[37] Just make sure that you are consistent with what is used before and after the string variable. You can't put a single quote before the variable and a double quote after the variable.

the single quote within the string constant. This is acceptable as well, but I prefer using the Chr() function because the single quote is hard to read when it is located next to a double quote.

The third example concatenates a string constant with a report field. Again, notice how the quotes are used around the text. Since the formula is telling Crystal Reports to concatenate string together, the & operator is used. Lastly, the InvoiceNumber field is a number so we have to use the CStr() function to tell Crystal Reports to convert it from a number to a string. If you are just concatenating two strings together, the CStr() function isn't necessary

Dates

Dates are similar to numbers in that they must be converted to their string equivalent. The tricky part is that you have to use the proper syntax so that Crystal Reports knows you are assigning a date to the formula. You can use any of the date conversion functions that come with Crystal Reports or surround it with #.

Listing 16-3. Assigning dates to formulas

[VB.NET]
```
'Assign today's date to the formula called PrintDate
myReport.DataDefinition.FormulaFields("PrintDate").Text = _
"#" & DateTime.Now.ToShortDateString() & "#"
'Assign the date variable InvoiceDate to the formula called PrintDate.
myReport.DataDefinition.FormulaFields("PrintDate").Text = _
"CDate(" & Chr(39) & InvoiceDate & Chr(39) & ")"
```

[C#]
```
//Assign today's date to the formula called PrintDate
myReport.DataDefinition.FormulaFields["PrintDate"].Text =
"#" + DateTime.Now.ToShortDateString() + "#";
//Assign the date variable InvoiceDate to the formula called PrintDate.
myReport.DataDefinition.FormulaFields["PrintDate"].Text =
"CDate(" + (char)39 + InvoiceDate.ToShortDateString() & (char)39 + ")";
```

The first example surrounds the date with # to tell Crystal Reports it is a date constant. The second example is a little more tricky because it uses the CDate() function to convert the string to a date. The tricky part isn't the use of CDate(), it's the fact that since CDate() requires a string constant to be passed to it, you need to surround the string with quotes. If you don't include the Chr(39) function before and after the string, you will get a very strange date on your report.

"The remaining text does not appear to be part of the formula"

When there are problems with modifying a formula during runtime, you get this error. Unfortunately, the error doesn't give you any indication of what is wrong. The easiest way to debug formulas is to use the report designer. It gives you the exact error message and is much easier to figure out. Go into debug mode in Visual Studio and use the Command Window to print the Text property of the formula. Copy this text to the Notepad program and stop your application. Open the report and use the Formula Editor to copy this text to the formula and save it. Crystal Reports will check the formula's syntax and give you an error message that is more descriptive.

Modifying the Current Values in a Parameter

A problem with parameters is that the user interface for prompting the user to enter a value isn't very exciting. Crystal Reports uses its own dialog box to prompt the user and it is generic and bland. Fortunately, Crystal Reports .NET lets you override a parameter's default behavior. When opening a report with parameters, you can use a form in your project that prompts the user for all the relevant data and pass this directly to the report. Or you could use business logic to determine the data passed to the parameter. This gives your reports a consistent interface with your application so that the user feels that the two are truly integrated. You also get the benefit of validating user input prior to printing the report. This reduces the chances of an error occurring when running reports.

Note

Parameters have two different ways to classify values: Current and Default. Current values are the data that the user types into the Enter Parameters dialog box when printing the report. Default values are the data that is presented to the user in a list format so that he can pick which data he wants the report filtered on. Default values are usually set when the report is being designed and don't change very often. The following sections discuss the code necessary to set a parameter's current values. The code for overriding the default values is discussed later in this chapter.

To modify a report parameter, call the SetParameterValue() method of the ReportDocument class. Pass it the parameter name and the new parameter value.

myReport.SetParameterValue("Country", "USA")

The SetParameterValue() method also lets you pass it a subreport name if you need to modify a parameter that is in a subreport.

myReport.SetParameterValue("Country", "USA", "Subreport1")

Invalid Index Error

When referring to a parameter name in your .NET application, don't put a ? in front of the name. Although this is required when referencing parameters from within a report using Basic syntax, it isn't used by .NET when referencing report objects via the object model. You'll get the Invalid Index error if you do so. However, if this is a report parameter that is also used as a stored procedure parameter, you need to put "@" in front of the name. This is required by the SQL Server naming convention.

The SetParameterValue() method is very flexible. It accepts any data type and assigns it to the parameter (assuming you use a compatible data type). Unlike the previous section on overriding formulas, you don't have to convert the data to its string equivalent or worry about surrounding string data with quotes.

Since the SetParameterValue() method is so easy to use, it does have it's limitations. They are listed below.

- Can't modify a parameter's default values list.

- Can't be used to set parameters with the ASP.NET or Windows report viewer classes.

- Can't modify any properties of the parameter object model.

Luckily, these are not significant limitations because the majority of the work you do with parameters won't be affected. I would say that for most people, the SetParameterValue() method is all that you need to learn. If you find that these limitations don't let you perform the work you need to do, a more thorough discussion of how to use the parameter classes to do advanced customization is discussed later in the following section.

Parameters have many different types of data that can be assigned to them. A parameter can hold a discrete value (a number, string, etc) or it can hold more complex values such as range values, multiple values, and a combination of discrete and range values. Assigning data to a parameter becomes increasingly complex as you exploit all of the types of data it can hold. In the next few sections we're going to learn how to assign the different data to a parameter. As the data becomes more complex, you will need to increase your understanding of the classes that manage parameters and see how Crystal Reports stores parameters. We'll start off simple and build from there.

Note

The code samples in the following sections all use the ReportDocument class. The CrystalReportsViewer class has different methods and properties than the ReportDocument class and this code will not work with it. Modifying parameters using the CrystalReportsViewer class is discussed later in this chapter.

Discrete Values

Discrete values consist of a single value that is a simple data type. It can be a number, string date or Boolean. To assign it to a parameter, you only need the parameter name and the new value. The first example assigns a string value to the parameter and the second example assigns today's date to the parameter.

Listing 16-4. Assign discrete values to parameters

[VB.NET]

```
myReport.SetParameterValue("Country", "USA")
myReport.SetParameterValue("PrintDate", DateTime.Now())
```

[C#]

```
myReport.SetParameterValue("Country", "USA");
myReport.SetParameterValue("PrintDate", DateTime.Now());
```

Range Values

Assigning range values to a parameter is a little more complicated because there isn't a compatible data type in the .NET syntax. Instead, you have to declare and instantiate an object variable using the **ParameterRangeValue** class. When using this class, there are two properties used for setting the range: **StartValue** and **EndValue**.

Listing 16-5. Assign range values to parameters

[VB.NET]

```
Dim myParameterName as String = "IdRange"
Dim myParameterRangeValue As New CrystalDecisions.Shared.ParameterRangeValue()
'Assign the start and end values to the parameter object
myParameterRangeValue.StartValue = 1000
myParameterRangeValue.EndValue = 1999
'Reference the actual parameter stored in the report's ParameterFields collection
myReport.SetParameterValue(myParameterName, myParameterRangeValue)
```

[C#]

```
string myParameterName = "IdRange";
CrystalDecisions.Shared.ParameterRangeValue myParameterRangeValue = new
CrystalDecisions.Shared.ParameterRangeValue();
//Assign the start and end values to the parameter object
myParameterRangeValue.StartValue = 1000;
myParameterRangeValue.EndValue = 1999;
'Reference the actual parameter stored in the report's ParameterFields collection
myReport.SetParameterValue(myParameterName, myParameterRangeValue);
```

This listing first declares two variables: one for storing the parameter name and one for storing the range value. The next two lines assign the start and end points for the range value. Both of these properties are declared as an Object and you can pass them any simple data type. Lastly, this code uses the **SetParameterValue()** method to assign the range value to the parameter. Once it's finished, you can preview the report and it will have the new parameter value.

Multiple Values

You can pass multiple values to a parameter using an array. Simply create and populate the array and pass it to the SetParameterValue() method.

Listing 16-6. Assign multiple values to a parameter

[VB.NET]

```
Dim InvoiceDates(1) As Date
InvoiceDates(0) = Date.Parse("2/1/2001")
InvoiceDates(1) = Date.Parse("2/5/2001")
'Assign the array to the parameter value
myReport.SetParameterValue("InvoiceDatesParam", InvoiceDates)
```

[C#]

```
DateTime[] InvoiceDates = new DateTime[2];
InvoiceDates[0] = DateTime.Parse("2/1/2001");
InvoiceDates[1] = DateTime.Parse("2/5/2001");
//Assign the array to the parameter value
myReport.SetParameterValue("InvoiceDatesParam", InvoiceDates);
```

This listing creates an array that stores two dates. This array is passed to report using the SetParameterValue() method prior to previewing the report.

Passing an array is very powerful because the array can consist of simple data types, the ParameterRangeValue class, or a combination of the two. For example, if you wanted to pass multiple range values to the parameter, declare the array using the ParameterRangeValue class and use the code in listing 16-5 to instantiate and assign data to each range value.

Crystal Reports also lets you combine multiple discrete and range values in a single parameter. To populate this type of parameter in your code, declare the array using the Object class and assign whatever combination of data you want to it. For example, you could assign date constants to some of the elements in the array and assign ParameterRangeValue objects to the other elements (assuming that each range also uses the date data type). You need to be careful that the array doesn't accidentally have different data types. For example, you can't store a number in some of the elements and string in the others.

Best Of The Forum

Question: In my Windows application, I assign the parameters to the report prior to the user viewing it. But when the user clicks the refresh button, the Enter Parameter Values dialog box pops up and makes the user re-enter them. How do I prevent this?

Answer: If this were an ASP.NET application, you could set the viewer property ReuseParameterValuesOnRefresh to True and this wouldn't happen.

However, as mentioned in Chapter 3, the Windows viewer doesn't have this property. You have to handle the RefreshReport() event and assign the parameters to the ReportDocument object again. You also have to set the e.Handled property to True so the viewer knows that you already loaded the parameters. Here is a simple code snippet that demonstrates this.

```
'Common code to load a report and set a parameter value
Private Sub LoadReport()
    Dim myReport As New CrystalReport1()
    myReport.SetParameterValue("NameFilter", TextBox1.Text)
    CrystalReportViewer1.ReportSource = myReport
End Sub
'Handle the ReportRefresh() event
Private Sub CrystalReportViewer1_ReportRefresh(ByVal source As System.Object, _
    ByVal e As CrystalDecisions.Windows.Forms.ViewerEventArgs) _
    Handles CrystalReportViewer1.ReportRefresh
    LoadReport()
    'Tell the viewer that the event was handled
    e.Handled = True
End Sub
```

Learning the Parameter Classes

Up to this point in the chapter, all the work you've done with parameters used the SetParameterValue() method. This method is useful because it is easy to use and it covers over 90% of the work that most people will do with parameters. If the previous sections showed you everything you need to update parameters in your application, you don't need the rest of this chapter and you can skip forward. However, as mentioned earlier, the SetParameterValue() method does have its limitations. If you find that you need to do advanced parameter customization, you need to learn the parameter object model in detail so that you understand each parameter class and the methods and properties available. The remainder of this chapter focuses on explaining the parameter object model and giving you sample code to work with its methods and properties.

The parameter object model is designed to give you complete control over almost every property of parameter. The majority of its properties have write access. This lets you modify parameters during runtime so that you can set the current value and the user isn't prompted to enter it via the parameter dialog boxes. If you still want the user to use the parameter dialog boxes, you can modify the default values so that you have control over what values the user chooses from.

The object model uses three different collections to manage parameters. These collections are listed in Table 16-1. The ParameterFieldDefinitions collection manages the parameters in the ReportDocument class. The ParameterFields collection manages the parameters in the CrystalReportViewer class. A parameter can store one value or multiple values. Since a parameter can store multiple values, a collection is used to save this data. This collection is called the ParameterValues collection. It is shared between both

ParameterFieldDefinitions and ParameterFields for storing CurrentValues and DefaultValues collections (both are a ParameterValues collection).

Table 16-1. The three types of parameter collections.

Collection	Purpose
ParameterFieldDefinitions	Manages the parameters in the ReportDocument class. It is fully populated with all the parameters. Found in the CrystalDecisions.CrystalReports. Engine namespace.
ParameterFields	Manages parameters in the CrystalReportViewer class. It is empty by default. Found in the CrystalDecisions.Shared namespace.
ParameterValues	Manages the values stored within each parameter object. The ParameterFieldDefinitions collection and the ParameterFields collection both use this class. Found in the CrystalDecisions.Shared namespace.

Caution

The naming convention for the parameter classes gives them the potential to be confusing to learn. The class DataDefinition uses the classes ParameterFieldDefinitions and ParameterFieldDefinition. The CrystalReportViewer class has similar class names: ParameterFields and ParameterField. The names are almost the same except that the DataDefinition classes have the word 'Definition' appended to them. This helps make it clear which class each is associated with. However, the property name in the DataDefinition class for the ParameterFieldDefinitions collection is called ParameterFields. This is the same name as the collection class in the viewer classes. Having a property that has the same name as a non-compatible class can be very confusing. If you aren't careful, you might see the ParameterFields property in the DataDefinition class and accidentally look at the object model for the ParameterFields class in the CrystalReportViewer class instead.[38]

The parameter classes are designed with two approaches in mind. The first approach is that you are using the CrystalReportViewer control to preview the report. The second approach

---

[38] When I first stared working with parameters, I didn't notice that the names were identical, but the classes were different. This caused me many headaches until I realized what the problem was.

is modifying parameters with the ReportDocument object. Both approaches can be used to modify the current value or the default values. But they do so in different ways.

The object model in Figure 16-1 shows two columns of classes. The left column has the classes related to the ReportDocument object. The right column has the classes for the CrystalReportViewer class. At the bottom of the diagram are the classes that store the actual parameter values. These classes are shared by both columns.

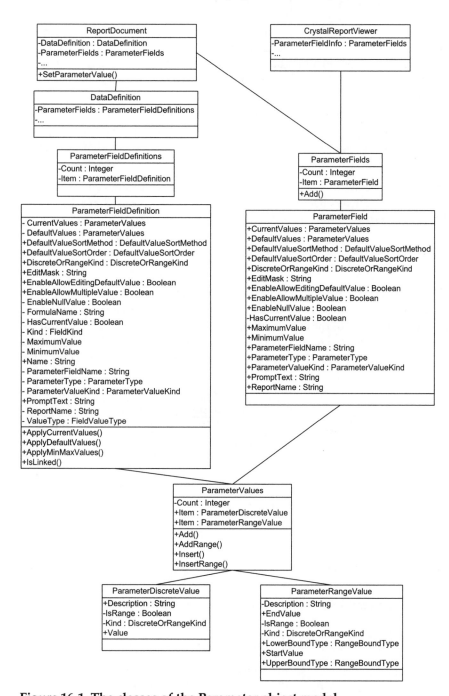

Figure 16-1. The classes of the Parameter object model.

When looking at the individual classes of both columns in more detail, you see that there are a lot of similarities between them. Let's start at the top and work our way down. The top most classes are the ReportDocument class and CrystalReportViewer class. Below the ReportDocument class is the DataDefinition class. Below each class is a collection class that stores the parameters. Under the collection class is the actual parameter field class. The two parameter field classes, ParameterFieldDefinition and ParameterField, have all the properties that you set when using the Create New Parameter dialog box in design mode (e.g. prompt text, min and max values, sort order, etc.). You can see that they have many properties in common.

The parameter field classes use a collection class to store the current values and the default values. The ParameterValues collection holds ParameterValue objects. Since the current value and default value of a parameter can store either a single discrete value or a range of values, there are two classes that are used to represent this. The ParameterDiscreteValue class only holds a single value. The ParameterRangeValue class stores a range value (it has an upper and lower range).

All of the parameter classes have a variety of properties that are enumeration data types. These enumerations are used to store a pre-determined set of values that the property can have. Since there are so many of the enumeration types, they are listed separately from the main parameter object model. See Figure 16-2 for each enumeration used. Since these represent the options that you can set for a parameter, they have already been discussed in Chapter 5.

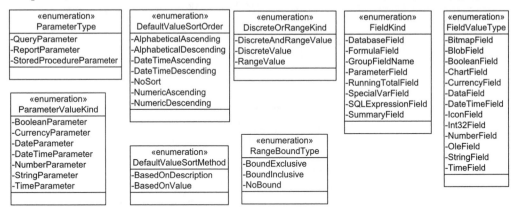

Figure 16-2. The enumeration constants of the Parameter object model.

Defining Default Values and Current Values

Before you can use the parameter classes to pass values to the parameter objects, you need to understand how values are classified. When a report with parameters loads, the user is shown a dialog box to enter values for each parameter. The dialog box frequently shows a pre-populated list of values to choose from. The values in the list are called Default Values.

When the user enters a value for a parameter, it could be a single value or possibly multiple values. The value that the user enters is called the Current Value.

A .NET program can modify either the default values or the current values. To design your application so that the user enters all the values on a .NET form and doesn't get the parameter dialog box, set the current values with your application. On the other hand, you might let the user get prompted with the parameter dialog box and you will set the default values listed. For example, you can simulate a data-bound listbox by setting the default value list to show data stored in a table. This is done by overriding the default values that were assigned to the parameter when the report was designed.

Note

When setting parameter values, either set the current value or the default values, but not both. Setting the current value and setting the default values are mutually exclusive operations. If you set a parameter's current value, the user never sees the dialog box and the default values are ignored. When you want the user to enter a parameter, set the default values but not the current values. Since there is no current value, the user will be prompted to enter it.

Considering that the parameter field classes of the ReportDocument class and the CrystalReportViewer class look so similar, you might assume that once you learn how to program with one class, you automatically know how to program with the other class. Unfortunately, this is not the case. Although there are many similarities, the differences are significant enough that you have to be very careful to make sure you understand the nuances between them. Paying close attention to the code examples in this section will save you headaches.

Tip

From a conceptual standpoint, the parameter objects in the ReportDocument class and the CrystalReportViewer class are the same. Both of them can modify the current values and default values of a parameter. This leads to the question of which one should you use in your application. This is determined by the other functionality your application implements. For most scenarios, you should use the ReportDocument class for manipulating reports. The CrystalReportViewer class is primarily used for setting display properties. Although it does have some functionality for modifying a report, it is very limited. It can be useful when using web services, but other than that you are better off always using the ReportDocument class. You should also note that SAP technical documents officially state that you cannot make report modifications with both classes simultaneously. You have to use one or the other. Thus, stick with the ReportDocument class at all times and you'll be fine.

Programming with the ReportDocument Class

The ReportDocument class manages every report object in the report. It has a collection class that is fully populated with every report parameter. Each parameter object can be assigned a value prior to printing the report.

To set a parameter's value, first get a reference to parameter field object. In the ReportDocument class, a parameter field is represented with the ReportFieldDefinition class. Once you have a reference to it, you can modify any of its properties.

The ReportFieldDefinition class has two properties that you are most concerned with: the CurrentValues and DefaultValues collections. Both of these collection objects are of the ParameterValues class. If you recall from Chapter 5, a parameter can have a single value or it can have multiple values. Since it can have more than one value, a collection is needed to store the values. The ParameterValues collection class is where these values are stored.

A parameter is either a discrete value or a range value and each is represented by a different class. The ParameterDiscreteValue class is for discrete values. The ParameterRangeValue class is for range values.

The ParameterDiscreteValue class only has one property to set: Value. This is the parameter's value. It is of type Object so that you can assign any data type to it as long as it is compatible with the data type that the parameter uses.

The ParameterRangeValue class has four values to set: StartValue, EndValue, LowerBoundType and UpperBoundType. The two value parameters are used to define the lower and upper bounds of the range. The two bound-type parameters are used to set whether the endpoint is inclusive or exclusive. If it is inclusive, the value is included as part of the range. If it is exclusive, the endpoint is not included as a part of the range. For example, let's say the range is 0 to 10 and the LowerBoundType is BoundExclusive and the UpperBoundType is BoundInclusive. This range would include all numbers from 1 to 10. If the bound-type is NoBound, there will be no bounds for that parameter and you do not need to enter a value for it.[39]

After populating the ParameterValues collection with one or more values, you have to assign it to either the CurrentValues property or the DefaultValues property. Do this by calling the ApplyCurrentValues() method or the ApplyDefaultValues() method. Pass each method the ParameterValues collection object.

Programming parameters with the ReportDocument class consists of 8 steps:

---

[39] See Chapter 5 for a discussion of bound-types.

1. Get a reference to the parameter field object that you want to modify. Use caution when declaring the variables because you have to declare an object of the ParameterFieldDefinition class, but get a reference to it using the ParameterFields property.

2. Instantiate a ParameterValues collection object.

3. Instantiate a parameter value object. This will either be of the ParameterDiscreteValue class or the ParameterRangeValue class.

4. Set the properties of the new parameter value object.

5. Add the parameter value object to the ParameterValues collection using the Add() method.

6. Repeat steps 3-5 for each parameter value object.

7. Assign the ParameterValues collection to the appropriate parameter field property using either the ApplyCurrentValues() method or the ApplyDefaultValues() method.

8. Set the ReportSource property of the CrystalReportViewer object so that the report gets displayed.

Listing 16-7 illustrates these steps. It modifies the DefaultValues collection by creating two discrete parameters and adding them to the collection. This gives the user a choice of two options to choose from when selecting the parameter value. Since we want the user to be prompted with the new default values, there is no need to modify the CurrentValues property. The inline comments explain the steps that are taking place.

Listing 16-7. Use the report document to modify a discrete parameter.

[VB.NET]

```
Dim myReport As new CrystalDecisions.CrystalReports.Engine.ReportDocument
myReport.Load("SampleReport.rpt")
'Use the ReportDocument object to create two default parameters
Dim myParameterFieldDefinition As _
    CrystalDecisions.CrystalReports.Engine.ParameterFieldDefinition
Dim myParameterValues As CrystalDecisions.Shared.ParameterValues
Dim myParameterDiscreteValue As _
    CrystalDecisions.Shared.ParameterDiscreteValue
'Step 1:Get a reference to the parameter field to modify
myParameterFieldDefinition = _
    myReport.DataDefinition.ParameterFields("Location")
'Step 2: Instantiate a ParameterValues collection object.
myParameterValues = New CrystalDecisions.Shared.ParameterValues()
'Step 3: Instantiate a ParameterValue object.
'This example uses a discrete value
myParameterDiscreteValue = _
    New CrystalDecisions.Shared.ParameterDiscreteValue()
'Step 4: Assign a value to the object
myParameterDiscreteValue.Value = "Louisville, KY"
```

```
'Step 5: Add it to the ParameterValues collection using the Add() method
myParameterValues.Add(myParameterDiscreteValue)
'Step 6: Repeat steps 3-5 for additional parameters
myParameterDiscreteValue = _
   New CrystalDecisions.Shared.ParameterDiscreteValue()
myParameterDiscreteValue.Value = "San Diego, CA"
myParameterValues.Add(myParameterDiscreteValue)
'Step 7: Assign the ParameterValues collection to the parameter field.
'Do this with either the CurrentValues or DefaultValues collection
myParameterFieldDefinition.ApplyDefaultValues(myParameterValues)
'Step 8: Print or Preview the report
CrystalReportViewer1.ReportSource = myReport
```

[C#]

```
CrystalDecisions.CrystalReports.Engine.ReportDocument myReport = new
CrystalDecisions.CrystalReports.Engine.ReportDocument();
myReport.Load("SampleReport.rpt");
CrystalDecisions.Shared.ParameterDiscreteValue ParameterDiscreteValue;
CrystalDecisions.Shared.ParameterValues ParameterValues;
//Use the ReportDocument object to create two default parameters
CrystalDecisions.CrystalReports.Engine.ParameterFieldDefinition ParameterFieldDefinition;
//Step 1: Get a reference to the property field to modify
ParameterFieldDefinition = myReport.DataDefinition.ParameterFields["Location"];
//Step 2: Instantiate a ParameterValues collection object
ParameterValues = new CrystalDecisions.Shared.ParameterValues();
//Step 3: Instantiate a ParameterValue object
//This example uses a discrete value
ParameterDiscreteValue = new CrystalDecisions.Shared.ParameterDiscreteValue();
//Step 4: Assign a value to the object
ParameterDiscreteValue.Value = "Louisville, KY";
//Step 5: Add it to the ParameterValues collection using the Add() method
ParameterValues.Add(ParameterDiscreteValue);
//Step 6: Repeat steps 3-5 for additional parameters
ParameterDiscreteValue = new CrystalDecisions.Shared.ParameterDiscreteValue();
ParameterDiscreteValue.Value = "San Diego, CA";
ParameterValues.Add(ParameterDiscreteValue);
//Step 7: Assign the ParameterValues collection to the parameter field
//Do this for either the CurrentValues or DefaultValues collection
ParameterFieldDefinition.ApplyDefaultValues(ParameterValues);
//Step 8: Print or Preview the report
crystalReportViewer1.ReportSource = myReport;
```

Programming the CrystalReportViewer Control

As mentioned earlier in this chapter, the viewer control should only be used to modify the display properties of the viewer and shouldn't be relied upon to make report changes. However, the viewer does have this functionality built into it, so we'll cover it here so that you know how to use it if the need arises.

Programming with the viewer has some similarities to programming with the ReportDocument class, but there are differences. From a high level, the viewer is similar because you have to get a reference to the parameter object and assign a value to its CurrentValues collection. From an implementation standpoint, the viewer is different because the names of the parameter classes are different.

The viewer is also different in how you assign the current/default value collection. It requires that you override the existing values collection with the new values collection. The ReportDocument class has you call the ApplyCurrentValue() method to do this.

The viewer uses the ParameterFields collection to manage the properties of each parameter in a report. The ParameterFields collection manages the ParameterField object.

Programming with the CrystalReportViewer consists of 8 steps:

1. Assign the report to the ReportSource property of the viewer.

2. Get a reference to the ParameterField object via the ParameterFieldInfo collection.

3. Instantiate a parameter value object. This will either be the ParameterDiscreteValue class or the ParameterRangeValue class.

4. Set the properties of the new parameter value object.

5. Use the ParameterValues.Add() method to add the parameter value to collection of values.

6. Override the CurrentValues collection with the new ParameterValues collection.

Caution

In Step 2 (getting a reference to the ParameterField object), if you are using the viewer object and programming in C#, the parameter name is case sensitive. Passing a string to the ParameterFieldInfo() indexer that doesn't match the parameter name casing results in the error System.ArgumentOutOfRange being raised.

Listing 16-8 illustrates these steps. It creates a parameter that is a range value and assigns it to the CurrentValues collection. The in-line comments explain the steps that are taking place.

Listing 16-8. Use the viewer to modify a range parameter.

[VB.NET]

```
Dim myParameterValues as New CrystalDecisions.Shared.ParameterValues
Dim myParameterField As CrystalDecisions.Shared.ParameterField
Dim myParameterRangeValue As CrystalDecisions.Shared.ParameterRangeValue
'Step 1: Assign the report object to the viewer
CrystalReportViewer1.ReportSource = Server.MapPath("Invoice.rpt")
'Step 2: Reference the ParameterField object
myParameterField = CrystalReportViewer1.ParameterFieldInfo("DateRange")
```

```
'Step 3: Create a ParameterValue object.
myParameterRangeValue = New CrystalDecisions.Shared.ParameterRangeValue
'Step 4: Assign a value to the object
myParameterRangeValue.StartValue = DateTime.Parse("1/4/1997")
myParameterRangeValue.EndValue = DateTime.Parse("2/2/1997")
'Step 5: Add the ParameterValue object to the values collection
myParameterValues.Add(myParameterRangeValue)
'Step 6: Override the CurrentValues collection with the new values collection
myParameterField.CurrentValues = myParameterRangeValue
```

[C#]

```
CrystalDecisions.Shared.ParameterFields ParameterFields;
CrystalDecisions.Shared.IParameterField ParameterField;
CrystalDecisions.Shared.ParameterRangeValue ParameterRangeValue;
//Step 1: Assign the report object to the viewer
CrystalReportViewer1.ReportSource = Server.MapPath("Invoice.rpt");
//Step 2: Reference the ParameterField object
ParameterFields = crystalReportViewer1.ParameterFieldInfo["DateRange"];
//Step 3: Create a ParameterValue object
ParameterRangeValue = new CrystalDecisions.Shared.ParameterRangeValue();
//Step 4: Assign a value to the object
ParameterRangeValue.StartValue = DateTime.Parse("1/4/1997");
ParameterRangeValue.EndValue = DateTime.Parse("1/20/1997");
//Step 6: Override the CurrentValues collection with the new values collection
ParameterField.CurrentValues = ParameterRangeValue;
```

Modifying Subreport Parameters

As you saw earlier in this chapter, if you want to modify the parameters in a subreport, you can pass the subreport name to the **SetParameterValue()** method. Of course, this method is only available with the **ReportDocument** class.

If you want complete access to all the properties of a subreport's parameters, you need to get a reference to the actual parameter. The ReportDocument.ParameterFields() indexer is overloaded so that you can pass it the subreport name as the second parameter. This returns the parameter from the subreport as a ParameterFieldDefinition object and you have access to all of its properties. As an example, Step 1 from Listing 16-7 has been modified to demonstrate getting a parameter from a subreport.

```
'Step 1:Get a reference to the parameter field to modify
myParameterFieldDefinition = _
    myReport.DataDefinition.ParameterFields("Location", "Subreport1")
```

For the rare times you want to modify a subreport parameter using the viewer object, the **ParameterFieldInfo** property of the viewer object has an overloaded indexer. In addition to passing it the parameter name, you can also pass the name of a subreport. Passing the subreport name gives you access to all the parameters on a subreport. If you pass an empty string as the subreport name, the main report's parameters are referenced.

As an example, Step 2 from Listing 16-8 has been modified to demonstrate getting a parameter from a subreport. The rest of the code in Listing 16-8 works as is and modifies the subreport parameter as expected.

```
'Step 2: Reference the ParameterField object
myParameterField = CrystalReportViewer1.ParameterFieldInfo("DateRange", "Subreport1")
```

Chapter 13 showed you how to connect to data sources using the Visual Studio IDE. This consisted of using the report wizards to select the data source, specify the fields to print, and work with SQL statements. This chapter focuses on showing you how to log on to secure data sources and change the data source of an existing report during runtime. Using the Crystal Reports object model during runtime gives you more power than working solely with the Visual Studio IDE.

Connecting to databases during runtime gives a reporting solution great flexibility for using a single report to print with different data sources and dynamic queries. Reports can dynamically print data from different servers, different types of databases, and create customized queries.

To be honest, this chapter starts out pretty easy, but it gets challenging after that. There are many variations for performing data connectivity and it can be overwhelming at first. It's best to read through the headings in this chapter to find the area that applies to your situation. Each solution is independent of the others. Most of the code can be used with any report without modifications.

Logging Onto Databases Simplified

Crystal Reports is designed so that the user ID you entered at design time is saved with the report file, but not the password. If you are printing from a non-secure data source, this doesn't affect you. If the data source is secure, you are prompted with a dialog box to enter the login credentials. This is done so that the security of your database isn't compromised. You can prevent this dialog box from appearing by setting the user credentials during runtime. This lets you manage security in a way that conforms to your corporation's policies.

Crystal Reports makes it very easy to connect to a secure data source. Use the SetDatabaseLogin() method of the ReportDocument class to pass a User ID and Password to the database. Listing 17-1 shows a simple example that passes a User ID of "sa" and a Password of "1234" to the report.

Listing 17-1. Using the SetDatabaseLogin() method to login to a database.

[VB.NET]

```
Dim myReport As New CrystalDecisions.CrystalReports.Engine.ReportDocument
myReport.Load("report.rpt")
myReport.SetDatabaseLogin("sa", "1234")
```

```
CrystalReportViewer1.ReportSource = myReport
```

[C#]
```
CrystalDecisions.CrystalReports.Engine.ReportDocument myReport = new
CrystalDecisions.CrystalReports.Engine.ReportDocument();
myReport.Load("report.rpt");
myReport.SetDatabaseLogin("sa", "1234");
CrystalReportViewer1.ReportSource = myReport;
```

The SetDatabaseLogin() method also passes the security credentials to all subreports that are associated with the main report. Thus, you only have to call it once.

Note

If logging into a secure MS Access database, the SetDatabaseLogin() method only needs the password to log in. You can pass an empty string as the User ID.

Unfortunately, there are situations where the SetDatabaseLogin() method can't be used. They are as follows:

- Each table connects to a different database.

- Subreports use different security credentials.

- Changing the server name or database name during runtime.

- Using the CrystalReportsViewer class to pass security credentials.

In these circumstances, you need to work directly with the classes within database object model. By accessing the methods and properties of the individual classes, you get a control over which data sources the report connects to and the security credentials it uses to access the data.

The Database Object Model

The ReportDocument class, shown in Figure 17-1, manages the connections to your report's data sources. It gives you runtime access to the methods and properties to dynamically manipulate and optimize the connections.

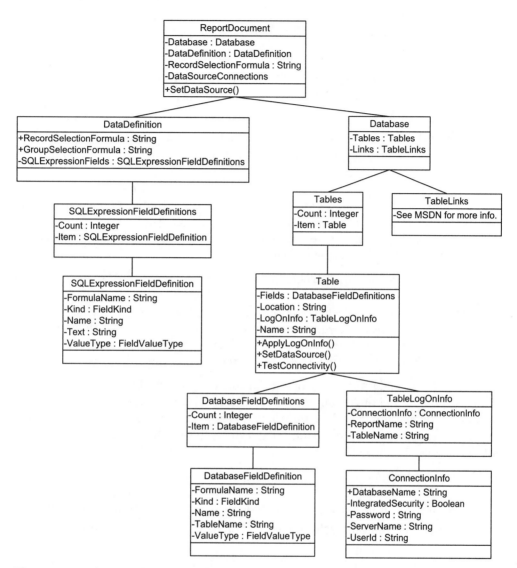

Figure 17-1. The Database class diagram.

This diagram shows the **ReportDocument** class and the two primary properties that work with data sources. The first is the **Database** property. It is a collection of tables and table links. Each table has properties that set the relevant information for connecting to the table as well as the fields in each table. This is the class that this chapter focuses on. The second property of the **ReportDocument** class is the **DataDefinition** class. It has the read-only collection of SQL expression fields.

Note

This section only applies to reports that use the Pull Model. The Pull Model saves connection information with the report and you have to modify the connection properties to set the user credentials. This doesn't apply if you are using the Push Model because you have to connect to the data source manually. The report doesn't save any of the connection information and consequently there is nothing for you to change. The Push Model is discussed later in this chapter.

Logging onto a secure data source uses two classes: **Table** and **ConnectionInfo**. The **Table** class is the primary class. The report object stores each table that it uses within a **Tables** collection. Loop through the **Tables** collection to reference each **Table** object. The **Name** property identifies which database table it is.

Within the **Table** object is the **TableLogOnInfo** object. This is only used to get a reference to the **ConnectionInfo** object. The **ConnectionInfo** object has the properties **UserID** and **Password**. The **UserID** property is already set to the user ID that you entered during design mode. If this is what you want, you do not have to change it. However, you probably want to reassign it with the current user's credentials. The **Password** property is always empty. You have to assign it with the current user's password.

When the **UserID** and **Password** properties are set, call the **ApplyLogOnInfo()** method of the **Table** object. After this is done for each table, Crystal Reports attempts to log on to the data source when it prints. If the information is valid, the user is logged in and the report prints. If the information isn't valid, a login dialog box is displayed so that new user information can be entered.

Tip

If you want to find out if the user credentials are valid before opening the report, call the **TestConnectivity()** method of the **Table** object. It returns **True** if there was a successful login.

Setting the logon properties is done differently depending upon whether you are doing so with the **ReportDocument** object or if you are using the viewer control. Although both use the same objects and properties, the way you get to this information is different. This is explained in detail in the next two sections.

Programmatically Changing the Data Source

Some programs require changing the data source of a table while the application is running. This can include changing the server name or database name. Although this isn't common, it does happen. An example is an application that wants to use the same report for multiple data sources. For example, a sales application could offer the user two reports: a sales report that shows current year data and a sales report that shows historical data. This historical data is archived on another server. As another example, you might use a test database for designing reports but the reports will use the production database when deployed. By changing the data source during run-time, you can design a single report that handles both options.

The data source can only be changed using the ReportDocument object. Modify the ServerName and DatabaseName properties to change the data source. These properties represent different values depending upon which data source you are connecting to. Table 17-1 shows what belongs in each property

Table 17-1 Setting the connection proerties for different data sources.

Data Source	ServerName	DatabaseName
MS Access	Leave it empty	The fully qualified file path
SQL Server	The server name	The database name
ODBC Driver	The DSN name	Leave it empty

Note

The data source isn't designed to have its connection type changed. For example, if the report is connected to SQL Server with an ODBC connection, you can't modify the connection during runtime to use OLE DB or any other type of connection. This would require the report engine to change the DLL it uses to process the data source. This is set when the application is compiled and can't be changed.

Listing 17-2 shows how to change the data source of a table as well as set the user credentials.

Listing 17-2. Changing the location of a data source.

[VB.NET]
```
Private Sub LogonToTables(ByVal myUserId As String, ByVal myPassword As String, _
    ByVal myServerName As String, ByVal myDatabaseName As String)
    Dim myReport As New CrystalDecisions.CrystalReports.Engine.ReportDocument
    myReport.Load("report.rpt")
    Dim myTableLogonInfo As CrystalDecisions.Shared.TableLogOnInfo
    'Set the database properties and security credentials
    Dim myConnectionInfo As New CrystalDecisions.Shared.ConnectionInfo
    myConnectionInfo.ServerName = myServerName
    myConnectionInfo.DatabaseName = myDatabaseName
    myConnectionInfo.UserID = myUserId
```

```
    myConnectionInfo.Password = myPassword
    'Apply the ConnectionInfo to the report tables
    Dim myTables As CrystalDecisions.CrystalReports.Engine.Tables
    myTables = myReport.Database.Tables
    For Each myTable As CrystalDecisions.CrystalReports.Engine.Table In myTables
        myTableLogonInfo = myTable.LogOnInfo
        myTableLogonInfo.ConnectionInfo = myConnectionInfo
        myTable.ApplyLogOnInfo(myTableLogonInfo)
    Next
    CrystalReportViewer1.ReportSource = myReport
End Sub
```

[C#]

```
private void LogonToTables(string UserId, string Password, string ServerName, string DatabaseName,
CrystalDecisions.CrystalReports.Engine.ReportDocument myReport)
{
    CrystalDecisions.Shared.TableLogOnInfo myTableLogonInfo;
    //Set the database properties and security credentials
    CrystalDecisions.Shared.ConnectionInfo myConnectionInfo = new
CrystalDecisions.Shared.ConnectionInfo();
    myConnectionInfo.ServerName = ServerName;
    myConnectionInfo.DatabaseName = DatabaseName;
    myConnectionInfo.UserID = UserId;
    myConnectionInfo.Password = Password;
    //Apply the ConnectionInfo to the report tables
    CrystalDecisions.CrystalReports.Engine.Tables myTables;
    myTables = myReport.Database.Tables;
    foreach (CrystalDecisions.CrystalReports.Engine.Table myTable in myTables)
    {
        myTableLogonInfo = myTable.LogOnInfo;
        myTableLogonInfo.ConnectionInfo = myConnectionInfo;
        myTable.ApplyLogOnInfo(myTableLogonInfo);
    }
    crystalReportViewer1.ReportSource = myReport;
}
```

Caution

You should make sure that the ServerName and DatabaseName properties are the proper case. I've noticed in some projects that these are case sensitive and that Crystal Reports won't accept them. Unfortunately, I have not been able to find any pattern to this problem. Sometimes it works; other times it doesn't. To be on the safe side, assume that these properties are always case sensitive.

This code loops through each table in the ReportDocument.Database.Tables collection and gets a reference to the TableLogOnInfo object. It uses the ConnectionInfo class to apply the database and login information that was passed to the procedure. After setting the properties, it calls the ApplyLogOnInfo() method of the Table class. This updates the table with the new login properties. The report viewer is assigned the report document and this forces the report to open the database connections using the user credentials and display the report.

Changing the Data Source with the Viewer Control

Changing the data source using the viewer control uses the same classes as the ReportDocument class, but it does so in a slightly different manner. Rather than having a collection object that stores a reference to every table in the report, the viewer stores a reference to each unique database connection. Thus, if a report uses three tables, but they are from the same database, the collection will only have a single object in it. If the report pulls data from two different databases, the viewer will have two objects in the collection. The TableLogOnInfos collection is the viewer's collection class of database connections. You have to get a reference to each TableLogOnInfo object within this collection and assign the proper connection properties. The viewer doesn't have an ApplyLogOnInfo() method. You simply overwrite the existing connection info and it takes effect.

Listing 17-3. Setting the Logon credentials with the viewer control.

[VB.NET]

```
Private Sub LogonToTables(ByVal UserId As String, ByVal Password As String, ByVal ServerName As
String, ByVal DatabaseName As String, ByVal ReportFilename As String)
    Dim myConnectionInfo As CrystalDecisions.Shared.ConnectionInfo = New
CrystalDecisions.Shared.ConnectionInfo()
    'Set the database connection info
    myConnectionInfo.ServerName = ServerName
    myConnectionInfo.DatabaseName = DatabaseName
    myConnectionInfo.UserID = UserId
    myConnectionInfo.Password = Password
    'Apply the connection info to every table
    CrystalReportViewer1.ReportSource = ReportFilename
    Dim myTableLogOnInfos As CrystalDecisions.Shared.TableLogOnInfos
    myTableLogOnInfos = CrystalReportViewer1.LogOnInfo
    For Each myTableLogOnInfo As CrystalDecisions.Shared.TableLogOnInfo In myTableLogOnInfos
        myTableLogOnInfo.ConnectionInfo = myConnectionInfo
    Next
End Sub
```

[C#]

```
private void LogonToTables(string UserId, string Password, string ServerName, string DatabaseName,
string ReportFilename)
{
    CrystalDecisions.Shared.ConnectionInfo myConnectionInfo = new
CrystalDecisions.Shared.ConnectionInfo();
    //Set the database connection info
    myConnectionInfo.ServerName = ServerName;
    myConnectionInfo.DatabaseName = DatabaseName;
    myConnectionInfo.UserID = UserId;
    myConnectionInfo.Password = Password;
    //Apply the connection info to every table
```

```
crystalReportViewer1.ReportSource = ReportFilename;
CrystalDecisions.Shared.TableLogOnInfos myTableLogOnInfos;
myTableLogOnInfos = crystalReportViewer1.LogOnInfo;
foreach (CrystalDecisions.Shared.TableLogOnInfo myTableLogOnInfo in myTableLogOnInfos)
{
    myTableLogOnInfo.ConnectionInfo = myConnectionInfo;
}
}
```

Caution

The choice of names for the viewer properties can be confusing if you aren't careful. The name of the collection class is called TableLogOnInfos(). Notice that it has an "s" at the end of it. It stores a collection of TableLogOnInfo() objects. Notice that this object name is singular. Now for the confusing part: the viewer's property name that represents the TableLogOnInfos() collection is called LogOnInfo. Notice that this name doesn't have the "s" at the end. Thus, the viewer's collection property doesn't have the same name as the collection class. Rather it has a similar name as the objects it manages. Be careful or else you might think that the collection is the object it stores.

Parameters and Stored Procedures

A common hurdle that developers have is figuring out how to print reports connected to stored procedures using parameters. It really isn't hard once you understand how it works. Reports that use stored procedures as their data source are no different than reports that use any other data source. When you open the report, it automatically calls the stored procedure, retrieves the data, and populates the report with this data. The difference between using a stored procedure and using a table is that stored procedures accept parameters as input.

When a report is designed with a stored procedure, Crystal Reports examines the stored procedure to see if it uses parameters. If so, the designer automatically creates a report parameter for each parameter in the stored procedure. There is a one-to-one mapping of report parameters to stored procedure parameters. When the report runs, the report engine takes the value of each of these parameters and automatically passes them to the stored procedure.

As you saw in Chapter 16, the user is always prompted to enter the parameters before the report can execute. Of course, you probably don't want to prompt the user for this information because your application has already done so via the user interface. To prevent this from happening, manually populate the parameter(s) via code with the information the user has already provided. After the parameters are filled, the report connects to the database, passes the parameters to the stored procedure and previews the report.

Listing 17-4 demonstrates how to connect to a report that uses a stored procedure with a parameter.

Listing 17-4. Connect to a stored procedure using a parameter.

[VB.NET]

```
Private Sub LogonToTables(ByVal myUserId As String, ByVal myPassword As String, _
    ByVal myServerName As String, ByVal myDatabaseName As String)
    Dim myReport As New CrystalDecisions.CrystalReports.Engine.ReportDocument
    myReport.Load("report.rpt")
    Dim myTableLogonInfo As CrystalDecisions.Shared.TableLogOnInfo
    'Set the database properties and security credentials
    Dim myConnectionInfo As New CrystalDecisions.Shared.ConnectionInfo
    myConnectionInfo.ServerName = myServerName
    myConnectionInfo.DatabaseName = myDatabaseName
    myConnectionInfo.UserID = myUserId
    myConnectionInfo.Password = myPassword
    'Apply the ConnectionInfo to the report tables
    Dim myTables As CrystalDecisions.CrystalReports.Engine.Tables
    myTables = myReport.Database.Tables
    For Each myTable As CrystalDecisions.CrystalReports.Engine.Table In myTables
        myTableLogonInfo = myTable.LogOnInfo
        myTableLogonInfo.ConnectionInfo = myConnectionInfo
        myTable.ApplyLogOnInfo(myTableLogonInfo)
    Next
    'Set the parameter value
    myReport.SetParameterValue("@ParameterName", "value")
    CrystalReportViewer1.ReportSource = myReport
End Sub
```

[C#]

```
private void LogonToTables(string UserId, string Password, string ServerName, string DatabaseName,
CrystalDecisions.CrystalReports.Engine.ReportDocument myReport)
{
    CrystalDecisions.Shared.TableLogOnInfo myTableLogonInfo;
    //Set the database properties and security credentials
    CrystalDecisions.Shared.ConnectionInfo myConnectionInfo = new
CrystalDecisions.Shared.ConnectionInfo();
    myConnectionInfo.ServerName = ServerName;
    myConnectionInfo.DatabaseName = DatabaseName;
    myConnectionInfo.UserID = UserId;
    myConnectionInfo.Password = Password;
    //Apply the ConnectionInfo to the report tables
    CrystalDecisions.CrystalReports.Engine.Tables myTables;
    myTables = myReport.Database.Tables;
    foreach (CrystalDecisions.CrystalReports.Engine.Table myTable in myTables)
    {
        myTableLogonInfo = myTable.LogOnInfo;
        myTableLogonInfo.ConnectionInfo = myConnectionInfo;
        myTable.ApplyLogOnInfo(myTableLogonInfo);
    }
    //Set the parameter value
```

```
myReport.SetParameterValue("@ParameterName", "value");
crystalReportViewer1.ReportSource = myReport;
}
```

Tip

If you want to pass a NULL value to a stored procedure parameter, set the parameter's Value property to Nothing in VB.Net and null in C#.

Things can get a little messy when using a stored procedure that uses DateTime parameters. Many tables only use the date part of a field and leave the time alone. When this happens, SQL Server automatically fills in a time of "00:00:00". However, since this isn't a proper time, it is the same as "12:00:00 AM". When Crystal Reports prints from a stored procedure using a DateTime parameter, the user is required to enter a time of "12:00:00 AM" in the Enter Parameter Value dialog box. This might cause confusion initially because the user is only trying to filter on the date.

To get around this, you could modify the stored procedure to use a varchar() datatype for the DateTime parameter. In a WHERE clause, SQL Server does implicit data type conversions so that you can compare a DateTime field to a varchar and the date is filtered properly. By doing this, Crystal Reports will create a string parameter in the report and let the user enter the date value without entering a time value. Unfortunately, since the parameter is now a string, there isn't any built-in error checking on the date. Using an edit mask is helpful, but it doesn't guarantee that the value is a proper date. Nonetheless, if you have capable users, this could be an acceptable alternative to making them enter a dummy time value every time they run your reports.

Set NoCount On

Although this chapter assumes you are already familiar with stored procedures, there is one statement that doesn't get much attention. I think it is very important to be aware of it.

SET NOCOUNT ON

The Set NoCount On statement prevents extraneous messages from being output by SQL Server. By default, SQL Server outputs status messages while it executes a stored procedure. These often state how many records were affected by the last statement. Unfortunately, these status messages confuse Crystal Reports and it thinks that they are part of the recordset. This obviously isn't the case and the report won't generate any output.

If you are working with simple stored procedures, the majority of them consist of a SELECT statement followed by a list of tables, fields and a join method. Crystal Reports handles this type of stored procedure fine. Once you start getting into writing more complex stored procedures you will find that you often need to execute multiple SQL statements within one stored procedure.

'SET NOCOUNT ON
INSERT INTO AuditLog …

SELECT * FROM tblSales WHERE ...

In the above code, the SET NOCOUNT ON statement is commented out. Running this code will generate two output messages for each statement. They will be in the format of **xx records affected**. This message is passed prior to the records being returned from the stored procedure. This conflicts with what the report is expecting. Thus, it doesn't use the data from the SELECT statement as the recordset. By removing the comment from the first line, you tell the database server not to report how many records are affected. This eliminates Crystal Reports from incorrectly using these messages as part of the database. Ideally, this statement would be the first statement in every stored procedure.

Note

If you use temp tables in a stored procedure, always use SET NOCOUNT ON. This is because temp tables always generate extraneous messages as the records are generated and saved to the temporary table.

Working with Subreports

As mentioned earlier in the chapter, when you use the SetDatabaseLogin() method to pass security credentials to a report, it logs into the main report's database as well as the database used by the subreports. Thus, you don't have to do anything extra to open a report that also uses subreports.

If you want to have more control over the database objects for a report, you need to reference them directly. This will let you do such things as change the data source. Fortunately, the subreport object is based on the same class as the main report (the ReportDocument class). Modifying the properties of a subreport uses the same code that was written for the main report. The only difference being that you have to use the OpenSubreport() method to get a reference to the subreport object.

Listing 17-5. Set subreport credentials

[VB.NET]

```
Dim myMainReport As New CrystalDecisions.CrystalReports.Engine.ReportDocument
Dim mySubReport As CrystalDecisions.CrystalReports.Engine.ReportDocument
myMainReport.Load("report.rpt")
mySubReport = myMainReport.OpenSubreport("subreport")
... insert your code to modify the SubReport object properties....
CrystalReportViewer1.ReportSource = myMainReport
```

[C#]

```
CrystalDecisions.CrystalReports.Engine.ReportDocument myMainReport = new
CrystalDecisions.CrystalReports.Engine.ReportDocument();
CrystalDecisions.CrystalReports.Engine.ReportDocument mySubReport;
myMainReport.Load("report.rpt");
mySubReport = myMainReport.OpenSubreport("subreport");
```

CrystalReportViewer1.ReportSource = myMainReport;

Implementing the Push Model

Reports can use either the Pull Model or the Push Model for retrieving data. The Pull Model links to a data source and retrieves the data automatically. The Push Model, discussed in the remainder of this chapter, is based upon generating reports from a manually populated data source. The data source can be a DataSet , DataTable, DataReader, DataView, XML or an object collection that implements the **IEnumerable** interface (e.g. an array or LINQ query). You have to create the data source, manually populate it with the appropriate data, and pass it to the report object for printing. You have complete control over the data and can optimize the data connections. Since there are so many ways to populate the data source, the Push Model gives you the flexibility to link to almost any type of data source as well as link to proprietary data sources. This isn't always possible with the Pull Model.

The Push Model is more complicated than the Pull Model, and as a result there are more steps to learn. The steps are also different depending upon what type of data you want to pass to the report. To make this easier, I'm going to list the steps separately based on the type of data used to populate the report. You can find the section that applies to your current report and jump directly to it.

Reporting From the DataSet, DataTable, DataView and XML

For purposes of simplifying this discussion, when referring to any of the above data types, I'll refer to them as only a dataset object. When there are any differences, I'll make a note of it.

There are three steps for reporting from a dataset. The first step consists of creating a dataset and specifying it as the report's data source. Then design the report using the fields from this dataset. The last step is passing the dataset to the report.

Steps

1. Define the dataset schema file.

2. Build the report using the dataset schema file as the data source.

3. Bind the dataset to the report.

Define the Dataset Schema File

When printing from any data source, Crystal Reports needs to know the tables and fields that it is printing from. When using a standard database, it can query the database to get this information. But when reporting from a dataset, it doesn't have this luxury. Instead, it uses a schema file to determine this information. It's your job to define the dataset's schema file and point the report to it.

A dataset schema is a fully compliant XML file that defines the properties of the data source. It usually has a file extension of '.xsd'. Listing 17-6 shows an excerpt of the XML code that is in the dataset file.

Listing 17-6. The XML schema from a dataset file.

```
<xs:element name="Customers">
   <xs:complexType>
      <xs:sequence>
         <xs:element name="CustomerID" type="xs:string" />
         <xs:element name="CompanyName" type="xs:string" />
         <xs:element name="ContactName" type="xs:string" minOccurs="0" />
      </xs:sequence>
   </xs:complexType>
</xs:element>
```

A dataset schema file can be created in two different ways. The first method uses the Visual Studio IDE and the second way uses ADO.NET methods to create it. The method you use depends upon your preferences.

Using the IDE to Create a Dataset File

The Visual Studio IDE makes it easy to create a dataset file. Select the menu options Project > Add New Item. The Add New Item dialog box lists the Dataset as an option. Click on this option, give it an appropriate file name and click Add. A blank dataset is created and added as an item in the Solution Explorer window. As you can see in Figure 17-2, the dataset is represented in the IDE as an empty screen.

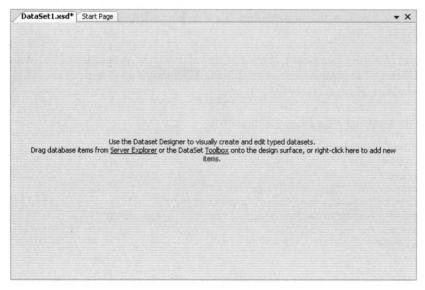

Figure 17-2. The default Dataset designer surface.

At this point, the IDE is ready to build a new dataset file from scratch. Open the Server Explorer and drill down to the appropriate data source to find the table(s) you need. Drag one or more tables from the Server Explorer window onto the dataset surface. Behind the scenes the IDE generates the appropriate code to represent the table(s) with XML. To see what the XML source looks like, save the file and view the .XSD file that is saved in the solutions folder on your hard drive.

Tip

When selecting a field in the dataset, you can set its properties in the Properties window. This lets you change things such as the data type, caption, default value, etc. If you have a table that is similar to the dataset you want to create, but not exact, add it to the dataset and make the necessary changes to its properties. This is easier than creating the dataset from scratch.

Once finished adding the appropriate tables to the dataset your screen will show the tables you added and their relationships.

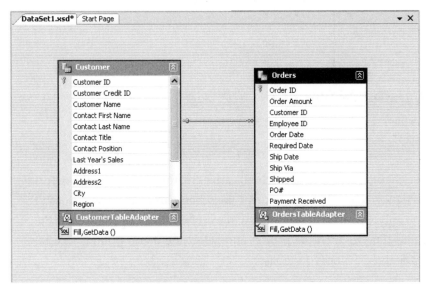

Figure 17-3. The Dataset designer surface with two sample tables.

Clicking on the Save button in the toolbar causes the IDE to save the XML source to the dataset file. The file is ready to be linked to the report.

Caution

It is easy to forget to save the schema file before linking it to the report. But if you don't save the file, the Report Expert won't know what the fields are. It will show an empty table with no fields listed. There must be a physical .xsd file prior to running the Report Expert.

Creating a DataSet Manually with the IDE

The previous method of building a dataset assumed that you have a table that can be dragged and dropped onto the designer. There are times you want to create a new table without having an existing data source. This could be a report based on user input or internal calculations. No worries, you can still use the IDE to create a dataset manually.

Just like before, add a **DataSet** object to your project. Right-click on the menu item Project > Add New Item. The Add New Item dialog box lists Dataset File as an option. Select this option, give it an appropriate filename and click Add.

The designer shows a blank screen. Right-click anywhere on the designer and select Add > DataTable. Right-click below the heading and select Add > Column. You can change the data type using the Properties window. In Figure 17-4 is a sample called DataTable1.

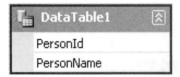

Figure 17-4. A new DataSet table.

After saving the file it can be referenced by a report.

Note

If you make changes to the dataset schema after creating the report, the report will not recognize these changes. It keeps the schema in its cache and doesn't refresh. The only way to force it to renew the cache is to completely close the Visual Studio IDE, re-open the project and select the menu options Crystal Reports > Database > Verify Database.

Creating a Dataset File with ADO.NET Methods

The last way to create a dataset file is to use the methods of the ADO.NET classes. The ADO.NET namespace is designed to make working with XML files almost effortless. It converts a dataset to and from its XML schema. Use the WriteXMLSchema() method to save the schema to a file. Simply pass it the filename to save it to.

First create a dataset object that links to the data you want to report on and populate it with some sample report data. You need to populate it with sample data so that it has the table structure in memory. How you populate the dataset isn't relevant because this is independent from the report itself. For example, some data sources you could load the data from are an SQL Server database, a MS Access database, an XML file, etc. Listing 17-7 shows how to load data from an SQL Server database.

Listing 17-7. Reading data from an SQL Server database

[VB.NET]

```
Dim myDataSet As DataSet
Dim myConnectionString As String
Dim myDataAdapter As SqlClient.SqlDataAdapter
Dim SQL As String
SQL = "SELECT Customers.*, Orders.* " & _
    "FROM Customers INNER JOIN Orders " & _
    "ON Customers.CustomerId = Orders.CustomerId"
myConnectionString = "Data Source=(local);UID=sa;pwd=pw;Database=Northwind"
myDataAdapter = New SqlClient.SqlDataAdapter(mySQL, myConnectionString)
myDataAdapter.Fill(myDataSet, "Customers")
```

[C#]

```
DataSet myDataSet;
string myConnectionString;
```

```
SqlClient.SqlDataAdapter myDataAdapter;
string SQL;
 SQL = "SELECT Customers.*, Orders.* " + "FROM Customers INNER JOIN Orders " + "ON
Customers.CustomerId = Orders.CustomerId";
myConnectionString = "Data Source=(local);UID=sa;pwd=pw;Database=Northwind";
myDataAdapter = new SqlClient.SqlDataAdapter(mySQL, myConnectionString);
myDataAdapter.Fill(myDataSet, "Customers");
```

If you need examples of how to connect to different types of data sources, you can reference the URL http://www.carlprothman.net/Default.aspx?tabid=81.

Once the dataset is created, call the WriteXMLSchema() method and pass it the filename. This saves the XML schema to the file to be used by your report. The code in listing 17-8 gives you a simple example of how to implement this. It is very generic and simply saves the dataset's schema to an XSD file. Make sure that the myDataSet object has been populated elsewhere in your application before calling the WriteXmlSchema() method.

Listing 17-8. Saving an XML schema file from a dataset object.

[VB.NET]
```
'Write a populated dataset object to an XML schema file
'Assume that the dataset has already been populated (see previous listing as an example)
myDataset.WriteXmlSchema("XmlData.xsd")
```

[C#]
```
myDataset.WriteXmlSchema("XmlData.xsd");
```

The key to using this code is that you only need to call it one time to create the schema file. In your code you should populate the dataset with the data you want to print, call this code to save the schema, and comment it out so that it isn't called again. You could also delete the code, but this isn't the best idea because if the structure of your data changes, you'll want to uncomment the code so that you can overwrite the older schema file.

Once you've saved the schema file, you can start designing your report from it.

Best Of The Forum

Question: I have many reports based on datasets that were built using Visual Studio 2003. When I upgraded to Visual Studio 2008, none of the reports print data anymore. Why not?

Answer: I solved my own question! I noticed that the XML schema file in 2008 is slightly different than the schema file in 2003. I rebuilt my dataset schemas and now everything works fine. You could also copy/paste the data tables from the old project to the new project and this will update them as well.

Build the Report Using the Dataset Schema File

For a report to use a dataset as its data source, it needs to know how the data is structured. It uses the schema file to determine the structure. The previous section showed three different ways to create the dataset schema file. The way that you created the dataset determines how it links to the report.

If you used the IDE to create a dataset, open the Database Expert[40], and expand the category Project Data > ADO.NET Datasets. This lists all the datasets in the project. Expand the dataset you created to see the list of tables within it.[41] Add the appropriate tables to the Selected Tables window on the right. Go to the Links tab to establish relationships between the tables.

If you created a dataset file manually, open the Database Expert and click on the category called Create New Connection. Under it you will see the ADO.NET node. Expand this node to select Make New Connection and the dialog box in Figure 17-5 will open.

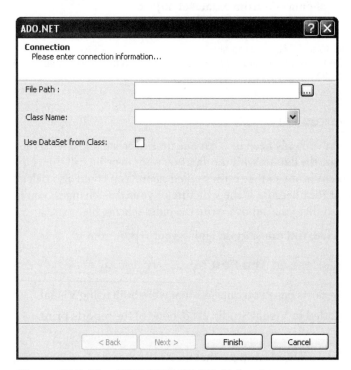

Figure 17-5. The ADO.NET (XML) dialog box.

---

[40] As mentioned earlier, the Database Expert can be reached by either using the Report Expert or by selecting the menu options Crystal Reports > Database > Database Expert.
[41] Remember that the dataset schema has to be saved to disk prior to opening the Database Expert. If you forget and later save the dataset, you can right-click anywhere on the Available Data Sources list and select Refresh. This tells Crystal Reports to clear its cache and requery the dataset file when you open it.

This dialog box lets you browse the schema files on your computer. You can select a dataset that was created with the IDE or one created using the WriteXmlSchema() method. After entering the file path for the schema, enter a class name (you can enter anything here and it doesn't matter).

Click the Finish button and design the report as normal. When finished with the report layout, go to the next steps to populate the dataset.

Note

Once the report is bound to a dataset file, the file is no longer used by the report. The schema information is saved within the report file. You can delete the dataset file after binding it and it will have no effect.

Bind the DataSet to the report

The last step in using the Push Model is writing the code to link the fully populated dataset to the report. The ReportDocument class has a SetDataSource() method that takes a populated dataset object and uses it as the data source for the report. After calling this method the report is bound to the dataset and is able to print the records.

Listing 17-9. Linking the dataset file to the report and previewing it.

[VB.NET]

```
Dim myReport as New CrystalReport1
Dim myDataSet As New DataSet()
'Populate myDataSet with the appropriate data (see Listing 17-7 for an example)
.....
myReport.SetDataSource(myDataSet)
CrystalReportViewer1.ReportSource = myReport
```

[C#]

```
CrystalReport1 myReport = new CrystalReport1();
DataSet myDataSet = new DataSet();
//Populate myDataSet with the appropriate data (see Listing 17-7 for an example)
.....
myReport.SetDataSource(myDataSet);
CrystalReportViewer1.ReportSource = myReport;
```

The code first creates an instance of the report and assigns it to the myReport object variable. Then it creates a new DataSet object and populates it. Again, you can populate the dataset using the appropriate data source for your application. The SetDataSource() method is passed the populated dataset. This binds the data to the report.

Tip

It is common to bind the report to the dataset and get the error "Logon Failed". This occurs when the table name wasn't specified when the dataset was populated with the data. It can also occur when the table name doesn't match what the report is expecting. Examine the dataset object in debug mode and see what those table names are. It is also helpful to pass the datatable object to the report rather than the dataset. For example, you can pass myDataSet.Tables(0) or myDataSet("tablename") instead.

As mentioned earlier, I've been saying that you have to pass the report a dataset object to simplify the explanations in this section. You can also pass the SetDataSource() method a DataTable object or even a DataView object.

> ### Caution
>
> When using an XML data source that has date fields, Crystal Reports will not print the dates correctly on the page. There is some type of bug with how Crystal Reports interprets the dates in a dataset that is derived from an XML file. It can't format the output correctly. The workaround for this bug is to read the XML schema into the dataset object prior to reading the XML data. Here is an example:

```
myDataSet.ReadXmlSchema("SampleData.xsd")
myDataSet.ReadXml("SampleData.xml")
```

Printing from a DataView object is the same as printing from a DataSet object. Since a dataview is based on an existing dataset, build the report using the dataset. Pass this dataset to the report's SetDataSource() method. Here is a sample that would be used to filter the data in a dataset.

```
Dim myDataView As DataView
myDataView = New DataView(myDataSet.Tables(0), "CustomerId=123", "",
DataViewRowState.CurrentRows)
myReport.SetDataSource(myDataView)
```

If you want to print the data from a datagrid, follow the same steps for printing a dataset. However, you first have to get the data from the datagrid and cast it as a dataset:

[VB.NET]
```
myDataSet = CType(myDataGrid.DataSource, DataSet)
```

[C#]
```
myDataSet = (DataSet)myDataGrid.Datasource
```

Reporting from an Object Collection

One of the data types that the SetDataSource() method accepts is System.Collections.IEnumberable. This lets you print data that is stored within an object collection. For example, it's easy to report from an ArrayList because it implements the

IEnumerable interface. You can even create a custom collection class as a data source as long as it follows this rule.

There are two requirements for using an object collection. The first is that the project declares a class with public properties. Crystal Reports uses the public class properties to define the fields in the report. The second requirement is that the collection class implements the IEnumerable interface. Let's walk through an example to see how this works.

In the Solution Explorer, right-click on the project name and select Add > New Item. In the Add New Item window, select Class and enter the name User. Then click the Add button to add it to your project.

For this simple example, there will only be two properties: FirstName and Lastname. Enter the following code for the class.

Listing 17-10. Code for the User class.

[VB.NET]

```
Public Class User
   Private _FirstName As String
   Private _LastName As String
   Sub New(ByVal FirstName As String, ByVal LastName As String)
     _FirstName = FirstName
     _LastName = LastName
   End Sub
   Public Property FirstName() As String
     Get
        Return _FirstName
     End Get
     Set(ByVal value As String)
        _FirstName = value
     End Set
   End Property
   Public Property LastName() As String
     Get
        Return _LastName
     End Get
     Set(ByVal value As String)
        _LastName = value
     End Set
   End Property
End Class
```

[C#]

```
public class User
{
   private string _FirstName;
   private string _LastName;
   public User(string FirstName, string LastName)
   {
```

```
      _FirstName = FirstName;
      _LastName = LastName;
   }
   public string FirstName
   {
      get { return _FirstName; }
      set { _FirstName = value; }
   }
   public string LastName
   {
      get { return _LastName; }
      set { _LastName = value; }
   }
}
```

The next step is to create a report and use this class as the data source. Right-click on the project and select Add > New Item and choose Crystal Report. In the Report Wizard, get to the Data tab and open the Project Data node. Then open the .NET Objects node. Find the name of the User class in this list and double-click it to add it to the Selected Tables list on the right.

Note

Crystal Reports doesn't always recognize when you add a new class to the project. If the new class isn't shown in the .NET Objects list, right-click on that node and select Refresh. Selecting Refresh forces it to re-examine your project and rebuild the list of classes.

After adding the class to the Selected Tables list, click the Next button and add the fields to the Fields To Display list. Click the Next button or the Finish button, depending upon whether you want to customize the report or not.

At this point, you have a report that was built using the class properties to define the fields that will be displayed. Now you need to create an array to store a collection of those objects and pass this array to the SetDataSource() method of the ReportDocument object. The code in listing 17-11 can be put in the form's Load() event or attached to a button. Make sure the form has a viewer control on it as well.

Listing 17-11. Create an object collection and pass it to the report.

[VB.NET]

```
Imports System.Collections
...
'Create the list of names
Dim UserNames As New ArrayList
UserNames.Add(New User("Napolean", "Serna"))
UserNames.Add(New User("Yitzel", "Serna"))
UserNames.Add(New User("Brian", "Bischof"))
'Load the report
```

```
Dim myReport As CrystalDecisions.CrystalReports.Engine.ReportDocument
myReport = New CrystalDecisions.CrystalReports.Engine.ReportDocument
myReport.Load("..\..\CrystalReport1.rpt")
'Pass the collection to the report's data source
myReport.SetDataSource(UserNames)
'Preview the report
CrystalReportViewer1.ReportSource = myReport
```

[C#]

```
using System.Collections;
...
//Create the list of names
List<User> UserNames = new List<User>{
   new User("Napolean", "Serna"),
   new User("Yitzel ", "Serna"),
   new User("Brian", "Bischof")
};
//Load the report
CrystalDecisions.CrystalReports.Engine.ReportDocument myReport;
myReport = new CrystalDecisions.CrystalReports.Engine.ReportDocument();
myReport.Load(@"..\..\CrystalReport1.rpt");
//Pass the collection to the report's data source
myReport.SetDataSource(UserNames);
//Preview the report
crystalReportViewer1.ReportSource = myReport;
```

In this listing, the **UserNames** variable is the array list for storing the collection of **User** objects. The first part instantiates this variable and fills it with sample names using the **Add()** method. For your own reports, you would build the collection in whatever way is appropriate for your application.

After creating the list of names, the report is loaded into memory and passes the **UserNames** collection to the report using the **SetDataSource()** method. The last line passes the report to the viewer and it displays the data in the **UserNames** collection on the report.

As you can see, the **SetDataSource()** method makes it easy to build reports using object collections.

Reporting From LINQ Objects

Microsoft created LINQ (.NET Language Integrated Query) so that programmers can query data sources within their application. This lets you apply SQL-like queries to non-traditional data sources such as a data view or an object collection. Being able to easily filter data within an object collection is quite powerful!

The LINQ libraries give you numerous ways for querying data from different data sources. It is a complex topic and beyond the scope of this book to discuss in detail. If you search the internet for "scott guthrie linq pdf", you will find a free online book that gives you a complete tutorial on how to implement LINQ in your own applications.

Caution

Microsoft released the LINQ language features for both .NET 2005 and .NET 2008. In .NET 2005 it is an optional install, and in .NET 2008 it is installed by default. Crystal Reports only added support for LINQ in .NET 2008. The code in this section will not work for .NET 2005.

LINQ lets you query a data source in your application and it returns the result set in an IEnumerable collection. As you learned in the previous section, Crystal Reports can report from IEnumerable. Consequently, it is very easy to build reports using LINQ.

Reporting from a LINQ query is almost identical to reporting from an object collection. With LINQ you use the LINQ query syntax to select data from a data source and return it in an IEnumerable collection. Pass this collection to the SetDataSource() method to generate a report with it.

In this example, we are going to create a UserNames collection like we did in Listing 17-11. But this time we will use LINQ to filter the data on last name and sort it by first name. Afterwards, we will assign it to the report and preview it.

Follow all the steps in the previous section, "Reporting From an Object Collection", but replace Listing 17-11 with the code in Listing 17-12.

Listing 17-12.

[VB.NET]

```
'Create the list of names
Dim UserNames As New ArrayList
UserNames.Add(New User("Napolean", "Serna"))
UserNames.Add(New User("Yitzel", "Serna"))
UserNames.Add(New User("Brian", "Bischof"))
'Use LINQ query to filter and sort the array list
Dim NewUsers = From myUser In UserNames _
        Where myUser.LastName = "Serna" _
        Order By myUser.FirstName _
        Select myUser
'Load the report
Dim myReport As CrystalDecisions.CrystalReports.Engine.ReportDocument
myReport = New CrystalDecisions.CrystalReports.Engine.ReportDocument
myReport.Load("..\..\CrystalReport1.rpt")
'Pass the collection to the report's data source
myReport.SetDataSource(NewUsers)
'Preview the report
CrystalReportViewer1.ReportSource = myReport
```

[C#]

```
using System.Collections;
using System.Linq;
...
//Create the list of names
```

```
List<User> UserNames = new List<User>{
    new User("Napolean", "Serna"),
    new User("Yitzel", "Serna"),
    new User("Brian", "Bischof")
};
//Use LINQ query to filter and sort the array list
IEnumerable<User> NewUsers;
NewUsers = from myUser in UserNames
        where myUser.LastName == "Serna"
        orderby myUser.FirstName
        select myUser;
//Load the report
CrystalDecisions.CrystalReports.Engine.ReportDocument myReport;
myReport = new CrystalDecisions.CrystalReports.Engine.ReportDocument();
myReport.Load(@"..\..\CrystalReport1.rpt");
//Pass the collection to the report's data source
myReport.SetDataSource(NewUsers);
//Preview the report
crystalReportViewer1.ReportSource = myReport;
```

The code first creates the list of names, **UserNames**. Secondly, it declares the LINQ variable, **NewUsers**, that stores the results of our LINQ query and assigns it the query text. You can see that the last name is filtered to only show "Serna" and the list is ordered by first name. The **PreviewReport()** method takes the **NewUsers** object and passes it to the report object using the **SetDataSource()** method. Lastly, it passes it to the viewer to preview it.

Note

The VB.NET code is a little less intuitive than the C# code. First of all, the **NewUsers** object variable is not strongly typed. This is because VB.NET automatically assigns the LINQ query type to it. Second, the **UserNames** variable is a generic **ArrayList** object and it doesn't have the User class properties exposed. When entering the LINQ query, intellisense will not work for the **FirstName** and **LastName** properties. Nonetheless, type them in and the compiler will recognize them during runtime when the LINQ query executes.

You can see in this example, that it is very easy to create a report using LINQ.

Reporting from the DataReader

Many people process data using the **DataReader** class and they want to run reports from it as well. Crystal Reports gives you the ability to do this. The **DataReader** class is another one of the many data types that can be passed to the **SetDataSource()** method.

Using the DataReader as a data source has some limitations to it that make it more difficult to use than the other data sources. They are as follows:

- The data must be returned from a method that uses the **IDataReader** interface.

- The method must be Shared (Visual Basic) or static (C#).

- The data provider must be the OleDB .NET data provider.

- The method must be part of a separate class library that is compiled into an assembly.

With the exception of the last bullet point, these requirements are all fairly easy to implement. The last bullet point is the most restrictive of the four listed. It says that you can't use a **DataReader** that is in the same project that the report is in. You have to create a separate library project and compile it into an assembly before Crystal Reports can reference it. In other words, if you want to report from a **DataReader**, you have to create a separate DLL just for the purpose of returning the **DataReader** from a shared method. Since this isn't a requirement for using the other data source types, the question that immediately comes to my mind is, "Why?"

Behind the scenes, Crystal Reports uses this DLL to determine the report's data source structure. Crystal Reports instantiates the class in the DLL and calls the appropriate method to get an instance of the fully populated **DataReader** object. It analyzes this object to determine the data structure and create the list of fields that you can report from. If this weren't a stand-alone DLL, there would be no way for Crystal Reports to determine its data structure at design time. Creating a separate library project is a necessary evil if you want to report from a **DataReader** object.

Let's look at the steps for creating a report using a **DataReader**. Although the requirements are a bit unusual, you'll see that they are very easy to implement and you will be able to do it quickly.

The first step is to create a new project using the Class Library template. In this example, I named my project, MyDataReader. After creating the project, I deleted the default Class1.vb file that was created automatically and added a new class called **DataSource**. The code is in listing 17-13.

Listing 17-13. Source code for the MyDataReader project.

[VB.NET]

```
Imports System.Data
Imports System.Data.OleDb
Public Class DataSource
    'Note: Use your own connection string here
    Private Const CONNECTION_STRING As String = _
    "provider=sqloledb;Data Source=vmware;Initial Catalog=xtreme;User Id=sa;Password=pw"
    Private Const CUSTOMER_TABLE As String = _
     "SELECT [Customer ID], [Customer Name], [Contact Last Name], City FROM Customer"
    Public Shared Function GetCustomers() As IDataReader
        Dim myOleDbConnection As OleDbConnection = New
OleDbConnection(CONNECTION_STRING)
        myOleDbConnection.Open()
        Dim myOleDbCommand As OleDbCommand
        OleDbCommand = New OleDbCommand(CUSTOMER_TABLE, myOleDbConnection)
```

```
      Dim myIDataReader As IDataReader = myOleDbCommand.ExecuteReader()
      Return myIDataReader
   End Function
End Class
```

[C#]

```csharp
using System.Data;
using System.Data.OleDb;
public class DataSource
{
   //Note: Use your own connection string here
   private const string CONNECTION_STRING = "provider=sqloledb;Data Source=vmware;Initial
Catalog=xtreme;User Id=sa;Password=pw";
   private const string CUSTOMER_TABLE = "SELECT [Customer ID], [Customer Name], [Contact
Last Name], City FROM Customer";
   public static IDataReader GetCustomers()
   {
      OleDbConnection myOleDbConnection = new OleDbConnection(CONNECTION_STRING);
      myOleDbConnection.Open();
      OleDbCommand myOleDbCommand;
      myOleDbCommand = new OleDbCommand(CUSTOMER_TABLE, myOleDbConnection);
      IDataReader myIDataReader = myOleDbCommand.ExecuteReader();
      return myIDataReader;
   }
}
```

This class creates a shared function called **GetCustomers()**. It is declared using the **IDataReader** interface from the **System.Data.OleDB** library. This fulfills the first three bullet points listed above. The rest of the code is the standard code for creating the appropriate connection string and SQL query and calling the **ExecuteReader()** method.

After you enter this code, compile it so that it saves it as a DLL file. Now it's ready to be used as a data source for Crystal Reports.

The second step is creating the project (or open an existing one) and add a report to it that consumes the DLL. When you create the report using the Report Wizard, on the Data tab click the Create New Connections node and click the ADO.NET node. This opens the ADO.NET window where you can enter the connection information (refer back to Figure 17-5).

For the file path, click the ellipses button to open the Open File dialog box. Change the File Type dropdown to ".NET Data Provider DLL". Navigate to where the DLL is located and select it. On the Class Name option, click the dropdown list and select the **MyDataReader.DataSource** class. Click the Finish button to save your changes and close the window.

The Data window now shows your DLL as a data source and the **GetCustomers** method is shown as the table name. Double-click on the **GetCustomers** table so that it is added to the Selected Tables list.

Click the Next button to go to the Fields tab. Here you will see that all the fields from the DataReader are listed. Behind the scenes, Crystal Reports instantiated the DLL, called the GetCustomers() method, and examined the data to determine the fields available.

At this point, creating the report follows the standard steps of using the Report Wizard to pick the fields to print and going through the remaining steps.

After you have finished creating the report, it has stored an internal reference to the DLL. Printing the report is simply a matter of getting a reference to the report and passing it to the viewer. There is no need to call the SetDataSource() method. For example, here is sample code which opens the report and previews it.

Listing 17-14. Previewing the report that uses the DataReader as a data source.

```
Dim myReport As New CrystalDecisions.CrystalReports.Engine.ReportDocument
myReport.Load("CrystalReport1.rpt")
CrystalReportViewer1.ReportSource = myReport
```

Note

It is a good idea to test your code prior to using it as a data source for your report. This ensures that there are no bugs and that the security credentials are valid. For example, you can do something like calling the method and seeing if it returns any errors and correcting them if necessary. Here is something simple that I used to test the above code.

```
Dim Test As System.Data.OleDb.OleDbDataReader
Test = MyDataReader.DataSource.GetCustomers()
```

Reporting from DataSets in a DLL

Crystal Reports also gives you the ability to report from DataSets that are within a separate DLL. In a multi-tier architecture, this lets you build reports directly from the data layer without having to write extra code to encapsulate the dataset in a local object variable.

The steps for doing this are almost identical to reporting from the IDataReader interface.[42] When creating the report, use the DLL as the data source and select the proper class and method that returns the dataset object.

Let's do a walk-through of the steps to report from a DLL that has a public method which returns a dataset. I assume that you already have a project library created, but for illustration

---

[42] If you skipped over the section about reporting from the IDataReader interface, please refer back to that section for a more detailed explanation

purposes I'll go through the steps of creating one from scratch so that you can test it on your computer.

The first step is to create a new project using the Class Library template. In this example, I named my project, MyDataSet. After creating the project, I deleted the default Class1.vb that was created automatically and added a class called **DataSource**. The code is in Listing 17-15. The class creates a public function called **GetCustomersDS()** which returns a **DataSet** object.

Listing 17-15. Source code for the MyDataSet project.

[VB.NET}

```
Imports System.Data
Public Class DataSource
    Private Const CONNECTION_STRING_DS As String = _
    "Data Source=vmware;Initial Catalog=xtreme;User Id=sa;Password=pw"
    Private Const CUSTOMER_TABLE As String = _
    "SELECT [Customer ID], [Customer Name], [Contact Last Name], City FROM Customer"
    Public Function GetCustomersDS() As DataSet
        Dim myDataSet As DataSet
        Dim myAdapter As System.Data.SqlClient.SqlDataAdapter
        myAdapter = New SqlClient.SqlDataAdapter(CUSTOMER_TABLE, CONNECTION_STRING_DS)
        myDataSet = New DataSet()
        myAdapter.Fill(myDataSet, "Customers")
        Return myDataSet
    End Function
End Class
```

[C#]

```
Using System.Data;
...
public class DataSource
{
    //Note: Use your own connection string here
    private const string CONNECTION_STRING = "provider=sqloledb;Data Source=vmware;Initial
Catalog=xtreme;User Id=sa;Password=pw";
    private const string CUSTOMER_TABLE = "SELECT [Customer ID], [Customer Name], [Contact
Last Name], City FROM Customer";
    public static IDataReader GetCustomers()
    {
        OleDbConnection myOleDbConnection = new OleDbConnection(CONNECTION_STRING);
        myOleDbConnection.Open();
        OleDbCommand myOleDbCommand;
        myOleDbCommand = new OleDbCommand(CUSTOMER_TABLE, myOleDbConnection);
        IDataReader myIDataReader = myOleDbCommand.ExecuteReader();
        return myIDataReader;
    }
}
```

After you enter this code, compile it so that it saves it as a DLL file. Now it's ready to be reported on.

The second step is to create a project, or open an existing one, and add a report to it that consumes the DLL. When you create the report using the Report Wizard, on the Data tab, click the Create New Connections node and click the ADO.NET node. This opens the ADO.NET window where you can enter the connection information (refer back to Figure 17-5).

For the file path, click the ellipses button to open the Open File dialog box. Change the File Type dropdown to ".NET Data Provider DLL". Navigate to where the DLL is located and select it. On the Class Name option, click the dropdown list and select the myDataSet.DataSource class.

Before clicking the Finish button, you need to tell Crystal Reports that the DLL has a method which returns a DataSet. Click the Use DataSet from Class checkbox. This causes a new dropdown box to appear which lists the methods in the class that return a dataset. Click the arrow and select the GetCustomerDS method.

Figure 17-6. Specifying the GetCustomerDS method as a data source.

Click the Finish button to save your changes and close the window.

The Data window now shows you the DLL as a data source and the GetCustomersDS method is shown as the table name. Double-click on the GetCustomersDS table so that it is added to the Selected Tables list.

Click the Next button to go to the Fields tab. Here you will see all the fields from the DataSet that are listed. Behind the scenes, Crystal Reports instantiated the DLL, called the GetCustomersDS method, and examined the data to determine the fields available.

At this point, creating the report follows the standard steps of using the Report Wizard to pick the fields to print and going through the remaining tabs.

After you have finished creating the report, it has stored an internal reference to the DLL. Printing the report is simply a matter of getting a reference to the report and passing it to the viewer. There is no need to call the SetDataSource() method. For example, here is sample code which opens the report and previews it.

Listing 17-16. Previewing the report that uses the DataReader as a data source.

[VB.NET]

```
Dim myReport As New CrystalDecisions.CrystalReports.Engine.ReportDocument
myReport.Load("..\..\CrystalReport1.rpt")
CrystalReportViewer1.ReportSource = myReport
```

[C#]

```
CrystalDecisions.CrystalReports.Engine.ReportDocument myReport;
myReport = new CrystalDecisions.CrystalReports.Engine.ReportDocument();
myReport.Load(@"..\..\CrystalReport1.rpt");
CrystalReportViewer1.ReportSource = myReport
```

Caching Data

If you are building an ASP.NET website, it is important to optimize the web server's memory. Reports can be quite large, and when you have many users on the site, then they can consume a lot of the server's resources. You can optimize reports by caching them. This saves them to memory so that the same report can be used across page views as well as shared between multiple users. Otherwise, the report would have to be processed each time it is referenced on a page. This creates unnecessary overhead for the web server as well as the database server which is servicing the queries.

There are two ways to cache reports and the method that you choose is dependent upon the report's shareability. A report that is used by multiple users within a relatively small time frame has high shareability. A report that is only needed by a single user is deemed to have a low shareability.

Note

When discussing whether a report is needed by more than one user, there is more to it than whether just the report itself is being used. Shareability takes into consideration the parameters that the report uses as well as the data that is returned from the database. For a report to have high shareability, every aspect of it must be identical across all users requesting that report. If a user enters one set of parameters for a report and another user enters a different set of parameters for that same report, the reports are considered to be different and can't be shared.

Reports that have low shareability are only used by a single user at a time. Thus, the report only needs to be persisted across page views for that one user. In this case, you can persist the report across page views by saving the report to the Session collection. This is discussed in detail in Chapter 14.

Reports that have high shareability will be used by multiple users on a regular basis. You shouldn't store the report to the Session collection because each user has their own instance of this object. Instead, persist the report using the Cache object. There is only a single instance of the Cache object on the server and all users share it.

The following code demonstrates saving a report to the Cache or retrieving it if it already exists.

Listing 17.17. Using the Cache to share a report.

[VB.NET]

```
Protected Sub Page_Init(ByVal sender As Object, ByVal e As System.EventArgs) Handles Me.Init
    Dim myReport As New CrystalDecisions.CrystalReports.Engine.ReportDocument
    'Check if the report already exists or not
    If Cache("CustomerReport") IsNot Nothing Then
        'The report is already in the Cache, so load it
        myReport = CType(Cache("CustomerReport"), _
        CrystalDecisions.CrystalReports.Engine.ReportDocument)
    Else
        'Create the report and save it to the Cache
        myReport.Load(Server.MapPath("CustomerReport.rpt"))
        Cache.Insert("CustomerReport", myReport)
    End If
    CrystalReportViewer1.ReportSource = myReport
End Sub
```

[C#]

```
protected void Page_Init(object sender, System.EventArgs e)
{
    CrystalDecisions.CrystalReports.Engine.ReportDocument myReport = new
CrystalDecisions.CrystalReports.Engine.ReportDocument();
    //Check if the report already exists or not
    if (Cache["CustomerReport"] != null)
    {
        //The report is already in the Cache, so load it
        myReport = (CrystalDecisions.CrystalReports.Engine.ReportDocument)Cache["CustomerReport"];
    }
    else
    {
        //Create the report and save it to the Cache
        myReport.Load(Server.MapPath("CrystalReport.rpt"));
```

```
      Cache.Insert("CustomerReport", myReport);
    }
    CrystalReportViewer1.ReportSource = myReport;
}
```

The code first checks to see if the Cache object has an instance of the Customer Report in its collection. If so, it assigns it to the **myReport** variable. Notice that it uses the **CType()** function to cast the object as a **ReportDocument** class.

If the report doesn't exist in the Cache object, a new copy of the report is instantiated and saved into the Cache object using the **Insert()** method.[43] It is now available to be reused by the current user as well as any other user on the site.

You might be surprised to see that this code doesn't test whether the **Page.IsPostBack()** property is true or false. Typically, web pages check if a page is being posted back to itself or not to determine whether it is necessary to reload certain objects or not. Since the Cache object is server based and not user based, it doesn't matter whether the user is loading the current page for the first time or not. It is only necessary to check whether the report is in the Cache object and act accordingly.

Working with Subreports

If a subreport uses the Push Model, you have to pass a populated dataset to the subreport. Just like the main report, this is accomplished using the **SetDataSource()** method and passing it the dataset object (or any of the applicable data types). The code for working with subreports is in Listing 17-5.

Printing Dynamic Images

I've received many email requests from people wanting to know how to print dynamic images on a report. If you've used previous versions of Crystal Reports with VB6, you know that there is a method that lets you load a new image onto the report for every record printed. Many people want that functionality back. Others want to have a field that serves as a link to an image. Rather than printing the link, they want the report to print the image that the link points to. Unfortunately, neither of these options is possible with .NET.[44] There are only two ways to print dynamic images on a report. The first way is to store the image in a blob field in SQL Server or MS Access. Add this field to the report just like any other field and it is printed on the report.

---

[43] The Cache.Insert() method has many optional parameters that let you specify how to cache the report. For example, you can set the dependency keys and an expiration policy. Please refer to MSDN for more information on the Insert method.

[44] If you have CR9, you can dynamically load images during runtime like you did with VB6. See Chapter 20 for more information.

If the images aren't stored in the database table, they have to be located on the local computer or network drive. To print these files you have to create a **DataTable** in memory and load these images into each row of the **DataTable**.

Note

The following steps are very involved and it is easy to make a mistake. With the release of Crystal Reports XI (and 2008), it is now possible to print dynamic images without writing any code in .NET. This process has been simplified so much, it is worth upgrading to Crystal Reports 2008 for this feature alone.

I'm going to show you an example of how to implement the second option where the images are loaded into a datatable. But this example requires that you modify it for your particular circumstance. It's not possible to illustrate all the ways you could add dynamic images to a report. More than likely you will have the file path stored in one of the fields in a table. I'm going to assume that is the case in this example and if you get your field names from somewhere else (e.g. hard-coded in the project, by reading the file list from the current directory, etc.), you can modify the example for your needs.

The overall process works as follows:

Load the existing dataset into memory. This is probably done by calling one of the **FillDataSet()** methods shown earlier.

Add a new column to the **DataTable** with a data type of **Byte()**. This column is where the image is stored.

Save this new table structure as an XML file using the **DataSet.WriteXmlSchema()** method (only do this the first time).

Create a new report using the schema file. Place all fields (including the image field) on the report.

When the application runs, read each record in the table and get the file path of the image. Use the file path to load the image into memory and save it to the new column of the row.

After looping through each row assign the **DataTable's DataSet** to the **ReportSource** property of the report.

Preview or print the report.

Wow! That's a lot of steps. I'm going to show you the final code that makes all this work and try to explain it as concisely and clearly as possible.

First of all, let's create a new **DataSet** and load a **DataTable**. I'm going to make this simple by creating a new **DataTable** manually and populate it with a couple records. In your application, replace this code with a call to **FillDataSet()**.

Listing 17-19. Printing dynamic images with a DataSet object.

[VB.NET]

```vbnet
Dim MyDataSet As New DataSet
Dim MyDataTable As DataTable
Dim MyDataRow As DataRow
Dim MyDataColumn As DataColumn
MyDataTable = New DataTable("ImageTable")
' Create first column
MyDataColumn = New DataColumn("PicNumber", GetType(System.Int32))
MyDataTable.Columns.Add(MyDataColumn)
'Field that points to the image file
MyDataColumn = New DataColumn("ImagePath", GetType(System.String))
MyDataTable.Columns.Add(MyDataColumn)
'Populate the table with dummy data
'Make sure your C Drive has two files called Image1.jpg and Image2.jpg
MyDataRow = MyDataTable.NewRow()
MyDataRow("PicNumber") = 1
MyDataRow("ImagePath") = "C:\Image1.jpg"
MyDataTable.Rows.Add(MyDataRow)
MyDataRow = MyDataTable.NewRow()
MyDataRow("PicNumber") = 2
MyDataRow("ImagePath") = "C:\Image2.jpg"
MyDataTable.Rows.Add(MyDataRow)
MyDataSet.Tables.Add(MyDataTable)
'Add the image column to the table - See Listing 17-19.
AddImageColumn(MyDataTable)
'Only do this when you first design the report
MyDataSet.WriteXmlSchema("ImageTable.xsd")
'Open the report and preview it
Dim MyReport as New CrystalReport1
MyReport.SetDataSource(MyDataSet)
CrystalReportViewer1.ReportSource = MyReport
```

[C#]

```csharp
public void LoginToTables(string UserId, string Password, string ServerName, string DatabaseName)
{
   CrystalReport1 MyReport = new CrystalReport1();
   CrystalDecisions.Shared.TableLogOnInfo MyLogonInfo;
   CrystalDecisions.Shared.ConnectionInfo MyConnectionInfo = new
CrystalDecisions.Shared.ConnectionInfo();
   if (ServerName != "")
   {
      MyConnectionInfo.ServerName = ServerName;
      MyConnectionInfo.DatabaseName = DatabaseName;
   }
   MyConnectionInfo.UserID = UserId;
   MyConnectionInfo.Password = Password;
   foreach (CrystalDecisions.CrystalReports.Engine.Table MyTable in MyReport.Database.Tables)
   {
      MyLogonInfo = MyTable.LogOnInfo;
      MyLogonInfo.ConnectionInfo = MyConnectionInfo;
      MyTable.ApplyLogOnInfo(MyLogonInfo);
      //Note: The next line is only necessary for SQL Server
```

```
    if (ServerName != "")
    {
        MyTable.Location = MyTable.Location.Substring(MyTable.Location.LastIndexOf(".")+1);
    }
}
crystalReportViewer1.ReportSource = MyReport;
}
```

This code creates a **DataTable** with two columns: **PicNumber** and **ImagePath**. The ImagePath column points to the location of the image. I put two images on the root directory of the C drive.

The next step adds a column to the table to hold the image. The following code is in a generic method so you can easily drop it into your own project with no modifications.

Listing 17-20. Create a table column for the image.

[VB.NET]

```
Public Shared Sub AddImageColumn(ByVal MyDataTable As DataTable, ByVal FieldName As String)
    'Create the column to hold the binary image
    Dim MyDataColumn As DataColumn = New DataColumn(FieldName, GetType(System.Byte()))
    MyDataTable.Columns.Add(MyDataColumn)
End Sub
```

[C#]

```
public void AddImageColumn(DataTable MyDataTable, string FieldName)
{
    //Create the column to hold the binary image
    DataColumn MyDataColumn = new DataColumn(FieldName, Type.GetType("System.Byte[]"));
    MyDataTable.Columns.Add(MyDataColumn);
}
```

This procedure takes a **DataTable** object and the name of the column that holds the binary image. It creates a new column of type **Byte()**.

After adding the new column, write the XML schema file and build the report using this schema file. Don't forget to comment out this line after you create the schema file!

Note

Even though the new column is of type **Byte()**, when this is saved to an XML schema file the column data type is automatically changed to **base64Binary**. If you are creating the **DataSet** manually with the IDE you have to specify the data type to be **base64Binary**.

Once the report is designed, open the **DataTable** again and load in the images.

Listing 17-21. Process each row in the table.

[VB.NET]

```
Public Shared Sub LoadAllImages(ByVal MyDataTable As DataTable, ByVal FilePathField As String,
ByVal ImageField As String)
    'Loop through all the rows and load the images
    For Each MyDataRow As DataRow In MyDataTable.Rows
        LoadImage(MyDataRow, ImageField, MyDataRow.Item(FilePathField))
    Next
End Sub
```

[C#]

```
public void LoadAllImages(DataTable MyDataTable, string FilePathField, string ImageField)
{
    //Loop through the rows and load the images
    foreach(DataRow MyDataRow in MyDataTable.Rows)
    {
        LoadImage(MyDataRow, ImageField, MyDataRow[FilePathField].ToString());
    }
}
```

The LoadAllImages() procedure loops through each row in the DataTable and calls the
LoadImage() procedure to load a single image. Pass the LoadAllImages() procedure the
DataTable object, the name of the column that has the image location, and the name of the
column that will hold the binary image.

Listing 17-22. Load a single image into a DataRow.

[VB.NET]

```
Public Shared Sub LoadImage(ByVal MyDataRow As System.data.DataRow, ByVal FilePath As String,
ByVal ImageField As String)
    Dim fs As New System.IO.FileStream(FilePath, IO.FileMode.Open, System.IO.FileAccess.Read)
    Dim Image(fs.Length) As Byte
    fs.Read(Image, 0, fs.Length)
    fs.Close()
    MyDataRow.Item(ImageField) = Image
End Sub
```

[C#]

```
public void LoadImage(DataRow MyDataRow, string ImageField, string FilePath)
{
    System.IO.FileStream fs = new System.IO.FileStream(FilePath, System.IO.FileMode.Open,
    System.IO.FileAccess.Read);
    Byte[] Image = new Byte[fs.Length];
    fs.Read(Image, 0, (int)fs.Length);
    fs.Close();
    MyDataRow[ImageField] = Image;
}
```

The LoadImage() procedure creates a new FileStream object and loads the image into a
Byte array. Then it saves this Byte array to the DataRow in the column.

Once all the rows have been updated with their appropriate image, pass the DataSet to the
report and preview or print it.

Best Of The Forum

Question: I am able to load pictures dynamically based on the examples in Brian's book. But, how can I change the image size as well?

Answer: Unfortunately, there aren't any properties that let you modify this. You have to use the same size for every image.

Report Web Services

Creating reports as Report Web Services (RWS) enables you to deliver reports using SOAP via an HTTP protocol. There are no issues with worrying about the report being blocked by security or network constraints.

There are two parts to viewing reports as a web service. The first part is to build the web service application and publish the report. The second is creating an application that consumes the report. Fortunately, Visual Studio .NET makes creating and consuming web services almost trivial.

First create a new Web Services project using the Visual Studio IDE. Click on the menu options File > New > Web Site.

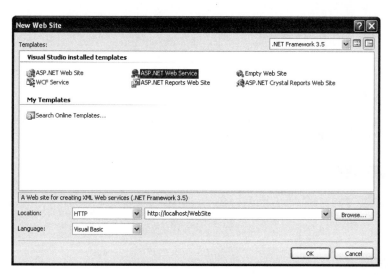

Figure 18-1. Create new web services project

Caution

Be careful to set the Location property to HTTP. This tells Visual Studio to update the IIS Settings so that the report is in the INetPub/WWWRoot folder and runs under LocalHost. If you use the File option, the URL uses a temporary URL each time the project runs and this can't be referenced directly by another application. You will have to update IIS manually to create a new virtual directory that accesses the web service directly.

When the web site opens, add a new report to it. You can either use the Report Wizard to build the report from scratch or add an existing report.

In my example, I selected the EmployeeList report I built in an earlier chapter. Right click on the project name in the Solution Explorer window and select Add > Add Existing Item. After the dialog box opens, browse to where your report is located and select it.

To publish the report as a web service, right-click on it in the Solution Explorer window and select Publish as Web Service.

Figure 18-2. Publish the report as a web service.

This adds a new web service class to your project. It is automatically named the same as the report name with "service" appended to it. The file extension is .asmx.

Figure 18-3. The new report web service class.

That's all there is to it! Test the report web service by right-clicking on it in the Solution Explorer and selecting Set As Start Page. Then run the application. A web browser will open up with the following page displayed.

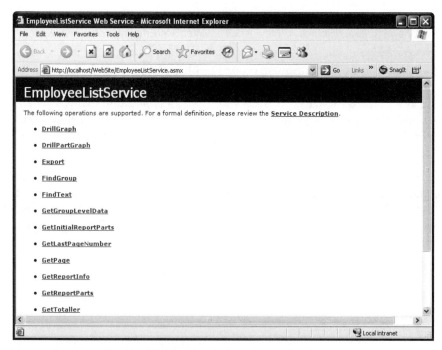

Figure 18-4. Testing the Report Web Service with a browser.

The browser shows you all the operations that the report supports. You can click on each one and see a sample SOAP request and response. Look in the address bar for the full URL of the report web service. This is the URL that is assigned to the viewer control of the application that consumes this service.

Consuming the Report Service

The second part is creating an application to consume the report's web service. To create an application that consumes the web service, open a new instance of the Visual Studio IDE and create a new Windows application (or an ASP.NET application).

Add a CrystalReportViewer control to your form and bind it to the web service. This is done by assigning the web service URL to the viewer's ReportSource property. The following code performs the binding.

Listing 18-1. Consuming a project's web service

[VB.NET]

```
Private Sub Form1_Load(ByVal sender As System.Object, ByVal e As System.EventArgs) Handles _
    MyBase.Load
    CrystalReportViewer1.ReportSource = "http://localhost/WebSite/EmployeeListService.asmx"
End Sub
```

[C#]

```
private void Form1_Load(object sender, System.EventArgs e)
```

```
{
    crystalReportViewer1.ReportSource = "http://localhost/WebSite/EmployeeListService.asmx";
}
```

Notice that when setting the **ReportSource** property with a URL, the viewer doesn't need to have any special properties set. In other words, a viewer can display any web service report as long as it's passed the URL. This lets you create an application that is a generic report viewer and display a number of reports. You could have one web service which returns a list of all the reports on the server and an application which retrieves this list and previews whichever one the user chooses.

Web services can only be consumed by the viewer control. Passing the web service URL to a **ReportDocument** results in an error. The only time you really need to use a **ReportDocument** object is when you want to print the report without previewing it first. To get around this problem, load the report into the viewer, call the **PrintReport()** method, and assign the **ReportSource** property to **Nothing**.

Listing 18-2. Print a web service report without previewing it.

[VB.NET]
```
Private Sub Form1_Load(ByVal sender As System.Object, ByVal e As System.EventArgs) _
Handles MyBase.Load
    CrystalReportViewer1.ReportSource = "http://localhost/WebSite/EmployeeListService.asmx"
    CrystalReportViewer1.PrintReport()
    CrystalReportViewer1.ReportSource = Nothing
End Sub
```

[C#]
```
private void Form1_Load(object sender, System.EventArgs e)
{
    crystalReportViewer1.ReportSource ="http://localhost/WebSite/EmployeeListService.asmx";
    crystalReportViewer1.PrintReport();
    crystalReportViewer1.ReportSource = null;
}
```

Making Client Side Runtime Modifications

Report web services can have a minor number of modifications made to them during runtime. As you learned in Chapter 14, the most flexible way to make runtime report modifications is by using the **ReportDocument** class. It is far more robust than the viewer control which only has a few properties. Unfortunately, a web service report is generated on the server and consequently this is where the **ReportDocument** object is instantiated. The client is restricted to using the viewer control and doesn't have any access to the **ReportDocument** object.

Only being able to use the viewer control is disappointing. It can only do three things: set the record selection formula, set parameters, and set user credentials for logging into the data source.[45] It can't get direct access to all the report objects and their properties.

All the code samples that use the viewer to make runtime modifications will work unchanged for report web services.

Making Server Side Report Modifications

The last section showed how the client is limited to using the viewer control for making runtime modifications. This doesn't give you many options for making runtime modifications. But that doesn't mean that it is impossible to make changes using the ReportDocument class. You just have to do it on the server within the web service application.

Making changes on the server side is very powerful because you get full access to the ReportDocument class. You can make changes to the report objects so that the report is completely dynamic. And you don't have to learn any new coding practices because you can use same code shown throughout this book. The only difference is how you reference the ReportDocument object. That is the tricky part!

Before showing you how to make server side modifications, you need to understand that there is one major problem with this approach. The server can't communicate with the client because the client can't pass information to the report web service. If this were a typical application, the user would enter information on a form and this information would be used to modify the ReportDocument object prior to printing the report. But you can't do this with report web services. If you try to pass information on the query string, the web service returns an error. You also can't use cookies because these are strictly client based. You are restricted to making changes to the ReportDocument object that aren't user specific.

The one trick around this is to use multiple web services that open the same report. Each web service can perform a different modification to the report object prior to previewing it. For example, you could have one web service show the default report and another web service modify the default grouping of a report. This lets one report be used by different web services and the end user thinks that they are looking at different reports. As another example, you could also have different web services specific to individual clients. Each client gets the same report, but you can charge them an additional fee if they want it customized to match their corporate image.

Modifying the ReportDocument object is done by overwriting the existing code in the instantiator method. For VB.NET, this is the New() method. It is within the web service's underlying .asmx.vb file (.asmx.cs for C# programs).

---

[45] Each of these was discussed in a prior chapter along with complete source code.

Here is the New() method code for the EmployeeList web service report that was created earlier in this chapter. It creates a ReportDocument object, loads the Employee List into it, and assigns a new report title to it.

Listing 18-3. Setting report properties on the client

[VB.NET]

```
Public Sub New()
    Dim myReport As new CrystalDecisions.CrystalReports.Engine.ReportDocument
    myReport.Load(Server.MapPath("EmployeeListx.rpt"))
    myReport.SummaryInfo.ReportTitle = "New Report Title"
    Me.ReportSource = myReport
End Sub
```

[C#]

```
Public EmployeeListService()
{
    CrystalDecisions.CrystalReports.Engine.ReportDocument myReport;
    myReport = new CrystalDecisions.CrystalReports.Engine.ReportDocument();
    myReport.Load(Server.MapPath( "EmployeeListx.rpt" ));
    myReport.SummaryInfo.ReportTitle = "New Report Title";
    this.ReportSource = myReport;
}
```

Being able to modify the ReportDocument on the server is crucial if you have a report based on a DataSet. If you recall from Chapter 17, datasets have to be manually populated by the application and assigned to the report using the SetDataSource() method of the ReportDocument object. You also know from the previous section that the viewer class can only set login credentials for a report. It can't set the data source property. If a report uses a dataset and you make it into a web service, the viewer is going to give you an error.

19
Exporting and Deploying Reports

Crystal Reports gives you two ways of delivering reports. The first way is exporting them to different formats and file types. For example, you could export reports as PDF or MS Word files. You could also export them as email attachments. The second way of delivering reports is by deploying them with your application. This involves modifying the setup files so that the reports and related libraries are included on the destination computer. This chapter covers both exporting and deploying reports.

Exporting Reports

Printing and previewing reports is a great way of presenting data to users. But there is one big problem: the user has to have a copy of your application to do it. If you want to show someone what a report looks like, you can't email them your application or ask everyone to sit at your computer. That is where exporting comes in. You can export reports in a variety of formats that are displayed by common applications that most people already have (Adobe Acrobat, Excel, HTML, etc.). This lets people see and understand your data without having a copy of the application on their computer. For example, the PDF format is the most common way of presenting data via the web. In fact, it has become the de facto standard and most users already have the Adobe Acrobat viewer installed on their computer. If you want to deliver reports that let users work with the data so that it is dynamic, you can export them to an Excel spreadsheet and give your users the ability to perform more advanced data analysis.

In one respect, exporting a report could seem like a frivolous task. Consider that a report is just output data that you had to assimilate with your code. Rather than generate a report, you could skip that step entirely and use an SQL query to export the raw data into another table or as XML. However, using Crystal Reports gives you many advantages. The most obvious advantage is that it has the export functionality built-in and this saves you time programming. A less obvious benefit is that it gives you the ability to quickly customize how the data is presented. Use the powerful report engine to perform the sorting and grouping and other functionality without having to worry about the implementation details. Without a doubt, being able to export report data to different formats is a very powerful feature.

Crystal Reports gives you many different formats for exporting your reports. They are as follows: MS Excel, HTML 3.2/4.0, PDF, Rich Text, MS Word, Microsoft Mail (MAPI), and Exchange Folder.

There are two ways to export a report. The first is using the built-in export capabilities of the viewer control. The second is to write the code to export the report. Although the second method is more work, you'll see in a later section that it gives you more control over the exporting process.

Exporting with the Viewer

The easiest way to export a report is to have the users do it themselves by using the report viewer. The viewer has a built-in export button that lets the user export the current report to the file format of their choice.

Figure 19-1. The Export button on the Windows Report Viewer toolbar.

When the user clicks on the export button, the Export Report dialog box appears. The user selects the file format and enters the filename. When the OK button is clicked, the report gets exported to the file. There is nothing for you as a programmer to do.

The formats that you can export to are Crystal Reports (a standard .rpt file), Adobe Acrobat PDF, MS Excel, MS Excel Data Only, MS Word, and Rich Text Format.

Note

The Export button does not support exporting to HTML.

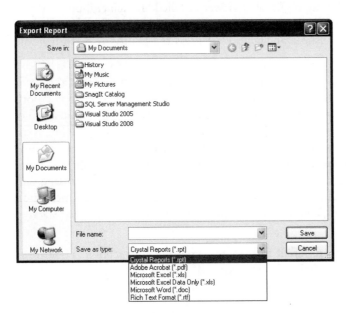

Figure 19-2. The Windows Export Report dialog box.

When exporting from a web page, a pop-up window appears with the export options in it. Exporting from the web lets you export to the same file type as Windows, but it also lets you specify the pages. The Windows export doesn't let you specify a page range and it always exports all report pages. Figure 19-3 shows the web export dialog box.

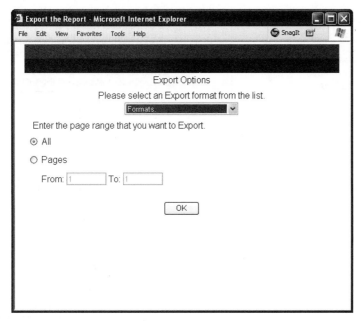

Figure 19-3. The web export page.

Exporting with Programming Code

Using the built-in export feature of the Crystal Reports viewer is nice, but as in most things related to programming, what you get in ease of use you give up in functionality. To get the most functionality for exporting a report, you have to write the programming code yourself.

Caution

It is common to export a report and find out that either the parameters or login information is lost. This is because these parameters were set using the viewer object and the ReportDocument object is used to do the exporting. These objects are exclusive of each other. When exporting, always set all properties with the ReportDocument object.

Before exporting a report, you have to consider two questions. The first questions is, "What is the destination type?" There are four destination types to choose from: Disk file, Exchange folder, Email attachment and an Http Response. The second question is , "What is the format that the report should be exported to?" There are seven formats that reports can be converted to: PDF files, RTF, MS Word, MS Excel, MS Excel data only, HTML 3.2 and HTML 4.0. These two questions are independent of each other and are programmed differently. Figure 19-4 shows the exporting object model and how the different classes work together.

ExportOptions
-DestinationOptions : DiskFileDestinationOptions
-DestinationOptions : ExchangeFolderDestinationOptions
-DestinationOptions : MicrosoftMailDestinationOptions
-ExportDestinationType : ExportDestinationType
-ExportFormatType : ExportFormatType
-ExportFormatOptions : ExcelFormatOptions
-ExportFormatOptions : HTMLFormatOptions
-ExportFormatOptions : PdfRtfWordFormatOptions
+CreateDiskFileDestinationOptions()
+CreateExcelFormatOptions()
+CreateExchangeFolderDestinationOptions()
+CreateHTMLFormatOptions()
+CreateMicrosoftMailDestinationOptions()
+CreatePdfRtfWordFormatOptions()

DiskFileDestinationOptions
-DiskFileName : String

ExchangeFolderDestinationOptions
-DestinationType
-FolderPath : String
-Password : String
-Profile : String

«enumeration» ExportDestinationType
-DiskFile
-ExchangeFolder
-MicrosoftMail
-NoDestination

MicrosoftMailDestinationOptions
-MailCCList : String
-MailMessage : String
-MailSubject : String
-MailToList : String
-Password : String
-UserName : String

«enumeration» ExportFormatType
-Excel
-HTML32
-HTML40
-NoFormat
-PortableDocFormat
-RichText
-WordForWindows

ExcelFormatOptions
-ExcelAreaGroupNumber : Integer
-ExcelAreaType : AreaSectionKind
-ExcelConstantColumnWidth : Double
-ExcelTabHasColumnHeadings : Boolean
-ExcelUseConstantColumnWidth : Boolean

HTMLFormatOptions
-FirstPageNumber : Integer
-HTMLEnableSeperatedPages : Boolean
-HTMLBaseFolderName : String
-HTMLFileName : String
-HTMLHasPageNavigator : Boolean
-LastPageNumber : Integer
-UsePageRange : Boolean

«enumeration» ExchangeDestinationType
-ExchangePostDocMessage

PdfRtfWordFormatOptions
-FirstPageNumber : Integer
-LastPageNumber : Integer
-UsePageRange : Boolean

Figure 19-4. The Export object model.

The ReportDocument class has various methods and properties that are used to implement the export functionality of Crystal Reports. Table 19-1 lists each method available.

Table 19-1. Export methods of the ReportDocument class.

Method	Description
Export()	Exports a report to any of the available export formats using the properties of the ExportOptions object.
ExportToDisk(ExportFormatType, Filename)	Exports a report to a disk file with no additional coding.
ExportToHttpResponse(ExportOptions, HttpResponse, Boolean, String)	Exports a report via the HTTP Response object. Has the option to export the report as a file attachment.

Easy Exporting To Disk

There is one method that makes exporting easy: ExportToDisk(). Without a doubt, the ExportToDisk() method is the most popular way of exporting a report because you are only required to specify the format type and the filename. The following code shows an example of saving a report as a PDF file. You can see that only one line of code is required to export the report to a PDF formatted file.

```
myReport.ExportToDisk(CrystalDecisions.Shared.ExportFormatType.PortableDocFormat,
"C:\Report.PDF")
```

The first parameter uses the ExportFormatType enumeration to specify the format the file should be saved in and the second parameter is the file name. The ExportToDisk() method supports the most common formats used for viewing files. Table 19-2 lists the format and enumeration constants associated with each. They are within the namespace CrystalDecisions.Shared.ExportFormatType.

Table 19-2. Enumeration constants for the export format.

Format	File Extension	Enumeration Constant
Adobe Acrobat	.PDF	PortableDocFormat
Rich Text Format	.RTF	RichText
HTML 3.2	.HTM / .HTML	HTML32
HTML 4.0	.HTM / .HTML	HTML40
MS Word	.DOC	WordForWindows
MS Excel	.XLS	Excel

MS Excel	.XLS	ExcelRecord (data only)
Crystal Reports	.RPT	CrystalReport

The drawback to using the ExportToDisk() method is that it doesn't have any parameters for customizing the export format. For example, there is no way to specify the page range. To customize the report format that gets exported, you have to use the more advanced features found in the Export() method.

Advanced Exporting

When you want to do more than a simple export to disk, use the Export() method. It has many classes and properties for customizing the export process. Consequently, having additional classes and properties makes this method more complicated to learn and use. This chapter gives you many examples that make it easy to copy and paste the code listings into your application.

Exporting a report consists of the following steps:

1. Create an ExportOptions object and set its properties.

2. Assign the type of destination where the export should be sent (e.g. disk file, email, MS Exchange Server).

3. Set the format type (Excel, PDF, etc.).

4. Assign the formatting options specific to each format type.

5. Call the ReportDocument.Export() method and pass it the ExportOptions object.

Although these steps are the same for every type of export, their implementation varies. Within the code listings of the following sections, you will see the details of how to perform each step. However, one aspect that is common to them all is that they all use the ExportDestinationType enumeration. This specificies the destination for the export. This could be a disk file, an email, or a MS Exchange Server folder. You have to specify the destination type so that Crystal Reports knows where to send the export. Table 19-3 shows the values for the CrystalDecisions.Shared.ExportDestinationType enumeration.

Table 19-3. Enumeration constants for ExportDestinationType.

Destination	Enumeration Constant
Disk File	DiskFile
Exchange Folder	ExchangeFolder
Email (MAPI)	MicrosoftMail

The following sections show you how to perform each type of export available in Crystal Reports. They cover exporting to PDF, RTF, Word, Excel, HTML, email, and MS Exchange Server.

Exporting to PDF, RTF, and Word Documents

The process for exporting to PDF, RTF, and MS Word shares the same classes for all three. In fact, the code is identical except for the property that sets the export format type, which specifies which of the three types to use.

Exporting a report to PDF, RTF or Word gives you the option to specify the page range. You can set the starting and ending page or simply print out the entire report. Note that all pages must be consecutively numbered. For example, you can't export the first few pages of a report and the last few pages of a report. Table 19-4 shows the properties used for setting the page range.

Table 19-4. PdfRtfWordFormatOptions Properties.

Property	Description
UsePageRange	Boolean that enables/disables the use of page ranges
FirstPageNumber	The first page number to export
LastPageNumber	The last page number to export

The following listing first creates an ExportOptions object variable, myExportOptions, and tells it that the export file will be saved to a disk file using the DiskFileDestinationOptions object.

After that, it sets the format type to PDF. If you want to export to RTF or Word, change this line to be the appropriate enumeration. After setting the format type, create a format options object and set the page range. If all the pages are going to be exported, set the UsePageRange property to False. Otherwise, set it to True and also set the FirstPageNumber and LastPageNumber properties.

Finally, assign the format options object to the myExportOptions object and call the ReportDocument.Export() method.

Note

The following code listings assume that you already instantiated a ReportDocument object and loaded the report into memory. This report object is one of the parameters listed in the method declaration. The other parameters specify the values for the exporting process (filename, which pages to print, etc.). These parameters are self-explanatory.

Listing 19-1. Set the export formatting to PDF

[VB.NET]

```vbnet
Public Sub ExportPdfRtfWord(ByVal Filename As String, ByRef myReport As
CrystalDecisions.CrystalReports.Engine.ReportDocument, ByVal UsePageRange As Boolean, ByVal
FirstPageNumber As Integer, ByVal LastPageNumber As Integer)
  Dim myExportOptions As New CrystalDecisions.Shared.ExportOptions
  'Set the export to a disk file
  myExportOptions.ExportDestinationType = _
  CrystalDecisions.Shared.ExportDestinationType.DiskFile
  Dim myDestinationOptions As CrystalDecisions.Shared.DiskFileDestinationOptions
  myDestinationOptions = CrystalDecisions.Shared.ExportOptions.CreateDiskFileDestinationOptions
  myDestinationOptions.DiskFileName = Filename
  myExportOptions.ExportDestinationOptions = myDestinationOptions
  'Change the next line if you want the format to be RTF or Word
  myExportOptions.ExportFormatType = _
  CrystalDecisions.Shared.ExportFormatType.PortableDocFormat
  'The following lines stay the same regardless of formatting
  Dim myFormatOptions As CrystalDecisions.Shared.PdfRtfWordFormatOptions
  myFormatOptions = CrystalDecisions.Shared.ExportOptions.CreatePdfRtfWordFormatOptions()
  myFormatOptions.UsePageRange = UsePageRange
  If UsePageRange Then
    myFormatOptions.FirstPageNumber = FirstPageNumber
    myFormatOptions.LastPageNumber = LastPageNumber
  End If
  myExportOptions.FormatOptions = myFormatOptions
  myReport.Export(myExportOptions)
End Sub
```

[C#]

```csharp
public void ExportPdfRtfWord(string Filename, ref
CrystalDecisions.CrystalReports.Engine.ReportDocument myReport, bool UsePageRange, int
FirstPageNumber, int LastPageNumber)
{
  CrystalDecisions.Shared.ExportOptions myExportOptions = new
CrystalDecisions.Shared.ExportOptions();
  //Set the export to a disk file
  myExportOptions.ExportDestinationType = CrystalDecisions.Shared.ExportDestinationType.DiskFile;
  CrystalDecisions.Shared.DiskFileDestinationOptions myDestinationOptions;
  myDestinationOptions =
CrystalDecisions.Shared.ExportOptions.CreateDiskFileDestinationOptions();
  myDestinationOptions.DiskFileName = Filename;
  myExportOptions.ExportDestinationOptions = myDestinationOptions;
  //Change the next line if you want the format to be RTF or Word
  myExportOptions.ExportFormatType =
CrystalDecisions.Shared.ExportFormatType.PortableDocFormat;
  //The following lines stay the same regardless of formatting
  CrystalDecisions.Shared.PdfRtfWordFormatOptions myFormatOptions;
  myFormatOptions = CrystalDecisions.Shared.ExportOptions.CreatePdfRtfWordFormatOptions();
  myFormatOptions.UsePageRange = UsePageRange;
  if (UsePageRange) {
    myFormatOptions.FirstPageNumber = FirstPageNumber;
```

```
      myFormatOptions.LastPageNumber = LastPageNumber;
  }
  myExportOptions.FormatOptions = myFormatOptions;
  myReport.Export(myExportOptions);
}
```

Question: I need to export multiple reports into a single PDF file. How do I merge them together into a single file?

Answer: Unfortunately, Crystal Reports can't do this. One workaround is to create a blank main report and add all the reports you want to merge as subreports. That lets them print out consecutively and you can export this new report to PDF. The other way is to download a third-party Crystal Reports/PDF tool. I haven't used one myself, but I see them advertised in Google search results.

Exporting to Excel

Exporting a report to an Excel spreadsheet gives you options to work with the report areas and how the columns are formatted. The columns can be formatted so that they have headers and that they are all the same width. Table 19-5 shows the properties used for setting the Excel formatting.

Table 19-5. ExcelFormatOptions Properties.

Property	Description
ExcelAreaGroupNumber	The base area group number if the area type is group area.
ExcelAreaType	The area type if you aren't using constant column width.
ExcelConstantColumnWidth	The width of each column (if using constant column width).
ExcelTabHasColumnHeadings	Boolean that determines if the columns have headings listed.
ExcelUseConstantColumnWidth	Boolean that determines if the columns are the same width.

The following listing is very similar to the previous listing. It first creates an ExportOptions object variable, myExportOptions, and tells it that the export file will be saved to a disk file using the DiskFileDestinationOptions object. The difference is that the format options object is specific to Excel and sets the properties listed in Table 19-5. After setting those properties, it calls the Export() method as the previous listing did.

Listing 19-2. Setting the format to be an Excel spreadsheet.

[VB.NET]

```
Public Sub ExportToExcel(ByVal Filename As String, ByRef myReport As
CrystalDecisions.CrystalReports.Engine.ReportDocument, ByVal UseConstantColumnWidth As
Boolean, ByVal ColumnWidth As Integer, ByVal UseColumnHeadings As Boolean)
    Dim myExportOptions As New CrystalDecisions.Shared.ExportOptions
    'Set the export to a disk file
    myExportOptions.ExportDestinationType = CrystalDecisions.Shared.ExportDestinationType.DiskFile
    Dim myDestinationOptions As CrystalDecisions.Shared.DiskFileDestinationOptions
    myDestinationOptions = CrystalDecisions.Shared.ExportOptions.CreateDiskFileDestinationOptions
    myDestinationOptions.DiskFileName = Filename
    myExportOptions.ExportDestinationOptions = myDestinationOptions
    'Set the Excel formatting properties
    myExportOptions.ExportFormatType = CrystalDecisions.Shared.ExportFormatType.ExcelRecord
    Dim myFormatOptions As CrystalDecisions.Shared.ExcelFormatOptions
    myFormatOptions = CrystalDecisions.Shared.ExportOptions.CreateExcelFormatOptions()
    myFormatOptions.ExcelConstantColumnWidth = ColumnWidth
    myFormatOptions.ExcelUseConstantColumnWidth = UseConstantColumnWidth
    myFormatOptions.ExcelTabHasColumnHeadings = UseColumnHeadings
    'Assign the formatting properties to the report and export it
    myExportOptions.FormatOptions = myFormatOptions
    myReport.Export(myExportOptions)
End Sub
```

[C#]

```
public void ExportToExcel(string Filename, ref
CrystalDecisions.CrystalReports.Engine.ReportDocument myReport, bool UseConstantColumnWidth,
int ColumnWidth, bool UseColumnHeadings)
{
    CrystalDecisions.Shared.ExportOptions myExportOptions = new
CrystalDecisions.Shared.ExportOptions();
    //Set the export to a disk file
    myExportOptions.ExportDestinationType = CrystalDecisions.Shared.ExportDestinationType.DiskFile;
    CrystalDecisions.Shared.DiskFileDestinationOptions myDestinationOptions;
    myDestinationOptions = CrystalDecisions.Shared.ExportOptions.CreateDiskFileDestinationOptions;
    myDestinationOptions.DiskFileName = Filename;
    myExportOptions.ExportDestinationOptions = myDestinationOptions;
    //Set the Excel formatting properties
    myExportOptions.ExportFormatType = CrystalDecisions.Shared.ExportFormatType.ExcelRecord;
    CrystalDecisions.Shared.ExcelFormatOptions myFormatOptions;
    myFormatOptions = CrystalDecisions.Shared.ExportOptions.CreateExcelFormatOptions();
    myFormatOptions.ExcelConstantColumnWidth = ColumnWidth;
    myFormatOptions.ExcelUseConstantColumnWidth = UseConstantColumnWidth;
    myFormatOptions.ExcelTabHasColumnHeadings = UseColumnHeadings;
    //Assign the formatting properties to the report and export it
    myExportOptions.FormatOptions = myFormatOptions;
    myReport.Export(myExportOptions);
}
```

Best Of The Forum

Question: I need to export 64 columns of data to an Excel spreadsheet. But Crystal won't let me because this is bigger than what can fit on a page. How do I send all my data to Excel?

Answer: You need to trick Crystal Reports into thinking that you have a very large printer installed on your computer. This lets you have a wide page format and export it to Excel. To do this, open the Control Panel and add a new printer. Select Local Printer and uncheck the option "Automatically detect and install". Click the Next button. Select the option "Create a New Port" and leave it at Local Port. Click the Next buton. Enter a dummy name and click the OK button. Select the printer "Hewlett-Packard HP-GL/2 Plotter" and click Next. After installing the new printer, go into your report and select the menu options Crystal Reports > Design > Printer Setup. Select the HP Plotter printer and select the paper size "DIN CO 917 x 1297 mm". Click the OK button to save your changes. You can now export a large number of columns to Excel.

Exporting to HTML

HTML output is inherently different from exporting to the other file formats. HTML files are meant to be viewed in a web browser and this can impose certain requirements on how you present the data to the user. You have the option of displaying the entire report in a single browser window or breaking it up into separate web pages. If you display the report on a single page, the user can view all the data at one time. But this requires a lot of scrolling to see everything. If you decide to break up the report into separate pages, you have to decide whether you will provide your own interface for navigating between the pages or whether you want page navigation links to be automatically added to the bottom of each page. Of course, doing it automatically is a much easier solution to implement, but you have to consider whether this fits in with the design of your entire web site. Luckily, each of these options is easy to set and you can quickly play around with each one and decide what works best for each project.

Note

The report viewer control doesn't have HTML listed in its dropdown list of available export file types. Exporting to HTML always requires writing your own code.

Table 19-6 lists the HTML export specific properties that control the output of the HTML pages.

Table 19-6. HTMLFormatOptions Properties.

Property	Description
FirstPageNumber	The first page number to export.
HTMLEnableSeparatedPages	Boolean that sets whether the HTML output will put each report page on its own web page.
HTMLBaseFolderName	The folder for storing the HTML files.
HTMLFileName	The filename used for saving the HTML output.
HTMLHasPageNavigator	Boolean that sets whether the bottom of each page should have navigation links.
LastPageNumber	The last page number to export.
UsePageRange	Boolean that enables/disables the use of page ranges.

Listing 19-3. Setting the format options for HTML.

[VB.NET]

```
Public Sub ExportToHTML(ByVal HTMLBaseFolderName As String, ByVal Filename As String, ByRef
myReport As CrystalDecisions.CrystalReports.Engine.ReportDocument, ByVal EnableSeparatedPages
As Boolean, ByVal HasPageNavigator As Boolean)
    Dim myExportOptions As New CrystalDecisions.Shared.ExportOptions
    'Set HTML specific formatting properties
    myExportOptions.ExportFormatType = CrystalDecisions.Shared.ExportFormatType.HTML40
    Dim myFormatOptions As CrystalDecisions.Shared.HTMLFormatOptions
    myFormatOptions = CrystalDecisions.Shared.ExportOptions.CreateHTMLFormatOptions()
    myFormatOptions.HTMLBaseFolderName = HTMLBaseFolderName
    myFormatOptions.HTMLFileName = Filename
    myFormatOptions.HTMLHasPageNavigator = HasPageNavigator
    myFormatOptions.HTMLEnableSeparatedPages = EnableSeparatedPages
    'Assign the formatting properties to the report and export it
    myExportOptions.FormatOptions = myFormatOptions
    myReport.Export(myExportOptions)
End Sub
```

[C#]

```
public void ExportToHTML(string HTMLBaseFolderName, string Filename, ref
CrystalDecisions.CrystalReports.Engine.ReportDocument myReport, bool EnableSeparatedPages,
bool HasPageNavigator)
{
    CrystalDecisions.Shared.ExportOptions myExportOptions = new
CrystalDecisions.Shared.ExportOptions();
    //Set HTML specific formatting properties
    myExportOptions.ExportFormatType = CrystalDecisions.Shared.ExportFormatType.HTML40;
    CrystalDecisions.Shared.HTMLFormatOptions myFormatOptions;
    myFormatOptions = CrystalDecisions.Shared.ExportOptions.CreateHTMLFormatOptions();
```

```
    myFormatOptions.HTMLBaseFolderName = HTMLBaseFolderName;
    myFormatOptions.HTMLFileName = Filename;
    myFormatOptions.HTMLHasPageNavigator = HasPageNavigator;
    myFormatOptions.HTMLEnableSeparatedPages = EnableSeparatedPages;
    //Assign the formatting properties to the report and export it
    myExportOptions.FormatOptions = myFormatOptions;
    myReport.Export(myExportOptions);
}
```

Unlike the previous code listings, this listing doesn't specify a disk file destination type. This is because HTML output is stored in a separate folder and these properties are already part of the format options object. A separate object isn't necessary to specify them.

There are two properties that deal with the filename that should be mentioned. The **HTMLBaseFolderName** property sets the folder that the HTML output is saved in. However, this is a little deceiving because the export process creates another folder within the base and puts the HTML files in this sub-folder. Unfortunately, you don't have any control over the name of this sub-folder. It is always given the report name. For example, if the report is called "EmployeeList.rpt", the subfolder is named "EmployeeList". If you leave the **HTMLBaseFolderName** property empty, only the subfolder is created.

You also have to be aware of how the HTML files are named. If the property **HTMLUseSeparatedPages** is **True**, the pages will be named according to the following rules:

- The first page is the filename you specified (e.g. Report.htm).

- The next pages have a number concatenated at the end (e.g. Report1.htm, Report2.htm…)

- The last page has the word "Last" concatenated at the end (e.g. ReportLast.htm).

Caution

If you print a page range, the numbers will not match the actual page number. The first page has no number and the second page printed is numbered as "1", regardless of its actual page number on the report. As an example, if you print pages 5 through 10, page 5 is named Report.htm; page 6 is named Report1.htm; and page 10 is named ReportLast.htm.

As an example of how confusing the folder names are, Figure 19-5 shows a snapshot of an HTML report that used a base folder name of "Crystal HtmlFiles"; the report name is "EmployeeList"; and the HTML file name is "Employees".

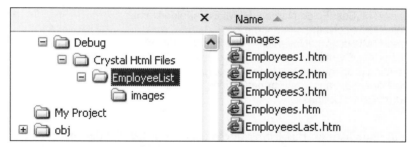

Figure 19-5. The folder/file naming convention for exporting HTML.

Exporting to Email

Exporting a report to an email creates the report as a separate file and attaches it to an email message. This email message is automatically sent out to the recipient. Table 19-7 shows the properties for exporting to email. Each of these properties relates to the typical settings you find when sending an email message.

Table 19-7. MicrosoftMailDestinationOptions Properties.

Property	Description
MailCCList	The list of emails to send a carbon copy to.
MailMessage	The text portion of the email message.
MailSubject	The text subject heading of the email message.
MailToList	The email(s) of those receiving the report.
Password	The password used when logging on to the email account.
UserName	The user name used when logging on to the email account.

Listing 19-4. Send a report as an attachment of an email.

[VB.NET]

```
Public Sub ExportToEmail(ByVal myReport As
CrystalDecisions.CrystalReports.Engine.ReportDocument, ByVal MailTo As String, ByVal CCList As
String, ByVal Subject As String, ByVal Message As String, ByVal UserName As String, ByVal
Password As String)
    'Set the destination type to Email
    Dim myExportOptions As New CrystalDecisions.Shared.ExportOptions
    myExportOptions.ExportDestinationType =
CrystalDecisions.Shared.ExportDestinationType.MicrosoftMail
    myExportOptions.ExportFormatType =
CrystalDecisions.Shared.ExportFormatType.PortableDocFormat
    'Instantiate an Email options object and set its properties
    Dim myOptions As CrystalDecisions.Shared.MicrosoftMailDestinationOptions
```

```
    myOptions = CrystalDecisions.Shared.ExportOptions.CreateMicrosoftMailDestinationOptions()
    myOptions.UserName = UserName
    myOptions.Password = Password
    myOptions.MailSubject = Subject
    myOptions.MailMessage = Message
    myOptions.MailToList = MailTo
    myOptions.MailCCList = CCList
    'Assign the options object to the report
    myExportOptions.DestinationOptions = myOptions
    myReport.Export(myExportOptions)
End Sub
```

[C#]

```
public void ExportToEmail(CrystalDecisions.CrystalReports.Engine.ReportDocument myReport, string
MailTo, string CCList, string Subject, string Message, string UserName, string Password)
{
    //Set the destination type to Email
    CrystalDecisions.Shared.ExportOptions myExportOptions = new
CrystalDecisions.Shared.ExportOptions();
    myExportOptions.ExportDestinationType =
CrystalDecisions.Shared.ExportDestinationType.MicrosoftMail;
    myExportOptions.ExportFormatType =
CrystalDecisions.Shared.ExportFormatType.PortableDocFormat;
    //Instantiate an Email options object and set its properties
    CrystalDecisions.Shared.MicrosoftMailDestinationOptions myOptions;
    myOptions = CrystalDecisions.Shared.ExportOptions.CreateMicrosoftMailDestinationOptions();
    myOptions.UserName = UserName;
    myOptions.Password = Password;
    myOptions.MailSubject = Subject;
    myOptions.MailMessage = Message;
    myOptions.MailToList = MailTo;
    myOptions.MailCCList = CCList;
    //Assign the options object to the report
    myExportOptions.DestinationOptions = myOptions;
    myReport.Export(myExportOptions);
}
```

This procedure sets the report object's destination type to be MicrosoftMail. Then it creates a new options variable and assigns the parameters to the appropriate properties. The last step assigns the options object to the DestinationOptions property of the report object and calls the Export() method.

Exporting to Exchange Folders

Crystal Reports lets you export a report to an Exchange folder. Table 19-8 shows the properties that need to be set for this to work.

Table 19-8. ExchangeFolderDestinationOptions Properties.

Property	Description
DestinationType	The export destination type
FolderPath	The path of the Exchange folder
Password	The Exchange password
Profile	The user profile for accessing the Exchange folder

Listing 19-5. Export a report to an Exchange folder.

[VB.NET]

```
Public Sub ExportToExchange(ByVal myReport As
CrystalDecisions.CrystalReports.Engine.ReportDocument, ByVal FolderPath As String, ByVal
Password As String, ByVal Profile As String)
    'Set the destination type to ExchangeFolder
    Dim myExportOptions As New CrystalDecisions.Shared.ExportOptions
    myExportOptions.ExportDestinationType =
CrystalDecisions.Shared.ExportDestinationType.ExchangeFolder
    myExportOptions.ExportFormatType =
CrystalDecisions.Shared.ExportFormatType.PortableDocFormat
    'Instantiate an ExchangeFolder options object and set its properties
    Dim myOptions As CrystalDecisions.Shared.ExchangeFolderDestinationOptions
    myOptions = CrystalDecisions.Shared.ExportOptions.CreateExchangeFolderDestinationOptions()
    myOptions.DestinationType =
CrystalDecisions.Shared.ExchangeDestinationType.ExchangePostDocMessage
    myOptions.FolderPath = FolderPath
    myOptions.Password = Password
    myOptions.Profile = Profile
    myExportOptions.DestinationOptions = myOptions
    myReport.Export(myExportOptions)
End Sub
```

[C#]

```
public void ExportToExchange(CrystalDecisions.CrystalReports.Engine.ReportDocument myReport,
string FolderPath, string Password, string Profile)
{
    //Set the destination type to ExchangeFolder
    CrystalDecisions.Shared.ExportOptions myExportOptions = new
CrystalDecisions.Shared.ExportOptions();
    myExportOptions.ExportDestinationType =
CrystalDecisions.Shared.ExportDestinationType.ExchangeFolder;
    myExportOptions.ExportFormatType =
CrystalDecisions.Shared.ExportFormatType.PortableDocFormat;
    //Instantiate an ExchangeFolder options object and set its properties
    CrystalDecisions.Shared.ExchangeFolderDestinationOptions myOptions;
    myOptions = CrystalDecisions.Shared.ExportOptions.CreateExchangeFolderDestinationOptions();
```

```
    myOptions.DestinationType =
CrystalDecisions.Shared.ExchangeDestinationType.ExchangePostDocMessage;
    myOptions.FolderPath = FolderPath;
    myOptions.Password = Password;
    myOptions.Profile = Profile;
    myExportOptions.DestinationOptions = myOptions;
    myReport.Export(myExportOptions);
}
```

This procedure sets the report object's destination type to be **ExchangeFolder**. Then it creates a new options object and assigns the parameters to the appropriate properties. The last step assigns the options object to the **DestinationOptions** property of the report object and calls the **Export()** method.

Printing with ASP.NET

The Crystal Reports web viewer control gives you a print button to send your reports directly to the printer. But there are times when you want to view them in a different format, or save them to a separate file. For example, many people like to view reports as a PDF file because they feel that it gives the report a more professional look.

The **ReportDocument.ExportToHttpResponse()** method exports files directly to the Http Response object. This lets the user view the file directly in the browser window or save it to their local computer.

The code for using the **ExportToHttpResponse()** method is very similar to calling the **Export()** method. The primary difference is that you don't need to specify the destination option because it is always being exported to Http. Second, there are a couple new arguments to pass to it. The method is overloaded with two declarations:

```
ExportToHttpResponse(ExportFormatType, HttpResponse, Attachment (Boolean), Filename)
ExportToHttpResponse(ExportOptions, HttpResponse, Attachment (Boolean), Filename)
```

The first declaration is the more simplistic of the two. The first parameter is the format type (PDF, Excel, etc.). The second parameter is the **System.Web.HttpResponse** object. It is used to stream the file directly to the browser. The third parameter is a Boolean that specifies if the file should be a separate attachment or not. If this is True, the user is prompted with the File Download dialog box. The fourth parameter is the default filename presented to the user when they save the file. Do not use a file extension with the filename because this is done automatically depending upon the file type.

The second method declaration is more complex because the first parameter expects an **ExportOptions** object. This allows you to create a **FormatType** object specific to the file type and set its properties. For example, a PDF file can specify the page range to print. You can't do this when using the first declaration.

Caution

The normal method of viewing an ASP.NET report is very efficient because pages are generated as they are displayed and this conserves resources. This isn't the case when exporting to a file. The entire report has to be generated to create the file and it has to be sent to the user's browser to be displayed. For large reports, your users might have a longer than normal delay.

The following two listings show an example of how to call each method declaration. The first, Listing 19-6, performs a simple export to a PDF file. The second listing, 19-7, shows how to export using an ExportOptions object and it only prints the first three pages of the report.

To thoroughly illustrate both export options available to you, the VB.NET code exports directly to the browser window. The C# code exports the file as an attachment and saves it to the file "EmployeeList.pdf"

Listing 19-6. Export a file using the ExportFormatType enumeration.

[VB.NET]

```
Public Sub ExportToPdfHttp()
    Dim myReport As New CrystalDecisions.CrystalReports.Engine.ReportDocument
    myReport.Load(Server.MapPath("EmployeeList.rpt"))
    Dim myExportOptions As New CrystalDecisions.Shared.ExportOptions
    myReport.ExportToHttpResponse( CrystalDecisions.Shared.ExportFormatType.PortableDocFormat,
Response, False, "")
End Sub
```

Class [C#]

```
public void ExportToPdfHttp()
{
    CrystalDecisions.CrystalReports.Engine.ReportDocument myReport = new
CrystalDecisions.CrystalReports.Engine.ReportDocument();
    myReport.Load(Server.MapPath("EmployeeList.rpt"));
    myReport.ExportToHttpResponse(CrystalDecisions.Shared.ExportFormatType.PortableDocFormat,
Response, true, "EmployeeList");
}
```

Listing 19-7. Export a file using an ExportOptions object.

[VB.NET]

```
Public Sub ExportToPdfHttp()
    Dim myReport As New CrystalDecisions.CrystalReports.Engine.ReportDocument
    myReport.Load(Server.MapPath("EmployeeList.rpt"))
    Dim myExportOptions As New CrystalDecisions.Shared.ExportOptions
    Dim myFormatOptions As CrystalDecisions.Shared.PdfRtfWordFormatOptions
    myFormatOptions = CrystalDecisions.Shared.ExportOptions.CreatePdfRtfWordFormatOptions()
    myFormatOptions.UsePageRange = True
    myFormatOptions.FirstPageNumber = 1
```

```
  myFormatOptions.LastPageNumber = 3
  myExportOptions.ExportFormatOptions = myFormatOptions
  myExportOptions.ExportFormatType =
CrystalDecisions.Shared.ExportFormatType.PortableDocFormat
  myReport.ExportToHttpResponse(myExportOptions, Response, False, "")
End Sub
```

Class [C#]

```
public void ExportToPdfHttp()
{
  CrystalDecisions.CrystalReports.Engine.ReportDocument myReport = new
CrystalDecisions.CrystalReports.Engine.ReportDocument();
  myReport.Load(Server.MapPath("EmployeeList.rpt"));
  CrystalDecisions.Shared.ExportOptions myExportOptions = new
CrystalDecisions.Shared.ExportOptions();
  myExportOptions.ExportFormatType =
CrystalDecisions.Shared.ExportFormatType.PortableDocFormat;
  CrystalDecisions.Shared.PdfRtfWordFormatOptions myFormatOptions;
  myFormatOptions = CrystalDecisions.Shared.ExportOptions.CreatePdfRtfWordFormatOptions();
  myFormatOptions.UsePageRange = true;
  myFormatOptions.FirstPageNumber = 1;
  myFormatOptions.LastPageNumber = 3;
  myExportOptions.FormatOptions = myFormatOptions;
  myReport.ExportToHttpResponse(myExportOptions, Response, true, "EmployeeList");
}
```

Exporting to a New Browser Window

I frequently see people on the forum asking how to export reports to a new browser window. This keeps the report output separate from your web application's browser. The reason that this is important is because users have a tendency to close the browser window when finished reading a report. They don't click the Back button to go to the previous page that launched the report. If you have the report in the same browser window as your application, this will close your application and the user has to start over again.

Printing a report in a new browser window is actually a function of .NET and not Crystal Reports. It requires knowing how to build the web page in such a way that the report links will open a new browser window. Nonetheless, we'll look at how to modify your web application to use this functionality with your reports.

.NET has two methods of opening a report in a new browser window. Both methods are easy to use. The first method uses a Hyperlink control. Simply put the hyperlink control on your web form and set the following two properties:

- NavigateUrl: The .aspx page that prints the report.

- Target: Set to "_blank"

When the user clicks the link, it opens the web page hosting your report in a new window. The second method of opening the report in a new browser window uses javascript code.

When the user clicks the link, it opens the web page hosting your report in a new window. The second method of opening the report in a new browser window uses javascript code. This is necessary when you want to open the report in response to an event of a web control. For example, you could open the report when the user clicks on a button. The JavaScript code calls the window.open() method to open the new browser window. Here is sample code associated with the Click event of a button. When you use this code in your application, change the name of the web page, "ShowReport.aspx" to the name of the page in your application which is hosting the report.

Listing 19-8. Use Javascript to open a report in a new browser window.

[VB.NET]
```
Protected Sub LinkButton1_Click(ByVal sender As Object, ByVal e As System.EventArgs) Handles LinkButton1.Click
    Response.Write("<script type='text/javascript'>window.open('ShowReport.aspx');</script>")
End Sub
```

[C#]
```
protected void Button1_Click(object sender, EventArgs e)
{
    Response.Write("<script type='text/javascript'>window.open('ShowReport.aspx');</script>");
}
```

It's as simple as that! Remember to put the code that instantiates and exports your report in the Page_Init() method of the new web page.

Deploying Reports

After working hard to build your reporting solution and test it on your computer, you will certainly want to deploy it to the end users computer. Although Microsoft advertises that .NET installations are no more difficult than an "XCOPY" deployment, this is only true if you use 100% .NET managed components. If your application has any non-managed components, you are required to create a deployment package to install it on the client's computer. This creates setup files that include all the managed and non-managed components and is responsible for installing them on the client computer.

Prior to Visual Studio 2005, installing Crystal Reports on a client's computer typically consisted of creating a deployment package and including the appropriate merge modules within the package. The merge modules selected for deployment depended upon which functionality of Crystal Reports you used. Unfortunately, this caused two big problems. The first problem is that people were required to decipher which merge modules were necessary and they could install the wrong ones. Secondly, since the merge modules were optional, you never knew what had been previously installed on a client's computer and you could assume something was there when it wasn't. And the fact that this deployment process allowed merge modules to be of different versions compounded the trouble even more. Programmers who have been around a while know all too well what a mess this was.

With the release of Visual Studio 2005, Business Objects decided to get away from merge modules and encourage programmers to use redistributable packages instead. A redistributable package has a .MSI extension. It can be run separately or as part of a bootstrap installation (a custom action in the setup.exe program runs it for you during the installation process). By giving you only a single redistributable file, this will eliminate the majority of problems caused by the use of merge modules. The other benefit is that it only needs to be installed once per computer.

Consequently, creating a deployment package for a Crystal Reports application is no different than creating one for any other type of application. The only thing you have to do prior to installing it on the client's computer is to make sure that the Crystal Reports redistributable package is installed beforehand.

Note

One of the most frequent complaints I hear regarding deploying reports is that after deploying a project to a user's computer, the reports don't work anymore. This problem is due to versioning issues when the client computer already has another version of Crystal Reports on their computer. Before deploying a reporting solution to a user's computer, make sure that both computers have the same versions of Crystal Reports. Additional confusion arises if you have the stand-alone edition of Crystal Reports installed on your computer. Due to the nature of software, both Visual Studio .NET and Crystal Reports have regular service packs available. This makes it confusing to know which version you have on your computer. It's possible that you installed the most recent Crystal Reports service pack on your development computer, but you haven't downloaded the most recent redistributable package. Always check the support site to ensure that your software is up to date. There are many downloads to choose from, so read the descriptions carefully to ensure that you click on the right one. The URL for the latest Crystal Reports downloads is: https://www.sdn.sap.com/irj/sdn/businessobjects-downloads

Required Installation Files

Much to my dismay, I couldn't find anything in the documentation that states where the redistributable packages were copied to during the installation of Visual Studio. The only way to track them down was to use Windows Explorer and search for all the .MSI files on my computer. To save you this trouble, here is where they are located:

Visual Studio 2005

C:\Program Files\Microsoft Visual Studio
8\SDK\v2.0\BootStrapper\Packages\CrystalReports\CRRedist2005_x86.msi

Visual Studio 2008

C:\Program Files\Microsoft SDKs\Windows\v6.0A\Bootstrapper\Packages\CrystalReports10_5\
CRRedist2008_x86.msi

Deploying a Windows Application

Since Crystal Reports no longer uses merge modules to create deployment projects, creating a deployment package for your reporting application is the same as creating one for any .NET application. Nonetheless, we'll walk through the steps here so that you can see how it works.

To create a deployment project for your application, first open your application in design mode. Then select the menu options File > New > Project. This opens the New Project dialog box.

Open the Other Project Types node and select Setup and Deployment. On the right side, click the Setup Project template. At the bottom of the dialog box, give it an appropriate name and set the file location. You should also select the option Add To Solution so that the setup project stays within the same solution as your reporting application. This is shown in Figure 19-6.

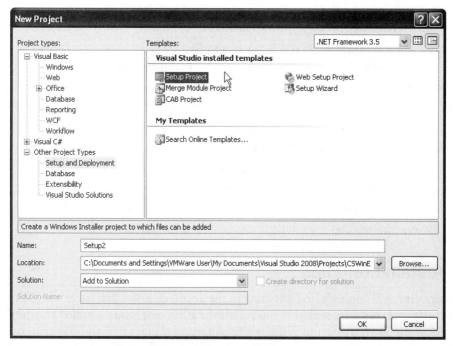

Figure 19-6. New Windows deployment project.

This adds the setup project to the current application's Solution Explorer window. Right-click on setup project's name and select Add > Project Output. This opens the Add Project Output Group window, shown in Figure 19-7.

Figure 19-7. Adding the Primary Output option to the project.

Click the Primary Output option and click the OK button. This adds the application's executable file to the setup project.

If you are using embedded reports, this is all that is required to create the deployment project. Your report classes are compiled within the application and will be deployed with it. Simply build your project and Visual Studio will create the .EXE and .MSI files you need to deploy this application to a client computer.

If you are using non-embedded reports, the reports are separate from your application and need to be added to the deployment project. This is done in one of two ways. If a report is listed in the Solution Explorer window, click on it and look at the Properties window. The first property is Build Action. Click on it and select Content. This tells Visual Studio that the report file is part of the applications content collection.

Next, right-click on the setup project's name and select Add > Project Output. This opens the Add Project Output Group window again. Select the Content Files option and click the OK button. Since the report was flagged as Content in the Build Action property, it is now included in the deployment project. If you want to confirm this, look for the Content Files node under the setup project's name and right-click on it. Select the Outputs menu option and you should see the report listed as one of the output files.

If you are using non-embedded reports and they aren't listed in the Solution Explorer window, you can manually add them to the deployment project. Right-click on the setup project's name and select Add > File. Browse to where the report is located and select it. This adds it to the deployment project's output.

Once all the report files are added to the project, rebuild the project to create the setup files and use them to install the application on the client computer.

Deploying an ASP.NET Application

Deploying a web application is very similar to deploying a Windows application. As far as Crystal Reports is concerned, the primary difference is that the project is going to be installed on a web server.

Caution

When deploying to a web server for the first time, make sure that the ASPNET user has full rights to the \Windows\Temp folder. Crystal Reports reads and writes temporary files to this folder while generating reports. If you're deploying to Windows Server 2003, use the NetworkServices account instead.

To create a deployment project for your web application, first open your application in design mode. Then select File > New > Project. This opens the New Project dialog box.

Open the Other Project Types node and select Setup and Deployment. On the right side, click the Web Setup Project template. At the bottom of the dialog box, give it an appropriate name and set the file location. You should also select the option Add To Solution so that the setup project stays within the same solution as your reporting application. This is shown in Figure 19-8.

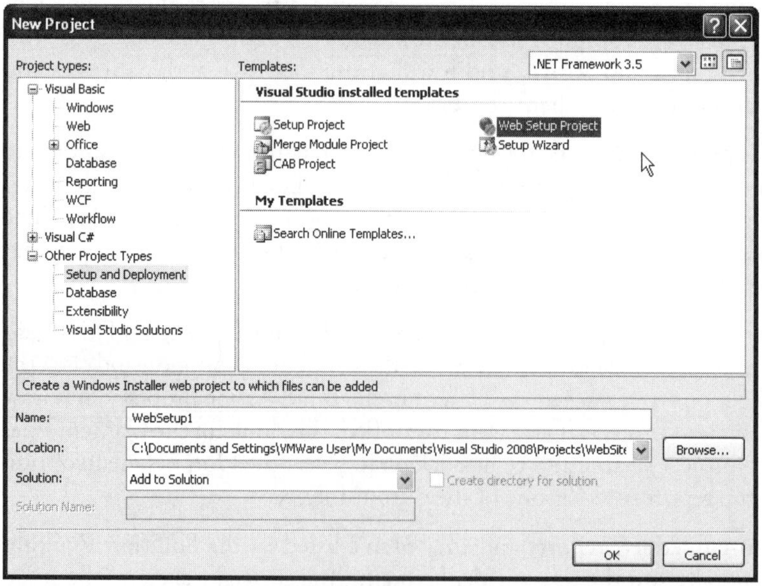

Figure 19-8. New Project window for a Web Setup Project.

This adds the setup project to the current application's Solution Explorer window. Right-click on setup project's name and select Add > Project Output. This opens the Add Project Output Group window, shown in Figure 19-9.

Figure 19-9. Adding content files to the web deployment project.

Select the Content option and click the OK button. Unlike the Windows setup process, selecting the Content option automatically adds every report in your web site to the deployment output. To confirm this, look for the Content Files node under the setup project's name and right-click on it. Select the Outputs menu option and you should see the report listed as one of the output files.

If the reports aren't listed in the Solution Explorer window (e.g. they are stored in a common reporting library), you can manually add them to the deployment project. Right-click on the setup project's name and select Add > File. Browse to where the reports are located and select them. This adds them to the deployment project's output.

Once all the report files are added to the project, rebuild the project to create the setup files and use them to install the application on the client computer.

Best Of The Forum

Question: I deployed my web application to a new server, but the Crystal Reports viewer is missing its icons. How do I install them on the server?

Answer: If the server doesn't have the Crystal Reports icons installed, you have to manually copy them from your development computer to the web server. Each version of Crystal Reports puts the icons in different folders so that there aren't versioning issues. Look on your computer in the following folders and copy them to the same location on your web server.

Visual Studio .NET 2005 Folder

File path when using IIS:

C:\Inetpub\wwwroot\aspnet_client\system_web\2_0_50727\CrystalReportWebFormViewer3

File path when using ASP.NET Development Server:

[Windows folder]\Microsoft.NET\Framework\v2.0.50727\ASP.NETClientFiles\
CrystalReportWebFormViewer3

Visual Studio .NET 2008 Folder

File path when using IIS:

C:\Inetpub\wwwroot\aspnet_client\system_web\2_0_50727\CrystalReportWebFormViewer4

File path when using ASP.NET Development Server:

[Windows folder]\Microsoft.NET\Framework\v2.0.50727\ASP.NETClientFiles\
CrystalReportWebFormViewer4

Best Of The Forum

Question: I'm going to use a third-party company to host my website. How do I deploy my reports on their server?

Answer: Most third-party hosting companies don't support Crystal Reports on their web servers. Since the Crystal Reports components are not 100% managed code, you can't transfer them via FTP to your site and expect it to work. The only way to print reports in this scenario is to talk to your hosting company and ask them to install the Crystal Reports runtime for your site. Unfortunately, it is highly unlikely that this will happen due to security concerns (not to mention licensing issues).

ClickOnce Deployment

ClickOnce deployment lets users install your application via a link on your website. You get the benefit of not having to install your application on multiple computers across your company. You copy the ClickOnce deployment package to a designated web page on the company web server and link to that page. Updating your application is simply a matter of copying the new deployment package to the server and letting your users know that they need to get the latest copy. You also have the option to have your application check for updates online and install them automatically. ClickOnce deployment makes it much easier to manage your release cycle.

To implement click-once deployment for your application, first open the application in design mode. Right-click on the project name and select Properties. Along the left-hand side are a series of tabs. Click on the Security tab and select Enable ClickOnce Security Settings. This is shown in Figure 19-10.

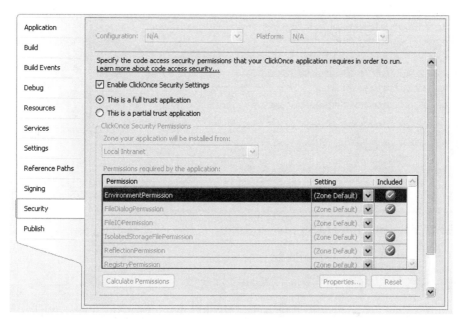

Figure 19-10. Enable ClickOnce Security Settings checkbox.

Secondly, select the Publish tab at the bottom and click the Prerequisites button to the right. This gives a list of prerequisites that need to be installed with your application. Make sure that ".NET Framework 3.5" and "Crystal Reports Basic for Visual Studio 2008" are checked. This is shown in Figure 19-11.

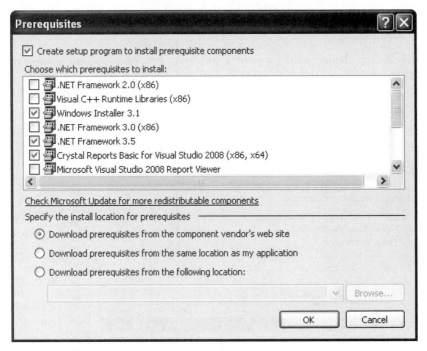

Figure 19-11. Selecting the proper prerequisites.

Click the OK button to save your changes.

Note

If you're using Visual Studio 2005, select the following prerequisites: ".NET Framework 2.0" and "Crystal Reports for .NET Framework 2.0".

Click the Updates button at the right and select the options "The application should check for updates" and "Before the application runs". This tells the application to check for updates each time the application runs.

To publish your application to the web server, save your changes and right-click on the project name and select Publish. This opens the Publish Wizard, which walks you through the process of specifying where to deploy your application. It prompts you for the location and asks if the files should be available both online and offline. If installed online, the applicaton is run directly from the link on the web page. If installed offline, the application is added to the Start Menu and the user can uninstall it with the Add/Remove Programs tool.

After publishing it to the web server, it's best to double check that the page is set up correctly and that the link works as expected.

Note

The .NET Framework and Crystal Reports redistributable package require a very large amount of bandwidth to download from the web server. For optimum performance, your users should download and install the .NET Framework and Crystal Reports redistributable package in advance. This is much more efficient because ClickOnce deployment is smart enough to recognize which prerequisites are already installed on the client machine and not download them a second time.

Printing for Mobile Devices

Mobile devices are becoming prevalent in our corporate lives and personal lives. With the faster data connections available and better browser interfaces, more and more people are becoming reliant on them as a primary source of information. In the corporate world, executives want timely business data and sales people want instant access to their latest sales figures. It's no surprise that Crystal Reports has a means of getting data to your users' mobile devices.

The Report Parts Viewer in Crystal Reports is designed for mobile devices and portals with a very limited viewing area. It only prints individual report objects and confines them to a limited report size. As the user clicks on data within the page, it drills-down into more data. You, the report designer, use hyperlinks to specify which report part is displayed next.

Having the user click on the report objects and link to other report parts is similar to how you navigate a typical report with drill down capabilities. The difference with report parts is that the resulting data is kept to a minimum and you control the "navigation path" the user follows.

Let's see how this works by building a web page that uses the report parts viewer and looking at the output. We're going to take the sample report, Group.rpt, that is installed with Visual Studio and display it with the report parts viewer.

First, create a new web site. Once you're in design mode, go to the Solution Explorer and right click on the web-site name. Select the menu option Add Existing Item.

Navigate to the Crystal Reports sample directory, "Featured Examples", and select the report Group.rpt. The report should be in this directory:

C:\Program Files\Microsoft Visual Studio 9.0\Crystal Reports\Samples\En\Reports\Feature Examples

Double-click on the report to open it in design mode. This report is grouped by the Country field. Within each country are listed the customers and last year sales. For the report parts viewer, we'll show the countries on the first page and let the user drill down to see sales detail for each customer.

The first thing we need to do is tell Crystal Reports which report object it should show on the first page of the report. This will be the Country field in the group header.

Right-click on the group header field (the country name) and select copy. Next, select the menu options Crystal Reports > Report > Report Options. This opens the Report Options dialog box.

At the bottom is the section titled Initial Report Part Settings. This is where you tell Crystal Reports which report object should be shown on the opening page. Click the Paste Link button and it copies the name of the group header field to the Object Name property. This is shown in Figure 19-12.

Figure 19-12. Assigning the initial report part settings.

Click the OK button to save your changes and close the dialog box.

The next step is to tell Crystal Reports what to do when the user clicks on the country name. If there were multiple groups, you might want the user to drill-down through each group. In this example, we'll just have it show the detail sales records.

Right-click on the Group Header #1 report object again and select Format Object. This opens the Format Editor dialog box. Click on the Hyperlink tab.

To display the detail records, click on the Report Part Drilldown radio button. The bottom of the dialog boxes changes to show the fields that you can select for displaying on the report.

Click the Details node to expand it. Then select the fields Field4 (customer name) and Field14 (last year's sales) and add them to the Fields To Display list on the right. This is shown in Figure 19-13.

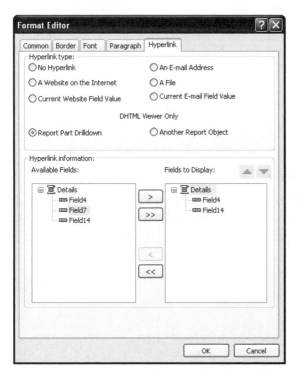

Figure 19-13. Specifying the detail records to show.

At this point, the report is ready to be displayed in a report parts viewer. We just need to add the viewer to the default web page and we'll be ready to go!

Open the web page Default.aspx in design mode and drag and drop the CrystalReportPartsViewer control onto the form. Use the SmartLinks button (in the top-right corner of the control) to open a new Report Source and specify the Group.rpt report. Click the OK button when you are finished.

Run the report and you should see a small version of the report appear on the web page. This is shown in Figure 19-14.

Figure 19-14. The report parts web page.

Notice at the bottom of the page that the previous and next buttons are already on the page and they are positioned in such a way that they will still be displayed on a mobile device.

You can click on one of the countries to drill down into the sales information. This is shown in Figure 19-15.

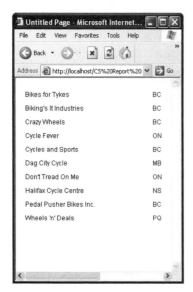

Figure 19-15. The detail records of the report parts viewer.

You can see from this example how easy it is to convert your reports into a format that is formatted for viewing on a PDA or portal site.

RAS - Dynamic Report Modification

If you've gotten this far in the book, you are very familiar with all the ins and outs of using Crystal Reports Basic. You also know that although Crystal Reports Basic can create powerful reporting solutions, it has features removed from it that users of the stand-alone Crystal Reports product expect. This includes robust reporting components and an object model that gives you unlimited runtime customization. When you find that you are trying to build reporting solutions that Crystal Reports Basic won't allow, it is time to look at upgrading to the stand-alone version of Crystal Reports 2008. With the release of Crystal Reports 2008, you no longer have to choose which version you need to buy. There is only a single version and it includes the .NET 2008 developer upgrade that you need.

Upgrade Compatibility

It's very important to realize that not every version of Crystal Reports is compatible with every version of Visual Studio. Since Business Objects is a separate company from Microsoft, each has their own timetables for when to release new upgrades and determining the functionality in different versions. Since Crystal Reports is a stand-alone product that has a light version included in Visual Studio, it can get confusing to talk about which version you are using and figuring out which version of Visual Studio is compatible with Crystal Reports. This section hopes to shed some light on this issue and make it easier for you to determine what will work in your environment.

Table 20-1 matches each version of Visual Studio with a compatible version of Crystal Reports. The first column lists the Visual Studio version and the second column shows the Crystal Reports version.

Table 20-1. Visual Studio .NET Compatibility Chart

Visual Studio .NET Version	Crystal Reports Compatibility
Visual Studio 2005	Crystal Reports XI R2
	Crystal Reports 2008
Visual Studio 2008	Crystal Reports 2008 R0

It's important to recognize when the second column of this table shows an "Rx" version number next to Crystal Reports. For example, Visual Studio 2005 isn't compatible with the orginal release of Crystal Reports XI. You have to download and install the R2 update to make it compatible with Visual Studio 2005. On the other hand, the original release of Crystal Reports 2008 is perfectly compatible with Visual Studio 2005.

The stand-alone version of Crystal Reports is typically released at a slightly earlier date than the release of Visual Studio. Although the developers were very close to finalizing the Visual Studio release, it isn't 100% complete and they can't guarantee compatibility between the two products. To make it possible to release Crystal Reports in a timely fashion, and still adhere to the Microsoft release timeline for Visual Studio, Business Objects waits until the latest version of Visual Studio is released to production and they issue a 'Release X' update to Crystal Reports. The update has been tested with the most recent release of Visual Studio and is a required download for the two products to be compatible.

It's also important to note that since Visual Studio 2008 is the latest release, it isn't compatible with Crystal Reports XI. If you want to integrate Visual Studio 2008 with Crystal Reports, you have to upgrade to Crystal Reports 2008 and install Release 0. Business Objects has not released an update to make Crystal Reports XI compatible with Visual Studio 2008.

> If you need to check on whether a new release is available, you can go to the download site and search on your product. The URL is:
>
> https://www.sdn.sap.com/irj/sdn/businessobjects-downloads

Upgrading to Crystal Reports 2008

Crystal Reports 2008 is a powerful reporting solution for all types of developers. Developers with prior experience programming Crystal Reports with other development tools (VB6, VC++, Delphi, etc.) are probably familiar with integrating the Report Designer Component (RDC) with their application. This has been phased out and is no longer available with Crystal Report 2008.[46]

When upgrading to Crystal Reports 2008, there are two ways you can use it. You can either use .NET with existing Crystal Reports 2008 reports, or use the RAS library for advanced runtime customization the standard .NET libraries don't give you. These two options are summarized next.

Use .NET with Crystal Reports 2008 reports:

After installing Crystal Reports 2008, your .NET application is upgraded so that it can open and print reports built with Crystal Reports 2008. The .NET IDE is still limited to creating less feature-rich reports, but they will be compatible with Crystal Reports 2008 as well. To build the most advanced reports, you will have to use the Crystal Reports 2008

---

[46] The RDC gave you complete access to the report object model and allowed you to modify hundreds of properties during runtime. Many developers have been spoiled by this, and even though Crystal Reports 2008 gives you many advanced customization options, it still doesn't have the full RDC functionality.

stand-alone report writer separately and only use .NET for opening them within your application.

Although installing Crystal Reports 2008 upgrades the underlying libraries to be compatible with the latest reports, there are only a few minor changes made within the IDE (e.g. printing a histogram chart, exporting to editable Word). You won't notice any significant changes to the report designer in Visual Studio after installing Crystal Reports 2008 and for the most part it will all appear the same.

Upgrade to Crystal Report 2008 RAS:

The RAS (Report Application Server) is a library that adds the ability to dynamically modify reports during runtime. It has an API (application programming interface) which exposes many methods and properties that you can access from your .NET application. The RAS can either be integrated into your .NET application or it can be run on a stand-alone server and work directly with the Business Objects enterprise software.

Note

Crystal Reports XI R2 makes the RAS library available for Visual Studio .NET 2005. All the code in this chapter is compatible with the XI R2 release.

Before looking at the different upgrade options with Crystal Reports, you first have to install it on your computer. This is easy to do, but you have to be careful. There are a few things that you need to be aware of to make the process go smoothly. This includes making sure you have the correct version of Crystal Reports and making sure you install the tools in the correct order.

For Crystal Reports 2008 to work with .NET, you have to install the tools in the proper order. Failing to do so means that your .NET applications won't be compatible with Crystal Reports 2008. You must install Crystal Reports 2008 AFTER Visual Studio .NET has been installed. When the stand-alone version of Crystal Reports is installed, it looks for an existing copy of Visual Studio .NET on your computer. If it finds Visual Studio .NET, it overwrites the default .NET components with the upgraded versions. These upgraded components give you new features and more functionality that make .NET compatible with Crystal Reports 2008 reports.

If you unknowingly installed .NET after installing Crystal Reports, you have to reinstall Crystal Reports again. Visual Studio .NET doesn't look for an existing copy of Crystal Reports on your computer. Even if it did, there is nothing that it could do differently because the upgraded components are included on the Crystal Reports installation CD. There is no way for .NET to install them.

If you later decide not to use Crystal Reports on your computer anymore, uninstalling it will corrupt the .NET reporting components. Uninstalling removes the upgraded components from your computer, but doesn't replace them with the original .NET components. The only way to get them back is to reinstall Visual Studio .NET and select

Repair. This restores the reporting components to their original state prior to installing the stand-alone version of Crystal Reports.

Programming with the RAS

The Report Application Server (RAS) is the recommended tool for developing enterprise caliber reporting solutions. It can communicate with enterprise software to deliver a high performance, highly scalable reporting solution, or it can be integrated into a Windows thick-client application to utilize advance reporting techniques. RAS also gives you the ability to do dynamic report creation during runtime. This means that your application can create reports from scratch or add/delete report objects during runtime. These powerful features aren't available if your application only uses Crystal Reports Basic.[47]

This chapter gives you an overview of the RAS and shows you sample code for creating and implementing RAS enabled applications within the .NET environment. Due to the complexity and broad reach of the RAS API, it is beyond the scope of this chapter to give a thorough analysis and tutorial of the entire RAS object model. Instead, the goal is to show you how to create a new RAS application and demonstrate common coding solutions that you will most likely encounter on the job. This provides you with a solid foundation to expand upon for building more complex applications. If you want more information, the RAS software installs ample help files to study and the SAP website has great information on it.

RAS Overview

The RAS server is implemented as part of a larger enterprise reporting solution. This could be Crystal Enterprise, Crystal Reports Server, or Business Objects Enterprise. This is referred to as managed reporting because the reports are managed by the enterprise software and the RAS retrieves them from the enterprise software prior to working with them. You can also use unmanaged reports which are loaded directly from the server using a fully qualified file path or URL. The RAS server component is optional and is only applicable for large corporations that need to scale reports across the enterprise. It's also important to have the necessary staff to support it.

The final piece of the RAS puzzle is the RAS SDK (software development kit). It has an application programming interface (API) that lets your .NET application talk to the RAS and modify reports. This is also referred to as InProc RAS because the necessary library files are installed transparently to the user's computer and your application invokes the report engine in process. This is strictly for applications that need a greater degree of control over report objects or when it is necessary to create report objects dynamically during runtime.

---

[47] As mentioned earlier in the book, Crystal Reports Basic is the official term for the scaled down version of Crystal Reports that comes included with Visual Studio .NET for free.

The version of RAS that you use is very clearly dictated by your reporting environment. Large corporations will use the version of RAS that works with enterprise software. Small reporting solutions will use InProc RAS for reports that need dynamic reporting customization.

Licensing

Disclaimer: The licensing contract that Crystal Decisions provides with RAS is complex and subject to change at the discretion of Business Objects. It is also subject to variation for different customers depending upon their software contract. This section is intended to give you a general understanding of the license as of the time of publication (November 2008) and how it might impact you. I am not a lawyer and this is not meant to be a legal interpretation of how your company can use the software. You need to have legal council review the contract in relation to your company's needs.

Thick client .Net applications that include the .Net runtime engine can be freely redistributed internally and externally to third parties. Web applications that include the .Net runtime engine can be freely redistributed internally only. If you wish to redistribute a web application to an external third-party, you will have to acquire a copy of Crystal Reports 2008 for each company the application is distributed to.

RAS ReportClientDocument Overview

Crystal Reports .NET references reports using the **ReportDocument** class. RAS references reports using the **ReportClientDocument** class. These two objects are designed to be used in conjunction with each other. A report can be referenced with either object model, or both simultaneously, and all changes are applied correctly. They are not mutually exclusive. The benefit of this is that you can write new code to call the RAS API without changing any existing code that used the **ReportDocument** class. Simply add the appropriate RAS code you need to take advantage of its report creation capabilities.

Caution
One word of caution when using both SDKs simultaneously: the ReportDocument class and ReportClientDocument class use similar class names and collections. If you are importing the namespace ('using' in C#), the compiler will give error messages that it can't resolve the class names since they appear in multiple namespaces. The best way to avoid this problem is to either work with only one SDK at a time, or use fully qualified class names which specify the entire namespace.

Before using the RAS SDK, you need to add the appropriate references to your application. Each one gives you different functionality and we'll discuss which ones are necessary within the applicable sections. It can be useful just to add all the references to your project and go back and delete the unused ones prior to putting your project into production. The references are as follows:

```
CrystalDecisions.ReportAppServer.ClientDoc
CrystalDecisions.ReportAppServer.DataDefModel
CrystalDecisions.ReportAppServer.Controllers
CrystalDecisions.ReportAppServer.ReportDefModel
```

It's also important that you check the version numbers for your existing CrystalDecisions.* references. Occasionally, the references will refer to the older 10.x versions and these are not compatible with RAS. When this happens, delete all CrystalDecision.* libraries from the references list and add back the most recent versions.

Note

There are numerous ways that you can work with the RAS SDK and it is impossible for me to predict what you need to do. So I created a library of common functions that will be beneficial to the most number of users. Each code listing is written so that you can copy and paste it into any application without any changes. Any required information is passed to it as a method argument. This allows you to pick and choose which methods you need to use for your application and get them working with a minimal amount of effort. Just remember that the first method, **OpenReportClientDocument()**, needs to be called first because it opens the report and gets a reference to the **ReportClientDocument** that is used by all the other methods.

I found that there are a few specific use cases that most programmers want to know about for using the RAS SDK. Of course, there are countless applications that the RAS can be with, but it's not possible to cover everything in this chapter. The use cases are as follows:

- Opening a report
- Logging on to a data source
- Adding fields to a report (e.g. database fields, formulas, and parameters)
- Modifying the record selection formula
- Modifying parameters and formulas
- Saving your changes to a report file

Each use case is covered throughout the remainder of this chapter.

Opening a Report

How you open a report is dependent upon how you installed RAS. We will create code templates that open a report and return a reference to it that you can use in your program. But before we do that, let's look at the code that will control this process by declaring the appropriate report object variables and assigning the report to the viewer.

Listing 20-1 is a template for opening a report and modifying the report using the ReportClientDocument object. The code to modify the report isn't included because we'll cover those details later in the chapter. This is just a simple template that demonstrates how to get access to both report objects and preview the report afterwards. We'll add more complexity with each new topic discussed.

Listing 20-1. Template for working with the ReportClientDocument

[VB.NET]

```
Private Sub Form1_Load(ByVal sender As System.Object, ByVal e As System.EventArgs) Handles
MyBase.Load
    Dim myReportDocument As CrystalDecisions.CrystalReports.Engine.ReportDocument = Nothing
    Dim rcd As CrystalDecisions.ReportAppServer.ClientDoc.ISCDReportClientDocument = Nothing
    OpenReportClientDocument("C:\myReport.rpt", myReportDocument, rcd)
    'Insert code to modify the report here
    CrystalReportViewer1.ReportSource = myReportDocument
End Sub
```

[C#]

```
private void Form1_Load(object sender, EventArgs e)
{
    CrystalDecisions.CrystalReports.Engine.ReportDocument myReportDocument = null;
    CrystalDecisions.ReportAppServer.ClientDoc.ISCDReportClientDocument rcd = null;
    RAS_SDK.OpenReportClientDocument(@"C:\myReport.rpt", ref myReportDocument, ref rcd);
    //...insert code to modify the report using the rcd object variable...
    crystalReportViewer1.ReportSource = myReportDocument;
}
```

This code instantiates a ReportDocument object and a ReportClientDocument object. Both of these are passed to the method OpenReportClientDocument(), shown in Listing 20-2. When it returns, the two objects each have their own copy of the report in memory. You can modify the ReportClientDocument object to add any new report objects to it. The last step passes the ReportDocument object to the ReportSource property of the report viewer. This displays it to the user with any changes you made to the ReportClientDocument.

If you are not using InProc RAS, you will only be working with ReportClientDocument object. You do not need to declare and instantiate a ReportDocument object. When this is the case, you can assign a reference to the ReportClientDocument object directly to the viewer. Replace the viewer code with this:

```
CrystalReportViewer1.ReportSource = rcd.ReportSource
```

The next three sections show you a variation of the OpenReportClientDocument() method that is called from Listing 20-1. The one you use in your application is determined by how you are using RAS. Each of the three possible methods is discussed here.

InProc RAS SDK

The InProc RAS SDK is used when your reporting solution isn't working with larger enterprise software. When using InProc RAS, you open the report as you normally would, with a ReportDocument object. There are various ways of doing this depending upon your application and all of them work with RAS. All the code samples throughout this book work without any changes. With RAS installed, the .NET ReportDocument class has a new property called ReportClientDocument. This is used to pass a reference of the currently open report to the RAS.

Listing 20-2. Create a ReportClientDocument using the ReportDocument object

[VB.NET]

```
Public Shared Sub OpenReportClientDocument(ByVal ReportFilePath As String, ByRef
myReportDocument As CrystalDecisions.CrystalReports.Engine.ReportDocument, ByRef rcd As
CrystalDecisions.ReportAppServer.ClientDoc.ISCDReportClientDocument)
    'Use the ReportDocument object to load the report
    myReportDocument = New CrystalDecisions.CrystalReports.Engine.ReportDocument()
    myReportDocument.Load(ReportFilePath)
    'Pass the report from the ReportDocument to the rcd
    rcd = myReportDocument.ReportClientDocument
End Sub
```

[C#]

```
public static void OpenReportClientDocument(string ReportFilePath, ref
CrystalDecisions.CrystalReports.Engine.ReportDocument myReportDocument,
    ref CrystalDecisions.ReportAppServer.ClientDoc.ISCDReportClientDocument rcd)
{
    //Use the ReportDocument object to load the report
    myReportDocument = new CrystalDecisions.CrystalReports.Engine.ReportDocument();
    myReportDocument.Load(ReportFilePath);
    //Pass the report from the ReportDocument to the rcd
    rcd = myReportDocument.ReportClientDocument;
}
```

This is a generic method you can use in any report to get a reference to a new RAS ReportClientDocument using the report's fully qualified file path. The first couple of lines simply use the Load() method of the ReportDocument to open the report and load it into memory. The last line passes a reference of the report to the ReportClientDocument object variable, rcd. Notice that the argument list for the method references the ISCDReportClientDocument interface rather than working directly with the class name. It's important to remember that you have to use the class interface when declaring the variables, and use the class name when instantiating the object.

Since both objects are passed to the method by reference, the calling method can use these objects to make changes to them or print the report.

Using Unmanaged RAS

Opening a report using unmanaged RAS is more efficient than using InProc RAS. This is because InProc RAS requires two steps to open a report. The first is to load it into memory and the second passes the report reference to RAS. When using unmanaged RAS you only need to call the ReportClientDocument.Open() method. This immediately loads it into RAS and it is ready for use. Let's look at the code that does this.

Listing 20-3. Open a report using unmanaged RAS.

[VB.NET]

```
Public Shared Sub OpenReportClientDocument(ByVal ReportFileName As Object, ByRef rcd As
CrystalDecisions.ReportAppServer.ClientDoc.ISCDReportClientDocument)
    'Pass the report from the ReportDocument to the rcd
    rcd = New CrystalDecisions.ReportAppServer.ClientDoc.ReportClientDocument
    rcd.Open(ReportFileName, 1)
End Sub
```

[C#]

```
public static void OpenReportClientDocument(object ReportFilePath, ref
CrystalDecisions.ReportAppServer.ClientDoc.ISCDReportClientDocument rcd)
{
    //Pass the report from the ReportDocument to the rcd
    rcd = new CrystalDecisions.ReportAppServer.ClientDoc.ReportClientDocument();
    rcd.Open(ref ReportFilePath, 1);
}
```

As you can see, the code is similar to the InProc RAS listing, but it's shorter. It simply instantiates the ReportClientDocument object and calls the Open() method to load the report into memory. One important thing to note is that the rcd variable is declared using the interface, but it is instantiated using the class name. This is because you can't use the New keyword with an interface class.

Using Managed RAS

Managed RAS opens reports that are managed by your enterprise software. As you can see, this code is much more involved than the previous code samples. It requires you to login to the enterprise software, query the server, and create the ReportClientDocument object. The detailed notes are shown within the code listing.

Listing 20-4. Open a report using managed RAS.

[VB.NET]

```
Public Shared Sub OpenReportClientDocument(ByVal ReportFileName As Object, ByRef rcd As
CrystalDecisions.ReportAppServer.ClientDoc.ISCDReportClientDocument)
    Dim mySessionMgr As New CrystalDecisions.Enterprise.SessionMgr
    Dim myEnterpriseSession As CrystalDecisions.Enterprise.EnterpriseSession
```

```
    Dim myReportAppFactory As CrystalDecisions.ReportAppServer.ClientDoc.ReportAppFactory
    Dim myInfoStore As CrystalDecisions.Enterprise.InfoStore
    Dim myInfoObjects As CrystalDecisions.Enterprise.InfoObjects
    Dim myInfoObject As CrystalDecisions.Enterprise.InfoObject
    Dim myEnterpriseService As CrystalDecisions.Enterprise.EnterpriseService
    Dim mySampleReportName As String
    Dim myObject As Object
    'Logon to the enterprise server using your credentials and server info
    myEnterpriseSession = mySessionMgr.Logon("administrator", "", "localhost", "secEnterprise")
    myEnterpriseService = myEnterpriseSession.GetService("InfoStore")
    myInfoStore = New CrystalDecisions.Enterprise.InfoStore(myEnterpriseService)
    'Instantiate the sample report and query for the Id in the Enterprise CMS
    mySampleReportName = ReportFileName
    myInfoObjects = myInfoStore.Query("Select SI_ID From CI_INFOOBJECTS Where SI_NAME='" +
mySampleReportName + "' And SI_INSTANCE=0")
    myInfoObject = myInfoObjects(1)
    'Create the ReportAppFactory that is based on the enterprise session
    myObject = myEnterpriseSession.GetService("", "RASReportFactory").Interface
    myReportAppFactory = CType(myObject,
CrystalDecisions.ReportAppServer.ClientDoc.ReportAppFactory)
    'Use the OpenDocument method to instantiate the ReportClientDocument object
    rcd = myReportAppFactory.OpenDocument(myInfoObject.ID, 0)
End Sub
```

[C#]

```
public static void OpenReportClientDocument(string ReportFilePath,
CrystalDecisions.ReportAppServer.ClientDoc.ISCDReportClientDocument rcd)
{
    CrystalDecisions.Enterprise.SessionMgr mySessionMgr;
    mySessionMgr = new CrystalDecisions.Enterprise.SessionMgr();
    CrystalDecisions.Enterprise.EnterpriseSession myEnterpriseSession;
    CrystalDecisions.ReportAppServer.ClientDoc.ReportAppFactory myReportAppFactory;
    CrystalDecisions.Enterprise.InfoStore myInfoStore;
    CrystalDecisions.Enterprise.InfoObjects myInfoObjects;
    CrystalDecisions.Enterprise.InfoObject myInfoObject;
    CrystalDecisions.Enterprise.EnterpriseService myEnterpriseService;
    Object myObject;
    //Logon to the enterprise server using your credentials and server info
    myEnterpriseSession = mySessionMgr.Logon("administrator", "", "localhost", "secEnterprise");
    myEnterpriseService = myEnterpriseSession.GetService("InfoStore");
    myInfoStore = new CrystalDecisions.Enterprise.InfoStore(myEnterpriseService);
    //Instantiate the sample report and query for the Id in the Enterprise CMS
    myInfoObjects = myInfoStore.Query("Select SI_ID From CI_INFOOBJECTS Where SI_NAME='" +
ReportFilePath + "' And SI_INSTANCE=0");
    myInfoObject = myInfoObjects[1];
    //Create the ReportAppFactory that is based on the enterprise session
    myObject = myEnterpriseSession.GetService("", "RASReportFactory").Interface;
    myReportAppFactory = (CrystalDecisions.ReportAppServer.ClientDoc.ReportAppFactory)myObject;
    //Use the OpenDocument method to instantiate the ReportClientDocument object
    rcd = myReportAppFactory.OpenDocument(myInfoObject.ID, 0);
}
```

Understanding the RAS Classes

Using the RAS SDK requires having an understanding of a variety of report classes and their methods. But the hardest part can be figuring out where to find them within the object model. Looking at the help files can create even more confusion because none of the examples have the class namespaces defined. In theory, this is acceptable because if you reference every RAS DLL available and import every namespace, you'll be covered. But doing this can be wasteful, and if you wish to use any classes from the Crystal Reports Basic library, there will be errors with naming conflicts. Not knowing the namespaces makes these problems very difficult to resolve.

The class you will use with every project is the **ClientDoc** class. This is because it is where the **ReportClientDocument** class is located. The **ReportClientDocument** class gives you access to all the other methods and properties you'll be using. In other words, it is the RAS equivalent to the ReportDocument class in the .NET SDK.

The **ReportDefModel** class defines all the report objects. This includes all the areas and sections of a report as well as all the report objects that are displayed within those sections. Basically, everything that appears within the Design tab is managed by the **ReportDefModel** class.

DateDefModel defines the classes that work with a report's data source. This includes the tables and fields available to the report. It's important to note that even if a field isn't used on the report, it is still managed by the **DataDefModel** class. This gives you the ability to add new fields to the report. Basically, all the database tables and fields listed in the Field Explorer window are here.

The code listings in this book always state the complete namespace for a class so that you don't have to guess how to reference it. Of course, this is only necessary for training purposes. Having an **Imports** statement (**using** in C#) in your own project will make your code shorter and more readable.

Adding Database Fields

Since the primary purpose of a report is to display information from a data source to the user, it's no surprise that the most common task that people want to do is add new fields to their report. RAS makes it easy to do this, but it's not a trivial process. Adding a database field involves the following steps:

- Selecting the table and field to display.
- Set the font properties (optional).
- Select the area and section to place the object as well as the coordinate.
- Add it to the report

Not only are these steps necessary for adding a database field to the report, they are also used for many other common tasks. For example, almost anytime you add a report object to the report that displays text, numbers or a data, you should set the font properties for that object. Since these individual steps are used extensively for different use cases, I put each one in a separate method. This lets you build a library of common RAS functions that can be used on any report. Each method uses the Shared keyword (static in C#) so that it can be put into a new class and be called from anywhere in your project without instantiating a new object. The following sections will look at the individual steps in detail and at the end it will show the code listing that pulls them together to add the database field to the report.

Selecting a Field from a Data Source

The report's data source points to all the tables and fields that can be printed. Even if a field isn't displayed on the report, it will still be in the data source if the report's query specifies it to be available. The RAS object model has methods within the ReportClientDocument.Database class that make it easy to find the table and field you need. As you can see in the comments within the code listing, you first get a reference to the table using the FindAlias() method and pass it the table name. It returns the index of the table in the Tables collection. The next step calls the Table.DataFields.Find() method and passes it the field name. This returns the index of the field in the DataFields collection. A reference to this field is returned to the calling method.

Listing 20-5. Get a reference to a field in the data source.

[VB.NET]

```
Public Shared Function GetField(ByVal TableName As String, ByVal FieldName As String, ByVal rcd
As CrystalDecisions.ReportAppServer.ClientDoc.ISCDReportClientDocument) As
CrystalDecisions.ReportAppServer.DataDefModel.Field
    Dim FieldIndex As Integer
    Dim TableIndex As Integer
    'Find the table's location in the table collection
    Dim myTable As CrystalDecisions.ReportAppServer.DataDefModel.Table
    Dim myField As CrystalDecisions.ReportAppServer.DataDefModel.Field
    TableIndex = rcd.Database.Tables.FindByAlias(TableName)
    Dim temp As CrystalDecisions.ReportAppServer.DataDefModel.ISCRTable
    temp = rcd.Database.Tables(TableIndex)
    'Get a reference to the table object
    myTable = DirectCast(temp, CrystalDecisions.ReportAppServer.DataDefModel.Table)
    'Find the field's location in the field collection
    FieldIndex = myTable.DataFields.Find(FieldName,
CrystalDecisions.ReportAppServer.DataDefModel.CrFieldDisplayNameTypeEnum.crFieldDisplayName
Name, CrystalDecisions.ReportAppServer.DataDefModel.CeLocale.ceLocaleUserDefault)
    'Get a reference to the field object
    myField = DirectCast(myTable.DataFields(FieldIndex),
CrystalDecisions.ReportAppServer.DataDefModel.Field)
    Return myField
End Function
```

[C#]

```
public static CrystalDecisions.ReportAppServer.DataDefModel.Field GetField(string TableName, string
FieldName,
    CrystalDecisions.ReportAppServer.ClientDoc.ISCDReportClientDocument rcd)
{
    int FieldIndex, TableIndex;
    CrystalDecisions.ReportAppServer.DataDefModel.Table myTable;
    CrystalDecisions.ReportAppServer.DataDefModel.Field myField;
    //Find the table's location in the table collection
    TableIndex = rcd.Database.Tables.FindByAlias(TableName);
    CrystalDecisions.ReportAppServer.DataDefModel.ISCRTable temp;
    temp = rcd.Database.Tables[TableIndex];
    //Get a reference to the table object
    myTable = (CrystalDecisions.ReportAppServer.DataDefModel.Table)temp;
    //Find the field's location in the field collection
    FieldIndex = myTable.DataFields.Find(FieldName,

CrystalDecisions.ReportAppServer.DataDefModel.CrFieldDisplayNameTypeEnum.crFieldDisplayName
Name,
        CrystalDecisions.ReportAppServer.DataDefModel.CeLocale.ceLocaleUserDefault);
    //Get a reference to the field object
    myField = (CrystalDecisions.ReportAppServer.DataDefModel.Field)myTable.DataFields[FieldIndex];
    return myField;
}
```

Adding a FontClass to a Report Object

Every report object that displays data, whether it is dynamic or static information, uses a FontColor object to store the font related information. Instantiating a FontClass object and assigning properties to it is very trivial. The only unusual part is that it breaks out the font properties into two categories. The first category includes the standard font properties that you find in any Windows application: font name, font size, bold, and italic. For these properties, there is a separate Font object that must be instantiated and assigned to the FontColor.Font property. The second category includes the properties that are unique to Crystal Reports objects. Some of these include the Color, CSS Class and conditional formulas. These have their own properties within the FontColor class.

The following code listing is a generic method for creating a new FontClass object and populating the standard font properties. The argument list in the method declaration lets the user pass in the formatting options they want to set. The method returns a FontClass object that can be assigned to the FontClass property of any report object.

Listing 20-6. Creating a FontClass object and setting its properties.

[VB.NET]

```
Public Shared Function NewFontColor(ByVal Size As Integer, ByVal Name As String, ByVal Bold As
Boolean, ByVal Italic As Boolean) As CrystalDecisions.ReportAppServer.ReportDefModel.FontColor
    Dim myFont As CrystalDecisions.ReportAppServer.ReportDefModel.Font
    myFont = New CrystalDecisions.ReportAppServer.ReportDefModel.FontClass()
    myFont.Size = Size
    myFont.Name = Name
```

```
    myFont.Bold = Bold
    Dim myFontColor As CrystalDecisions.ReportAppServer.ReportDefModel.FontColor
    myFontColor = New CrystalDecisions.ReportAppServer.ReportDefModel.FontColorClass()
    myFontColor.Font = myFont
    Return myFontColor
End Function
```

[C#]

```
public static CrystalDecisions.ReportAppServer.ReportDefModel.FontColor NewFontColor(int Size,
string Name, bool Bold, bool Italic)
{
    CrystalDecisions.ReportAppServer.ReportDefModel.Font myFont;
    myFont = new CrystalDecisions.ReportAppServer.ReportDefModel.FontClass();
    myFont.Size = Size;
    myFont.Name = Name;
    myFont.Bold = Bold;
    CrystalDecisions.ReportAppServer.ReportDefModel.FontColor myFontColor;
    myFontColor = new CrystalDecisions.ReportAppServer.ReportDefModel.FontColorClass();
    myFontColor.Font = myFont;
    return myFontColor;
}
```

Selecting a Report Area and Section

As you learned earlier in the book, a report consists of areas and within each area there can be one or more sections. Each report object has to be located within a specific section. When using the RAS SDK to dynamically add a report object, you have to specify the section that the new report object belongs in.

Adding a report object to the report requires first identifying which area to put it in and which section within that area. Both the areas and sections are stored in a collection that is zero based. So the first area/section has an index of zero and the next will have an index of one. When specifying the section number, it is usually zero because most areas only have one section.

To specify the area number, you could use a number if the number of areas is fixed. But this is more prone to error since it changes based upon how many groups are in a report. Adding a group will re-order the index numbers of all the areas. It is more reliable to use the area name to find its current index number. In the code sample below, the **Areas** collection is iterated through and the **Name** property is tested to see if it matches the given area name. If so, it uses the current index number to get a reference to that **Area** object. To make this work in your own application, you need to know how Crystal Reports names each area. The naming convention is to use the area name followed by the word, "Area", followed by the number 1. The exception to the rule is groups. Since there can be more than one group in a report, each group uses the next consecutive number available. The first group will use the number 1 and the second group will use the number 2, and so on. The following is a list of the area names in a typical report. It is important to note that these names are case sensitive and that there are no spaces in the name.

ReportHeaderArea1

PageHeaderArea1

GroupHeaderArea1 (optional)

GroupHeaderArea2 (optional)

DetailArea1

GroupFooterArea2 (optional)

GroupFooterArea1 (optional)

PageFooterArea1

ReportFooterArea1

Listing 20-7 is a method that accepts the name of an area and a section number and returns a Section object. This object is used to tell the RAS where you want to put a new report object. The code loops through the Areas collection looking for the area with a matching name. When found, it uses the section number to get a reference to the correct section object within that area.

Listing 20-7. Get a reference to a section object using the area name and section number.

[VB.NET]
```
Public Shared Function GetSection(ByVal AreaName As String, ByVal SectionNumber As Integer,
ByVal rcd As CrystalDecisions.ReportAppServer.ClientDoc.ISCDReportClientDocument) As
CrystalDecisions.ReportAppServer.ReportDefModel.Section
    Dim mySection As CrystalDecisions.ReportAppServer.ReportDefModel.Section = Nothing
    For AreaIndex As Integer = 0 To rcd.ReportDefinition.Areas.Count - 1
        If rcd.ReportDefinition.Areas(AreaIndex).Name = AreaName Then
            mySection = rcd.ReportDefinition.Areas(AreaIndex).Sections(SectionNumber)
        End If
    Next
    Return mySection
End Function
```

[C#]
```
public static CrystalDecisions.ReportAppServer.ReportDefModel.Section GetSection(string AreaName,
int SectionNumber, CrystalDecisions.ReportAppServer.ClientDoc.ISCDReportClientDocument rcd)
{
    CrystalDecisions.ReportAppServer.ReportDefModel.Section mySection = null;
    for (int AreaIndex = 0; AreaIndex < rcd.ReportDefinition.Areas.Count; AreaIndex++)
    {
        if (rcd.ReportDefinition.Areas[AreaIndex].Name == AreaName)
        {
            mySection = rcd.ReportDefinition.Areas[AreaIndex].Sections[SectionNumber];
        }
    }
    return mySection;
}
```

Add Database Field to the Report

The code to add the database field to the report creates a new field object and uses the objects created in the previous code listings to set its properties. To try and keep the method as simple as possible, the FontClass object and Section object must be created prior to calling this method. That code will be shown in the next section.

The arguments in this method are pretty self-explanatory. You pass it the table name and field name of the database field you want to put on the report. Next you give it the object coordinates and dimensions. After that are the Section and FontColor objects.

Listing 20-8. Adding the database field to the report.

[VB.NET]

```
Public Shared Sub AddDatabaseField(ByVal TableName As String, ByVal FieldName As String, ByVal
Top As Integer, ByVal Left As Integer, ByVal Height As Integer, ByVal Width As Integer, ByVal Section
As CrystalDecisions.ReportAppServer.ReportDefModel.Section, ByVal FontColor As
CrystalDecisions.ReportAppServer.ReportDefModel.FontColor, ByVal rcd As
CrystalDecisions.ReportAppServer.ClientDoc.ISCDReportClientDocument)
    'Find the data source field to add to the report
    Dim myField As CrystalDecisions.ReportAppServer.DataDefModel.Field
    myField = GetField(TableName, FieldName, rcd)
    'Create the report object that will be added to the report
    Dim myFieldObject As CrystalDecisions.ReportAppServer.ReportDefModel.ISCRFieldObject
    myFieldObject = New CrystalDecisions.ReportAppServer.ReportDefModel.FieldObjectClass()
    myFieldObject.Kind =
CrystalDecisions.ReportAppServer.ReportDefModel.CrReportObjectKindEnum.crReportObjectKindFiel
d
    myFieldObject.FieldValueType = myField.Type
    myFieldObject.DataSource = myField.FormulaForm
    myFieldObject.Left = Left
    myFieldObject.Top = Top
    myFieldObject.Width = Width
    myFieldObject.Height = Height
    myFieldObject.FontColor = FontColor
    'Add the report object to the correct section
    rcd.ReportDefController.ReportObjectController.Add(myFieldObject, Section, 0)
End Sub
```

[C#]

```
public static void AddDatabaseField(string TableName, string FieldName, int Top, int Left, int Height, int
Width, CrystalDecisions.ReportAppServer.ReportDefModel.Section Section,
    CrystalDecisions.ReportAppServer.ReportDefModel.FontColor FontColor,
    CrystalDecisions.ReportAppServer.ClientDoc.ISCDReportClientDocument rcd)
{
    //Find the data source field to add to the report
    CrystalDecisions.ReportAppServer.DataDefModel.Field myField;
    myField = GetField(TableName, FieldName, rcd);
    //Create the report object that will be added to the report
    CrystalDecisions.ReportAppServer.ReportDefModel.FieldObject myFieldObject;
    myFieldObject = new CrystalDecisions.ReportAppServer.ReportDefModel.FieldObjectClass();
```

```
    myFieldObject.Kind =
CrystalDecisions.ReportAppServer.ReportDefModel.CrReportObjectKindEnum.crReportObjectKindFiel
d;
    myFieldObject.FieldValueType = myField.Type;
    myFieldObject.DataSource = myField.FormulaForm;
    myFieldObject.Left = Left;
    myFieldObject.Top = Top;
    myFieldObject.Width = Width;
    myFieldObject.Height = Height;
    myFieldObject.FontColor = FontColor;
    //Add the report object to the correct section
    rcd.ReportDefController.ReportObjectController.Add(myFieldObject, Section, 0);
}
```

To keep this code as understandable as possible, I left out many of the advanced formatting properties available. For example, you can set the properties EnableCanGrow, EnableSuppress, EnableKeepTogether, etc. These properties are found in the ISCRFieldObject.Format class. If you want to set these properties as well, in the previous listing you can add code similar to the following:

```
myFieldObject.Format.EnableCanGrow = True
myFieldObject.Format.HyperlinkText = "http://www.CrystalReportsBook.com"
myFieldObject.Format.EnableSuppress = False
```

As you can see, the RAS SDK exposes many properties that let you customize the formatting of a report object. To see a complete list of properties, please consult the help file.

Demonstrate Adding a Database Field to the Report

Finally, we get to see how everything works by demonstrating the code which creates all the necessary objects and calls the AddDatabaseField() method to put the object on the report. This code uses the Form_Load() event so that the report is built immediately when the form opens. Of course, you can copy and paste this code into the appropriate method for your application.

Listing 20-9. Demonstrating adding a database field to the report.

[VB.NET]

```
Private Sub Form1_Load(ByVal sender As System.Object, ByVal e As System.EventArgs) Handles
MyBase.Load
    'Declare both the reporting objects
    Dim myReportDocument As CrystalDecisions.CrystalReports.Engine.ReportDocument = Nothing
    Dim rcd As CrystalDecisions.ReportAppServer.ClientDoc.ISCDReportClientDocument = Nothing
    OpenReportClientDocument("C:\CrystalReport1.rpt", myReportDocument, rcd)
    'Create the fontcolor object
    Dim FontColor As CrystalDecisions.ReportAppServer.ReportDefModel.FontColor
    FontColor = NewFontColor(10, "Times New Roman", True, False)
    'Get a reference to the section where the object will be placed
    Dim mySection As CrystalDecisions.ReportAppServer.ReportDefModel.Section
```

```
    mySection = GetSection("DetailArea1", 0, rcd)
    'Add the object to the report
    AddDatabaseField("Orders", "Ship Via", 0, 1000, 221, 1000, mySection, FontColor, rcd)
    CrystalReportViewer1.ReportSource = myReportDocument
End Sub
```

[C#]

```
private void Form1_Load(object sender, EventArgs e)
{
    // Declare both of the reporting objects
    CrystalDecisions.CrystalReports.Engine.ReportDocument myReportDocument = null;
    CrystalDecisions.ReportAppServer.ClientDoc.ISCDReportClientDocument rcd = null;
    //Load the report into memory
    OpenReportClientDocument(@"C:\CrystalReport1.rpt", ref myReportDocument, ref rcd);
    //Create the fontcolor object
    CrystalDecisions.ReportAppServer.ReportDefModel.FontColor FontColor;
    FontColor = NewFontColor(10, "Times New Roman", true, false);
    //Get a reference to the section where the report object will be placed
    CrystalDecisions.ReportAppServer.ReportDefModel.Section mySection;
    mySection = GetSection("DetailArea1", 0, rcd);
    //Create the report object and place it on the report
    AddDatabaseField("Orders", "Ship Via", 0, 1000, 221, 1000, mySection, FontColor, rcd);
    //Preview the report in the viewer
    crystalReportViewer1.ReportSource = myReportDocument;
}
```

Adding a Special Field to the Report

Crystal Reports has special fields that give you more in-depth information about a report. Some of these include Page Number, Page N of M, Print Time, etc. The complete list is found in the Field Explorer window in the Special Fields node.

Adding a special field to a report is almost identical to adding a database field. The difference is that the special field is an internal field and not associated with an external data source. Because of this, rather than set the **DataSource** property to the name of a table's field, you assign it a pre-defined constant. Crystal Reports will recognize that it is a special field and place it on the report.

Each pre-defined constant name is almost identical to its related special field name. The pre-defined constant has the spaces removed. In a few unique cases, the name is an abbreviation of the special field name. To make it easy, the name of every special field is listed in Table 20-2. The left column is the special field name and the right column is the value you assign to the **DataSource** property.

Table 20-2. Special Fields and their pre-defined constants.

Special Field	DataSource Name
Data Date	DataDate

Data Time	DataTime
File Author	FileAuthor
File Path and Name	FileName
Group Number	GroupNumber
Group Selection Formula	GroupSelection
Modification Date	ModificationDate
Modification Time	ModificationTime
Page N of M	PageNofM
Print Date	PrintDate
Print Time	PrintTime
Record Number	RecordNumber
Record Selection Formula	RecordSelection
Report Title	ReportTitle
Total Page Count	TotalPageCount
Content Locale	ContentLocale
Data Time Zone	DataTimeZone
Print Time Zone	PrintTimeZone
Horizontal Page Number	HPageNUmber

The following code creates the report object which holds a special field. To use it in your program, you can take the code in Listing 20-9 and replace the call to AddDatabaseField() with a call to AddSpecialField(). When calling the AddSpecialField() method, the first argument is the special field name that designates which field you want to put on the report. Use the name from column two in Table 20-2.

Listing 20-10. Add a Special Field to the report.

[VB.NET]

```
Public Shared Sub AddSpecialField(ByVal Name As String, ByVal Top As Integer, ByVal Left As
Integer, ByVal Height As Integer, ByVal Width As Integer, _
 ByVal Section As CrystalDecisions.ReportAppServer.ReportDefModel.Section, ByVal FontColor As
CrystalDecisions.ReportAppServer.ReportDefModel.FontColor, _
 ByVal rcd As CrystalDecisions.ReportAppServer.ClientDoc.ISCDReportClientDocument)
    Dim myFieldObject As CrystalDecisions.ReportAppServer.ReportDefModel.ISCRFieldObject
    myFieldObject = New CrystalDecisions.ReportAppServer.ReportDefModel.FieldObject()
    myFieldObject.DataSource = Name
```

```
    myFieldObject.Left = Left
    myFieldObject.Top = Top
    myFieldObject.Width = Width
    myFieldObject.Height = Height
    myFieldObject.FontColor = FontColor
    'Add the report object to the correct section
    rcd.ReportDefController.ReportObjectController.Add(myFieldObject, Section, 0)
End Sub
```

[C#]

```
public static void AddSpecialField(string Name, int Top, int Left, int Height, int Width,
CrystalDecisions.ReportAppServer.ReportDefModel.Section Section,
    CrystalDecisions.ReportAppServer.ReportDefModel.FontColor FontColor,
    CrystalDecisions.ReportAppServer.ClientDoc.ISCDReportClientDocument rcd)
{
    CrystalDecisions.ReportAppServer.ReportDefModel.ISCRFieldObject myFieldObject;
    myFieldObject = new CrystalDecisions.ReportAppServer.ReportDefModel.FieldObject();
    //This is the name of the special field
    myFieldObject.DataSource = Name;
    myFieldObject.Left = Left;
    myFieldObject.Top = Top;
    myFieldObject.Width = Width;
    myFieldObject.Height = Height;
    myFieldObject.FontColor = FontColor;
    //Add the report object to the correct section
    rcd.ReportDefController.ReportObjectController.Add(myFieldObject, Section, 0);
}
```

Adding Formulas and Parameters

After going through the examples for adding database fields and special fields to a report, you should be an expert at how the code works to add objects to a report. Of course, you will most likely want to add formulas and parameters to your report. So let's just look at the general rules for adding formulas and parameters to the report and leave it to you to make the necessary changes.

Adding formulas and parameters to a report uses the similar code as the AddDatabaseField() method, but with two exceptions. The two properties, FieldValueType and DataSource have to be customized.

The FieldValueType has to be set so that Crystal Reports knows what type of data to display. For example, you need to tell it whether it is a string, number, date, etc. It uses the enumerated data type CrystalDecisions.ReportAppServer.DataDefModel. CrFieldValueTypeEnum to specify the field type. You can use intellisense to browse the complete list of data types available.

The DataSource property is assigned the name of the formula or parameter. It requires that you use proper Crystal syntax and include the curly brackets and full name. The following code snippet shows how to set the properties for a string formula and a numeric parameter.

```
'Properties for a string formula
myFieldObject.FieldValueType =
CrystalDecisions.ReportAppServer.DataDefModel.CrFieldValueTypeEnum.crFieldValueTypeStringFiel
d
myFieldObject.DataSource = "{@SampleFormula}"
'Properties for a number parameter
myFieldObject.FieldValueType =
CrystalDecisions.ReportAppServer.DataDefModel.CrFieldValueTypeEnum.crFieldValueTypeNumberFi
eld
myFieldObject.DataSource = "{?SampleParameter}"
```

You can use the code for adding a database field to a report and replace it with either of the two samples above to add a formula or parameter.

Changing the Record Selection Filter

The record selection filter tells Crystal Reports which records you want to include in the report's output. Any records not matching the record selection filter are excluded. The RAS lets you change the filter with a single statement: RecordFilterController.SetFormulaText(). To change the grouping formula, use the GroupFilterController.SetFormulaText() method. The next two listings demonstrate this.

Listing 20-11. Changing the record selection formula.

[VB.NET]

```
Private Sub ModifyFilter(ByVal NewFilter As String, ByVal rcd As ISCDReportClientDocument)
    rcd.DataDefController.RecordFilterController.SetFormulaText(NewFilter)
End Sub
```

[C#]

```
private void ModifyRecordFilter(string NewFilter, ISCDReportClientDocument rcd)
{
    rcd.DataDefController.RecordFilterController.SetFormulaText(NewFilter);
}
```

Listing 20-12. Change the group selection formula.

[VB.NET]

```
Private Sub ModifyFilter(ByVal NewFilter As String, ByVal rcd As ISCDReportClientDocument)
    rcd.DataDefController.GroupFilterController.SetFormulaText(NewFilter)
End Sub
```

[C#]

```
private void ModifyGroupFilter(string NewFilter, ISCDReportClientDocument rcd)
{
    rcd.DataDefController.RecordFilterController.SetFormulaText(NewFilter);
}
```

Modifying Report Parameters

Parameters in RAS use a totally different architecture than parameters in .NET. The RAS uses a ParameterFieldController to manage a report's parameters. The ParameterFieldController is found in the DataDefController namespace. Modifying a parameter requires you getting a copy of the existing parameter object. Make changes to this copy and tell the controller to use the copy to update the actual parameter in the report.

Before looking at the details of how to modify parameters, you need to understand how to work with the two types of parameters: discrete value and ranged value. Each type requires using a different report object and each works slightly different than the other.

Discrete parameters use the ParameterFieldDiscreteValue class. They are the easiest to change. Simply assign a value to the parameter using the Value property.

Range parameters use the ParameterFieldRangeValue class. You have to set both the beginning and ending values (the boundary) of the range. This is done using two properties: BeginValue and EndValue. Each of these values can either be inclusive or exclusive. Each range boundary is set using the properties LowerBoundType and UpperBoundType. There are three possible settings for determining whether a value is included in the range or not. These settings are listed in Table 20-3.

Table 20-3. Possible values for the bounds type.

Value	Description
crRangeValueBoundTypeNoBound	There are no bounds for this value. For lower bounds, the smallest possible value will be included in the range. For upper bounds, the largest value will be part of the range.
crRangeValueBoundTypeExclusive	The value is not included in the range. The next possible value that is either higher or lower will be used.
crRangeValueBoundTypeInclusive	The value is included in the range.

The only part of the table that might need clarifying is the value crRangeValueBoundTypeNoBound. This setting isn't available in .NET. It is used for ignoring either the lower or upper bounds. For example, if used for the lower bound, there will be no lower bound and the range will only be limited to the upper bound.

Now that you've seen how to work with the different types of parameters, let's build upon this information and look at the steps for modifying parameters during runtime. The RAS object model doesn't let you modify a parameter directly. You have to temporarily build a new parameter field and set its properties. Pass this new parameter to the

ParameterFieldController object and it updates the existing parameter to have the new values. The detailed steps of how to implement this are as follows.

Declare two parameter field objects. One is for the existing report parameter and the other is for creating the new parameter. Each object variable is of type **ParameterField**.

Get a reference to the existing parameter from the **ParameterFields** collection. The **ParameterFields** collection is found in the report's **DataDefinition** class. The following line of code passes the value 0 so that the first parameter in the collection is retrieved.

```
OldParameter = myReport.DataDefinition.ParameterFields.Item(0)
```

This line of code requires that you know the field's index number in the collection.[48] If you don't know the index number, you can get it by calling the collection's **Find()** method. The **Find()** method is passed a string that is used for identifying the parameter you want. It returns an integer that is the index number of where that parameter is within the **ParameterField** collection.

The string that is used to find a parameter can actually be different things. A few examples of what the string could represent are the parameter name, its header, or its formula. Since the string could represent a variety of things, you also have to pass an enumerator that states how to use the string. The following line of code finds a parameter field with the name "EmpId". The first parameter is the string name and the second parameter is the enumerator.

```
Dim ParameterIndex as Integer
ParameterIndex = myReport.DataDefinition.ParameterFields.Find("EmpId",
CrystalDecisions.ReportAppServer.DataDefModel.CrFieldDisplayNameTypeEnum.
crFieldDisplayNameName)
```

Tip

Due to the dynamic nature of reports as they are developed, it isn't practical to track the index number of each parameter object. To make your application easier to read and maintain, you should always use the **Find()** method.

After getting a reference to the existing parameter object, copy it to the new parameter object. This is done by instantiating the new parameter field and calling the **CopyTo()** method of the existing parameter. The **CopyTo()** method copies all the properties of the existing parameter into the new parameter.

```
OldParameter.CopyTo(NewParameter, True)
```

Modify the new parameter object so that it stores the new value(s). To do this you have to instantiate a new value object based upon the type of parameter and assign a value to it. As mentioned earlier, since a parameter can store either discrete values or range values, this code to update the parameter value(s) is different for each type.

---

[48] The ParameterFields collection is zero based.

Programming the discrete value only requires setting the Value property. The following code creates a discrete value object and assigns it a value from the generic variable **myValue**.

```
myParameterValue = New
CrystalDecisions.ReportAppServer.DataDefModel.ParameterFieldDiscreteValue
myParameterValue.Value = myValue
```

Programming the range value requires setting the **BeginValue** and **EndValue** properties. You also have to specify whether the bounds are inclusive or exclusive using the **LowerBoundType** and **UpperBoundType** properties. The following code creates a range value object and assigns it the generic variables **myBeginValue** and **myEndValue**. Both the lower and upper bounds are set to be inclusive.

```
myParameterValue = New
CrystalDecisions.ReportAppServer.DataDefModel.ParameterFieldRangeValue
myParameterValue.BeginValue = myBeginValue
myParameterValue.LowerBoundType = _
CrystalDecisions.ReportAppServer.DataDefModel.CrRangeValueBoundTypeEnum.
crRangeValueBoundTypeInclusive
myParameterValue.EndValue = myEndValue
myParameterValue.UpperBoundType = _
CrystalDecisions.ReportAppServer.DataDefModel.CrRangeValueBoundTypeEnum.
crRangeValueBoundTypeInclusive
```

After creating either the discrete value or range value, you have to assign it to the values collection of the new parameter object.

```
NewParameter.CurrentValues.Add(myParameterValue)
```

At this point, the new parameter has been created and assigned the new values. Now you have to copy this parameter back into existing parameter and overwrite the existing parameter's values. The report object has a **ParameterFieldController** object which manages the parameters. Call the **Modify()** method and pass it both the existing parameter object and the new parameter object.

```
myReport.DataDefController.ParameterFieldController.Modify(OldParameter, NewParameter)
```

After calling the **Modify()** method, the parameter will have the current value(s) that the report needs to run. If there are more parameters in the report, you have to call this code again for each parameter.

The following examples tie all the code samples into a single listing so that it is easier for you to see how all the objects work together.

Listing 20-13 is a generic method for modifying a discrete parameter in a report. Pass it the parameter name, the parameter value, and the report object that you are working with.

If you remember from the description of Listing 20-1, which shows how to load and preview a report, prior to setting the **ReportSource** property you should call any code that performs runtime modification on the report object. This is where you would call this procedure.

Listing 20-13. Modifying a discrete parameter.

[VB.NET]

```
Public Shared Sub SetDiscreteParameter(ByVal ParameterName As String, ByVal NewValue As
Object, ByVal rcd As CrystalDecisions.ReportAppServer.ClientDoc.ISCDReportClientDocument)
    Dim OldParameter As CrystalDecisions.ReportAppServer.DataDefModel.ParameterField, _
    NewParameter As CrystalDecisions.ReportAppServer.DataDefModel.ParameterField
    Dim myParameterValue As _
    CrystalDecisions.ReportAppServer.DataDefModel.ParameterFieldDiscreteValue
    'Get a reference to the existing parameter
    Dim ParameterIndex As Integer
    ParameterIndex = rcd.DataDefinition.ParameterFields.Find(ParameterName, _
CrystalDecisions.ReportAppServer.DataDefModel.CrFieldDisplayNameTypeEnum.crFieldDisplayName
Name, CrystalDecisions.ReportAppServer.DataDefModel.CeLocale.ceLocaleUserDefault)
    OldParameter = DirectCast(rcd.DataDefinition.ParameterFields(ParameterIndex),  _
    CrystalDecisions.ReportAppServer.DataDefModel.ParameterField)
    'Create the new parameter and base it off the existing parameter
    NewParameter = New CrystalDecisions.ReportAppServer.DataDefModel.ParameterFieldClass()
    OldParameter.CopyTo(NewParameter, True)
    'Create the value object that will go in the parameter object
    myParameterValue = New
CrystalDecisions.ReportAppServer.DataDefModel.ParameterFieldDiscreteValueClass()
    myParameterValue.Value = NewValue
    'Save the parameter
    NewParameter.CurrentValues.Add(myParameterValue)
    rcd.DataDefController.ParameterFieldController.Modify(OldParameter, NewParameter)
End Sub
```

[C#]

```
public static void SetDiscreteParameter(string ParameterName, object NewValue,
CrystalDecisions.ReportAppServer.ClientDoc.ISCDReportClientDocument rcd)
{
    CrystalDecisions.ReportAppServer.DataDefModel.ParameterField OldParameter, NewParameter;
    CrystalDecisions.ReportAppServer.DataDefModel.ParameterFieldDiscreteValue myParameterValue;
    //Get a reference to the existing parameter
    int ParameterIndex;
    ParameterIndex = rcd.DataDefinition.ParameterFields.Find(ParameterName,
CrystalDecisions.ReportAppServer.DataDefModel.CrFieldDisplayNameTypeEnum.crFieldDisplayName
Name, CrystalDecisions.ReportAppServer.DataDefModel.CeLocale.ceLocaleUserDefault);
    OldParameter =
(CrystalDecisions.ReportAppServer.DataDefModel.ParameterField)rcd.DataDefinition.ParameterFields[
ParameterIndex];
    //Create the new parameter and base it off the existing parameter
    NewParameter = new CrystalDecisions.ReportAppServer.DataDefModel.ParameterFieldClass();
    OldParameter.CopyTo(NewParameter, true);
    //Create the value object that will go in the parameter object
    myParameterValue = new
CrystalDecisions.ReportAppServer.DataDefModel.ParameterFieldDiscreteValueClass();
    myParameterValue.Value = NewValue;
    //Save the parameter
    NewParameter.CurrentValues.Add(myParameterValue);
    rcd.DataDefController.ParameterFieldController.Modify(OldParameter, NewParameter);
```

}

Listing 20-14 shows a generic method for modifying a range parameter in a report. Pass it the parameter name, the beginning and ending values and the report object that you are working with. To make this example easier, it is assumed that each value uses inclusive bounds. It would be easy for you to modify it so that this is also passed as a parameter.

Listing 20-14. Modifying a range parameter.

[VB.NET]

```
Public Shared Sub SetRangeParameter(ByVal ParameterName As String, ByVal NewBeginValue As
Object, ByVal NewEndValue As Object, _
    ByVal rcd As CrystalDecisions.ReportAppServer.ClientDoc.ISCDReportClientDocument)
    Dim OldParameter As CrystalDecisions.ReportAppServer.DataDefModel.ParameterField,
NewParameter As _
    CrystalDecisions.ReportAppServer.DataDefModel.ParameterField
    Dim MyParameterValue As
CrystalDecisions.ReportAppServer.DataDefModel.ParameterFieldRangeValue
    'Get a reference to the existing parameter
    Dim ParameterIndex As Integer
    ParameterIndex = rcd.DataDefinition.ParameterFields.Find(ParameterName, _

CrystalDecisions.ReportAppServer.DataDefModel.CrFieldDisplayNameTypeEnum.crFieldDisplayName
Name, _
    CrystalDecisions.ReportAppServer.DataDefModel.CeLocale.ceLocaleUserDefault)
    OldParameter = DirectCast(rcd.DataDefinition.ParameterFields(ParameterIndex), _
    CrystalDecisions.ReportAppServer.DataDefModel.ParameterField)
    'Create the new parameter and base it off the existing parameter
    NewParameter = New CrystalDecisions.ReportAppServer.DataDefModel.ParameterFieldClass()
    OldParameter.CopyTo(NewParameter, True)
    'Create the value object that will go in the parameter object
    MyParameterValue = New
CrystalDecisions.ReportAppServer.DataDefModel.ParameterFieldRangeValueClass()
    MyParameterValue.BeginValue = NewBeginValue
    MyParameterValue.EndValue = NewEndValue
    MyParameterValue.LowerBoundType = CrystalDecisions.ReportAppServer.DataDefModel.
CrRangeValueBoundTypeEnum.crRangeValueBoundTypeInclusive
    MyParameterValue.UpperBoundType = CrystalDecisions.ReportAppServer.DataDefModel.
CrRangeValueBoundTypeEnum.crRangeValueBoundTypeInclusive
    'Save the parameter
    NewParameter.CurrentValues.Add(MyParameterValue)
    rcd.DataDefController.ParameterFieldController.Modify(OldParameter, NewParameter)
End Sub
```

[C#]

```
public static void SetRangeParameter(string ParameterName, object NewBeginValue, object
NewEndValue, CrystalDecisions.ReportAppServer.ClientDoc.ISCDReportClientDocument rcd)
{
    CrystalDecisions.ReportAppServer.DataDefModel.ParameterField OldParameter, NewParameter;
    CrystalDecisions.ReportAppServer.DataDefModel.ParameterFieldRangeValue MyParameterValue;
    //Get a reference to the existing parameter
    int ParameterIndex;
```

```
    ParameterIndex = rcd.DataDefinition.ParameterFields.Find(ParameterName,

CrystalDecisions.ReportAppServer.DataDefModel.CrFieldDisplayNameTypeEnum.crFieldDisplayName
Name,
        CrystalDecisions.ReportAppServer.DataDefModel.CeLocale.ceLocaleUserDefault);
        OldParameter = (CrystalDecisions.ReportAppServer.DataDefModel.ParameterField)
rcd.DataDefinition.ParameterFields[ParameterIndex];
        //Create the new parameter and base it off the existing parameter
        NewParameter = new CrystalDecisions.ReportAppServer.DataDefModel.ParameterFieldClass();
        OldParameter.CopyTo(NewParameter, true);
        //Create the value object that will go in the parameter object
        MyParameterValue = new
CrystalDecisions.ReportAppServer.DataDefModel.ParameterFieldRangeValueClass();
        MyParameterValue.BeginValue = NewBeginValue;
        MyParameterValue.EndValue = NewEndValue;
        MyParameterValue.LowerBoundType = CrystalDecisions.ReportAppServer.DataDefModel.
CrRangeValueBoundTypeEnum.crRangeValueBoundTypeInclusive;
        MyParameterValue.UpperBoundType = CrystalDecisions.ReportAppServer.DataDefModel.
CrRangeValueBoundTypeEnum.crRangeValueBoundTypeInclusive;
        //Save the parameter
        NewParameter.CurrentValues.Add(MyParameterValue);
        rcd.DataDefController.ParameterFieldController.Modify(OldParameter, NewParameter);
}
```

Modifying Formulas

The concepts that apply to modifying parameters are the same concepts for modifying
formulas. RAS uses a similar object model for making changes to a formula. Rather than
use the ParameterFieldController class, you use the FormulaFieldController. Listing 20-15
is the complete code listing.

Listing 20-15. Modifying the value of a formula.

[VB.NET]

```
Public Shared Sub SetFormula(ByVal FormulaName As String, ByVal FormulaText As String, _
    ByVal rcd As CrystalDecisions.ReportAppServer.ClientDoc.ISCDReportClientDocument)
    Dim OldFormula As CrystalDecisions.ReportAppServer.DataDefModel.FormulaField, _
    NewFormula As CrystalDecisions.ReportAppServer.DataDefModel.FormulaField
    'Get a reference to the existing formula
    Dim FormulaIndex As Integer
    FormulaIndex = rcd.DataDefinition.FormulaFields.Find(FormulaName, _
CrystalDecisions.ReportAppServer.DataDefModel.CrFieldDisplayNameTypeEnum.crFieldDisplayName
Name, _
    CrystalDecisions.ReportAppServer.DataDefModel.CeLocale.ceLocaleUserDefault)
    OldFormula = DirectCast(rcd.DataDefinition.FormulaFields(FormulaIndex), _
    CrystalDecisions.ReportAppServer.DataDefModel.FormulaField)
    'Create the new formula and copy the old formula into it
    NewFormula = New CrystalDecisions.ReportAppServer.DataDefModel.FormulaField()
    OldFormula.CopyTo(NewFormula, True)
    'Set the new formula text
    NewFormula.Text = FormulaText
```

```
    rcd.DataDefController.FormulaFieldController.Modify(OldFormula, NewFormula)
End Sub
```

[C#]
```
public static void SetFormula(string FormulaName, string FormulaText,
    CrystalDecisions.ReportAppServer.ClientDoc.ISCDReportClientDocument rcd)
{
    CrystalDecisions.ReportAppServer.DataDefModel.FormulaField OldFormula, NewFormula;
    //Get a reference to the existing formula
    int FormulaIndex;
    FormulaIndex = rcd.DataDefinition.FormulaFields.Find(FormulaName,

CrystalDecisions.ReportAppServer.DataDefModel.CrFieldDisplayNameTypeEnum.crFieldDisplayName
Name,
        CrystalDecisions.ReportAppServer.DataDefModel.CeLocale.ceLocaleUserDefault);
    OldFormula =
(CrystalDecisions.ReportAppServer.DataDefModel.FormulaField)rcd.DataDefinition.FormulaFields
[FormulaIndex];
    //Create the new formula and copy the old formula into it
    NewFormula = new CrystalDecisions.ReportAppServer.DataDefModel.FormulaField();
    OldFormula.CopyTo(NewFormula, true);
    //Set the new formula text
    NewFormula.Text = FormulaText;
    rcd.DataDefController.FormulaFieldController.Modify(OldFormula, NewFormula);
}
```

Saving Your Report Changes

Crystal Reports lets you save the changes you made to a report to a new file. Call the ReportDocument.Save() method and pass it a fully qualified filename.

Custom Add-Ins for Crystal Reports 2008

New to Crystal Reports 2008 is the ability for .NET developers to create custom Add-Ins. A custom Add-In allows you to extend the functionality of Crystal Reports 2008 by writing a library of functions that the user can call directly from the menu bar. Prior to this, you could create a User Function Library (UFL)[49] and these functions could be called by a formula within Crystal Reports. Custom Add-Ins are different because they are called directly by the user via the menu bar. This is illustrated in Figure 20-1.

---

[49] See Chapter 7 for a full discussion of creating a User Function Library.

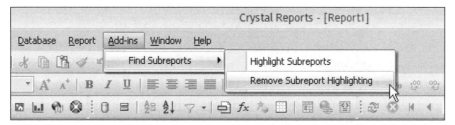

Figure 20-1. The Add-In option on the Crystal Reports 2008 menu bar.

When Crystal Reports 2008 opens, it looks in its AddIns subfolder for any DLL files that start with "csc". It examines each one to find out which menu commands should be added and lists them under the Add-Ins menu option.[50] This is done using the DotNetExternalCommandAdapter.DLL library. This DLL handles all communication between Crystal Reports and the .NET Add-In files. When a user selects an item in the Add-Ins menu, Crystal Reports calls your Add-In and passes the menu item that was clicked and the filename of a temporary copy of the report. Your Add-In does whatever processing is necessary and saves the changes back to the temporary copy of the report. This new report is displayed to the user and any changes made by your Add-In are now in effect.

Two parts of this process need to be examined in more detail so that you get a better understanding of what is happening. The first part is how Crystal Reports communicates with your Add-In. When it first searches the AddIns subfolder and finds your DLL, it requests a list of all commands that it can process. These are identified within an object array that gives each option a numeric ID, description and bitmap. When the user chooses an Add-In, Crystal Reports uses the numeric ID to tell your DLL which command they chose. You use this ID to perform the necessary processing.

Note

You cannot pass parameters from Crystal Reports to your .NET class. Crystal Reports only passes a single number to .NET and this number represents the Add-In command that the user selected.

The second part of the process that needs more explaining is how your DLL handles the report. When Crystal Reports calls your Add-In, it creates a temporary copy of the report that the user is viewing and passes your Add-In the filename of this temporary report file. You have to load the report copy into memory and process it accordingly. Use the RAS library provided in the .NET SDK to work with the report. You have full access to all the report properties and methods. Now you can traverse the object collections and make changes to any report object. When finished, save the report back to the temporary file and exit. Crystal Reports takes your temporary report copy and refreshes the report viewer with it.

---

[50] When Crystal Reports finds a DLL in the AddIns subfolder for the first time, it won't show the Add-Ins command in the menu. You have to close Crystal Reports and re-open it for the menu option to appear.

Caution

When Crystal Reports makes a temporary copy of the report so that your Add-In can load it into memory and process it, it saves the data with the report. Since the temporary copy will override the report that the user is currently looking at, all the data must be saved with it so that it can be re-displayed when the Add-In is finished.

If the report is designed so that it only loads a single page into memory at a time, the user will have to wait for the report to process all the remaining records prior to calling your Add-In. They will see a message in the status bar at the bottom that the report is processing additional records. Reports that print thousands of records will require a long wait.

Now that you understand how the process works, lets walk through the steps of creating a new Add-In using Visual Studio .NET. For this example, we'll keep it simple and create an Add-In that sets the record selection filter showing order amounts greater than $5,000. There will also be a second option to remove the record selection formula.

Create a new Visual Studio .NET project and choose Class Library from the templates. Remember that the project name must start with "csc". Name the project "cscSalesAmount" and click the OK button.

Delete the Class1.cls file that was created by default.

Right-click on the References node in the Solution Explorer and select Add Reference. Add the following references:

- CrystalDecisions.ReportAppServer.ClientDoc

- CrystalDecisions.ReportAppServer.Controllers

- CrystalDecisions.Shared

- CrystalDecisions.CrystalReports.Engine

- DotNetExternalCommandAdapter. You will need to browse for it in the C:\Program Files\Business Objects\BusinessObjects Enterprise 12.0\win32_x86 directory.)

- System.Drawing

- System.Windows.Forms

After adding the above references, the first step is to create the class that works with the report to carry out the Add-In commands. In this example, the commands will either create a new record selection formula that filters on the order amount, or clear the existing record selection formula.

Right-click on the project name in the Solution Explorer and select Add > Class. Name it "OrderAmounts" and click the OK button to create it.

Enter the code in Listing 20-16.

Listing 20-16. Open the temporary report and modify the record selection formula.

[VB.NET]

```
Imports System
Imports System.Windows.Forms
Imports CrystalDecisions.CrystalReports.Engine
Imports CrystalDecisions.ReportAppServer.ClientDoc
Imports CrystalDecisions.Shared

Class OrderAmounts
    Private myReportDocument As New ReportDocument()
    Private rdc As ISCDReportClientDocument

    Public Sub New(ByVal FileName As String)
        myReportDocument.Load(FileName)
        rdc = myReportDocument.ReportClientDocument
    End Sub
    Public Sub SetFilter()
        Try
            rdc.DataDefController.RecordFilterController.SetFormulaText("{Orders.Order Amount} > 5000")
            rdc.Save()
            myReportDocument.Close()
        Catch e As System.Exception
            System.Windows.Forms.MessageBox.Show(e.Message)
        End Try
    End Sub
    Public Sub ClearFilter()
        Try
            rdc.DataDefController.RecordFilterController.SetFormulaText("")
            rdc.Save()
            myReportDocument.Close()
        Catch e As System.Exception
            System.Windows.Forms.MessageBox.Show(e.Message)
        End Try
    End Sub
End Class
```

[C#]

```
using System;
using System.Windows.Forms;
using CrystalDecisions.CrystalReports.Engine;
using CrystalDecisions.ReportAppServer.ClientDoc;
using CrystalDecisions.Shared;

namespace cscOrderAmounts
{
    class OrderAmounts
```

```
    {
        private ReportDocument myReportDocument = new ReportDocument();
        private ISCDReportClientDocument rdc;

        public OrderAmounts(string FileName)
        {
            myReportDocument.Load(FileName);
            rdc = myReportDocument.ReportClientDocument;
        }
        public void SetFilter()
        {
            try
            {
                rdc.DataDefController.RecordFilterController.SetFormulaText("{Orders.Order Amount} >
5000");

                rdc.Save();
                myReportDocument.Close();
            }
            catch (System.Exception e)
            {
                System.Windows.Forms.MessageBox.Show(e.Message);
            }
        }
        public void ClearFilter()
        {
            try
            {
                rdc.DataDefController.RecordFilterController.SetFormulaText("");
                rdc.Save();
                myReportDocument.Close();
            }
            catch (System.Exception e)
            {
                System.Windows.Forms.MessageBox.Show(e.Message);
            }
        }
    }
}
```

The code in this listing is the same as the code you've seen throughout the entire chapter. It uses the RAS SDK to open the report, modify the record selection formula, and save it back to disk. After it is saved to disk, Crystal Reports will open it and use it to override the existing report in the designer. The key points are that there is one method for each command in the Add-In menu. This code is not called directly by Crystal Reports. Instead, it is called by the next class we'll create.

The next step is to add the class that talks directly with Crystal Reports. Right-click on the project name in the Solution Explorer and select Add > Class. Name it "Main".

Enter the code in Listing 20-17. This is the basic template for all your Add-Ins.

Listing 20-17. Template for a .NET Add-In.

[VB.NET]

```vbnet
Imports System
Imports System.Text
Imports System.Drawing
Imports System.Windows.Forms
Imports BusinessObjects.CrystalReports.DotNetExternalCommand
Public Class myCommand
    Implements ICommand
    Private name As String
    Private commandID As Integer
    Private bitmap As Bitmap = Nothing
    Private largeBitmap As Bitmap = Nothing
    Private description As String
    Public Sub New(ByVal name_ As String, ByVal commandID_ As Integer, ByVal bitmap_ As Bitmap, _

    ByVal largeBitmap_ As Bitmap, ByVal description_ As String)
        name = name_
        commandID = commandID_
        bitmap = bitmap_
        largeBitmap = largeBitmap_
        description = description_
    End Sub
    Public Function getDisplayName() As String Implements _
    BusinessObjects.CrystalReports.DotNetExternalCommand.ICommand.getDisplayName
        Return name
    End Function
    Public Function getCommandID() As Integer Implements _
    BusinessObjects.CrystalReports.DotNetExternalCommand.ICommand.getCommandID
        Return commandID
    End Function
    Public Function getBitmap() As Bitmap Implements _
    BusinessObjects.CrystalReports.DotNetExternalCommand.ICommand.getBitmap
        Return bitmap
    End Function
    Public Function getLargeBitmap() As Bitmap Implements _
    BusinessObjects.CrystalReports.DotNetExternalCommand.ICommand.getLargeBitmap
        Return largeBitmap
    End Function
    Public Function getDescription() As String Implements _
    BusinessObjects.CrystalReports.DotNetExternalCommand.ICommand.getDescription
        Return description
    End Function
End Class
```

[C#]

```csharp
using System;
using System.Text;
using System.Drawing;
using System.Windows.Forms;
using BusinessObjects.CrystalReports.DotNetExternalCommand;
namespace cscOrderAmounts
{
```

```
public class myCommand : ICommand
{
    private string name;
    private int commandID;
    private Bitmap bitmap = null;
    private Bitmap largeBitmap = null;
    private string description;
    public myCommand(string name_, int commandID_, Bitmap bitmap_, Bitmap largeBitmap_, string description_)
    {
        name = name_;
        commandID = commandID_;
        bitmap = bitmap_;
        largeBitmap = largeBitmap_;
        description = description_;
    }
    public string getDisplayName()
    {
        return name;
    }
    public int getCommandID()
    {
        return commandID;
    }
    public Bitmap getBitmap()
    {
        return bitmap;
    }
    public Bitmap getLargeBitmap()
    {
        return largeBitmap;
    }
    public string getDescription()
    {
        return description;
    }
}
}
```

This code is the base class that Crystal Reports uses to define each command that appears under the Add-Ins menu. It implements the **ICommand** interface. It has properties for command name, command ID, description, and bitmaps. It uses public methods to expose them to Crystal Reports. This code should stay the same for every Add-In you build.

The next piece of code that we will add is specific to your project. Although the general template is the same for every Add-In, it defines each command listed in the Add-In menu, and these commands will be different for every Add-In. For each command, it declares and instantiates an **OrderAmounts** object variable, and calls the appropriate method.

Insert the code in Listing 20-18 so that it is the last method of the Main class.

Listing 20-18. Create the Add-In menu items and implement the commands.

[VB.NET]

```vb.net
Public Class myCommandDll
    Implements ICommandDll
    'Main menu name
    Private strDisplayName As String = "Filter Order Amounts"
    Public Sub New()
    End Sub
    Public Function getAllCommands() As ICommand() Implements
BusinessObjects.CrystalReports.DotNetExternalCommand.ICommandDll.getAllCommands
        Dim commands As ICommand() = {New myCommand("Orders > $5,000", 0, Nothing, Nothing,
"Show Order Amounts greater than $10,000."), New myCommand("Remove Filter", 1, Nothing,
Nothing, "Remove order amount filter.")}
        Return commands
    End Function
    Public Function doCommand(ByVal CmdID As Integer, ByVal arguments As Object()) As Integer
Implements BusinessObjects.CrystalReports.DotNetExternalCommand.ICommandDll.doCommand
        Try
            'Declare and instantiate the class that implements the commands
            Dim orderAmounts As New OrderAmounts(DirectCast(arguments(0), String))
            ' Handle the commands
            Select Case CmdID
                Case 0
                    ' User selected Highlight subreports
                    orderAmounts.SetFilter()
                    Exit Select
                Case 1
                    ' User selected to remove highlighting
                    orderAmounts.ClearFilter()
                    Exit Select
                Case Else
                    Exit Select
                    ' If this is called then there was a command exposed that is not handled here.
            End Select
        Catch e As System.Exception
            MessageBox.Show(e.Message)
            Throw New DotNetExternalCommandException(e.Message, e)
        Finally
        End Try
        Return CRCError.CRCNoError
    End Function
    Public Function initialize(ByVal version As UShort) As Integer Implements
BusinessObjects.CrystalReports.DotNetExternalCommand.ICommandDll.initialize
        Return CRCError.CRCNoError
    End Function
    Public Function getLastErrorString() As String Implements
BusinessObjects.CrystalReports.DotNetExternalCommand.ICommandDll.getLastErrorString
        Return Nothing
    End Function
    Public Function getDisplayName() As String Implements
BusinessObjects.CrystalReports.DotNetExternalCommand.ICommandDll.getDisplayName
        Return strDisplayName
    End Function
```

```
    Public Sub terminate() Implements
BusinessObjects.CrystalReports.DotNetExternalCommand.ICommandDll.terminate
    End Sub
    Public Function canDoCommand(ByVal CmdID As Integer, ByVal arguments As Object()) As Integer
Implements BusinessObjects.CrystalReports.DotNetExternalCommand.ICommandDll.canDoCommand
        Return CRCError.CRCNoError
    End Function
End Class
```

[C#]

```csharp
public class myCommandDll : ICommandDll
{
    //Main menu name
    private string MenuName = "Filter Order Amounts";
    public myCommandDll()
    {
    }
    public ICommand[] getAllCommands()
    {
        ICommand[] commands = {
        new  myCommand("Orders > $10,000", 0, null, null , "Show Order Amounts greater than $5,000."),
        new  myCommand("Remove Filter", 1, null, null , "Remove order amount filter."),

    };
        return commands;
    }
    public int doCommand(int CmdID, object[] arguments)
    {
        try
        {
            //Declare and instantiate the class that implements the commands
            OrderAmounts orderAmounts = new OrderAmounts((string)arguments[0]);
            // Handle the commands
            switch (CmdID)
            {
                case 0:
                    orderAmounts.SetFilter();
                    break;
                case 1:
                    orderAmounts.ClearFilter();
                    break;
                default: break;
            }
        }
        catch (System.Exception e)
        {
            MessageBox.Show(e.Message);
            throw new DotNetExternalCommandException(e.Message, e);
        }
        finally
        {}
        return CRCError.CRCNoError;
```

```
    }
    public int initialize(ushort version)
    {
        return CRCError.CRCNoError;
    }
    public string getLastErrorString()
    {
        return null;
    }
    public string getDisplayName()
    {
        return MenuName;
    }
    public void terminate()
    {

    }
    public int canDoCommand(int CmdID, object[] arguments)
    {
        return CRCError.CRCNoError;
    }
}
```

This code implements the **ICommandDLL** interface, used for communicating with the Crystal Reports Add-In manager. The string variable **MenuName** is the name of the sub-menu item that appears directly under the Add-Ins menu item. The commands that you create will appear under this sub-menu item.

The method **getAllCommands()** builds the list of menu items that will appear on the menu bar under the Add-In option. It creates an object array of **ICommand** objects and sets the properties for each menu command. The **doCommand()** method is called by Crystal Reports after the user selects which Add-In they want to run. It uses a case statement to call the appropriate method of the **OrderAmounts** class. When finished, it returns a **CRCNoError** constant if everything ran okay.

The .NET Add-In is now finished. Build the solution to create the DLL.

The DLL needs to be within the Crystal Reports Addins subfolder so that it knows about it. If this is the first Add-In on your computer, you will need to create the Addins folder manually. Here is where it should go:

C:\Program Files\Business Objects\BusinessObjects Enterprise 12.0\ win32_x86\Addins

After creating this folder, copy the cscOrderAmounts.dll file to it. Open Crystal Reports and look for the Add-Ins menu option. Click on it and you should see the sub-menu item you declared using the variable **MenuItem**. Click on it, and you'll see two commands. The first sets the record selection filter and the second clears the record selection filter.

Note

You can't add a new Add-In to Crystal Report while it is open. Crystal Reports only checks for new Add-Ins when you open it. If you later update an Add-In and want to refresh it in Crystal Reports, you have to close Crystal Reports to release its lock on the DLL so that you can overwrite it.

To test the Add-In, create a simple report that uses the Xtreme.mdb sample database and print the field **Orders.Orders Amount** in the Details section. When you preview the report you will see every record in the database. After running the Add-In, only the records greater than $5,000 will be shown. Run the other Add-In command to clear the filter and see all the records again.

Caution

After Crystal Reports calls the Add-In and updates the report, it is supposed to go back into preview mode. Unfortunately, some changes don't refresh the report in the background prior to saving it. When this happens, the report stays in design mode and the user has to click the Preview button again. I'm unable to track down what exactly causes this, but the only way to fix it is to export the report prior to saving it. Hopefully, they will fix this problem in a future update. If this is happening to your Add-In, use the following code to force the report to refresh itself.

```
myReportDocument.ExportToDisk(ExportFormatType.PortableDocFormat,
"C:\temp.pdf")
```

Chapter 8 taught programming using Basic syntax as the primary language. This appendix builds on that chapter by showing you the Crystal syntax. It should be used as a companion tutorial with Chapter 8. It strictly shows what is unique about Crystal syntax compared to Basic syntax. It doesn't try to teach you programming all over again. The best way to use this appendix is to read through Chapter 8 first and become familiar with all the concepts. Then come back and read this appendix to see what the differences are with Crystal syntax.

The end of this appendix has conversion tables from Basic syntax to Crystal syntax. You'll notice that most of the functions are identical and there are only a few differences. The tables list the function names only. If you need more information about how the functions work, look at the table captions to get their reference number and flip back to Chapter 8 or 9 to see the details.

Writing Comments

Crystal syntax uses // within a line to comment out the remaining characters.

```
//This is a comment
```

Line Terminators

Crystal syntax uses the semicolon to mark the end of a line. A programming statement can use multiple lines with no special characters. If there are multiple statements within a formula, then use the semicolon to separate the lines. If a formula only has one line of code, no semicolon is needed (but you can put it there if you wish).

```
X := 5;  \\ This is a single line
Y := "This is also "
& "a single line";
```

Returning a Value

To return a value with Crystal syntax, put the value on a line by itself. Nothing else should appear on the line. The following code returns True if the employee received a bonus. If not then False is returned.

```
If {Employee.Bonus} > 0 Then
    True
Else
    False
```

Declaring Variables

Crystal syntax lists the variable scope and data type before the variable name.

Local datatype var

A variable's scope determines which formulas have access to that variable. There are three operators that you use to declare scope:

1. **Local** (**Dim** for Basic syntax): The variable can only be seen within the current formula. In a sense, a variable declared using the Dim keyword effectively defaults to Local scope.
2. **Global**: The variable can be seen within any formula inside the same report. Subreports do not have access to the variable.
3. **Shared**: Simlar to Global, but the variable can also be seen within subreports.

Local HireDate As Date
Shared AffiliateCities() As String

In Crystal syntax the default scope is **Global**, not **Local**. This is the exact opposite of how Basic syntax handles the default scope.

Variable Assignment

Crystal syntax uses the := for assignment.

X := 5

Array Data Types

Crystal syntax uses square parentheses to specify the array bounds.

X[1] := 5

To declare an array with Crystal syntax, use the Array keyword after the data type.

Local NumberVar Array X
Local NumberVar Array Y[10]

Assigning values to an array is done in different ways. If you know what the values of an array are during the development process, you can initialize the array with these values using the **MakeArray()** function. Pass the **MakeArray()** function all the elements as a comma delimited list and it returns an array that is fully populated with these elements. When using the **MakeArray()** function you don't have to specify the array size. The compiler figures that out for you.

Range Data Types

Crystal syntax puts the **Range** keyword after the data type.

Local datatype Range var

Conditional Structures

Crystal syntax does not have an End If statement. It also considers the entire If block a single statement. Put the line terminator after the Else block to terminate it. The Else If keyword is actually two words. If there is more than one statement within a code block, then enclose the statements within parentheses and use the semicolon to terminate each statement. The standard comparison operators are =, >, <, >=, <=, <>.

```
If condition1 Then
   ...code...
Else If condition2 Then
   (
   ...code...;
   ...code...;
   )
Else
   ...code;
```

Here is an example.

```
If {Employee.HoursWorked} = 40 Then
(
   Message = "";
   True;
)
Else
(
   Message := "Overtime alert";
   False;
)
```

Crystal syntax Select statements are slightly different than Basic syntax. The Case keyword is only used for testing the conditions. Put a colon at the end of the condition. If no conditions match the value being tested, the program executes the Default case. There is no End keyword.

```
Select var
   Case condition1:
      ...code...
   Case condition1, condition2:
      ...code...
   Default:
      ...code...
```

For Next Loop

Crystal syntax uses := to assign the loop range and it has the **Do** keyword at the end of the line. Rather than terminating the loop with the **Next** keyword, it requires parentheses to surround the code block.

```
For var := start To end Step increment Do
(
    ...code...
    If condition Then
        Exit For
    End If
)
```

While and Do Loops

Crystal syntax has few looping structures to choose from. It has the **While..Do** loop and the **Do..While** loop. It uses parentheses to define the code block.

Code template for **While … Do**:

```
While true_condition Do
(
    ...code...
)
```

Code template for **Do..While**:

```
Do
(
    ...code...
) While true_condition
```

Table 8-1. Data Type Default Values

Basic Data Type	Crystal Data Type	Default Value
Number	NumberVar	0
Currency	CurrencyVar	$0
Boolean	BooleanVar	False
String	StringVar	""
Date	DateVar	Date(0,0,0) – The Null Date value00/00/00
Time	TimeVar	No default valueNull
DateTime	DateTimeVar	No default valueNull

Table 9-1. String Analysis Functions

Basic Syntax	Crystal Syntax
AscW(str)	AscW(str)
ChrW(val)	ChrW(val)
Len(str)	Length(str)
IsNumeric(str)	N/A
InStr(start, str1, str2, compare)	InStr(start, str1, str2, compare)
InStrRev(start, str1, str2, compare)	InStrRev(start, str1, str2, compare)
StrCmp(str1, str2, compare)	StrCmp(str1, str2, compare)
Val(str)	Val(str)

Table 9-3. String Parsing Functions

Basic Syntax	Crystal Syntax
Trim(str)	Trim(str)
LTrim(str)	TrimLeft(str)
RTrim(str)	TrimRight(str)
Mid(str, start, length)	Mid(str, start, length)
Left(str, length)	Left(str, length)
Right(str, length)	Right(str, length)

Table 9-4. String Manipulation Functions

Basic Syntax	Crystal Syntax
Filter(str, find, include, compare)	Filter(str, find, include, compare)
Replace(str, find, replace, start, count, compare)	Replace(str, find, replace, start, count, compare)
StrReverse(str)	StrReverse(str)

ReplicateString(str, copies)	ReplicateString(str, copies)
Space(val)	Space(val)
Join(list, delimiter)	Join(list, delimiter)
Split(str, delimiter, count, compare)	Split(str, delimiter, count, compare)
Picture(str, template)	Picture(str, template)

Table 9-5. Conversion Functions

Basic Syntax	Crystal Syntax
CBool(number), CBool(currency)	CBool(number), CBool(currency)
CCur(number), CCur(string)	CCur(number), CCur(string)
CDbl(currency), CDbl(string), CDbl(boolean)	CDbl(currency), CDbl(string), CDbl(boolean)
CStr()	CStr()
CDate(string), CDate(year, month, day), CDate(DateTime)	CDate(string), CDate(year, month, day), CDate(DateTime)
CTime(string), CTime(hour, min, sec), CDate(DateTime)	CTime(string), CTime(hour, min, sec), CDate(DateTime)
CDateTime(string), CDateTime(date), CDateTime(date, time), CDateTime(year, month, day)	CDateTime(string), CDateTime(date), CDateTime(date, time), CDateTime(year, month, day)
CDateTime(year, month, day, hour, min, sec)	CDateTime(year, month, day, hour, min, sec)
ToNumber(string), ToNumber(boolean)	ToNumber(string), ToNumber(boolean)
ToText()	ToText()
IsDate(string), IsTIme(), IsDateTime()	IsDate(string), IsTIme(), IsDateTime()
IsNumber(string)	N/A
ToWords(number),	ToWords(number),

ToWords(number, decimals)	ToWords(number, decimals)

Table 9-8. Math Functions

Basic Syntax	Crystal Syntax
Abs(number)	Abs(number)
Fix(number, decimals)	Truncate(number, decimals)
Int(number), numerator \ denominator	Int(number), numerator \ denominator
Pi	Pi
Remainder(numerator, denominator), numerator Mod denominator	Remainder(numerator, denominator), numerator Mod denominator
Round(number, decimals)	Round(number, decimals)
Sgn(number)	Sgn(number)
Sqr(number), Exp(number), Log(number)	Sqr(number), Exp(number), Log(number)
Cos(number), Sin(number), Tan(number), Atn(number)	Cos(number), Sin(number), Tan(number), Atn(number)

Table 9-10. Date and Time Functions

Basic Syntax	Crystal Syntax
CurrentDate, CurrentTime, CurrentDateTime	CurrentDate, CurrentTime, CurrentDateTime
DateSerial(year, month, day), DateTime(hour, minute, second)	DateSerial(year, month, day), DateTime(hour, minute, second)
DateAdd(interval, number, date)	DateAdd(interval, number, date)
DateDiff(interval, startdate, enddate, firstdayofweek)	DateDiff(interval, startdate, enddate, firstdayofweek)
DatePart(interval, date, firstdayofweek, firstweekofyear)	DatePart(interval, date, firstdayofweek, firstweekofyear)
MonthName(date, abbreviate)	MonthName(date, abbreviate)

Timer	Timer
WeekDay(date, firstdayofweek)	DayOfWeek(date, firstdayofweek)
WeekdayName(weekday, abbreviate, firstdayofweek)	WeekdayName(weekday, abbreviate, firstdayofweek)

APPENDIX B
Report Object Model Diagrams

The reporting classes are mapped throughout the book in various chapters. This appendix shows the diagrams in a single location to make it easier for you to visualize their relationship. Each one is labeled with the original caption that was used in the chapter so that it is easy to go back and read more about it.

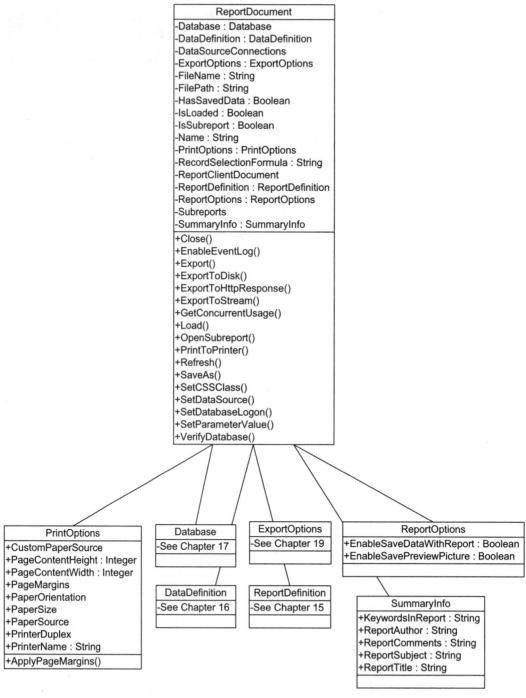

Figure 14-2. The ReportDocument object model.

CrystalReportViewer (Windows)
+ActiveViewIndex : Integer
+BackColor
+BackgroundImage
+BackgroundImageLayout
+DisplayBackgroundEdge : boolean
+DisplayGroupTree : boolean
+DisplayStatusBar : boolean
+DisplayToolbar : boolean
+EnableDrillDown : boolean
+EnableToolTips : boolean
-LogOnInfo : TableLogonInfos
-ParameterFieldInfo : ParameterFields
+ReportSource
+RightToLeft
+SelectionFormula : String
+ShowCloseButton : boolean
+ShowExportButton : boolean
+ShowGotoPageButton : boolean
+ShowGroupTreeButton : boolean
+ShowPageNavigationButtons : boolean
+ShowPrintButton : boolean
+ShowRefreshButton : Border
+ShowTextSearchButton : boolean
+ShowZoomButton : boolean
-ViewCount : Integer
+CloseView()
+DrillDownOnGroup()
+ExportReport()
+GetCurrentPageNumber()
+PrintReport()
+RefreshReport()
+SearchForText()
+ShowFirstPage()
+ShowGroupTree()
+ShowLastPage()
+ShowNthPage()
+ShowPreviousPage()
+Zoom()

CrystalReportViewer (Web)
+AutoDataBind : boolean
+BestFitPage : boolean
+BorderStyle
+ClientTarget : String
+CssFileName : String
+DisplayGroupTree : boolean
+DisplayPage : Boolean
+DisplayToolbar : boolean
+EnableDatabaseLoginPrompt : boolean
+EnableDrillDown : boolean
-EnableParameterPrompt : Boolean
+EnableToolTips : boolean
+GroupTreeImagesFolderUrl : String
+GroupTreeStyle
+HasCrystalLogo : boolean
+HasDrillUpButton : boolean
+HasExportButton : boolean
+HasGotoPageButton : boolean
+HasPageNavigationButton : boolean
+HasPrintButton : boolean
+HasRefreshButton : boolean
+HasSearchButton : boolean
+HasToggleGroupButton : boolean
+HasViewList : boolean
+HasZoomFactorList : boolean
+HyperlinkTarget : String
-LogOnInfo : TableLogOnInfo
+PageToTreeRatio : double
+PageZoomFactor : int
-ParameterFieldInfo : ParameterFields
+ReportSource
+ReuseParameterValuesOnRefresh : boolean
+RightToLeft
+SelectionFormula : String
+ToolbarImagesFolderUrl : String
-SeparatePages : Boolean
+RefreshReport()
+SearchAndHighlightTest()
+SearchForText()
+ShowFirstPage()
+ShowLastPage()
+ShowNextPage()
+ShowNthPage()
+ShowPreviousPage()
+Zoom()

Figure 14-3. The CrystalReportViewer object model.

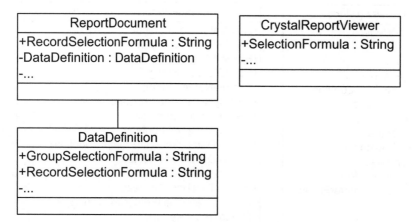

Figure 15-1. Properties used in selecting records.

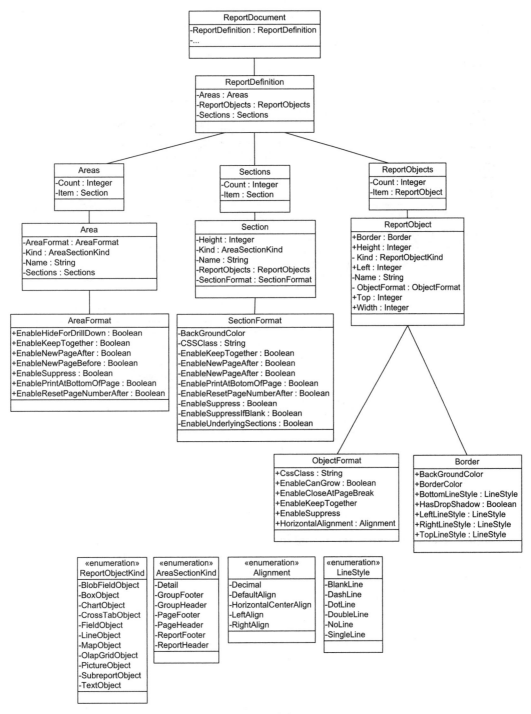

Figure 15-2. The ReportDefinition object model

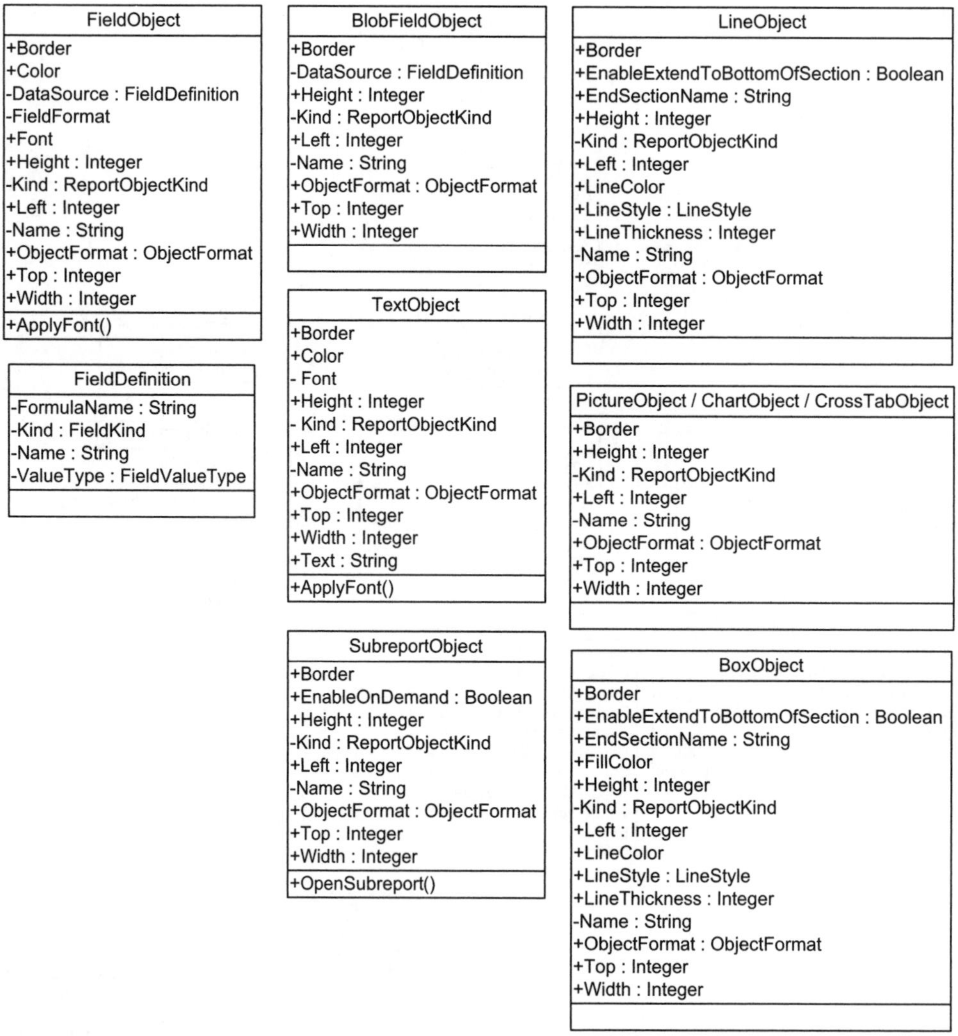

FieldObject

+Border
+Color
-DataSource : FieldDefinition
-FieldFormat
+Font
+Height : Integer
-Kind : ReportObjectKind
+Left : Integer
-Name : String
+ObjectFormat : ObjectFormat
+Top : Integer
+Width : Integer

+ApplyFont()

FieldDefinition

-FormulaName : String
-Kind : FieldKind
-Name : String
-ValueType : FieldValueType

BlobFieldObject

+Border
-DataSource : FieldDefinition
+Height : Integer
-Kind : ReportObjectKind
+Left : Integer
-Name : String
+ObjectFormat : ObjectFormat
+Top : Integer
+Width : Integer

TextObject

+Border
+Color
- Font
+Height : Integer
- Kind : ReportObjectKind
+Left : Integer
-Name : String
+ObjectFormat : ObjectFormat
+Top : Integer
+Width : Integer
+Text : String

+ApplyFont()

SubreportObject

+Border
+EnableOnDemand : Boolean
+Height : Integer
-Kind : ReportObjectKind
+Left : Integer
-Name : String
+ObjectFormat : ObjectFormat
+Top : Integer
+Width : Integer

+OpenSubreport()

LineObject

+Border
+EnableExtendToBottomOfSection : Boolean
+EndSectionName : String
+Height : Integer
-Kind : ReportObjectKind
+Left : Integer
+LineColor
+LineStyle : LineStyle
+LineThickness : Integer
-Name : String
+ObjectFormat : ObjectFormat
+Top : Integer
+Width : Integer

PictureObject / ChartObject / CrossTabObject

+Border
+Height : Integer
-Kind : ReportObjectKind
+Left : Integer
-Name : String
+ObjectFormat : ObjectFormat
+Top : Integer
+Width : Integer

BoxObject

+Border
+EnableExtendToBottomOfSection : Boolean
+EndSectionName : String
+FillColor
+Height : Integer
-Kind : ReportObjectKind
+Left : Integer
+LineColor
+LineStyle : LineStyle
+LineThickness : Integer
-Name : String
+ObjectFormat : ObjectFormat
+Top : Integer
+Width : Integer

Figure 15-3. The report classes that inherit from the ReportObject class.

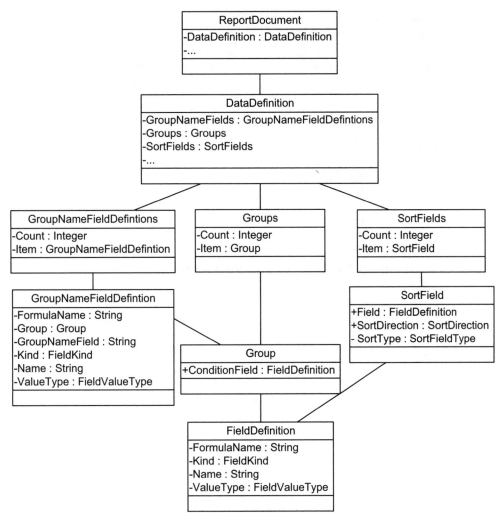

Figure 15-6. The Sorting and Grouping object model.

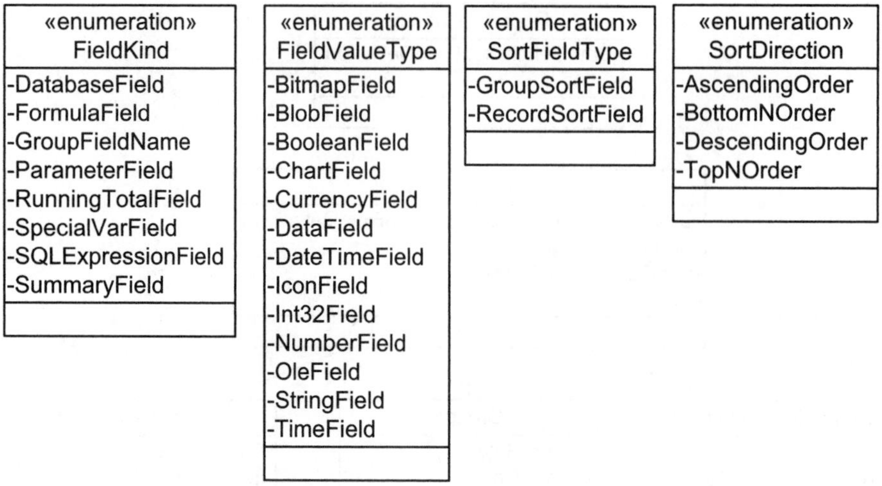

«enumeration» FieldKind	«enumeration» FieldValueType	«enumeration» SortFieldType	«enumeration» SortDirection
-DatabaseField	-BitmapField	-GroupSortField	-AscendingOrder
-FormulaField	-BlobField	-RecordSortField	-BottomNOrder
-GroupFieldName	-BooleanField		-DescendingOrder
-ParameterField	-ChartField		-TopNOrder
-RunningTotalField	-CurrencyField		
-SpecialVarField	-DataField		
-SQLExpressionField	-DateTimeField		
-SummaryField	-IconField		
	-Int32Field		
	-NumberField		
	-OleField		
	-StringField		
	-TimeField		

Figure 15-7. Sorting and Grouping enumeration constants.

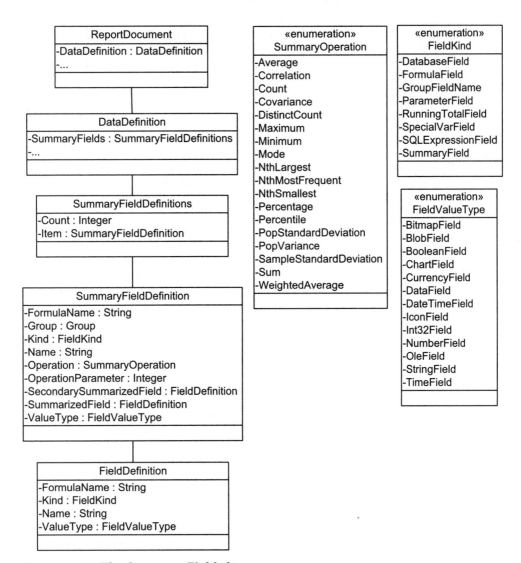

Figure 15-13. The Summary Field classes.

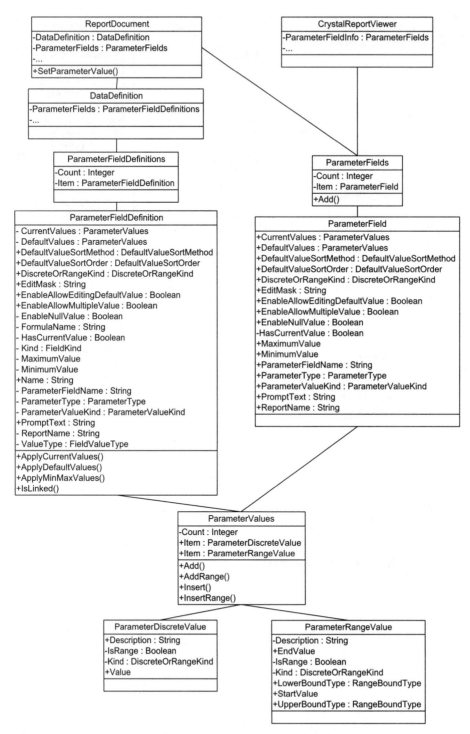

Figure 16-1. The classes of the Parameter object model.

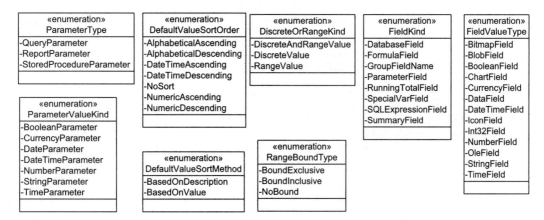

Figure 16-2. The enumeration constants of the Parameter object model.

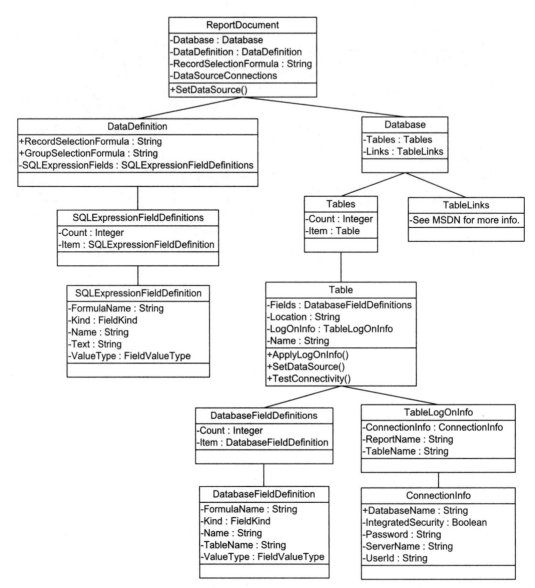

Figure 17-1. The Database class diagram.

```
┌─────────────────────────────────────────────────────┐
│                    ExportOptions                     │
├─────────────────────────────────────────────────────┤
│ -DestinationOptions : DiskFileDestinationOptions     │
│ -DestinationOptions : ExchangeFolderDestinationOptions│
│ -DestinationOptions : MicrosoftMailDestinationOptions │
│ -ExportDestinationType : ExportDestinationType       │
│ -ExportFormatType : ExportFormatType                 │
│ -ExportFormatOptions : ExcelFormatOptions            │
│ -ExportFormatOptions : HTMLFormatOptions             │
│ -ExportFormatOptions : PdfRtfWordFormatOptions       │
├─────────────────────────────────────────────────────┤
│ +CreateDiskFileDestinationOptions()                  │
│ +CreateExcelFormatOptions()                          │
│ +CreateExchangeFolderDestinationOptions()            │
│ +CreateHTMLFormatOptions()                           │
│ +CreateMicrosoftMailDestinationOptions()             │
│ +CreatePdfRtfWordFormatOptions()                     │
└─────────────────────────────────────────────────────┘
```

```
┌─────────────────────────────────┐
│    DiskFileDestinationOptions    │
├─────────────────────────────────┤
│ -DiskFileName : String           │
│                                  │
└─────────────────────────────────┘
```

```
┌─────────────────────────────────────┐
│    ExchangeFolderDestinationOptions  │
├─────────────────────────────────────┤
│ -DestinationType                     │
│ -FolderPath : String                 │
│ -Password : String                   │
│ -Profile : String                    │
│                                      │
└─────────────────────────────────────┘
```

```
┌─────────────────────────────────┐
│      «enumeration»               │
│     ExportDestinationType        │
├─────────────────────────────────┤
│ -DiskFile                        │
│ -ExchangeFolder                  │
│ -MicrosoftMail                   │
│ -NoDestination                   │
│                                  │
└─────────────────────────────────┘
```

```
┌─────────────────────────────────────┐
│    MicrosoftMailDestinationOptions   │
├─────────────────────────────────────┤
│ -MailCCList : String                 │
│ -MailMessage : String                │
│ -MailSubject : String                │
│ -MailToList : String                 │
│ -Password : String                   │
│ -UserName : String                   │
│                                      │
└─────────────────────────────────────┘
```

```
┌─────────────────────────────────┐
│      «enumeration»               │
│      ExportFormatType            │
├─────────────────────────────────┤
│ -Excel                           │
│ -HTML32                          │
│ -HTML40                          │
│ -NoFormat                        │
│ -PortableDocFormat               │
│ -RichText                        │
│ -WordForWindows                  │
│                                  │
└─────────────────────────────────┘
```

```
┌──────────────────────────────────────────────┐
│              ExcelFormatOptions               │
├──────────────────────────────────────────────┤
│ -ExcelAreaGroupNumber : Integer               │
│ -ExcelAreaType : AreaSectionKind              │
│ -ExcelConstantColumnWidth : Double            │
│ -ExcelTabHasColumnHeadings : Boolean          │
│ -ExcelUseConstantColumnWidth : Boolean        │
└──────────────────────────────────────────────┘
```

```
┌──────────────────────────────────────────────┐
│              HTMLFormatOptions                │
├──────────────────────────────────────────────┤
│ -FirstPageNumber : Integer                    │
│ -HTMLEnableSeperatedPages : Boolean           │
│ -HTMLBaseFolderName : String                  │
│ -HTMLFileName : String                        │
│ -HTMLHasPageNavigator : Boolean               │
│ -LastPageNumber : Integer                     │
│ -UsePageRange : Boolean                       │
└──────────────────────────────────────────────┘
```

```
┌─────────────────────────────────┐
│      «enumeration»               │
│    ExchangeDestinationType       │
├─────────────────────────────────┤
│ -ExchangePostDocMessage          │
│                                  │
└─────────────────────────────────┘
```

```
┌──────────────────────────────────────────────┐
│             PdfRtfWordFormatOptions           │
├──────────────────────────────────────────────┤
│ -FirstPageNumber : Integer                    │
│ -LastPageNumber : Integer                     │
│ -UsePageRange : Boolean                       │
│                                               │
└──────────────────────────────────────────────┘
```

Figure 19-4. The Export object model.

Books by Brian Bischof

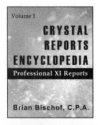

Crystal Reports Encyclopedia, Volume 1: Professional XI Reports

Make your reporting projects a success with this comprehensive, tutorial based guide. If you're just learning or are a seasoned expert, there is something here for you.

Crystal Reports Encyclopedia, Volume 2: Programming .NET 2005

Written for Visual Studio .NET developers, this book provides in-depth information for integrating Crystal Reports into windows and web applications alike.

Crystal Reports .NET Programming

Visual Studio .NET 2003 programmers can build first-class reports with this comprehensive guide that walks you through each step of the process. This is the missing manual that should have been included with Visual Studio .NET.

The .NET Languages: A Quick Translation Guide

This is the only book that shows you the programming code for VB6, VB.NET and C# side by side. Syntax translation tables make it easy to convert code between all languages.

Pro Visual Studio .NET

Co-authored by Brian Bischof, reveals and demystifies Visual Studio .NET to enable programmers to do their job more quickly and with fewer errors.